The Kirk, Satan and Salem:
A History of the
Witches of Renfrewshire

BARGARRAN HOUSE.

The Kirk, Satan and Salem:
A History of the
Witches of Renfrewshire

Edited by
Hugh V. McLachlan

The Grimsay Press

The Grimsay Press
an imprint of
Zeticula
57 St Vincent Crescent
Glasgow
G3 8NQ
Scotland.

http://www.thegrimsaypress.co.uk
admin@thegrimsaypress.co.uk

First published 2006
© Hugh McLachlan 2006

*Every effort has been made to trace possible copyright holders
and to obtain their permission for the use of any copyright
material. The publishers will gladly receive information enabling
them to rectify any error or omission for subsequent editions.*

ISBN 1 84530 035 1 Hardback
ISBN 1 84530 034 3 Paperback

To Sheila McLachlan, my tender enchantress.

*'How fair is thy love, my sister, my spouse!
how much better is thy love than wine!
and the smell of thine ointment than all spices.'*

Song of Solomon, Chapter 4, Verse 10.

Contents

Acknowledgements

I am grateful to Julian Goodare, Richard Godbeer, James Marr and Alan Reeves for helpful comments and to S.W. McDonald, Suzanne Trill and the National Archive of Scotland for permission to reprint, respectively: 'The Bargarran Witchcraft Trial: A Psychiatric Reassessment'; Extract from the Diary of Lady Ann Halkett; and Manuscript JC26/81/D9.

A Note on the Contents of this Edition

The core of this book was first published as *A History of the Witches of Renfrewshire* in 1809 and again in 1877 with additional material. This 3rd edition of *A History of the Witches of Renfrewshire* reprints the 2nd edition and contains, as well as the new introduction, the following additional material:

A Brief an True Narrative of some Remarkable Passages Relating to sundry Persons Afflicted by Witchcraft at Salem Village: Which happened from the Nineteenth of March to the Fifth of April, 1692. Collected by Deodat Lawson.

National Archives of Scotland Edinburgh. Manuscript JC26/81/D9.

Christ's Fidelity the Only Shield Against Satan's Malignity Asserted in a Sermon Deliver'd at Salem-Village the 24th March 1692. Being Lecture-day there and a time of Publick Examination of some suspected for Witchcraft. By Deodat Lawson, Minister;

Extract from the Diary of Lady Anne Halkett from Wednesday 12th October 1698. Kindly provided by and transcribed by Dr Suzanne Trill, School of Literatures, Languages and Cultures, University of Edinburgh.

Apendix to *Christ's Fidelity The Only Shield Against Satan's Malignity* by Deodat Lawson.

'The Bargarran Witchcraft Trial: A Psychiatric Reassessment', by S.W McDonald, A. Thom and A. Thom. From the *Scottish Medical Journal*, 1996, Vol. 41, pp. 152-158.

'Exonerate the Erskine One' by H.V. McLachlan and J.K. Swales. This paper was presented at: Twisted Sisters: Women, Crime and Deviance in Scotland Since 1400. Scottish Women's History Network Conference, Glasgow Caledonian University, 14th October, 2000. (see http://www.swhn.org.uk)

Introduction

'Witch hunt' is a term that is associated with irrationality, hysteria and cruelty. When people talk of the witchcraft cases of long ago, they tend to focus upon the apparent strangeness of it all. They talk as if people then thought and felt quite differently from people now. Witchcraft prosecution is often considered to have been, by its very nature, persecution. For instance, it is often said that the witchcraft trials were not proper trials at all: that they were unfair and unjust. In this regard, the famous 'swim-test' is frequently cited. The theory behind it was held to be that since witches had renounced their Christian baptism, of which water was the substance, water would thereafter reject them. If the suspected witches floated, then they were guilty and were executed. If they did not float, they sank and were drowned. Either way, so the story goes, they had no chance. It was as if a coin was tossed and accused witches were told by the courts: 'Heads we win; tails you lose'. However, it is this sort of story that is the real travesty: witchcraft accusation and prosecution were more subtle, complex and interesting than that. It was also fairer and more just or, if you like, less unfair and less unjust.

This book is about the famous outbreak of witchcraft allegations and prosecutions associated with Christian Shaw, the so-called 'Bargarran Impostor' in Renfrewshire, Scotland in the 1690s: much of the material it comprises was written then. In the consequent trial in Paisley in 1697, it was alleged that Christian, who was a young girl and the daughter of the Laird of Bargarran, had been bewitched by several people who, while being invisible to the other people present with her, were seen by the child to mock and torment her by, for instance, nipping and biting her. She was said to have fallen into fits during which she was unable to speak and to have removed from her mouth pins and other objects that had been placed there by her tormentors. The local clergy and the Presbytery of Paisley played an important part in instigating the trial and in appearing as witnesses.

Central to the historical discussion of the case has been the reported behaviour of Christian Shaw. This was contained in a book written shortly after the trial and execution of the witches concerned. It is worth noting that what was central to the actual trial and, possibly also, to the thoughts of the members of the jury might well have been quite different from the concerns and content of that book. Just as we do not know how juries think in present day cases and what particular considerations influence them, we do not know what were the deliberations of juries in the past. Such discussions are private and are not recorded. The book was called : *A True Narrative of the Sufferings and Relief of a Young Girle; Strangely molested by Evil spirits and their instruments in the West: With a preface and postscript containing Reflections on what is most Material or Curious either in the history or trial of the Seven Witches who were Condemn'd to be Execute in the country*. Published in Edinburgh in 1698, it is reproduced below. According to the *Narrative*, the whole affair started after Christian Shaw had fallen out with and been shouted at by one of her family's servants, Katherine Campbell, a young Highland woman who had come to Renfrewshire in search of work.

The *Narrative* is anonymous. Its authorship is a matter

16

of dispute. My own view is that it was written by the Rev. James Brisbane and/or the Rev. Andrew Turner, two local ministers. I comment more fully on this in the chapter called 'Exonerate the Erskine One' below. I think that the author (or authors) of the *Narrative* was (or were) familiar with the booklet written by the Rev. Deodat Lawson. This is the earliest narrative written about the Salem case. It is reprinted below. An older theory is that the *Narrative* was written by Lord Cullen, Francis Grant. He was the judge in the Paisley witchcraft trials. (For a fuller discussion of this and related issues, see McLachlan and Swales, 2002).

There are similarities and links between this Renfrewshire case and the Salem case in New England in 1692; some of them are clear and direct, others of them are not. For instance, the sorts of fits that alleged victims of witchcraft were said to have experienced are very similar. They both involve children as alleged victims. Clergymen play important parts in both cases. A previously unpublished manuscript will show them to be even more similar than they might appear to be. In this introduction, I shall sketch the background of witchcraft in New England as well as in old Scotland.

Witchcraft in New England: Salem and Escaping Salem

The most famous witchcraft prosecution of all time is that of Salem Village. In the public mind it is considered to typify witchcraft cases, which are thought of as being stupid, ignorant, superstitious, cruel, unfair and unjust. They are also thought of as being hysterical and mindless: driven by emotion rather than reflective reasoning. This has become the stereotypical view of witchcraft trials and accusations. However, whether or not what went on in Salem is in accord with this stereotypical view, Salem was not typical. It was an aberration. It was not even typical of New England witchcraft cases. Nonetheless, as Richard Godbeer notes in his recent book, *Escaping Salem: The Other Witch Hunt of 1692*: 'Although Salem was not typical of most outbreaks in colonial New England, it remains, by default, the archetype through which most Americans understand, or misunderstand the subject'. (Godbeer, 2005, p. ix) I would suggest that it is the archetype through which most English-speakers misunderstand the nature and extent of witchcraft prosecutions.

Salem Village was a smaller and poorer place than the town of Salem, which was itself tottering near the very edge of subsistence. It is perhaps significant in relation to the morale and attractiveness of the community that the turnover of its ministers was high: clergymen did not stay for very long when they could be prevailed upon to try to settle there. 1692 was a time of particular stress in the locality. For instance, there was much religious hostility and anxiety relating to dissenting Anglicans and Quakers.

There was fear and tension regarding possible attacks by Indians. Actual attacks had occurred recently nearby. The winter was a particularly cold one when Betty Parris, the nine-year-old daughter of the recently-installed minister of Salem Village, Samuel Parris, started to have strange fits. She dashed about the house inexplicably, was contorted with pain and complained of having a fever. Other people including - but not only - young girls began to show symptoms of similar fits: they complained of being bitten and pinched; they would seem to be contorted with pain and at other times they would be stock-still and totally silent. The Rev. Mr. Parris suggested fasting and prayer. He also consulted a physician, who was unable to offer a natural explanation for the ailments. Cotton Mather, another New England minister had published a book called *Memorable Providences* that described the behaviour of a supposedly bewitched person in Boston. This book had been read and much discussed in Salem. The idea soon gained currency that Betty Parris and the others were victims of witchcraft. They were encouraged to name those who were tormenting them. Samuel Parris had a Barbadian slave called Tituba. She was one of the first to be named. Others followed. Tituba confessed and cited other local witches.

Nineteen people - five men and fourteen women - were convicted and hanged. One man, an old man in his eighties was crushed to death by the weight of heavy stones heaped upon his chest. He refused to plead. Perhaps he did not understand what was being asked of him or was unable to articulate his plea. Several people died in prison. However, the outbreak was short-lived. Confidence in the courts evaporated quickly. More than a hundred other suspects were imprisoned. They were released when legal proceedings were suspended in Salem because they had come to lack credibility and perceived legitimacy. Tituba survived and was sold by Parris. About five years later, one of the judges involved, Judge Samuel Sewell, issued a public apology for his part in the proceedings. It was read aloud by the minister in front of the congregation of Judge Sewell's meeting-house while he stood contrite and humbly bowed his head. (See Francis, 2005)

Salem Village was not the only community in New England to have a witchcraft trial in 1692. South of Salem, around Stamford and Fairfield in Connecticut there was another witch hunt although a far less famous one. It started when a young woman called Katherine Branch, a servant in the household of Daniel and Abigail Wescot, a respected and fairly well-to-do couple in Stamford, had fits. As it says in the foreword of Godbeer's recent book, *Escaping Salem*, 'Readers may be surprised to learn that the men and women struggling to understand Katherine Branch's fits exhibited a broad range of emotions and ideas. They were not always eager to blame the Devil for Branch's affliction, on the one hand, or to assume on the other, that she was either an imposter or a woman beset by mental illness'. As with Scottish witchcraft cases, people were often doing their best to discover the truth, much as we do now and would, were we living then, have done then. There was, too, in Scotland a diversity of thought. Not everyone in the community thought the same thing about witchcraft in general or about particular supposed instances of it.

Kate had strange fits. She was tormented by people, whom she named, who were visible to her but invisible to the other people in the room. In her fits, her body became contorted and she had amazing strength. She was said sometimes to become as stiff as a board. It was very difficult to restrain her and could take several people to do so. Bruises appeared on her body and pins were found in her hands allegedly so placed by her invisible tormentors, the witches. As we have seen, by coincidence, there is also a young woman called Kate - Katherine Campbell - who features in the famous Renfrewshire witchcraft case and who was a servant in the household at the centre of the case. However, Katherine Campbell was not the alleged victim: she was an accused witch. She was accused of bewitching Christian Shaw, who was reported to have had fits very similar to those that Kate Branch was said to have had.

Unlike the Salem case, there was only one alleged victim of witchcraft in the Connecticut case of 1692. Kate named several people as her tormentors but, in the end, only two of them were tried as witches. Neither was executed. There was a hung jury, and when the trial was reconvened, one of the accused - Elizabeth Clawson - was found not guilty and the other one - Mercy Disborough - was found guilty. However, this latter verdict was quashed by a superior legal authority.

Godbeer paints a broader picture of witchcraft prosecution in New England than we normally look at when he writes:

'New England's legal system was rigorous and cautious in its handling of capital cases. Convincing oneself and one's neighbors of an individual's guilt was not the same as convincing a court. Of the sixty-one known prosecutions for witchcraft in seventeenth-century New England, excluding the Salem witch hunt, sixteen at most (perhaps only fourteen) resulted in conviction and execution, a rate of just over one-quarter (26.2 percent). Four of the accused individuals confessed, which made the court's job much easier. If those cases are omitted, the conviction rate falls to just under one-fifth (19.7 percent).' (Godbeer, 2005, p. 161).

Not every one who was tried for witchcraft in New England was executed – far from it. As we shall see, the same thing can be said of the Scottish witchcraft trials. Notice that in New England, in order to prove guilt in the case of witchcraft, it was necessary to prove that the accused person had an association with the Devil. It was not necessarily always so in Scotland.

Salem was an aberration and should not be thought of as a typical witchcraft outbreak. According to Godbeer:

'That other witch hunt of 1692 took a very different course from the panic in Massachusetts. Stamford townsfolk were for the most part remarkably cautious in reacting to Kate's accusations. The officials responsible for handling Connecticut's witch crisis refused to make hasty judgements about the accused and insisted on weighing carefully the evidence against them: if witch suspects were to hang, their guilt must be irrefutable. *Escaping Salem* provides a corrective to the stereotype of early New Englanders as quick to accuse and condemn. That stereotype originates with Salem, which was, in its scale and intensity of hysteria, unlike other outbreaks of witch hunting in New England. Stamford's witch hunt was more typical'. (Godbeer, 2005, pp. 7-8)

Although ministers often played a prominent part in

witchcraft cases, it would be a mistake to imagine that their intervention was always malign, dogmatic and foolish. Consider, for instance, this interesting view of Increase Mather, a New England minister and the son of Cotton Mather. He argued that use of the swim-test to detect witches was itself a form of superstition and akin to witchcraft. If some people did but others did not float in some particular stretch of water, then, Mather argued, this must be the result of some diabolical trick. It was not a test that should be relied upon. In any case, the supposed swim-test is based on dubious theological reasoning. He argued that not all water is the water of baptism but only that which has been set apart for the very act of baptism. There is no theological reason for thinking that water in general will, somehow or other, reject witches and prevent them from sinking even if there were a reason for thinking that baptismal water would so react. However, there is, he argued, no biblical warrant for thinking that even baptismal water would so behave. The swim-test is superstitious nonsense. As the Rev. Deodat Lawson – whose sermon and narrative about the Salem witchcraft case is reprinted in this book – would have expressed the point: we should not try to use the Devil's shield against the Devil's sword.

When there was a hung jury in the trials of Elizabeth Clawson and Mercy Disborough, a group of local ministers was asked to consider the evidence that had been presented regarding the accused women and submit a written report on it. It is cautious, reasonable and balanced. For instance, they say: '...we cannot but give our concurrence with the generality of divines that the endeavour of conviction of witchcraft by swimming is unlawful and sinful and therefore it cannot give any evidence,' (quoted in Godbeer, 2005, p. 116). Regarding the supposed evidence presented by Kate Branch, the afflicted servant maid, they were sceptical. Although they concluded that 'her affliction, being somewhat strange, well deserves a further inquiry', they were suspicious that there was at least an element of deception on her part even if there were more to her condition than mere deception. They were against relying on her accounts of invisible tormentors as credible evidence against the accused women because of 'the easy deception of her senses and subtle devices of the Devil...'. (quoted in Godbeer, 2005, p. 117) Furthermore, 'As to the other strange accidents such as the dying of cattle, etc, we apprehend the applying of them to these women as matters of witchcraft to be upon very slender grounds' (quoted in Godbeer, 2005, p. 118).

The reasoning of this group of ministers was, I suggest, not unlike the reasoning of many people – theists and atheists – today. Their reasoning is not impenetrable to us; it is not alien to us. One need not live in the same historical and social environment as other human beings in order to understand their thoughts. The notion that our reasoning is relative to our historical and social circumstances is one that might contain an element of truth but it should not be taken too literally or too seriously.

It is sometimes suggested – as, for instance, by Francis (2005) – that those in the past who opposed witchcraft prosecution had a 'modern' or scientific way of looking at things while those who were in favour of witchcraft prosecution had a different world-view. This is very dubious. Science and what they would have thought of as the scientific method was appealed to by many of those who approved of the prosecution of witches. As Godbeer notes:

'Daniel and Abigail Wescot's home had become the stage for a grim and perplexing drama. At its center was the luridly physical and yet mystifying spectacle of Katherine Branch's fits. Around the young woman there crowded a growing cast of characters, all determined to figure out who or what was causing her fits. The residents of Stamford were anything but hasty in concluding that witchcraft must be responsible for Kate's torments: differing points of view jostled and competed for ascendancy. At first, not even the Wescots assumed that their servant was bewitched. Their first step was to call in the local medical expert, not the town minister: they began by seeking a natural cause for Kate's affliction. Even once the Westcots became convinced that witches were in fact causing the woman's torments, not all of their neighbours followed suit: some suspected that Kate was faking her symptoms. Those who believed that she was under an evil hand, and those who did not, were equally determined to justify their points of view. Their approach was experimental: they converged upon the Wescots' home and turned it into a laboratory of the occult with Kate as the specimen under investigation. They watched her: they tested her; and they reached conclusions based on what they observed.'. (Godbeer, 2005, pp. 33-34.)

We will see a similar pattern with the Renfrewshire witches. The appeal made to the scientific evidence of Dr Matthew Brisbane, a physician and Mr Marshall, an apothecary is noteworthy and the discussion of it by McDonald, Thom and Thom below is particularly erudite and interesting. Witchcraft belief was not (and is not) inconsistent with an enthusiasm for science. On the contrary, because people were enthusiastic about and had confidence in the pronouncements of science, they were prone in some cases to cite witchcraft when science was unable to account for particular events and occurrences. That everything is explicable by science is not a scientific belief but a philosophical one. It seems to me to be a false philosophical belief. That everything that is explicable is explicable by science and that some things are inexplicable would be a more reasonable one. My one own view is that whether or not all things are explicable, not everything is correctly explicable by science. This is not, of course, to say that witchcraft beliefs can correctly explain that which science cannot.

Scottish Witchcraft

General Background

Lurking behind the prosecution of people for witchcraft in Sixteenth and Seventeenth Century Scotland, there was the following theological theory of witchcraft, which was considered as a sort of inversion (and perversion) of Christianity. It was believed that the Devil appeared to prospective witches in the form of a man. People were thought to become actual witches by the voluntary act of entering into a pact with him and renouncing Christ and their Christian baptism to him. They became the servants of the Devil and enemies of God rather than followers of Christ. To become a witch was a wilful act. Exercises of witchcraft – and this could be the use of diabolical power to help as well as to harm people (beneficium as well as maleficium) – were also thought of as wilful and, of course, sinful acts. Strictly speaking, witchcraft was not considered to be 'possession'. There was no particular shame attached to being possessed by an evil spirit and the remedy for it was exorcism. It was not thought of as a punishable condition. Witches were not thought to be possessed by demons or by the Devil: they were, rather, his willing accomplices; they were in league with him. They were enemies of God and of society. Death and damnation were considered to be their just deserts. Similarly, when witches harmed or helped people, they did not 'possess' them. When people sought the help of witches, then they were considered to have committed a sin and a crime.

However, there was no stigma attached to being the victim of witchcraft. It signified merely that, for whatever reason, God had allowed the Devil to cause the person to suffer at the behest of one of his servants, i.e. a witch.

This was the basis of the notion of witchcraft put forward in Scotland by its educated elite, but it would not have been held by all of them. Different members of the elite might have believed different things when they believed in witchcraft and, of course, not every one did believe in witchcraft. Apart from anything else, then as now, some (perhaps many) people were atheists. There were differences between the elite and the non-elite (or popular) beliefs relative to witchcraft (see Macdonald, 2002: 1-14; 195-8; Maxwell-Stuart, 2001: 1-29: 181 – 215). Beliefs about witchcraft could merge with other beliefs about fairies, brownies, little-people and so forth that did not always have an ominous, venomous, threatening or Satanic element. Even more readily than, say, money or property, beliefs and theories can flow between social groups and classes. This theological conception of witchcraft gained currency in Scotland, I would suggest, partly, at least, through clergymen. They acted as gates between the world of learning and the thoughts of the masses.

Beliefs and practices relative to 'witchcraft' were, I would suggest, harmless superstitions until the theologians and the politicians got their metaphorical hands on them. In this regard, the following argument was instrumental: *everything, comes from either God or Satan; 'witchcraft' does not come from God, therefore it must come from Satan.* The argument is fallacious and pernicious. Since we have free will, some things come from us. In addition, some things come from the interaction of human beings with each other and with their non-human environment. Consider, for instance, the economic phenomena of inflation, monetary stability and deflation. It would be a curious theology that insisted that they must all be either divine or diabolical. In any case, it is not the business of the courts or the politicians to decide what is Godly and what is ungodly and to praise or punish accordingly.

A theologically weak part of the theory seems to me to be the stress on the supposedly binding nature of the alleged pact with Satan. When people voluntarily make promises then, other things being equal, they are morally bound by them and ought to keep them. However, the duties created by our promises can clash with other duties, many of which might be stronger than and prior to those resulting from our promises. If, say, we promise someone that we will rob a bank with him and then change our mind, few people would argue that we ought to go through with the bank raid because we promised to do so. Who or what can be expected to enforce the deal if we renege on it? Would we say that God would enforce the promised arrangement? Surely not. Similarly, if in a moment of weakness, someone did – let us for the sake of the argument suppose – enter into a pact with Satan and promised to be his servant, why should this be thought of as a morally binding arrangement? If the person had a change of mind and decided not to be the Devil's servant any longer and thereby not to keep his side of the deal this, surely, would be Satan's loss and the end of the matter. To imagine that God would hold the person to his promise to Satan even if he no longer wanted to keep it would be bizarre.

The notion that witches would, by ill-treating their Christian victims, try to persuade them to become witches was not prevalent in Scottish witchcraft cases generally although it is central to the Renfrewshire case and crops up in the New England ones as well. It is a very strange idea. After all, no matter how bad any earthly pain might be, it would be less severe and shorter than the torments of hell. Any pain that the Devil inflicted through witchcraft would last only as long as God – for whatever purpose – allowed it to last. He was the believer's only sure hope. No Christian would trust the Devil to deliver his side of any bargain.

Witches were believed to hold meetings with other witches at which the Devil presided and was worshipped. Hence, in their confessions, accused witches often gave a list of the other witches who attended meetings with them and the Devil. You might well imagine that there would be a domino-effect whereby entire communities risked being wiped out by witchcraft accusations. However, it did not happen like that in Scotland. The lists of alleged fellow witches were always limited and usually fairly short. When, say, half a dozen accused witches confessed to having attended meetings with other witches at some place and time, they were likely each to specify that the other five attended the meetings with them.

Nowadays, some people, particularly those who think of themselves as present-day witches claim that the accused witches of old were followers of some sort of pre-Christian religion or fertility cult. They tend to argue that there were witchcraft meetings and a witchcraft organisation of some sort even if they were quite different in character and purpose from the way they were described by the courts. I am sceptical about this view. Apart from the confessions of accused witches, there is little or no evidence that such meetings took place. Perhaps there was some sort of reality behind the theory of the witches 'sabbaths' (as they were called in Europe): perhaps there was not. It would be, I suggest, a mistake to claim to *know* either way.

Was witch-hunting women-hunting?

Was witch-hunting the deliberate hunting of women? Was it some sort of manifestation of anti-feminism? It is not clear-cut. This is a live issue within the study of Scottish witchcraft and one I shall say much more about in a future book with J. Kim Swales called *Women, Crime and Witchcraft: Scotland After the Reformation and Before the Enlightenment.*

Of the 1,891 Scottish cases collated in *A Source-book of Scottish Witchcraft* (Larner, Lee and McLachlan, 2005) where individuals were known to have been tried as witches or merely to have had preliminary proceedings taken against them in pre-trial processes, the sex of the accused is known in 1,733 of them. Of these, 86% involved females and 14% involved males. There was clearly a sexual bias of some sort involved in the social interactions whereby it came about that the vast majority of those who were brought before the courts as accused witches were female. Thereafter, within the legal process, the existence of a sexual bias is not manifest. The Scottish courts did not seem to treat accused females more harshly than accused males.

It is worth noting in passing that Apps and Gow argue that in some parts of Europe, more men than women were accused on witchcraft. (See Apps and Gow, 2003.)

Prior to the bulk of the actual witchcraft hunts and trials, James VI and I had speculated that the ratio of female to male witches was 20:1, i.e. that only 4.8% of witches would be male. His explanation for the assumed preponderance of female witches was as follows:

'The reason is easie, for as that sexe is frailer than men is, so it is easier to be intrapped in these grosse snares of the Devil, as was over will proved to be true, by the Serpent's deceiving of Eva at the beginning, which makes him the homlier with that sexe sensine'. (James VI and I, 1597, pp. 43-44)

Was this view widely held? I do not know. It certainly does seem to a good example of what might be meant by the term 'sexist'.

Could the Devil make witches pregnant? James VI and I had an answer to this question. He said that when the Devil appears as a man, he occupies the body of a recently deceased person. Hence, he argued, the Devil will appear cold to the witches during sexual intercourse and will eject cold, sterile, semen. In Scotland, female suspected witches were typically accused of having sex with the Devil. For instance, Manie Halieburton, from West Fenton, Dirleton who was burnt as a witch in 1649 confessed that when she was at home: '... in come the Devil and lay with her (she being yet in bed) and had carnal copulation with her, his nature being cold. He desired her to renounce Christ and her baptism and become his servant which she did ...'. Male suspected witches in Scotland were not accused of having sex with the Devil although in other respects – the allegation of a pact with the Devil, meetings with other witches and the performing of *maleficia* – the pattern was the same.

There are problems in saying outright that witch-hunting was women hunting. For instance, most people who are accused of and tried for, say, murder are men. However, we do not normally say that this shows that the law is biased against males. For most crimes, in Scotland now and in the Sixteenth and Seventeenth Centuries, of those tried, most are and were male. We do not automatically conclude that criminal-hunting is man-hunting. (See McLachlan and Swales, 1994). Furthermore, if witch-hunting were woman hunting, the central question would not be 'What proportion of those accused of witches was female?' it would be, rather: 'What proportion of women was accused of being witches?' The answer is that only a tiny proportion of women was accused. If it were a hunt against women, witch-hunting does not seem to have been a very vigorous one. One of the conclusions of The Edinburgh University Survey of Scottish Witchcraft was that most parishes in Scotland never had a witchcraft case at any time. Another way to think of matter in its true proportions is this: if, say, as a rough estimate, two thousand Scottish soldiers were killed at the battle of Culloden then that would have been more men, perhaps very many more, than there were women who were ever executed as witches in Scotland between 1563, when the Witchcraft Act was passed and 1736, when the Scottish statutes against witchcraft were repealed. It was not a holocaust. It rarely, if ever, involved hysteria.

Perhaps women felt cowed and intimidated by the possibility that they might have been accused of witchcraft. However, I know of no evidence that they generally did feel that way. Perhaps men felt cowed and intimidated by the possibility that they might be accused of, say, murder, treason or theft. Such fears would have been more rationally (or less irrationally) based than would women's fears of being accused of witchcraft. There again, perhaps men also felt cowed and intimidated by the possibility that they might have been accused of witchcraft. The chances of any particular person being executed as a witch were so remote that the difference between the chances of particular men and of particular women being executed must have been negligible. Of course, fears are not always rationally based and, in any case, we must keep reminding ourselves that our present-day views of what witchcraft prosecution was like are not necessarily the same as those who lived at the time of it had. This is not because we are different sorts of people but because, for instance, we have read and been told different sorts of things about Scottish witchcraft than they read and were told about.

Rationality, Justice and Witchcraft Trials

Nowadays, the commonly held view of 16th and 17th century witchcraft trials and pre-trial investigations is that they were unfair, unjust and irrational procedures and that those who were accused were innocent but were invariably found guilty - often as a result of confessions induced by torture - and executed. However, Scottish witchcraft was not like this. The swim-test was not cited in the Scottish witchcraft trials. I have only ever come across one instance where mention is made of it in the official records of a pre-trial investigation and, by co-incidence, it is in the previously-unpublished manuscript that I have already mentioned and that can be read below. In that case, ropes seem to have been attached to those who were thrown into the water in order that those who did not float would not drown. Not everyone was a fool in Paisley in the 1690s. Notice too that the suspected witch who was thrown in the water did float but was not executed or even tried for witchcraft. Far greater thought and care went into the investigation of witchcraft cases than the popular, crude stereotypical view allows for. Furthermore, as a colleague and I have shown before with regard to early modern Scotland: 'The assertion that it was extremely uncommon to be acquitted in a witch trial is unsupported; and so is the claim that all those found guilty in such trial were executed'. (Swales and McLachlan 1979, p. 91) Our findings were that of all the then-known Scottish witchcraft trials between 1560 and 1730 where the fate of the accused witch was discovered, 53.9 per cent were executed; 4.8 per cent received non-capital punishments; 26.8 per cent were acquitted; and 14.5 per cent had miscellaneous fates – for instance, the suspect died in prison or fled (Swales and McLachlan,, 1979, p. 92 and Larner, Lee and McLachlan, 2005, pp. 236-41.)

The conclusion that not all those who were tried for witchcraft were executed is echoed by the recent Survey of Scottish Witchcraft of Edinburgh University which identifies 3,212 named accused witches in Scotland between 1563 and 1736 (not all of whom were actually put on trial for witchcraft). The question of how many accused witches were executed is answered in the Survey in the following way:

'It's hard to tell, but certainly not all. Of the 3,212 named individuals, we know of the sentence of a trial in only 305 cases. 205 of these were to be executed, 52 were acquitted, 27 were banished, 11 were declared fugitive, 6 were excommunicated, 2 were put to the horn (outlawed), 1 person was to be kept in prison and 1 person was to be publicly humiliated. In addition, a further 98 were recorded as having fled from prosecution'. (Goodare, Martin, Miller and Yeoman, 2003)

In many instances at least, witchcraft trials were what they purported to be: they were honest attempts, however clumsy, to discover the truth. They were about the arguments and the evidence that were presented and evaluated in order to establish whether accused people were guilty or not guilty of the specific charges levelled against them. This was so for witchcraft cases no less than it was for the trials for other crimes although, no doubt, miscarriages of justice sometimes occurred then just as they sometimes do now.

In terms of the Scottish Witchcraft Act of 1563, it was a crime – it was a capital offence – for any person to use 'Witchcraftis Sorsarie or Necromancie nor gif thame selfis furth to have any sic craft or knawledge thairof thairthrow abusand the pepill' (see Larner, Lee and McLachlan, 2005, p. 283) It was, that is, a crime not only to use witchcraft, sorcery and necromancy, it was a crime to purport to be able to do so. It was also a crime – a capital offence – to consult witches. In my view, although it was a product of misplaced religious zeal on the part of the new Scottish Presbyterians, the Witchcraft Act was, at least to an extent, paternalistic in nature. You might well say that the Act did not have a paternalistic effect but paternalistic legislation frequently fails to fulfil to hopes and intentions of those who framed it. Think, for instance, about legislation against drug-taking. Think about Prohibition. At least in part, the Act was passed in order to prevent gullible people from being fleeced by charlatans, I would argue. This, I think, is one of the reasons why few people, if any, were actually executed merely for having consulted witches. Witchcraft is referred to in the act as a 'vane superstition'. It is uncertain whether or not the legislators believed in the efficacy of witchcraft. They might not have done. It is possible, for instance, that they thought of it as a legacy of Popish superstition. Notice that the Reformation occurred in Scotland in 1560, three years before the Witchcraft Act was passed.

Goodare presents a tantalising case for saying that the Witchcraft Act was actually drafted by a minister (or by ministers) rather than by a parliamentary lawyer. According to him, 'The act originated with the leaders of the new Protestant Church....Although there is no conclusive evidence that the general assembly of December 1562 saw the drafting of a witchcraft act, the indications are there, and this is also the scenario that makes the most sense of what followed.' (Goodare, 2005, pp. 40-41) John Knox is suggested as a likely author of the act.

At least some of those who were found guilty of being witches were found guilty because they were guilty of being witches. In order to be a witch and to be correctly found guilty, beyond all reasonable doubt, of being a witch, it was not necessary to be a successful witch. It was sufficient that one had purported to be one. Those who thought that particular people were witches did not necessarily believe in witchcraft in the sense that they thought that it 'worked'.

Notice that the act talks, in the same breath of witchcraft, necromancy and sorcery. These general terms were used, I think, in order to cover all actions that the courts might want to consider as unacceptable dabbling with the supernatural. The terms did not necessarily always have precise, differentiated meanings. They were, I suspect, deliberately vague like a term such as 'breach of the peace'. Just as there is no 'essential' feature of an offence of breach of the peace, there was, perhaps, no essential feature to an offence of witchcraft, necromancy and/or sorcery. Sometimes, people in Scotland were charged with witchcraft and charming even although, as far as I can discover, this wording is more in line with the English legislation of 1604 than it is with Scots law. In any event, what did 'charming' mean exactly? It is not clear.

Maxwell-Stuart and the Cases of Tibbie Smart and Elizabeth Dunlop

It is the view of Maxwell-Stuart that some of those people who were found guilty of witchcraft were clearly guilty. Some, for instance, were professional witches. Moreover, he also argues that:

'... even when circumstances might appear to be particularly hostile to someone accused of witchcraft, the authorities were willing to acknowledge a person's innocence, or that the evidence presented to them was insufficient.' (Maxwell-Stuart, 2001, p. 92)

Consider, for instance, the case against Tibbie Smart from Mickle Coull, in South Aberdeenshire. (See Maxwell-

Stuart, 2001, pp. 94-6). She had a reputation as a witch and had been previously convicted as a witch and branded on the cheek as a punishment and as a public sign of her conviction. She had been accused of healing sick animals, causing the death of animals and claiming to be able to find lost goods. John Davidson – 'ane puir man' – was said to have found a purse belonging to Tibbie Smart. It contained, among other things, human bones. John Davidson burned the purse. When Tibbie Smart found out, she was furious and threatened that he would become ill. He became sick, wasted away and, within eight days was dead. John Dacre sowed grass on land that Tibbie Smart had wanted to use. She threatened that the sheep that he hoped to graze on the land would all die. They all died.

There was a feud in Ardo, Kincardineshire between the Findlaws and the Reids. In the course of it, in 1585, a Reid struck one of the Findlaw's shepherds. The Findlaws sent for Tibbie Smart and hid her in their house for three days and plotted revenge upon the Reids with her. In the charge against her it is said that: '... in the samin moneth of march and yeir of god foirsaid [the Reids] contractit and deidlie, terrible, and crewall sewerand seiknes and swalling in thair hairtis'. (Maxwell-Stuart 2001: 94) In May 1585, David Reid died. In September 1585, Richard Reid died. In December 1585, Christian Reid died. In April 1586, William Reid died.

At her trial in 1586, Tibbie Smart was acquitted, despite what must have seemed to be a strong case against her.

Maxwell-Stuart also draws attention to another particularly interesting case. It is the trial of Elizabeth Dunlop in 1567. (See Maxwell-Stuart, 2001, pp. 72-87) She was the spouse of Andrew Jack and she lived in Lyne, in Ayrshire. As Maxwell-Stuart says:

'Elizabeth's record is unusual in that it consists not so much of the final list of articles drawn up against her as of the questions she was asked and her fairly detailed answers during two separate interrogatory sessions, the second held in September, 1567 and the first undated but probably held in that same month as well.' (2001, pp. 76-7)

She confessed to many strange and to some unremarkable things. She said that she consulted with someone called Thomas Reid, who appeared to her as an elderly man, dressed in grey with a black bonnet and a white stick. He is said by Elizabeth to have died at the battle of Pinkie in 1547. She did not know him when he was alive. The ability to find lost or stolen goods was one of her claimed talents, as was the ability to cure illness in humans and animals. When she cured people and animals, Thomas would tell her what to do and sometimes pull herbs and give them to her for this use. For instance, she said that he gave her something like beetroot and told her to boil it and make a salve or else to dry it and make a powder of it. Many centuries before Lord of the Rings was written, she talked of 'middle earth'.

She had a clientele from the local gentry including Lady Thridpart and Lady Blair. They had items stolen from them and, after consulting Thomas Reid, she was able to tell them who the thieves were. The eldest daughter of William Blair of the Strand was going to marry the Laird of Baidland. Elizabeth said that Thomas Reid told her that, if the proposed marriage took place, it would be a disaster for the girl.

40

Henry Jameson and James Baird from the Mains of Waterstone asked her to discover what had happened to their coulter land share. She said that she would have to consult Thomas Reid. She said that Thomas Reid had told her that John and George Black, father and son - both of whom were blacksmiths - had stolen the items and hidden them in their father's house. She said they had bribed James Douglal, one of the sheriff's officers.

The dowager, Lady Kilbowie, asked her to help her crooked leg. Elizabeth said that Thomas told her that nothing could be done 'because the bone marrow was used up and the blood was rotten'. (Maxwell-Stuart 2001, p. 83)

Elizabeth was found guilty and executed. She might have been tortured and the confession might have been a product of that torture. However, as Maxwell-Stuart points out, this is mere speculation. As speculation, it is not particularly convincing. She did not confess to all that she was accused of and this might be surprising, were she tortured. Furthermore, not all of her reported answers were, by any means, what one might think that her interrogators would have been interested in hearing. For instance, to the question of whether or not she had sex with Thomas Reid, she answered that she did not. Her confessions were not the only evidence against her: there was the testimony of her clientele. I would speculate that she actually was guilty of witchcraft. Whether or not she was a charlatan or a sincere believer in her own abilities, she seems to me to have been a professional witch and, in the words of the Witchcraft Act, 'an abuser of the people'.

Notice that the notion that Elizabeth and her clientele

had about the nature of Elizabeth's alleged dabbling with the supernatural might well have been quite different from the theological theory of diabolical witchcraft that we have looked at. Popular views and those of the elite regarding such matters might well have diverged. Notice too that this case of 1586 is a very early one. The bulk of the cases occurred later, between, say, 1590 and 1660.

Torture and the Nature of the Scottish Witchcraft Trials

Russell says of the early modern European witchcraft trials that: 'They reflect a world of belief and practice that is almost entirely alien to us'. (2001, p. 122) This is potentially very misleading as a description of the Scottish witchcraft trials even although the particular trial in Eichstatt, Germany, that he gives an account of sounds bizarre in the extreme. In addition to other important considerations, Russell fails to make it clear that the sort of inquisitorial system that was used in the German case he talks of was not ubiquitous. Scotland, for instance, and other places that he seems to want his theories to be applied to had an accusatorial system. Notice that whether or not a system is inquisitorial is a different question from whether or not it involves a 'jury' of some kind.

In some respects, the practices of the 16th and 17th century Scottish courts were 'alien'. For instance, none of the court officials was female. None of the members of the jury was female. In most cases, the witnesses were males: the testimony of female witnesses was not admissible except in exceptional circumstances and exceptional types of cases such as treason and witchcraft. However, there was this fundamental similarity. It was the task of the pursuer, i.e. the advocate for the prosecution – not the judge – to convince the jury – not the judge – beyond all reasonable doubt that the accused person was guilty of one or other of the specific charges against him or her.

Russell gives the impression that witchcraft trials were some sort of power struggle between accused witches and the torturers of accused witches and that the aim of the tortures was to induce the accused witch to say what the torturers implored them to say. That impression is seriously misleading. In the Scottish cases at least, torture of this sort was not always nor, perhaps, even frequently used even if other types of cruel treatment were routine. Furthermore, even when they played a part, torturers were a small number in the total cast of those involved in the various processes of investigation and deliberation.

Commissions could be specifically granted in particular instances to authorise the use of torture in particular witchcraft trials and investigations. However, in the absence of such specific authorisation, the use of torture in witchcraft trials was not legal. It might, of course, have occurred illegally in some or many instances but there is no justification for saying that it always or typically did. Sleep deprivation in order to get the suspected witches to confess seems to have been used by the kirk sessions and others although not in the manner described by Russell as part of a trial for witchcraft but as a means of getting evidence in order to get a commission from the Privy Council to try suspects as witches. Whether – and if they did, to what extent – such 'confessions' formed part of the case against suspected witches at any subsequent trial is an interesting question but not an easy one to answer. Whether torture was used in the investigations is one thing, whether confessions provoked by it were used as evidence in the trials is another.

Consider the following extract from a letter from John, Earl of Loudon, chancellor of Scotland to George Home of Kimergem and others, 12th April, 1650. This letter was written to local commissioners regarding the trial of three witches in Berwickshire.

'Haveing issued furth a commissioun to yow against certane persons accused of the cryme of witchcraft, and being desirious that thair tryell may not be informall but upon sume well grounded evidentes, wee thought fitt heirby to recommend to your special care that, notwithstanding any confessiouns emitted by the parties before the ecclesiasticall judges, you would appoint tuo or on[e] at least of your number to repare to the parties with some of the ministers befor whom they formerly confest, and cause them renew their confessioun in thair presence'.(See Historical Manuscripts Commission, Fourteenth Report, Appendix, Part III, London, 1894: 109-110)

In some instances, it was even stated as, I would suggest, a reminder and a warning, in the particular commissions that torture must not be used. For instance, in the Commission granted by the Privy Council for the trial of Margarter Guthrie of Carnbee in Fife in 1664 for witchcraft, it is stipulated that she be tried: 'without any sort of torture or indirect means used to bring her to confession'. The same thing is said in the commission for the trial for witchcraft of Isobell Key in St. Andrews in 1666. (See *Register of the Privy Council*, 3rd Series, vol. 2, pp. 165 and 246)

What, in any case, is meant by 'torture'? Macdonald argues that we should clarify our terms in this area. He writes:

'Precise definitions are crucial.... We therefore need to distinguish between six elements: judicial torture (what Larner called direct torture, that is the application of physical coercion as part of the broadly understood legal process in order to extract a confession; searches for a witch-mark (witch-pricking); sleep deprivation (waking and watching); harsh jail conditions including cold, poor treatment by guards, and lack of food; mob violence; and finally, the method of execution, however cruel. These distinctions are not intended to downplay what must have been a brutal experience for those involved. Why they must be made is so that a fair comparison can be made between the Scottish witch-hunt and those in other parts of Europe'. (Macdonald, 2002, p. 127)

Russell is, as we have seen, clearly talking about 'judicial torture'. Macdonald has conducted a superb and extensive study of the available documentation concerning witchcraft cases in Fife between 1560 and 1710. He concludes:

'An examination of those accused as witches in Fife shows that they did indeed experience harsh conditions, mob actions, and, in many cases, sleep deprivation. There is strong evidence that some were searched by witch-prickers in order to search for the mark the Devil supposedly placed on their bodies. There is, however, no evidence that any of those in Fife accused of witchcraft ever underwent judicial torture.' (2002, p. 127)

In his study of Scottish 16th century witchcraft, Maxwell-Stuart says:

'In fact, the use of torture in Scottish witchcraft trials is, except for one or two undoubted instances, a highly debatable matter.... Close confinement, watching and frequent intimidation by men of consequence from the suspect's local community, together with the other hazards attendant upon imprisonment in hard, possibly harsh, conditions did not, however, constitute torture. Torture was a judicially approved process involving the use and application of instruments intended to inflict pain. Anything else amounted to maltreatment or ill-usage, but could not be defined legally as a process for extracting information, or confirming information already obtained'. (2001, pp. 72-73)

Notice that the definitional distinctions that Macdonald and Maxwell-Stuart make might not be significant in all circumstances. For instance, if someone is deprived of sleep, then some people would be inclined to call the sleep deprivation 'torture' whether or not it was a legally sanctioned process of inflicting pain in order to produce information and whether or not it was direct physical torture and whether or not it was done in order to produce a confession. If and when suspected terrorists are roughly treated, their interrogators are waiting and listening not merely for possible confessions but for anything that might be said that might help them in the investigation of crimes and for anything in particular that might incriminate the suspected person or other people. Nevertheless, torture cannot be said to be known to have been routine and pivotal in the Scottish witchcraft trials (although it still remains possible, even if unlikely, that it was).

Russell also stresses the role of confessions, which

he says were crucial. They were not crucial in Scotland although, then as now, the confessions of accused persons was regarded as important. However, if all that could be levelled against a witchcraft suspect was that, under torture, he or she had confessed to being a witch, I suggest that the person would, in all likelihood, have been acquitted if the case had come to court - when, of course, the person could have pleaded not guilty. It is more likely that such a case would not have reached a court.

Goodare's Five-Stage Model of Prosecution

Russell in his paper focuses on a particular aspect of the witchcraft prosecutions: a particular feature of a particular trial, i.e. the relationship between a particular accused witch and her torturer. Goodare's five-stage model of prosecution is a useful antidote to Russell's myopic, narrow gaze. According to Goodare, there were, in general, five stages in the successful prosecution of crimes in Scotland. There was: first of all, deliberation about the occurrence of some particular deviant act and the classification of it by the members of the community as a criminal act; secondly, there was the attempt by members of the community to ensure that a specific person was tried for a specific offence; thirdly, there was the decision by particular court officials that a particular person should be tried for a particular crime by their court; fourthly, there was the trial itself and the verdict of the jury; fifthly, there was the sentencing by the judge (see Goodare, 2002, pp. 123-4).

Goodare writes:

'A prosecution thus faced a series of hurdles, and could

fall at any one of them... Suspected witches and their relatives can sometimes be seen trying to persuade their neighbours not to take a case to court; we mainly know about the times when they failed, but they must often have succeeded. In the third stage, the clerk to the court might tell the aggrieved neighbours to go away because their prima facie case was too weak; this would not be recorded, and only rarely do we have evidence of such cases. At the fourth and fifth stages, the assize might acquit, or the judge might impose an unusually lenient sentence'. (Goodare 2002, p. 124)

The third stage, when central government was brought into the picture was the crucial one according to Goodare. He has some very interesting things to say about the trials that were conducted locally but authorised centrally by the Privy Council. He notes that there was a very low rate of acquittal in these trials. The trials were often, in a sense, a mere formality. In effect, he argues, the Privy Council was itself trying the cases, very cautiously and carefully, on the basis of the evidence that was submitted to it and granting commissions to the local applicants only when it was convinced that there was sufficient evidence properly to convict the suspects. To say that the trials were formalities does not mean that they were travesties. Consider an analogy. When they are running well, examination boards for the degree classification of students are usually formalities. The work has already been fairly and justly done before then.

Witches as Healers

Russell regards witchcraft as a non-elite body of

48

knowledge, one that the authorities were intent on suppressing and denying the reality of. He considers that the trials were like contests between or tests of the legitimacy of different sorts of knowledge. The trials involved the attempted suppression by representatives of the elite of competing claims to knowledge made by members of the non-elite. So Russell thinks. (See Russell, 2001.) This is in line with a view that is frequently expressed to me quite forcefully at my talks on Scottish witchcraft by members of the audience. It is that the accused witches were healers.

Sometimes, but not normally, accused Scottish witches seem to have been healers and were accused of healing as, for instance, in the case of Bessie Paine who was indicted for witchcraft in 1671. All the charges against her seem to relate to *beneficium* in curing people and animals of sicknesses rather than of *maleficium* i.e. the causing of harm. For instance, it is charged in her indictment that: 'Cuthbert Browne of Craigend his first wife being sick, he sent for Bessie Paine who before she was spoken to concerning the nature of the disease told her that Agnes Rowan had witched her and thereafter she went and cured her'. (See Larner, Lee and McLachlan 2005, pp. 269-71.) John Brugh from Kinross-shire was said to have made much money from curing sicknesses before being strangled and burnt in 1643. (See McLachlan and Swales, 1980, p. 148.) Janet Cock (or Cook) from Dalkeith, who was executed as a witch in 1661, was specifically accused of trying to heal people. Another instance of someone who was accused of trying to heal through the use of witchcraft was Issobell Haldane from Perth who was tried in 1625. It is worth noting in passing that, in the commission from the Privy Council authorising the provost and baillies of Perth to try her, there is a *proviso* that the punishment 'extend not to lyff nor members'. She was executed.

To the question: were the witches midwives or healers? the response of the Edinburgh Survey of Scottish Witchcraft team is:

'Not usually. We have recorded 9 individuals whose occupation was recorded as being a midwife, and for 10 people midwifery practices were included as part of the accusations of witchcraft levelled against them. This is a tiny percentage of the overall total. Folk healing was more common and featured in the witchcraft accusations of 141 people – about 4%. Even so, it is not something that the typical witch seems to have engaged in – though the beliefs that underpinned folk healing were closely related to witchcraft beliefs. If magic could be used to heal, it could also be used to harm'. (See Goodare, Martin, Miller and Yeoman, 2003)

The famous Paisley case of 1697 is particularly relevant to the assessment of Russell's theory insofar as professional medical practitioners gave evidence at the trial. However, their role in the case does not provide evidence for Russell's theory. The medical practitioners were Dr. Matthew Brisbane, a physician and Mr Marshall, an apothecary. They did not say that the accused witches were charlatans. If they had done so that might have been regarded as an attempt to suppress particular powers that the accused people had or to deny that they had particular powers (that, according to Russell they had). Brisbane and Marshall attributed powers to the accused that they did not have rather than denied that they had powers that they did have.

What their evidence amounted to was the assertion that not all of the ailments and experiences of Christian Shaw could be explained by them, i.e. by Brisbane and Marshall. They concluded that some of them must be supernatural. Their elite medical knowledge was insufficient to explain fully what was happening to Christian Shaw: therefore, they concluded, some causes other than natural ones must be in play. They were not saying that elite medical knowledge was superior to that of the witches. The trial was not a contest between elite and non-elite forms of knowledge.

Houston argues that for Brisbane, natural and supernatural explanations would: '...not have been in competition, for ultimately God provided all causes and remedies alike. Furthermore, in the Neoplatonic scheme of things, both demonic intervention and demonic possession were strictly manipulations of nature rather than something beyond it. In diagnosing Christian Shaw, Matthew Brisbane tried simply to select the correct level of explanation for particular phenomena. Learned and painstaking, Brisbane's analysis of the Shaw case shows the coexistence of different understandings of Christian's condition'. (Houston, 2000, p. 319)

Scotland and Witchcraft: Concluding General Remarks

Various particular trials for, say, murder, rape, treason or shop-lifting could be shown to be miscarriages of justice. However, we would not thereby conclude that all trials for such crimes are unjust. Hence, if some particular trial for witchcraft were a travesty of justice, it would not follow that all witchcraft trials were travesties of justice. It would not follow that, by their very nature, witchcraft trials were unfair and unjust procedures. Furthermore, it would not follow that the legal systems in which they occurred were necessarily, overall, poorer ones than legal systems tend to be. Even the very best of them have lapses from pure rationality, justice and fairness. Witchcraft should not have been a crime. The Scottish politicians who, with the encouragement of the Kirk, passed the Witchcraft Act of 1563 were unwise to do so. One can be sure that politicians are at this moment devising more and more laws to make particular actions – that have hitherto been perfectly legal – crimes. Not all such laws will be wise laws. Not all such laws will have the effects that their makers intended. That is the way it is now. That is the way it was in Scotland in the 16th and 17th centuries, when most of the trials for witchcraft occurred.

Even if witchcraft cases do in some respects seem very strange to us, at least some of the behaviour involved is very familiar. I suggest that it might be worthwhile to think about witchcraft prosecution of long ago as being, in some respects, akin to modern reactions to terrorism, threats of terrorism and fears of terrorism. Policies were devised and practices were followed in reaction to what people at the time or, rather, some people at the time believed, whether rightly or wrongly, to be real and unusual risks and dangers. Because the dangers seemed novel and strange, new laws were passed to meet the perceived problems. Normal safeguards and procedures were, to an extent suspended. When, as a young man, I first studied Scottish witchcraft as the research assistant of the late Professor Christina Larner – who I can still see now in my mind's eye looking like Merryl Streep with a dash of John Lennon's defiant eccentricity - I used to think that the use of torture and the use of female witnesses in witchcraft cases tended to show how desperate the authorities were for convictions in such trials. Maybe so. However, now, I tend to think that it showed more how keen they were to establish the truth in cases where the truth was thought to be particularly difficult to discover.

I used to think that torture was useless as a means of discovering the truth since, under torture, people might say whatever they think their torturer want them to say. I can see now that although torture is not much use as the sole means of verifying theories, it can still be a useful tool in interrogation as long as it is used carefully. Torturers do not and need not believe everything or anything that those they torture tell them. However, under torture, people can say things that they would not otherwise say or say so promptly: such things can then be checked by other means. Torture can be used to suggest theories that might not otherwise have been thought of even although it is not in itself a reliable means of testing the suggested theories. Who were your accomplices? Torture can speedily elicit answers to that question. Other investigations can test the veracity of them. In any case, it now seems that torture was not used in witchcraft cases as widely and indiscriminately as I used to think.

Is the use of torture justified? It is very interesting to note that this old question that teased people in the past, in particular with reference to witchcraft and treason cases, has been raised again recently in the light of the fear of terrorism. James VI of Scotland who, with the union of the crowns, became James I and went to England, neatly unites the issues. He not only wrote a book about witchcraft but was personally involved with the torturing of accused witches and traitors – terrorists in all but name – who were alleged to have tried to shipwreck him and his bride. Furthermore, Guy Fawkes, in one of history's best known acts of terrorism, tried to blow him up along with his ministers and children shortly after he came to live in England. Guy Fawkes was, as is well known, captured and tortured. Was the torturing of him morally justified? I do not know but I think that, at least, a case could be made in support of it. He was caught in manifestly suspicious circumstances while involved in a transparently treasonable conspiracy against the high officials of the state and put to the horrible torture of the rack. As a result of that torture, information was obtained that brought about the speedy identification and capture of his fellow conspirators. Consequently, the significant risk that they posed to the maintenance of the state and the safety of the populace was eliminated. Did Guy Fawkes have, as some people would claim, a 'human right' that was infringed by the torture? I think that he had (like the rest of us) a moral right not to be tortured but that he forfeited it by his idiotic, reckless behaviour and his murderous intentions.

Whether or not the use of torture can be in particular circumstances morally justified is an interesting question but it is not the crucially important one in this context. The important practical question is this: should torture by the state be, in any circumstances, legal? It should, perhaps, be illegal even in the particular circumstances where it might be morally justified.

The Renfrewshire Witchcraft Prosecution of 1697

The 1690s could be thought of as years of particular religious, social and political tension and crisis in Scotland. 1688 saw the 'Glorious Revolution' and the start of the reign of William of Orange and Mary. After a period of Episcopalianism, Presbyterianism was restored in Scotland. However, '... the diehard Presbyterians who were returned to power were disappointed at the low moral tone and lack of religious enthusiasm of many of their compatriots. This escalated to a feeling of crisis with the publication of John Toland's *Christianity Not Mysterious* in 1696'. (Wasser, 2002, p. 150) There was war with France, bad harvests and famines. There was the massacre of Glencoe in 1692, which had its origins in the issue of allegiance to King William and the continuing fear and threat of Jacobitism. In the latter half of the 1690s, there was the disastrous Darien scheme and the consequent draining of Scottish financial resources and confidence. According to Wasser:

'During the Bargarran case and for a number of years thereafter these crises found specific expression in the Renfrewshire region. For example, 6 December 1696 saw the beginning of a French invasion scare that continued for a number of months. This was not just a physical threat; the French represented the great Antichrist, the Roman Catholic church. As the Bargarran witches were being tried, taxes and troops were being levied in the west to repel the expected invaders. The Bargarran witchcraft narrative contains references to beggars coming to the house, and this must be seen against a backdrop of an ongoing famine

and the Privy Council's attempt to control food prices.'
(Wasser, 2002, p. 150)

Although Christian Shaw was brought up as a Presbyterian, she was born during the Episcopalian ascendancy in Scotland and it seems likely that she was baptised by an Episcopalian priest. This consideration might well have seemed important to those around her whether or not it had any significance for the child herself. It might help to illuminate the following conversation that, in the *Narrative* of her reported suffering reprinted below, she is supposed to have had with the Devil:

'Woudst thou have me renounce my Baptism? ... Dost thou say my baptism will do me no good, because thou alledgest he was not a sufficient Minister that baptized me? Thou art a liar. I'll be content to dye ere I renounce my Baptism.'

Thirty five people were accused of witchcraft of whom thirty were named – twenty women and ten men. However, not all those who were accused were tried. Seven people were tried – four women and three men. They were: Katherine Campbell; Agnes Naismith; Margaret Fulton; Margaret Lang; John and James Lindsay – aliases Bishop and Curate, respectively; and another John Lindsay from Barloch, who was a cotter, i.e. a tenant farmer on the Laird of Bargarran's land. Another man, John Reid, who was a blacksmith living in Inchinnan was found hanged in his cell when he was in prison awaiting trial. The presumption is that he committed suicide. He confessed that he renounced Christ and his baptism to the Devil. He renounced his renunciation of Christ and asked for God's mercy. At one of the witches' meetings in Bargarran Orchard when they were planning the death of Christian Shaw, the Devil, so it is said, gave them some flesh to eat so that, if interrogated, they would not confess. Reid did not eat the flesh and he subsequently confessed to being a witch. He said that a black dog led them to the meeting places. Marks that were insensible to pain had been found on the small of John Reid's back.

It is often said that six people were tried and executed. This is not so: there were seven. Perhaps the confusion arises from the fact that there were two John Lindsays or perhaps because of John Reid's death in prison. They were accused of the murder by witchcraft of a minister called John Hardie and several children as well as bewitchment of Christian Shaw. They were also accused of capsizing the Erskine ferry boat by witchcraft thereby drowning the Laird of Brighouse, John Glen the ferryman and several horses.

Allan Naismith, aged twenty-three, schoolmaster and Andrew Wallace, aged twenty-five , a minister, testified to the painful death of Mr Hardie. He threw himself around his death bed violently, his face, with a strange expression went bright red and he conversed with people who were not seen by other bystanders. He said: 'I live by faith in the Son of God, by whom I expect to be saved and on whom I depend'. When the witches made an image of John Hardie, out of, among other things, bees wax and hair, Agnes Naismith played a central role. It was dipped in a mixture of water and ale and roasted in a spit over a fire. This took place in the yard of John Hardie's manse. He was the minister at Dumbarton.

Of the crimes of witchcraft, sorcery, necromancy and charming, all except John Lindsay in Barloch were unanimously found guilty. He was found guilty by a majority vote. He had a mark on his back which a pin could only penetrate slightly and a similar mark on his shoulder that could not be penetrated even by a tailor's needle. Once, when he had happened to visit the Bargarran household, Christian Shaw fell into a fit. This had led to his being suspected as a witch. When he was found guilty at his trial, he seemed to be stupefied and dumb-struck. He is said not to have uttered another word in his (brief) life thereafter.

They were all hanged and then burnt. The usual Scottish practice was to strangle them and then burn them. To hang witches was the English custom. It is also what happened in Salem, Massachusetts. This was a very late Scottish case. Witchcraft cases were few and far between. Very few, if any, people in Renfrewshire in the 1690s would have had any idea what Scottish witchcraft trials were normally like. How would they have known? It is only now that such knowledge is becoming available. As a colleague and I have written:

'In Scotland in the later part of the seventeenth century, the only courts competent to deal with witchcraft cases were the High Court and those authorised by specific commissions from the Privy Council. In the records of the Privy Council, one has to go back as far as 1677 for even the mention of a witch – Annabel Stewart – in or remotely near Paisley. In the same year there was a commission for the trial of five accused witches across the Clyde in Dumbarton. Bessie Neveing was tried for witchcraft in the (High) circuit court in Renfrew in 1658.... We can find no High Court case which is prior and closer in both space and time to the Bargarran incidents – they occurred almost forty years later – than that'. (McLachlan and Swales,

2002, pp. 60-61)

It would be a mistake to imagine that present day stereotypes of 16th and 17th century witchcraft were stereotypes in Paisley in 1697.

It is a strongly held current local belief that the seven witches were buried at the junction of Maxwellton Street and George Street in Paisley, where there is a horse-shoe in the road that – supposedly – marks the spot. It is obvious to anyone who cares to look at it that the horse-shoe is a comparatively new one, and it has not been there continuously since 1697. The witches were not buried at that particular spot. They were hanged and burnt somewhere near there but almost certainly not precisely there, in the middle of what was or has become two roads. What would have been left of the bodies to be buried after they were burnt? Perhaps their skeletons or some of their bones would have remained. They might have been buried somewhere near the junction. The local belief is that the witches were buried at this crossroads in order to prevent them seeking and finding people to take their revenge upon in line with a supposed curse. This sounds rather much like 'trying to use Satan's shield against Satan's sword' and I doubt very much whether such a manifestly superstitious and whimsical strategy would have been publicly and officially adopted. I suspect that the local belief is, like the horseshoe, not a very old one.

Be careful when you come across the expression 'famous witnesses'. Specialist historians as well as general readers have been confused by it. If someone is called a 'famous witness' in the context of a Scottish witchcraft case, or some other cases of a similar vintage, it does not mean that he was necessarily a well-known person or a celebrity of some sort. What is meant is that the person is famous in the sense that he is not infamous. He is of good fame rather than notorious.

Similarly, be careful with the expression 'the Bargarran Impostor'. The implication is not that Christian Shaw was pretending to be someone other than who she was but that she was pretending to be something other than she was, namely genuinely tormented. One of the central issues at dispute in the literature about the case is the nature of the child's supposed suffering. According to the writer or writers of the *Narrative*, she was tormented by the Devil and by witchcraft and witches. The extract from the diary of Lady Anne Halkett, who lived in Fife in the latter part of the seventeenth century that is reprinted below shows that at least one contemporary person had some sympathy with that view. Those who call her the Bargarran Impostor claim that she was deliberately pretending to be afflicted and that she managed to fool credulous adults, court officials and jury-members into thinking that she was bewitched. This is the traditional orthodox explanation of the case. Others, most notably McDonald, Thom and Thom consider that she was suffering from a mental illness. Their paper on the topic is reprinted below. Isobel Adam also supports a similar position. (See Adam, 1978.) Her book is highly readable, balanced in judgement and very well researched. However, the novelistic style that she adopts does not allow the reader always to tell when she is merely inventing incidents and conversations for literary effect and when she is presenting and interpreting facts. (The same could be said, to a lesser extent, about Godbeer's *Escaping Salem*.)

My own view, developed with Kim Swales, is different. We think that both these theories might plausibly account for some of the elements and aspects of the case but they cannot account for all of them. The key, we suggest, is the realisation that some or other of the reports of the stunningly strange events are fabrications. We argue that they were inspired by an awareness of Lawson's account of Salem witchcraft. Whether or not they were deliberate, wilful fabrications remains a debatable issue. Our paper 'Exonerate the Erskine One' concludes this volume.

Christian Shaw became a very successful business woman and entrepreneur. She managed the Bargarran Thread Company. This was a basis for the cotton industry in Paisley, upon which much of its subsequent prosperity depended. I have written a brief account of her life for *The Biographical Dictionary of Scottish Women*.(Ewan, Innes, Reynolds and Pipes, 2006) It would be splendid if someone were to write a full biography of her. There should be a plaque or some such commemorative item in or near to Paisley in honour of this wonderful woman. The people of Renfrewshire can be surprisingly reticent when it comes to celebrating their heroes and heroines.

The Second Major Outbreak of Witchcraft Accusation in Renfrewshire in the 1690s

Many years ago, in Register House in Edinburgh, I came across a document which indicates that in and around Renfrewshire in the 1690s, various people other than Christian Shaw – including (but not only) other children – were involved with the sorts of bizarre behaviour which she was said to have indulged in. It is published for the first time ever below. The document is dated Glasgow May 1699. (See National Archives of Scotland, MS JC/26/81/D9)

Just as New England in 1692 has a famous and non-famous witch hunt, so too does Scotland in the 1690s. In both instances, awareness of the non-famous case sheds light on the other one and shows again that witch hunting was not as blindly irrational and enthusiastic as it is commonly thought to be and as the stereotype suggests. People were more circumspect and cautious regarding witchcraft accusations, prosecutions and convictions than they are commonly thought to have been. In the first Renfrewshire batch of witchcraft accusations, as we have seen, seven people were tried and executed as witches in Paisley in 1697 although, initially, over twenty people had been charged. In a very similar sort of over-lapping case (involving very similar types of evidence and even some of the original suspects and victims), twenty five people were charged with witchcraft as indicated in the discovered document and obliged to compear before their Lordships within the Tollbooth of Glasgow on 19th of May, 1700. The case was 'deserted' i.e. dropped. None of those charged was actually brought to trial. The procedures were not mechanical ones. Thought does seem to have been given by the authorities to the weight of evidence available against accused people in witchcraft cases. It would seem that the evidence was not thought to be sufficiently strong to secure reliable convictions. At least, there were other more pressing matters for the courts' attention.

If Christian was a deliberate hoaxer or was mentally ill then so too, one might suppose, were other alleged victims of witchcraft around the same time and at the same place. If other such alleged victims of witchcraft were not deliberate hoaxers and were not mentally ill, then one might suspect that Christian Shaw herself was not a hoaxer and not mentally ill. Let us have a brief preview of this other wave of witchcraft cases.

John Patersone from Geillie was charged with being a witch and was said to have been commonly reputed to be a warlock and to have been accused by other confessing witches '... and he has ane insensible mark and was named by Christian Shaw daughter to Bargarran and by Margrat Reid as on[e] of their tormentors and when Margrat Laird was in her insensible fits her foot did stand away as his did and she walked like him upon a staff'. At the time of the 1697 trial and the years of supposed bewitchment that led up to it, Christian Shaw was a pre-teenaged child. She would have been, during this time, between 10 or 11 and 12 years old. Margaret Laird was also a child. Margaret Reid was an adult. It is obviously possible that Margaret Laird was play-acting when she walked in a manner similar to John Patersone. But the following incidents are not so readily explained.

Margaret Laird named Janet Laing, the spouse of John Mathey elder in Penitorsone, as one of her tormentors and fell into a fit when Janet's name was mentioned to her. When Janet looked into a room where Margaret Laird was, the child fell into a fit even although it is said that the child could have had no way of knowing that Janet had looked into the room. A similar thing happened when Janet was covered by a blanket and Margaret Laird was, unbeknown by the child, brought into her presence.

Annabell Reid was the spouse of John Stewart. They lived in Inchinnan. She was charged with witchcraft and named by Margaret Laird as one of her tormentors. Annabell touched Margaret's hand and Margaret fell into a fit and her hand swelled and turned blackish. The Rev. Mr. James Brisbane challenged Annabell and claimed that she had laid a charm on Margaret's hand. Annabell said: 'The Lord Jesus Christ take it off for I cannot' and immediately, Margaret's hand returned to its normal colour, the swelling ceased and Margaret's pain went away. If this was a trick, it was quite a trick.

Issobel Houstone, spouse to George Wilson in Houston, was another of Margaret Laird's alleged tormentors. In the document, one reads:

'... when the s [ai]d Margaret Laird was in her fitts she saw the said Issobell Houstone in the roume and spoke to her and challenged her for tormenting her but the said Issobell Houstone was invisible to any other person in the roume as also the said Issobell Houstone tormented a chyld of Mr James Brisbane Minister at Kilmacomes by a pictur of wax untill the chyld dyed....'

This was not trickery nor was it mental illness on the part of the child.

It might be suggested that Janet Laing had a particular smell, but if the child could have detected it, so too could the other bystanders. If we are wary of this as a possible means of trickery on the part of the child, so too, we can imagine, would have been the observers of Margaret Laird's behaviour.

Other people, some of them children, were said to have had other strange experiences.

Jean Ross, an unmarried school teacher from Paisley and Janet Stewart had a quarrel in Paisley in the month of March, April or May in 1697 and Jean Ross went away murmuring something or other. That very same night, Janet's child had extraordinary pains, stiffness and convulsions. These fits lasted from about twelve o'clock at night until five in the morning. After the fits, the child was black and blue as if he had been buffeted and pinched. Between the fits, the child was fine. This lasted for about twelve days. It is said of his condition that: '... physitians and o[ther]r skilled persons could assigne no cause for it...'. Then, the child died. This, again, was not a trick on the part of the child. It does not sound like a mental illness.

It is said in the document that, in 1688, (i.e. years before Christian Shaw's alleged affliction and before the Salem outbreak) Jean Ross had a quarrel with Alexander Mure over his daughter who, it appears, attended Jean's school. It is said that within a week:

'... the chyld was troubled with a strange and extraordinary sickness as one distempered and out of her witts for she did climb up the walls with her feet and dashed herselfe to the bed so that he [i.e. Alexander Mure] could hardly hold her with all his strength and tymes she would have gone out of his hands as souple as a willow wand and the chyld continued under this distemper for three days and then she dyed and two or three nights befor the chyld fell sick the hous was infested by a multitude of cats....'

This could not be explained by trickery or by a supposed mental illness on the part of the child.

Some of the supposed evidence did not come from alleged victims as, for instance, in the following case.

Elspet Wood, from Overgourock was a widow. She was charged with witchcraft and, among other things, it was said against her that she spoke to the Rev. Mr. James Brisbane immediately after he came out of the kirk at Kilmacolm and she repeated part of the first prayer of the morning and discussed with him the sermon which he had delivered in the afternoon. Yet, she or the shape of her had been seen sitting for the whole of that same day in some church in another town.

Conclusion

People from different backgrounds and for various reasons want to know and enjoy reading about historical witchcraft cases. Hence, not every item that is contained in this book will be of equal interest to all readers or of interest to them all for the same reasons. One person's spam is another man's roast beef and yet another's broccoli. Nonetheless, there is here plenty of material that will reward the perusal and scrutiny of both the specialist scholar and the general reader.

A History of the Witches of Renfrewshire

Second Edition, 1877
in facsimile

A HISTORY

OF THE

WITCHES OF RENFREWSHIRE.

A NEW EDITION,

WITH AN

INTRODUCTION,

Embodying Extracts, hitherto unpublished, from the Records of the Presbytery of Paisley.

HARGARREN ARMS.

PAISLEY: ALEX. GARDNER.

1877.

INTRODUCTION.

WITCHCRAFT is a subject that has bulked largely in the history of mankind. A belief in it has been by no means confined to dark ages and barbarous nations. In Jewish history it held a prominent place. The first king of Israel banished wizards and witches from his borders, but could not set himself free from faith in their spells. Many of his successors had dealings with familiar spirits; and down to the days of Christianity, Gentiles as well as Jews all over the world attributed to certain men and women supernatural powers that were generally exercised for evil. Christianity, though it gave a blow to superstition, by no means eradicated it. The influence of heathen beliefs and practices did not cease to be operative when the majority of a nation formally surrendered them. The evil one has always been regarded as the great king and master of the wizard band; and faith in Witchcraft is yet to be found among certain followers of all religions that recognise the existence of the spirit of darkness. Bishop Hutchinson's curious "Historical Essay on Witchcraft" shews how much such superstitions have served to degrade and enslave the intellect, even during periods that have been characterised by great national progress. Pope Innocent VIII., in 1484, issued a bull which indicated the beliefs that in his day were entertained regarding the baleful influences exercised by those who were credited with having made a bargain with Satan, accepting certain gifts from him in return for the surrender of their soul's salvation. "They have intercourse with the infernal fiends`; they afflict both man and beast; they blight the marriage bed; destroy the births of women and the increase of cattle; they blast the corn on the ground, the grapes in the vineyard, the fruits of the trees, and the grass and herbs of the field." To punish these obnoxious men and women he issued most cruel edicts. The Alpine valleys witnessed thousands of victims slaughtered under excruciating tortures, accused of denying Christ, dishonouring his cross, and in Satan's company maintaining his devil's Sabbath. The strongest minds did not rise above the popular delusion. Luther gravely describes his interviews with the spirit of evil, and tells of many bitter nights and much restlessness which he caused him. "I no longer wonder," he says, "that the persons whom he assails are often found dead in their beds. I am of opinion that Gesner and Œcolampadius came in that manner to their deaths." Knox, too, though of stouter mental calibre than the German Reformer, was mainly instrumental in passing a statute which discharged all persons of whatsoever estate, degree, or condition to use any manner of witchcraft, sorcery, or necromancy under the pain of death, "as well to be execute against the user, abuser, as the seeker of the response or consultation." In Scotland the belief in Witchcraft was all but universal, and was sanctioned by the highest authority. It is one of the thousand marvellous proofs of Shakespere's fidelity to truth that his witches ply their vocation on Scottish soil. King James VI. was an ardent student of Witchcraft, which his "Daemonologie," in three books, gravely discusses as a science. His was not only a theoretic speculation, but a real experience as to demoniac antipathies. When he returned from Scandinavia with his bride, there was a strong muster of the Satanic army to oppose him. In his presence many poor victims confessed to being in league with Satan, and explained the schemes which had been planned by the powers of darkness to the prejudice and damage of his Scottish Majesty. When it was declared that a wretched woman named Symson had performed the feat, of sailing with two hundred companions from Leith to North Berwick in a sieve, James had her put to torture. She was subjected to the ordeal of the witch's bridle, and to other cruelties. James, by questioning with pitiless pertinacity, elicited the admission that she and her party had baptised a black cat, and raised a dreadful storm to sink the ship that held the king, for which unholy and regicidal effort she was condemned to be burned, and died protesting her innocence, and calling upon God for "the mercy that Christian men withheld." The Scottish enactments against Witchcraft he transferred to England on his accession, and under the statute many persons perished. This Act was not repealed until 1736, when it was obliterated, yet even in 1743 the Associate Presbytery enumerated amongst other national sins that had subjected the nation to Divine wrath, that "The penal sta-

tutes against Witches have been repealed by the Parliament, contrary to the express law of God ; for which a holy God may be provoked in a way of righteous judgment to leave those who are already ensnared to be hardened more and more ; and to permit Satan to tempt and seduce others to the same dangerous and wicked snare." The Associate Presbytery was composed of seceders from the Scottish Ecclesiastical Establishment, and was in time incorporated into the United Presbyterian Church. The testimony just quoted may be regarded as the last ecclesiastical protest in favour of witch hunting ; but it must not be supposed that among clergy of the Establishment and laymen generally there were few sympathisers with the seceders. The annals of the General Assembly bring before us several proofs that belief in Witchcraft was very general at the beginning of the 18th century. In 1699 an overture against Witchcraft or charming was transmitted to Presbyteries, and in 1707 the subject was the occasion of a protracted discussion, which resulted in an instruction to the commission to advise Presbyteries in regard to cases of witchcraft, sorcery, and charming. In 1730 William Forbes, advocate, Professor of Law in Glasgow University, methodically treated of the crime and its symptoms in a professional work, " The Institutes of the Law of Scotland," in which he excuses himself for declining to follow the English commentators who touch the matter as if it were an obsolete belief. " Nothing seems plainer to me than that there may be, and have been witches, and that perhaps such are now actually existing ; which I intend, God willing, to clear in a larger work concerning the criminal law." "Witch-craft is that black art whereby strange and wonderful things are wrought by a power derived from the Devil." Learning and eminence were no defence against the popular supersti-tion. Even Hale, wise and exemplary judge as he was, avowed his belief in Witchcraft on occasion of the trial of two women whom he sentenced to death in 1664; and John Wesley, in his journal, declared that surrender of belief in Witchcraft was tantamount to infidelity. "Giving up Witch-craft," he wrote, "is in effect giving up the Bible."

The explanation of the hold which such superstition retained over strong intellects is to be found in the extreme pertinacity with which the human mind associates the acci-dental surroundings of religion and its essential principles. There is an extreme repugnance to admit that any doctrine once accepted as a truth of revelation has occupied its posi-tion as an incidental accessory, and not as a substantial verity. The last witch-fire kindled in Scotland was in 1722, when a poor old woman, accused of transforming her daughter into a mare to carry her to witches' gatherings, and causing her to be shod by the Devil, so that she was lamed in hands and feet, was condemned, put into a tar-barrel, and burned at Dornoch. The poor creature is represented as having sat warming herself in the cold night at the fire which was being prepared for her execution, "while the other instruments of death were getting ready." The daughter escaped and be-came the mother of a son who was as lame as herself, though it does not appear that the same cause was assigned for the deformity, "and this son," wrote Sir Walter Scott in 1830, "was living so lately as to receive the charity of the present Marchioness of Stafford, Countess of Sutherland in her own right." This was the last execution for Witchcraft in Scotland, and the "Acts Anentis Witchcraft" were formally repealed, the indignant protest of the Associate Presbytery notwithstanding, in June 1736. But although Witchcraft then ceased to be regarded as a specific crime, the trials for fraudulent fortune-telling, which ever and anon are reported in the newspapers, and the many other proofs of superstitious credulity that meet us, suggest the unpleasant reflection that the belief in Witches is to a very considerable extent still prevalent. Without appealing to the evidence arising from recent trials of impostors who set up as spiritualists, and in return for hard cash professed to put their dupes in communication with the invisible world, the superstition that is still displayed in other forms may well occasion surprise. We do not hear so much of it in the busy centres of population, but in country places the credulity of many is surprising, and even in the cities any one who sets up pretentions to supernatural powers will find believers. Burns tells us that faith in the world, which his Tam O'Shanter so picturesquely describes, was not altogether a pretence on his part, but so influenced him that on dark nights, and at suspicious places his heart beat more quickly than it was wont to do in other circumstances. There are still alive Scottish peasants who maintain that there is a witch world around them with which certain men and women are in communication. The evil eye is not yet an obsolete superstition, and the horse shoe is not an extinguished charm against its influence. Southey, in his Common-Place Book, preserves a cutting from the *Scotsman* newspaper of July 1836, which describes a discovery made by boys who, while amusing themselves in searching for rabbit burrows on Arthur's Seat, noticed, in a very rugged and secluded spot, a small opening in one of the rocks, which attracted their attention. The mouth of this little cave was closed by three thin pieces of slate stone, rudely cut at the upper ends into a conical form, and so placed as to protect the interior from the effects of the weather. The boys having removed these tiny slabs, discovered an aperture in which were lodged seventeen Lilliputian coffins forming two tiers of eight each, and one on a third, just begun. Each of the coffins contained a miniature figure of the human form cut in wood, well executed. They were dressed from head to foot in cotton clothes, and decently laid out with a mimic representation of all the funereal trappings, which form the usual habiliments of the dead. Other circumstances, described in detail in the extract, justified the conclusion of the writer that the arrangements were made in consequence of a prevalent belief that there were still some of the weird sisters hovering about Mushat's Cairn or the Windy Gowl, who retained their ancient power to work the spells of death by entombing the likenesses of those they wished to destroy.

The history of the Witches of Renfrewshire furnishes an interesting and characteristic exposition of the beliefs and manners of the times. The extracts from the Records of the Pres-

bytery which follow are now, we believe, for the first time fully
published, and throw a striking sidelight on the narrative
which was drawn up with full ecclesiastical sanction. The
clergymen who took so prominent a part in the investigation
were, many of them, men of note in their day. Not to mention less distinguished iniquisitors, there were William Dunlop,
Principal of the University of Glasgow; Patrick Simpson,
minister of Renfrew, whose reputation was great, and who
was so much respected by his brethren that when age
and infirmity hindered him from leaving his manse, they
appointed some of their number to wait on him and consult him in connection with all matters that came before
them; Robert Millar, an eminent theologian and historical
writer; Thomas Blackwell, a learned scholar and author, who
was transferred from the Abbey of Paisley to Aberdeen, and
was afterwards appointed Principal of the northern University. All these and others entered with zest on the investigation, and the record of the manner in which they conducted
it, though quite in accordance with the spirit of the age, is a
sad chapter of local Scottish history. The subject was first
introduced to the presbytery by Mr. Andrew Turner, minister
of Inchinnan, who reported that Christian Shaw, daughter
of the laird of Bargarren, was suffering from Witchcraft, and
indicated the authors of her trouble. The wretched girl, whose
imposture is so palpable, that we wonder how it could for a
moment have deceived any being possessed of common sense,
seems never to have had her good faith called in question. If
any witchcraft was exercised, it was by the hysterical

80

Christian, who appears to have cast a glamour over parents, Presbytery, Lords of Privy Council, and all who had to do judicially with the case. From the first the poor victims of her wickedness or insanity had not a chance. Their guilt was a foregone conclusion, and the chief efforts made to obtain evidence consisted in appeals made to their consciences to confess guilt. We find no reference in the proceedings to witch-bridles or other instruments, such as King James caused to be applied to the water witches in order to extort confession; but the mental suffering to which they were subjected must have been a dreadful ordeal. The life of a reputed witch was one of constant persecution. In the case of the Renfrewshire witches, the tests usually employed to bring home conviction were probably applied. Among these, inability to shed tears; not sinking in water when thrown in with hands and feet tied across,—the right hand to the left foot, and the left hand to the right foot;—failure to repeat the Lord's Prayer without mistake or omission; excrescences on the body supposed to be the Devil's marks; their being seen with a familiar in the shape of some animal, differing from a real animal in that it could not be caught or killed, were signs accepted as infallible proofs of guilt. King James ingeniously justifies the water ordeal by stating that "God hath appointed (for a supernatural sign of the monstrous impiety of Witches) that the water shall refuse to receive them in her bosom that have shaken off them the sacred water of baptism, and wilfully refuse the benefit thereof; no, not so much as their eyes are able to shed tears, threaten and torture them

c

81

as ye please, albeit" adds his sapient majesty, "the women-kind especially be able otherways to shed tears at every light occasion, when they will; yea, although it were dissemblingly, like the crocodiles." James explains philosophically the reason why there were so many more witches than wizards, by the assertion that the serpent's success with Eve had "made him the homelier with that sex sensine."

Whether such tests found place in the investigations of the Presbytery of Paisley is not recorded, but the " dealing " with the accused parties to which reference is frequently made was no doubt the reason why some of them became, in ecclesiastical language, "confessants." The confession was probably brought about by the cruel treatment to which the poor creatures were exposed. Regarded as traitors to humanity, who had deserted to the standard of man's great enemy, reputed Witches received no sympathy. Every misfortune that visited a neighbourhood or homestead was attributed to their agency. Children fled when they appeared, or pursued them with yells and execrations. No one would give them shelter or sell them food. They were kept in perpetual motion, and if they broke down under the fatigue, their weakness was accepted as an evidence of guilt. The existence of a reputed Witch became so miserable that death was preferable to life. Sinclair, in his "Satan's Invisible World Discovered," tells of several Witches who were tried at Lauder in 1649, and all but one condemned to execution. The one who escaped sent for the minister and others and confessed that she had formed a league with Satan. She was not believed, and was urged to

82

retract her acknowledgment of guilt, but refused, and was condemned to die with the others. When she was carried to
the stake she exclaimed, " Now all you that see me this
day, know that I am now to die a Witch by my own confession, and I free all men, especially the ministers and magistrates, of the guilt of my blood. I take it wholly upon myself;
my blood be upon my own head. And as I must make
answer to the God of heaven presently, I declare I am as free
of Witchcraft as any child, but being delated by a malicious
woman, and put in prison under the name of a Witch, dis-
owned by my husband and friends, and seeing no ground
of my coming out of prison, or ever coming in credit again,
through the temptation of the devil I made up that confession
on purpose to destroy my own life, being weary of it, and
choosing rather to die than to live."

Unquestionably very many of the confessions made by reputed Witches were obtained by torture, and the forms they
took were moulded by the questions of the examiners. The
discovery of Witches became a profession. Manuals for the
guidance of inquisitors, such as the " Malleus Maleficarum "
of Sprenger, were published, containing full directions as to
the signs of guilt, and the forms of questioning the suspected
persons. The general use of these manuals explains the
family resemblance which most of the confessions assume.
Matthew Hopkins, who was honoured with the title of Witch-
finder General, is the most famous in the annals of Witch-hunting. In 1644 and the two following years his exploits gained
for him great fame and emolument. During that time many

scores of accused persons were executed through his energetic prosecutions. His fate affords an illustration of the "engineer hoist on his own petard." It is recorded by Hutchinson that " he went on searching and swimming the poor creatures till some gentlemen, out of indignation at the barbarity, took him and tied his own thumbs and toes as he used to tie others, and when he was put into the water, he himself swam as they did. This cleared the country of him." Butler, in his Hudibras, celebrates the retribution that overtook Hopkins.

> " Has not he within a year
> Hanged threescore of them in one shire ?
> Some only for not being drown'd ;
> And some for sitting above ground,
> Whole nights and days upon their breeches,
> And feeling pain were hanged for witches ;
> And some for putting knavish tricks
> Upon green geese and turkey chicks,
> Or pigs that suddenly deceased
> Of griefs unnatural, as he guessed,
> Who after proved himself a witch,
> And made a rod for his own breech."

While, however, as a general rule, the examinations gave shape to the acknowledgments, it cannot be denied that in some cases confession was made by poor creatures who believed that they were as guilty as others considered them. The mental condition in which such confession originated is by no means a rare psychological phenomenon. Belief in Witchcraft being almost universal, it is not wonderful that persons of a hysterical or morose temperament should attribute experiences and feelings that they could not understand to a direct influence exerted upon them by Satan. If, even

them by the Synod, therefore they appoint Mr. Turner to cause transcribe four copies, and to send one to Principall Dunlop and Mr. Ja. Brown, another to Mr. Balantyne, another to Mr. Mr. Wylie, and another to Mr. Wilson, allowing them to advise with any of the brethren of their respective presbyteries in the revising thereof, appointing them ere they leave to meet and appoint time and place of their next meeting that they may compare their animadversions, and put the wholl relation in a suteable dress.

The meeting considering that the Synod had recommended them to think upon the expediency of having a fast day, on this occasion through the Presbyteries of the Synod, as it had been in the Presbytery of Paisley, as they should find it consistent with the dyets and issue of the Commission; and the meeting finding that the Commission is to be adjourned for some time does judge it expedient and necessary, that betwixt and the next meeting of the Commission there be a fast day throwout the whole bounds of the Synod, leaving it to the particular presbytery to concert their own days to be observed, and if their ordinary meeting fall not in timeously that they call a Presbytery *pro re nata* and appoint Mr. Warner, Mr. Wilson, and Mr. Dav. Brown to draw up some causes of the same against the next meeting.

The meeting appoints all the members that are not upon the forementioned committees to meet to-morrow, at seven o'clock in the morning, for prayer at the Presbytery House, and adjourns till to-morrow after rising of the Commission.

At Pasley, Apr. 15, 1697.

Reported that the representation of the circumstances of the bounds was given in and approven, and put in the hands of the Commissioners.

Mr. Wilson produced the causes of a fast to be kept throw-

sturdie," "the cutting off a stirk's head, boiling it, burning the bones to ashes, and burying the ashes," a remedy which, as Dougall stoutly maintained before the Presbytery, was "most effectual." The accused had also offered "for a 14" to teach a man how to get a part of his neighbours' fishing and his own too. This feat was to be accomplished by taking the sailing pin out of his neighbour's boat. Dougall was declared by the presbytery to be a scandalous person, and sentenced to be publicly rebuked. That he found, however, many to accept his doctrine is proved by the care which the presbytery took to prohibit their parishioners from resorting to, and trafficking with him.

The Commissioners, in the report presented by them to the Privy Council on the 9th of March, 1697, stated that there were twenty-four persons, male and female, suspected of being concerned in the Bargarren case, and in the list a girl of fourteen and a boy under twelve find place. Twenty of the suspected persons were condemned, but only five appear to have been executed. Death was probably produced by burning. It has indeed been alleged that the Witches were hanged first, and their bodies afterwards committed to the flames; but against this the statement found in the presbytery records seems to militate, that "one or two of the brethren" were assigned to each of the sentenced persons "to deal with them, and wait upon them *to the fire.*"

Christian Shaw, whose early history was so painfully associated with Paisley, acquired a reputation of a more pleasant nature in her after life. To her the town is indebted for

86

originating the trade which now occupies in it so prominent a place,—the spinning and manufacture of linen thread. At the time of the investigations she was only 11 years of age, but manifested an amount of cunning and artifice extraordinary at her years. In his statistical account of Scotland, Sir John Sinclair describes the circumstances in which the thread manufacture at Bargarren originated. Christian having acquired great dexterity in the spinning of fine yarn, conceived the idea of manufacturing it into thread. With her own hands she executed almost every part of the process, manifesting great ingenuity in the bleaching and other preparation of material. Holland was at the time the seat of extensive thread manufactories, and Christian having contrived to procure information regarding the mode of conducting the processes in that country, introduced them into her own business, and established an extensive and profitable trade. Bargarren thread obtained a wide celebrity, and, guaranteed by a stamp, held the first place in the market. From this beginning, Paisley and its neighbourhood became celebrated for this branch of industry.

In the newspapers and other publications of the time, the following advertisement found place :—

" The Lady Bargarren and her daughters having attained to a great perfection in making, whitening, and twisting of SEWING THREED, which is as cheap and white, and known by experience to be much stronger than the Dutch, to prevent people's being imposed upon by other Threed, which may be sold under the name of 'Bargarren Threed,' the papers in which the Lady Bargarren and her daughters at Bargarren, or Mrs. Miller, her eldest daughter (Christian, now a widow), at Johnstone, do put up their Threed, shall, for direction, have thereupon their Coat of Arms, '*azure* three covered cups *or*.' Those who want the said Threed, which is to be sold from fivepence to six shillings per ounce, may write to the Lady Bargarren at Bargarren, or Mrs. Miller at Johnstone, near Paisley, to the care of the Postmaster at Glasgow; and may call for the samen in Edinburgh, at John Seton, merchant, his shop in the Parliament Close, where they will be served either in Wholesale or Retail; and will be served in the same manner at Glasgow, by William Selkirk, merchant, in Trongate."

About the year 1718 Christian Shaw became the wife of John Miller, a licentiate of the Presbytery of Paisley, then minister of Kilmaurs. She was soon left a widow, as her husband died in the autumn of 1721, when Mrs. Miller removed to Johnstone, and, in connection with her mother, the Lady Bargarren, and other members of the family, resumed business as a manufacturer of fine linen thread.

EXTRACTS FROM THE RECORDS OF THE PRESBYTERY.

At Pasley, December 30, 1696.

"This day Mr. Turner represented to the Presbytery a deplorable case of Christine Shaw, daughter to the laird of Bargarren, in the paroch of Erskine, who, since the beginning of September last, hath been under a very sore and unnatural-like distemper, frequently seized with strange fits, sometimes blind, sometimes deaf and dumb, the several parts of her body sometimes violently extended, and other times as violently contracted, and ordinarily much tormented in various parts of her body, which is attended with an unaccountable palpitation in those parts that are pained, and that those several weeks by past she hath degorged a considerable quantity of hair, folded up straw, unclean hay, wild-fowl-feathers, with divers kinds of bones of fowles and others, together with a number of coal cinders burning hot, candle grease, gravel-stones, etcetera, all which she puts forth during the forementioned fits, and in the intervals of them is in perfect health, wherein she gives an account of several persons, both men and women, that appeares to her in her fits, tormenting her, all which began with her upon the back of one Kathrine Campbell, her cursing of her, and though her father hath called physicians of the best note to her during her trouble, yet their application of medicine to her hath proven ineffectual, either to better or worse, and that they are ready to declare that they look upon this distemper as *toto genere* preter-natural. All which was attested by the minister who, by the Presbytery's recommendation, had visited her in her trouble, upon all which Mr. Turner desired that the Presbytery would do what they judged convenient in such a juncture. The Presbytery

D

being deeply sensible of the sad circumstances of that Damsel
and family, does appoint the exercise of fasting and prayer to
be continued as it is already set up by Mr. Turner in that
family every tuesday, leaving it to him to call to his assistance
whom he pleased, from time to time. And further, appoints
Mr. Turner and Mr. Birsbane to repaire to Bargarren, friday
next, there to take up a particular narrative of her whole
trouble, of its rise and progress; and also appoints Mr. John
Stirling and Mr. Andrew Turner to go to Edinburgh munday
next, and to lay the whole affair before the Lords of his
Maj.'s Privie Counsell, in order unto their obtaining a
commission for putting those who are suspected to be her
tormentors to a tryall, and in their way thitherward to go to
Dr. Birsbane, and to entreat him to give a declaration of his
sentiments of the foresaid trouble, in order to their more easy
obtaining a Commission as said is.

At Pasley, February 3, 1697.

Anent the business of Witchcraft it was reported that the
appointments anent the taking up of the narrative of Christine
Shaw's trouble, and the going to Edinburgh were obeyed, and
accordingly the Lords of his Majestie's Privie Counsell had
granted a commission to my Lord Blantyre and some other
gentlemen in the bounds for taking a precognition of that
affair, who are to meet at Renfrew, the 5 instant. The
Presbytery appoints Mrs. Symson, Turner, and Blackwell to
wait upon the commission on the foresaid day; and the Presbytery further considering that the trouble of Bargarren's
daughter continueth, therefore the Presbytery appoints thurs-
day-come-eight days for a public day of humiliation and fasting, and Mrs. Hutcheson and Symson are appointed to joyn
with Mr. Turner in that work, leaving it for them to call the
next Presbytery as they shall find convenient.

90

At Pasley, February 17, 1697.

Reported that the fast was kept at Erskine according to appointment, by Mr. Hutcheson and Mr. Sympson joyning with Mr. Turner, who finding that the Commissioners had apprehended several persons delated by James and Thomas Lindsays, and Elizabeth Anderson, now confessant, and accused by Christine Shaw as her tormentors, and that they were to sit at Renfrew to-morrow as their last meeting before their report to the Counsell. Therefore they had called the Presbytery this day that they might consider what was incumbent upon them at this juncture. The Presbytery approved of their being called, and finding that the Commission is to meet to-morrow at Renfrew, does adjourn thither to-morrow against ten of the clock.

At Renfrew, February 18, 1697.

The Presbytery considering what was incumbent upon them at this juncture did, at the desire of the Commissioners, think meet to wait upon them at their enquiries and examinations, and to deal with the consciences of the suspected, now prisoners, to see if they could be brought to a confession, which was done accordingly; and afterward meeting together, and finding Bargarren was desired by the Commissioners to go on with their report, which was to be put in the hand of Sir John Maxwell to present to the Counsell, did think fit that one of our number should go in company with Bargarren, and accordingly did appoint Mr. Thomas Blackwell, and, failing him, Mr. Robert Taylor, to go in to Edinburgh and to represent to the said Sir John Maxwell, and, with his concurrence, to His Majestie's Advocate and other Lords of His Majestie's Privie Counsell, the *lamentable condition* of this part of the country, upon the account of the great number that are delated by some that have confessed, and of the many *murders* and other *malefices* that in all probability are perpetrated by them, and to entreat their compassion in granting a Commission for putting these persons to a tryall, and for bringing the same to an effectual and speedy issue. And that they would order some way for maintaining those of them that have nothing of their own till the tryall be complete, or so long as they shall be detained in prison. And the three confessants, viz., Elizabeth Anderson, James and Thomas Lindsays, the Presbytery thought fit, upon the desire of the said Commissioners for enquiry, that they should be severally keeped by turns in the houses of the ministers of the Presbytery, and that they may have opportunity to instruct and deal with their consciences in the meantime, till further course be taken with them by authority.

At Pasley, March 17, 1697.

The Presbytery this day considering that upon the giving in of the Commission's report, appointed for taking a precognition of the business of witchcraft, the Lords of His Majestie's Privie Counsell had granted a Commission for putting those who are incarcerate or suspected to a tryall, and that those commissionat are to meet to-morrow at Renfrew : therefore the Presbytery appoints Mrs. Pat. Sympson, Dav. Brown, Jo. Stirling, Andrew Turner, Tho. Blackwell to wait upon their Lordships' day and place forsd.

At Pasley, March 24, 1697.

The Presbytery, considering the great rage of Satan in this corner of the land, and, particularly, the continued trouble of Bargarren's daughter, which is a great evidence of the Lord's displeasure, being provoked by the sins of the land (exprest as the cause of our former publike fasts), so to let Satan loose among us : therefore the Presbytery judged it very necessary to set apart a day of solemn humiliation and fasting, that we may humble ourselves under God's hand, and wrestle with God in prayer that He may restraine Satan's rage, and relieve that poor afflicted damsell and that family from their present distress, and that the Lord would break in upon the hearts of these poor obdured wretches that are indited, that they may freely confess, to the glory of God and the rescuing of their own souls out of the hands of Satan, and that the Lord would conduct and clear their way that are to be upon the tryall, in order to the giving of Satan's kingdom an effectuall strok : therefore the Presbytery appoints thursday-come-eight-days to be religiously and solemnly observed, upon the accounts foresaid, in all the congregations within their bounds, and the same to be intimate the Sabbath preceding. The Presbytery also appoints the wholl members to deall with those who are indited, as they shall have occasion, in order unto their being brought to a confession.

At Irvine, April 6, 1697.

The Presbytery considering that the Commissioners of Witchcraft are to meet again, April 13, at Pasley, and the Presbytery considering how requisite it would be to have a sermon before them at their down sitting upon such an occassion, and being informed also that the same is desired and expected by those concerned in the tryalls ; therefore the Presbytery appoints their clerk to write and send an express to Mr. Hutcheson, signifying that the Presbytery hath appointed and seriously recommended to him to preach before the Commissioners at Pasley, Aprile 13.

The Presbytery appoints their Moderator to apply to the Synod that they would appoint some of the grave and experienced brethren in the several Presbyteries to join with this Presbytery of Pasley during the time of the tryall for assisting and advising with them in anything incumbent upon them at this juncture.

At Pasley, Apr. 13, 1697.

Reported that application had been made to the Synod for appointing some experienced brethren to join with this Presbytery, and according to their appointment were present— Mrs. Will. Dunlop, J. Brown, Ro. Wylie, Pa. Warner, J. Wilson, Ro. Wallace, Jo. Ritchie, Tho. Linning, with several brethren of the neighbouring Presbyteries.

Mr. Hutcheson preached before the Commissioners according to appointment on Ex. xxii. 18. The meeting, at the desire of the Commissioners, appoints Mrs. Will. Dunlop, Ja Brown, Pa. Warner, Ro. Wylie, Jo. Wilson, Tho. Linning, Ja. Hutcheson, Pa. Sympson, And. Turner, Ja. Birsbane, to wait upon their Lordships, and to know their desires to this meeting; and further recommended it to them to deal with the consciences of those on whom the insensible marks are found, in order to their being brought to confession, as they shall, with the Commissioners, concert the method of the same.

At Pasley, Apr. 14, 1697.

Reported that those appointed to wait upon the Commissioners obeyed accordingly. The meeting considering the necessity of their representing unto the Commissioners their thoughts with respect unto this present affair, and specially of the circumstances of severals delated and suspected within the bounds, does therefore appoint Mrs. Sympson, Wyllie, and Dunlop to put the same in form against the next meeting, in order to its being represented to the Commissioners, and appoints all the brethren to give information of the particular circumstances of such persons in their respective paroches unto those appointed to draw the representation.

The meeting this day considering that the revising of the narrative of Christine Shaw's trouble was recommended unto prisoners as they had access, did leave it to the Presbytery of Paisley to meet themselves, or to call the whole meeting as they found cause.

At Pasley, May 19, 1697.

Mrs. M'Dowell, Da. Brown, Ja. Stirline, are appointed as frequently as they possibly can to converse with the seven persons that are condemned to die for witchcraft. Mr. Pa. Symson and Mr. Da. Brown are appointed to have each of them a lecture in the Tolbooth to those that are condemned, upon June 9, the day preceding their execution.

At Pasley, June 9, 1697.

Mr. Symson preacht this day in the Tolbooth to the condemned persons, on 2 Timothy, ii. 25, 26, and also Mr. Brown on 1 Tim. i. 16, according to appointment.

The Presbytery did appoint the whole members to spend some time this night with the condemned persons who are to dy to-morrow, and did allot to each one or two of the brethren one of the sentenced persons, to be dealt with by them, and waited upon to the Fire.

J. D.

A History of the Witches of Renfrewshire

who were burned on the Gallowgreen of Paisley
1809 Edition, in Facsimile

FROM AUTHENTIC DOCUMENTS.

A HISTORY

OF THE

WITCHES

OF

RENFREWSHIRE,

WHO WERE BURNED ON THE GALLOWGREEN
OF PAISLEY.

PUBLISHED BY

THE EDITOR OF THE PAISLEY REPOSITORY.

" *Magic Terrors, Spells of mighty power,*
" *Witches, who rove at midnight hour.*"

PAISLEY :

PRINTED BY J. NEILSON,
FOR JOHN MILLAR, BOOKSELLER.

1809.

The Publisher sincerely thanks his numerous subscribers for their liberal encouragement of this work, which has far exceeded his most sanguine expectations. While he has, at a considerable trouble and expense, collected old manuscripts and other materials on the subject, besides what were promised in his Prospectus, and by that means he has been enabled to make his work complete, he has the satisfaction to think that the most of his subscribers will be well pleased with the work. However, he is not of the opinion that his book will please every person, for that is what no book has ever yet done.

The Publisher cannot, with propriety, omit returning his warmest thanks to Thomas Bissland, Esq, of Ferguslie; William M'Kerrell, Esq., Maxwellton; Robert Paterson, Esq., Provost of Renfrew, and other landed gentlemen; the Faculty of Procurators, Paisley, and particularly, Messrs. William M'Walter and Henry Wilson, writers, for the pieces he received from them, and the interest they took in the work.

CONTENTS.

A

TREATISE ON WITCHCRAFT.

BY

Sir GEORGE MACKENZIE, of Rosehaugh,

Who was King's Advocate, and one of the Lords of the Privy Council in Scotland.

From his *"Laws and Customes of Scotland in Matters Criminal."*

Printed in 1678.

———◆———

CONTENTS.

THAT there are witches, divines cannot doubt, since the Word of God hath ordained that no witch shall live; nor lawyers in Scotland, seeing our law ordains it to be punished with death. And though many lawyers, in Holland

B

and elsewhere, do think that albeit there were witches under the law, yet there are none under the Gospel,—the devil's power having ceased as to these as well as in his giving responses by oracles.

I.—Wierus, that great patron of witchcraft, endeavours to maintain his opinion by these arguments :—1. That such as are accused of witchcraft are ordinarily silly old women whose age and sex disposeth them to melancholy, and whose melancholy disposeth them to a madness which should render their confessions very suspected, and in this crime there are seldom other proofs, whereas the things confessed are so horrid, that it cannot be imagined any reasonable creature would commit them.—2. God can only work the miracle ascribed to witches, He who is the author of nature being only able to alter or divert its course ; and the devil doth but delude the fancy of poor creatures, as fevers and melancholy misrepresent objects. Nor are such as are cheated in the one more guilty than they who are sick of the other. And it is severe to burn men and women for doing that which is concluded impossible to be done by them.—3. It is unjust to punish them for doing ill by charms, except it could be first proved that these charms produced the effects that are punishable ; and lawyers should argue thus, those who kill or hurt men or beasts by unlawful means, are punishable by death. But so it is, that witches and charmers kill men and beasts by unlawful means, and therefore ought to be punished by death, of which syllogism Wierus denies the minor ; for it can never be proved that verses, crosses, or laying flesh in the threshold, &c., can destroy men or beasts, these being causes very disproportionable to such effects, there being no contact betwixt the agent and patient in these cases.—4. These who execute the will of God are not punishable, for that is their duty, and so cannot be their crime. But so it is, that whatever the devil or witches do, is decreed by God either for trial or punishment expressly, and without his permission nothing can be done. And if the devil were not acting here by obedience, or were at liberty, he would not leave any one man undestroyed, or any of God's works undefaced.

But that there are witches, and that they are punishable capitally, not only when they poison or murder, but even for enchanting and deluding the world, is clear by an express text, Exod. xxii. verse 18.,—"Thou shalt not suffer a witch to live." And it is observable, that the same word which expresses a witch here, is that which is used in Exod. vii. to express those magicians who deluded only the people by transforming a rod into a serpent, as Moses had done, though no person was prejudged by their cheat and illusion. Likeas, Lev. xxix. and 27. It is ordained that "a man or a woman that hath a familiar spirit, or that is a wizard, shall surely be put to death; they shall stone them with stones; their blood shall be upon them." Which laws were in such observation amongst the Jews, that the witch of Endor, 1 Sam. xxviii., was afraid to use her sorcery before the king, because the king had cut off those who had familiar spirits and wizards out of the land. And so great indignation did the eternal God bear to this sin, that he did destroy the ten tribes of Israel because they were addicted to it.

Nor were the Jews only enemies to this vice, but even the Heathens, following the dictates of nature, punished witches as enemies to the author of it; for the Persians dashed their heads against stones, as Minsing observes, ad. Item lex Cornelia inst. de pub. and Tacitus, lib. ii. Annal. tells us that Publius Marcius and Pituanus were executed for this crime; for which likewise Valerius Maximus, lib. vi. cap. iii. tells us that Publicia and Lucinia were with threescore and ten other Romans hanged. But since it is expressly con-

demned in scripture, and many general councils, such as
Aurelian, Toletan, and Anaciritan, it should not be lawful
for us to debate what the law hath expressly condemned, by
the same reason, that we should deny witches, we must deny
the truth of all history, ecclesiastic and secular. It is sure
that the devil having the power and will to prejudge men,
cannot but be ready to execute all that is in witchcraft: And
it is as credible that God would suffer men to be convinced
by these means, that there are spirits, and that by these means
he would give continued proofs of his power in repressing the
devil, and of the necessity that silly men have of depending
upon his infinite power.

To the former arguments it may be answered, that as to the
first, all sins and vices are the effects of delusion; nor are
witches more deluded by melancholy, than murderers are by
rage and revenge. And though it hath never been seen, that
persons naturally mad, have been either guilty of, or punished
for this crime, the devil designing in this crime to gain only
such as can damn themselves by giving a free consent. Yet
if madness could be proved, or did appear; it would certainly
defend both against the guilt and punishment: And therefore
such a series of clear circumstances should concur before a
person be found guilty of this crime, as should secure the
panel, and satisfy the judge fully in the quærie. But since
daily experience convinces the world that there may be such
a crime, and that the law exacts either confession, or clear
proofs, who can condemn the law as rigorous in this case,
since, without believing these, there could be no justice administered, and whilst judges shunned to punish it in some
cases, they behoved to suffer it from the same arguments to
go unpunished in all cases.

To the second, it is answered, that though neither the devil
nor witches can work miracles, yet the offering to cheat the

world by a commerce with the devil, and the very believing that the devil is able to do such things for them, should be a sufficient crime; but much more when they believe all those things to be done by themselves, they giving their own express consent to the crime, and by concurring by all that in them is to the commission of it. Likeas, it is undeniable, that the devil knowing all the secrets of nature, may, by applying actives to passives that are unknown to us, produce real effects which seem impossible.

To the third, though charms be not able to produce the effects that are punishable in witches, yet since these effects cannot be produced without the devil, and that he will not employ himself at the desire of any who have not resigned themselves wholly to him, it is very just that the users of these should be punished, being guilty at least of apostacy and heresy.

The fourth argument is but a mere and silly sophism; for though God in his providence permits at least all things that are done, to be done, yet such as contemn either the commands of him or his vicegerents, ought to be punished.

I cannot but acknowledge that there are some secrets in nature which would have been looked upon in the first authors as the effects of magic; and I believe that in the duller nations a philosopher drawing iron with a loadstone might have run a great risk of being burned; and it is hard to give a judgment of Naudeus' learned book in favour of the Persian magicians, the Assyrian chaldeans, the Indian gymnosophists, and the druids of the Gauls; for it cannot be denied but that many true mathematicians and physicians have passed for magicians in the duller ages of the world; but as to this, there is now no fear, since learning hath so sufficiently illuminated the world, so as to distinguish betwixt these two. But I am still jealous of those sages who were frequented by familiar spirits, though they were otherwise very excellent men, such as Porphir, Jamblicus, Plotin, and others, who pretended by the purity of their lives to be so spiritual, as to deserve the friendship of spirits : for besides that the primitive fathers and doctors of the church have testified against such as mere magicians.   It is not intelligible how those spirits that frequented them could be good, since they were tempted to fall from the true religion to paganism, and did offer such sacrifices as the true God did never allow ; and if such impostures were allowed, it were easy for any to defend themselves, being truly witches.

II.—Albeit witchcraft be the greatest of crimes, since it includes in it the grossest of heresies, and blasphemies, and treasons against God, in preferring to the Almighty his rebel and enemy, and in thinking the devil worthier of being served and reverenced, and is accompanied with murder, poisoning, bestiality, and other horrid crimes : yet I conclude only from this, that when witches are found guilty, they should be most severely punished, not with scourging and banishment, as the custom of Savoy was related to be by Gothofred, hoc tit. but by the most ignominious of deaths.   Yet from the horridness of this crime, I do conclude, that of all crimes it requires the clearest relevancy, and most convincing probation.   And I condemn, next to the witches themselves, those cruel and too forward judges, who burn persons by thousands as guilty of this crime, to whom I shall recommend these considerations.

1. That it is not presumable that any who hear of the kindness of God to men, and of the devil's malice against them, of the rewards of heaven, and torments of hell, would deliberately enter into the service of that wicked spirit, whom they know to have no riches to bestow, nor power to help, except it be allowed by permission that he may tempt men : and that he being a liar from the beginning, his promises

deserve no belief, especially since in no man's experience he hath ever advantaged any person : whereas, on the contrary, his service hath brought all who entered in it to the stake.

2. Those poor persons who are ordinarily accused of this crime, are poor ignorant creatures, and oft-times women who understand not the nature of what they are accused of ; and many mistake their own fears and apprehensions for witchcraft ; of which I shall give you two instances, one of a poor weaver, who after he had confessed witchcraft, being asked how he saw the devil, he answered, "like flies dancing about a candle." Another of a woman, who asked seriously, when she was accused, if a woman might be a witch and not know it ? And it is dangerous that these, who are of all others the most simple, should be tried for a crime, which of all others is most mysterious.

3. These poor creatures, when they are defamed, become so confounded with fear, and the close prison in which they are kept, and so starved for want of meat and sleep, (either of which wants is enough to disorder the strongest reason) that hardly wiser and more serious people than they would escape distraction : and when men are confounded with fear and apprehension, they will imagine things very ridiculous and absurd ; and as no man would escape a profound melancholy upon such an occasion, and amidst such usages ; therefore I remit to physicians and others to consider what may be the effects of melancholy, which hath oft made men, who appeared otherwise solid enough, imagine they were horses, or had lost their noses, &c. And since it may make men err in things which are obvious to their senses, what may be expected as to things which transcend the wisest men's reason.

4. Most of these poor creatures are tortured by their keepers, who being persuaded they do God good service, think it their duty to vex and torment poor prisoners : and I know *ex cer-*

*tissima scientia,** that most of all that ever were taken, were tormented after this manner, and this usage was the ground of all their confession; and albeit the poor miscreants cannot prove this usage, the actors being the only witnesses, yet the judge should be afraid of it, as that which at first did elicit the confession, and for fear of which they dare not retract it.

5. I went when I was a justice-depute to examine some women who had confessed judicially, and one of them, who was a silly creature, told me under secrecy, that she had not confessed because she was guilty, but being a poor creature, who wrought for her meat, and being defamed for a witch, she knew she would starve, for no person thereafter would either give her meat or lodging, and that all men would beat her, and hound dogs at her, and that therefore she desired to be out of the world; whereupon she wept most bitterly and upon her knees called God to witness what she said. Another told me that she was afraid the devil would challenge a right to her, after she was said to be his servant, and would haunt her, as the minister said when he was desiring her to confess; and therefore she desired to die. And really ministers are ofttimes indiscreet in their zeal, to have poor creatures to confess in this; and I recommend to judges, that the wisest ministers should be sent to them, and those who are sent, should be cautious in this.

6. Many of them confess things which all divines conclude impossible, as transmutation of their bodies into beasts, and money into stones, and their going through close doors, and a thousand other ridiculous things, which have no truth nor existence but in their fancy.

7. The accusers here are masters, or neighbours who had their children dead, and are engaged by grief to suspect these

---

* From certain knowledge.

108

poor creatures. I knew one likewise burned because the lady was jealous of her with her husband : and the crime is so odious that they are never assisted or defended by their relations.

8. The witnesses and assizers are afraid that if they escape, that they will die for it, and therefore they take an unwarrantable latitude. And I have observed that scarce ever any who were accused before a country assize of neighbours did escape that trial.

9. Commissions are granted ordinarily to gentlemen, and others in the country who are suspected upon this account; and who are not exactly enough acquainted with the nature of this crime, which is so debateable amongst the most learned; nor have the panels any to plead for them, and to take notice who are led as witnesses ; so that many are admitted who are *testes inhabiles,** and suspected : and albeit their confessions are sent to, and advised by the counsel before such commissions be granted, yet the counsel cannot know how these confessions were emitted, nor all the circumstances which are necessary, and cannot be known at a distance. Very many of these poor silly women do re-seal at the stake from the confessions they emitted at the bar, and yet have died very penitent : and as it is very presumable that few will accuse themselves, or confess against their own life, yet very many confess this crime.

III.—The method I shall use in treating of this crime shall be—1. Upon what suspicion witches may be apprehended. 2. What judges are competent. 3. What ditties are relevant. 4. What probation is sufficient. 5. What is the ordinary punishment. As to the first, I know it is

---

* Improper witnesses.

C

ordinary in Scotland not only that Magistrates do apprehend witches almost upon any dilation; but even gentlemen and such as are masters of the ground do likewise make them prisoners, and keep them so till they transmit them at their pleasure to Justices of Peace, Magistrates, or some open prisons.   But all this procedure is most unwarrantable, for gentlemen, and such as are vested with no authority, should upon no account, without a special warrant, apprehend any upon suspicion that they are witches, since to apprehend is an act of jurisdiction; and, therefore, I think no prison should receive any as suspected of witchcraft until they know that the person offered to them be apprehended by lawful authority.   2. Since imprisonment is a punishment, and constantly attended with much infamy to the name and detriment to the affairs of him who is imprisoned, especially in witchcraft, I do conclude that there must some presumption precede all inquisition,—for the meanest degrees of inquisition, though without captor, does somewhat defame,—and that the person should not be apprehended except it appear, by the event of the inquisition, that she lies under either many or pregnant suspicions, such as—That she is defamed by other witches; that she hath been herself of an evil fame; that she hath been found charming, or that the ordinary instruments of charming be found in her house; and according to Delrio's opinion,— Lib. V., Sec. II.,—"*Ad assumendas informationes, sufficiunt levia judicia, fed gravia requiruntur ad hoc ut citetur reus, & ut judex specialiter inquirat.*" *

IV.—Witchcraft was *crimen utriusque fori* † by the canon

---

* In order to take information, light trials suffice, but particular ones are required to this one, that the person accused be summoned, and that the judge may make special enquiry.

† Crime examinable by both Courts.

law, and with us the Kirk Sessions used to inquire into it, in order to the scandal, and to take the confession of the parties, to receive witnesses against them, as is clear by the process of Janet Barker and Margaret Lawder, December 9th, 1643. But since so much weight is laid upon the depositions there emitted, Kirk Sessions should be very cautious in their procedures.

By the Act of Parliament, Q. M. 9 Parl., 73. Act. All sheriffs, lords of regalities, and their deputes, and all other judges having power to execute the same, are ordained to execute that Act against witchcraft, which can import no more but that they should concur to the punishment of the crime by apprehending or imprisoning the party suspected; but it doth not follow that because they may concur, that, therefore, they are judges competent to the cognition of the crime, since the relevancy in it is oft-times so intricate, and the procedure requires necessarily so much arbitrariness, and the punishment is so severe, that these considerations jointly should appropriate the cognition thereof solely to the Justice Court. Nor find I any instances wherein these inferior courts have tried this crime. And albeit the council do oft-times grant commissions to countrymen, yet that seems dangerous; nor can I see why, by express Act of Parliament, it should have been appointed that no commission should be granted for trying murder, and yet witchcraft should be so tried by commissions. The Justices, then, are the proper judges in witchcraft.

V.—As to the relevancy in this crime, the first article useth to be paction to serve the devil, which is certainly relevant *per se*, without any addition, as is to be seen in all the indictments, especially in that of Margaret Hutchison, August 10th, 1661. And by Delrio, carpz. p. 1. quest. 47. and others; but because the devil useth to appear in the similitude of a

111

man, when he desireth these poor creatures to serve him ; therefore they should be interrogate, if they knew him to be the devil when they condescended to his service.

Paction with the devil is divided by the lawyers, *in expressum & tacitum*, an express and tacit paction. Express paction is performed either by a formal promise given to the devil then present, or by presenting a supplication to him, or by giving the promise to a proxy or commissioner empowered by the devil for that effect, which is used by some who dare not see himself. The formula set down by Delrio, is—" I deny God, creator of heaven and earth, and I adhere to thee, and believe in thee." But by the journal books it appears, that the ordinary form of express paction confessed by our witness is a simple promise to serve him. Tacit paction is either when a person who hath made no express paction, useth the words or signs which sorcerers use, knowing them to be such, either by their books, or discourse ; and this is condemned as sorcery, Can. 26. quest. 5. and is relevant to infer the crime of witchcraft, or to use these words and signs, and though the user know them not to be such ; it is no crime, if the ignorance be probable, and if the user be content to abstain, Delrio, lib. ii. quest. 4.

VI.—Renouncing of baptism is by Delrio made an effect of paction ; yet with us it is *per se** relevant (as was found in the former process of Margaret Hutchison), and the solemnity confessed by our witches is by putting one hand to the crown of the head, and another to the sole of the foot,— renouncing their baptism in that posture. Delrio tells us that the devil useth to baptize them of new, and to wipe off their brow the old baptism ; and our witches confess always the giving them new names which are very ridiculous, as Redshanks, Sergeant, &c.

* By itself.

VII.—The devil's mark useth to be a great article with us ; but it is not *per se* found relevant, except it be confessed by them that they got that mark with their own consent,—*quo casu,** it is equivalent to a paction. This mark is given them, as is alledged, by a nip in any part of the body, and it is blue. Delrio calls it stigma, or character, lib. ii., quest. 4, and alledges that it is sometimes like the impression of a hare's foot, or the foot of a rat or spider,—l. v., sect. 4, num. 28. Some think that it is impossible there can be any mark which is insensible and will not bleed, for all things that live must have blood ; and so this place behoved both to be dead and alive at once, and behoved to live without aliment, for blood is the aliment of the body. But it is very easy to conceive that the devil may make a place insensible at a time, or may apply things that may squeeze out the blood.

This mark is discovered among us by a pricker, whose trade it is, and who learns it as other trades ; but this is a horrid cheat, for they alledge that if the place bleed not, or if the person be not sensible, he or she is infallibly a witch. But, as Delrio confesses, it is very hard to know any such mark *à nevo, clavo, vel impertigine naturali,*† and there are many pieces of dead flesh which are insensible even in living bodies ; and a villain who used this trade with us, being in the year 1666 apprehended for other villanies, did confess all this trade to be a mere cheat.

VIII. Threatening to do mischief, if any evil follow immediately, hath been too ordinarily found a relevant article to infer witchcraft with us. Thus Agnes Finnie was pursued in anno 1643, upon the general article of having witched several persons, and particularly for these articles, 1. That William Fairlie having nick-named and called her Annie Winnie, she

---

* In which case. † From a mark or a natural insensibility.

sware in rage he should go halting home, and within twenty-four hours he took a palsy. 2. That Beatrix Nisbit refusing to pay the said Agnes the annual rent of two dollars owing by Hector Nisbit her father, she told her she should repent it, and within an hour thereafter she lost her tongue, and the power of her right side. 3. That Janet Greintoun having refused to carry away two herrings she had bought from the said Agnes, and to pay for them, she told her it should be the last meat she should eat, and within a little after she fell sick; against which articles, it was there alledged that this libel was not relevant, and could not go to the knowledge of an inquest :—1. Because no means were condescended upon from which the witchcraft was inferred; and if this libel were relevant, it would be relevant to libel generally that the panel were a witch. 1. Assizers are only judges to the matter of fact, and not to what consists *in jure*;* but so it is, that if this libel were to pass to the knowledge of an inquest, all the debate *in jure* behoved to be before the assize before whom the panels' procurators behoved to debate how far *minæ & damnum sequutum*† are relevant, and how far any person is punishable as a witch, though no charms or other means commonly used by witches be condescended upon; and as to the threatenings, they were not relevant, seeing they had not all the requisites which are expressed by the doctors as requisite, for they were not specific, bearing the promise to do a particular ill, as that Fairlie should take a palsy or Nisbit lose her tongue. 2. There was not a preceding reason of enmity proved, nor is it probable that for so small a matter as a herring or the annual rent of two dollars she would have killed any person, and exposed herself to hazard; nor was

---

* In law.　† Threatening and damage following thereon.

the effect immediate, nor such as could have proceeded from any other natural cause, without all which had concurred. Delrio—lib. 5, sect. 3—is very clear that *minæ etiam cum damno sequuto* * are not so much as a presumption; but though all these did concur, it is very clear both from Delrio, ibid, and Farin., quest. 5, num. 37, that all these threatenings are not sufficient to infer the crime of witchcraft. Lastly, it was offered to be proved that some of these persons died of a natural disease, depending upon causes preceding that threatening; notwithstanding of all which, the libel was found relevant, and she was burned. But I think this decision very hard, and very contrary to the opinion of all received writers, who think that albeit *minæ* be *adminiculatæ*,† with all the former advantages and *probatæ de ea quæ solet minas exequi*,‡ yet the same are only sufficient to infer an arbitrary punishment, not corporal but pecuniary. And certainly such a wicked custom as threatening is in itself a crime, and thus it was only well found to be *crimen in suo genere* § in the process led against Katherine Oswald, Nov. 11th, 1629.

IX.—Sometimes articles are libelled wherein the malefice hath no dependence at all upon the means used; and thus it was libelled against Margaret Hutchison, August 20th, 1661, that John Clark's wife being sick, she came to the bedside when all the doors and windows were fast, and combed her head, several nights; and the last of these nights, she came to the bedside, and put her hand to the woman's pap, whereupon the child died,—which article was found relevant *per se*. And it was libelled against Janet Cock, September 7th, 1661,

---

* Even threatening with following damage. † Threats attested.

‡ And proven concerning her who was accustomed to execute these threatenings.

§ Crime in its own kind.

that a woman called Spindie being at enmity with her, she gave her a cuff, whereupon Spindie immediately distracted; and being reproved therefore by the minister of Dalkeith, he immediately distracted; which article was likewise found relevant, being joined with fame and delation: which decisions are, in my opinion, very dangerous, for they want a sure foundation, and are precedents whereby judges may become very arbitrary. And against these, I may oppone a third allegiance used in the former process against Agnes Finnie, wherein it was alledged that the conclusion of all criminal libels should be necessarily inferred from the deed subsumed, and that *conclusio semper sequitur debiliorem partem: nam libellus est syllogismus apodicticus, sed non probabilis;* * and, therefore, except the libel could condescend upon some means used by the panel, from which the malefice were necessarily inferred, it could not be concluded that these malifices were done by her, or that she was guilty of the wrong done. Thus, Bodin, lib. 4., does conclude, that *veneficæ non sunt condemnandæ licet sint deprehensæ cum busonibus, ossibus, aliisque instrumentis egredientes exovili licet oves immædiate moriantur.* † And, Perkins, cap. 6, asserts that neither defamation nor threatenings, albeit what is threatened does follow, nor *mala fama,* ‡ nor the defuncts laying the blame of their death upon the person accused (called *inculpatio* by the doctors) can infer this crime, though all these be conjoined; for, in his opinion, nothing can be a sufficient ground to condemn a witch, except the panel's own confession, or the depositions

---

* That a conclusion always follows the weaker party, for a libel is an apodictic syllogism; but is not at all probable.

† That witches are not to be condemned with toads, bones, or other instruments, and unless the sheep die immediately when they go out of the fold.

‡ Bad fame.

of two famous witnesses, deponing upon means used by the panel. And it is remarkable, that in the chapter immediately subsequent to that wherein witches are ordinarily to be put to death, God hath expressly ordained that "out of the mouth of two or three witnesses every word shall be established." And in the process deduced against Isobel Young for witchcraft, February 4, 1629, and against Katherine Oswald, November 11, 1629, this point is likewise debated, it being libelled against the said Katherine, that by her witchcraft she caused a cow give blood instead of milk, and caused a woman fall and break a rib in her side. Against which it was alleged, that there was no necessary connection there, *inter terminum à quo & ad quem inter causam & effectum:* * but, on the contrary, the cow's giving blood for milk might proceed from another natural cause, viz., from lying upon an ant or emmet hill; and, therefore, I think that because we know not what virtue may be in herbs, stones, or other things which may be applied, it were very hard to find cures performed by the application of these, without the using charms or spells, to be witchcraft. But when these outward applications are used to do hurt, as for instance,—If the said Margaret Wallace, being at enmity with John Clark, and after she was forbidden to frequent his house, did continue to frequent the same, and did throw in blood or any unusual thing upon his wife's pap; if the child who sucked the same had thereafter died, I think this article, joined with preceding defamation of her by another witch, might have been found relevant, because she was there *in re illicita.* † And since the law cannot know exactly what efficacy there is in natural causes, it may very well

---

* There were no necessary connection existed betwixt the cause and the effect.

† In an unlawful way.

D

discharge any such superstitious forbidden acts as it pleases, under the pain of witchcraft. Nor can those who are accused complain of severity since *sibi imputent*,* that use these forbidden things against the express commandment of the law: and, therefore, since the law and practice hath forbidden all charms, it is most just that these who use the same should be severely punished, whatever the pretext be upon which they are used, or after whatever way or manner, or to whatever end, whether good or bad.

X.—Albeit per leg. 4 cod. de mal. & Math. these magic arts are only condemned which tend to the destruction of mankind, but not these whereby men are cured or the fruits of the ground preserved, yet I have oft-times imputed this constitution to Tribonian, who was a Pagan and a severe enemy to Christians, or else that it behoved to be so interpreted, or that thereby remedies assisted by godly prayers were allowed, else what mean these words—*suffragia innocenter adhibita*. † But since, I am informed from the ecclesiastic historians, as Zozim. lib. 2, that Constantine was not yet turned Christian when he passed that constitution. But, however, this constitution is omitted in the Basilicks, and the Gloss says that ουκ ιδιχου ιν τη απωκαθαρ θιι it was not thought fit to be. mentioned in the repurgation of the law ; and that constitution was very well reprobated by Leo's 65 Novel. And by the canon law, *tit. de forti-legiis ;* and the general sanction of the former Act of Parliament leaves no place for this distinction. Suitable to all which, John Brough was convicted for witchcraft in Anno 1643 for curing beasts by casting white stones in water, and sprinkling them therewith ; and for curing women by washing their feet with south-running water, and putting odd money in the water. Several

---

* They may lay the blame on themselves.   † Aids innocently used.

other instances are to be seen in the processes led in Anno 1661; and the instance of Drummond is very remarkable, who was burned for performing many miraculous cures, albeit no malefice * was ever proved.

XI.—Consulting with witches is a relevant ditty with us, as was found against Allison Jollie, per. Oct. 1596; and this is founded upon the express words of the Act. The professing, likewise, skill in necromancy, or any such craft, is by the foresaid Act of Parliament a relevant article; for the full clearing of which Act it is fit to know that divination was either *per dæmono-mantiam,*—the invocation of Pagan gods; or *nanganiam,*—which was the prophecying for invocation of some sublunary thing. *Magnania* is divided in *necromantiam,* which was a prophecying by departed spirits; *udromantiam,* which was a divination by water, &c. All which species and kinds of divinations by any thing is comprehended under the general prohibition of necromancy, and such like acts, so that predictions and responses by the seive; and the shear, and by the book, and all such cheats and species of sorcery are punishable by death in this Act. Yet these forbidden practices may sometimes be excused by ignorance, or if it can be cleared by circumstances, that the user designed nothing but an innocent jest or recreation,—Delrio lib. 4, cap. 1, quæst. 4.

XII.—The last article in criminal libels useth ordinarily to be the being delated by other witches, which the doctors call *diffamatio,*† and we, common bruit, and open fame, which are never sustained as relevant *per se,* but only joined with other relevant articles; as is to be seen in the foresaid process of

---

* Malefice, in the Scots law, signifies an act or effect of witchcraft.

† Defamation.

Margaret Hutchison, though I think that *interloquutor* very severe, since if any of the former articles be *per se* relevant, they need not the assistance of fame and delation. Sometimes likewise, but with much more reason, articles that are of themselves irrelevant, are sustained relevant, being joined with fame and delation; an example whereof is to be seen in the 9th article of the indictment against Janet Cock, Sep. 7, 1661, in which article, she was accused for having recovered a child by charms, with the help of another witch, which other witch had confessed the same when she was confronted with the said Janet; likeas, both of them were found lying above the child, whispering one to another, and the blood of a dog was found standing in a plate beside them; which article was not sustained relevant *per se*, but was found relevant, being joined with fame and delation.

XIII.—The relevancy of this crime being thus discussed, the ordinary probation of it is by confession or witnesses; but the probation here should be very clear, and it should be certain that the person who emitted it is not weary of life or oppressed with melancholy. 2. Albeit, *non requiritur hic ut constet de corpore delicti*,*—this being a crime which consists oft-times *in animo*,†—yet it ought to be such as contains nothing in it that is impossible or improbable. And thus, albeit Isobel Ramsay did upon the 20th of Aug., 1661, confess that the Devil gave her sixpence, and said that God desired him to give it her, and at another time a dollar, which turned thereafter into a slate-stone,—the justices did not find this confession, though judicial, relevant. And to know what things are of themselves impossible for the Devil to do, or at least what is believed to be impossible, may be seen very

---

* Not required this as it may constitute the substance of the crime.

† In the mind.

fully treated of in Delrio's second book, where it is condescended that *succubi* & *incubi sunt possibiles,—id est*, that
the Devil may lie in the shape of a man with a woman, or in
the shape of a woman with a man, having first formed to
himself a body of condensed air; and upon such a confession
as this, Margaret Lawder and others were convicted. It is
likewise possible for the Devil to transport witches to their
public conventions from one place to another, which he may
really do by carrying them; and sundry witches were in
Anno 1665 burned in Culross upon such a confession as this.

XIV.—It may be, I confess, argued that spirits and im-
material substances cannot touch things material, and consequently can neither raise nor transport them; but if we
consider how the adamant raises and transports the iron,—and
how the soul of man, which is a spirit, can raise or transport
the body,—and that a man's voice, or a musical sound, is
able to occasion great and extraordinary motions in other
men,—we may easily conclude that devils who are spirits of
far more energy may produce effects surpassing very far our
understanding. And yet I do not deny but that the Devil
does sometimes persuade the witches that they are carried to
places where they never were, making those impressions upon
their spirits, and acquainting them what was done there,
which is done by impressing images upon their brain, and
which images are carried to the exterior senses by the animal
spirits, even as we see the air carries the species of colours
upon it, though in a very insensible way; and thus we see,
likewise, that the fumes of wine or melancholy will represent
strange apparitions, and make us think them real. Nor
ought it to be concluded that, because those witches are only
transported in spirit or in dreams, that therefore they ought
not to be punished, since none can be punished for dreaming;
and that, because those witches desire to have these dreams

and glory in them when they are awake; nor have any these dreams but such as have entered into a preceding paction. I know that the Canon Episcopi in the Council of Anacir (or the Aquilean Council, as others call it) does condemn these transportations as false, and mere delusions, which are impressed upon the fancy of poor creatures by the Devil, & *cum solus spiritus hæc patitur, nec non in animo sed in corpore inveniri opinantur;* * but that Act of that Council does not assert all transportations to be imaginary and dreams, but only declares those who thought they followed Diana and Herodias to these public meetings to be altogether seduced, for these indeed were seduced, for Herodias being dead long since could not be at their meetings. But, from that, it is unjustly concluded that there are no real transportations,— there being so many instances of these transportations given, both in sacred and profane story, and persons having been found wounded, and having really committed murders and other insolencies during these transportations.

XV.—Whether it be possible for a witch to cause any person be possessed by putting devils into their body, may be debated; and that it is possible appears from the history of Simon Magus and many others, and is testified to be true by St. Jerome in the life of St. Hilarion. And since witches have confessed that there are devils who obey one another, and that there are different degrees amongst them, why may not those of an inferior degree be forced, by virtue of a paction with those of a superior order, to possess men and women at the desire of witches? Witches themselves have confessed that this hath been done; and I find by a decision of the Parliament of Tholodus that devils have been heard to

---

* And when the spirit of itself suffers such things, they are supposed to afflict the body as well as the mind.

complain in those that were possessed that they were put there by the enchantment of such and such women. But, upon the other hand, it is not to be imagined that devils would obey mortal creatures, or that God would leave so great a power to any of them to torment poor mortals. And the Devil, who is a liar from the beginning, is not to be believed in saying that he is put there by enchantments; and though he makes such promises to witches, yet he does in these but cheat them: and if the Devil could possess at pleasure, we would see many more possessed than truly there are.

XVI.—The Devil cannot make one solid body to penetrate another, quest. 17; and therefore I think that article libelled against Margaret Hutchison of coming to John Clark's house when doors and windows were shut, should not have been admitted to probation, since it is very probable they would have searched the house after the second or third night's fear, and she could not penetrate doors nor walls.

XVII. — The Devil cannot transform one species into another, as a woman into a cat, for else he behoved to anni-hilate some of the substance of the woman, or create some more substance to the cat,—the one being much more than the other; and the Devil can neither annihilate or create, nor could he make the shapes return, *nam non datur regressus à privatione ad habitum.** But if we consider the strange tricks of jugglers, and the strange apparitions that Kercher and others relate from natural causes, we may believe that the Devil can make a woman appear to be a beast, & *è contra,*† by either abusing the sense of the beholders, or altering the medium, by inclosing them in the skin of the beast repre-sented, or by inclosing them in a body of air shaped like that

---

* When the shape is destroyed, it is impossible to restore it.

† On the other hand.

which he would have them represent, and the ordinary relation of the witnesses being wounded when the beast was wounded in which they were changed may be likewise true, either by their being really wounded within the body of air in which they were inclosed, or by the Devil's inflicting that wound really himself, which is Delrio's opinion. But it would seem hard to condemn any person upon the confession of what seems almost impossible in itself; and I cannot allow instances in the journal books where poor creatures have been burned upon such confessions, without other strong adminicles.

XVIII.—The Devil may make brutes to speak, or, at least, speak out of them, quest. 18.

He can also raise storms in the air, and calm these that are raised, quest. 11. And yet it being libelled against Janet Cock that she said to those who were carrying a witch to be executed—" Were it not a good sport if the Devil should take her from you?" likeas, a great storm did overtake them when they were carrying her to the place,—it having been a great calm both before and after; yet this article was not sustained relevant, since it might have proceeded from folly, or jest, or *vana jactantia.**

XIX.—The Devil may inflict diseases, which is an effect he may occasion *applicando activa passivis*,† and by the same means he may likewise cure : a clear instance whereof appears in the marriage-knot. And not only may he cure diseases laid on by himself, as Wierus observes, but even natural diseases, since he knows the natural causes and the origin of even those natural diseases, better than physicians can, who are not present when diseases are contracted, and who, being younger than he, must have less experience. And it is as un-true that Divus Thomas observes, who asserts that cures per-

---

* Vain boasting.   † By applying actives to passives.

formed by the Devil cannot continue, since his cures are not natural.

And since he both may make sick and make whole, it follows that he may transfer a disease from one person to another. And I find that it being libelled against Margaret Hutchison, that she took a disease off a woman to put it on a cat : it was alleged that this article was not relevant ; because, 1. *Una saga non potest esse ligans & solvens in eodem morbo;* * 2. That in such transactions as these the Devil never used to. interpose his skill, except where he was a gainer ; and, therefore, though he would transfer a disease from a brute beast to a rational creature, yet he would never transfer a disease from a rational creature to a brute beast: both these defences were repelled. Many witches likewise confess that they cannot cure diseases, because they are laid on by witches of a superior order, who depend upon spirits of a higher degree.

Some think that they may innocently employ a witch to take off the disease imposed by another, and lay it upon the witch who imposed it, even as men may innocently borrow money from a user to be employed for pious uses, or may cause an infidel swear by his false gods for eliciting truth : and that in this manner devils are rather punished than served. But since all commerce with devils is unlawful, this practice is justly reprobated by D. Autun, p. 2, discourse 48. But yet it is thought lawful to all who are bewitched to desire the bewitchers to take off the disease, if it can be removed without a new application to the Devil, but only by taking away the old charm ; or it is lawful to any to remove the charm or sign of it, if it be in their power, D. Autun, pag. 825.

---

* The same witch cannot both cause and cure a disease.

E

125

XX.—Witches may kill by their looks, which looks being full of venomous spirits, may infect the person upon whom they look, and this is called *fascinatio physica, sed fascinatio vulgaris, quæ dicitur fieri per oculos tenerorum puerorum vel parvorum porcorum vana est & ridicula,*[*] Del. lib. 3. q. 4. sect. 1.

I know there are who think all kinds of fascination by the eyes, either an effect of fancy in the person affected, or else think it a mere illusion of the Devil, who persuades witches that he can bestow upon them the power of killing by looks, or else the Devil really kills, and ascribes it falsely to their looks : whereas, others contend, that by the received opinion of all historians, men have been found to be injured by the looks of witches : and why may not witches poison this way, as well as the Basilisk doth: or why may not the spirits in the eye affect as well as the breath? or why may not looks kill as well as raise passions in the person looked upon? nor can it be denied but that blearedness is begot by blearedness ; and that menstruous women will spoil a mirror by looking upon it. Likeas, there seems even some ground for it in scripture ; for, Deut. xxviii. 54., " It is said that a man's eyes shall be evil towards his brother." And some likewise endeavour by consequence from Matth. xx. 15, " Is thine eye evil : " the word βασκαινω signifiying in Scripture both to bewitch and to envy. Some likewise think that St. Paul, Gal. iii. 1., alludes to this received opinion, but conjecture doth so much over-rule all this affair, that it were hard to fix crimes upon so slender grounds ; and, therefore, though where witches confess that they did kill by their looks, their confession and belief may, if they be otherwise of a sound judgment, make a very

---

[*] Natural witchcraft is the effects of natural causes, but that which is produced by the eyes of certain persons or animals, is vain and ridiculous.

considerable part of a crime, where it is joined with other probabilities, yet *per se* it is hardly relevant.

XXI.—It may be also doubted whether witches can, by amorous potions, inchant men or women to love ; and though it may seem that these being acts of the soul, cannot be raised by any corporeal means, yet l. 4. c. de. Malef. & Mathemat. makes this possible, and punishable, *eorum scientia punienda, & severissimis merito legibus vindicanda, qui magicis accincti artibus pudicos ad libidinem de fixisse animos deteguntur :* * but this law speaks only of lust, and not of love, as I conceive. Nor can it be denied, but that not only witches, but even naturalists may give potions that may incline men or women to lust. And, therefore, the question still remains, whether witches may incline men or women by potions to a fancy and kindness for any particular person ; and though potions may incline men to madness, yet it doth not follow that, therefore, they may incline them to love. And though D. Autun doth bring many arguments from history, and pretends that the Devil may raise and excite the old species of love which lies hidden in the body, and may thereby form a passion, yet these are too conjectural grounds to be the foundation of a criminal sentence. The Basilicks make the punishment of this to be deportation, and so supplies the former law.

XXII. Witches do likewise torment mankind, by making images of clay or wax, and when the witches prick or punce these images, the persons whom these images represent, do find extreme torment, which doth not proceed from any influence these images have upon the body tormented, but the devil doth by natural means raise these torments in the person tormented, at the same very time that the witches do prick or

---

* The several punishments ought to be inflicted on those who, by magic arts, force chaste persons to the commission of acts of impurity.

punce, or hold to the fire these images of clay or wax; which manner of torment was lately confessed by some witches in Inverness, who likewise produced the images, and it was well known they hated the person who was tormented, and upon a confession so adminiculate, witches may very judiciously be found guilty, since *constat de corpore delicti de modo de linquendi & inimicitiis præviis.* *

XXIII. — It is ordinarily doubted whether confessions emitted before the Kirk Sessions, in this case, be sufficient; but this I have treated more fully in the title of probation by confession. Only here I shall observe that Christian Stewart was found art and part of the bewitching Patrick Ruthven, by laying on him a heavy sickness with a black clout, which she herself had confessed before several ministers, notaries, and others, at diverse times,—all which confessions were proved; and upon these repeated confessions, she was burned Nov., 1596. Margaret Lawder was convicted upon confession emitted before the magistrates and ministers of Edinburgh, albeit past from in judgment Dec. 9, 1643,—see that book of adjournal, p. 349. And if the confession be not fully adminiculate, lawyers advise that confessors should be subjected to the torture, which is not usual in Scotland. And it is very observable that the justices would not put James Welsh to the knowledge of an inquest, though he had confessed himself a witch before the Presbytery of Kirkcudbright, because he was a minor when he confessed the crime, and the confession was only extra-judicial, and that he now retracted the same. But because he had so grossly prevaricated, and had delated so many honest persons, they ordained him to be scourged and put in the correction-house April 17th,

---

* It is evident from the nature of the crime mentioned just now, of their hatred and previous malice.

1662. It was proved against Margaret Wallace, March 20, 1622, that she said that if it could be proved that she was in Greg's house, she should be guilty of all the ditty; and, therefore, it being proved that she was in Greg's house, that probation was alleged by the advocate to be equivalent to a confession, as was found against Patrick Cheyn, to which it was replied that this could amount to no more than a lie : and in my opinion it could not have even the strength of an extra-judicial confession, but rather imported a denial of the crime.

XXIV.—The probation by witness in this crime is very difficult, and therefore *socii criminis* * or other confessing witches are adduced ; but though many of them concur, their depositions solely are not esteemed as sufficient, *ne vel ad pœnam extraordinariam imponendam,* † though some think the same sufficient to that end because of that general brocard, — *ex multiplicatis indiciis debilibus resultare indicia indubitata.* But Delrio asserts that the conjection of such testimonies is not sufficient ; "*nunquam enim,*" saith he, "*quæ sua natura dubia sunt possunt facere rem indubitatem ut nec multa agraunum sanum nec multa non alba unus album nec multa tepida unum callidum.*" ‡ And that the testimony of one confessing witch was not found sufficient to file the panel is clear by the process of Allison Jollie, who was assoilzied pen. Oct., 1596 ; albeit Janet Hepburn, another witch, confest that the said Allison had caused her bewitch Isobel Hepburn, whereof she died. But though witchcraft cannot be proved

---

* Accomplices in the crime.   † Not to impose extraordinary punishments.

‡ A multitude of weak evidences can never establish one undoubted fact, as many sick cannot make one in health, nor many black figures a white one, nor many cold substances a warm one.

*per socios criminis,** though dying and penitent witches, yet it
may be doubted if the consulting witches may not be proved
by two witches who were consulted, for, if this be not a
sufficient probation, it would be impossible to prove consulting
any other manner of way.

The persons to whom the injuries are done by the witches
are admitted to be witnesses; thus, Katherine Wardlaw was
admitted against Margaret Hutchison.   But sometimes they
are only admitted *cum nota*, if the probation be not otherwise
weak; and thus William Young and Agnes Hutchison were
only admitted *cum nota*, against Beatrix Leslie, August, 1661.
And in that process, likewise, they received only Agnes Ross
cum nota, because she was the mistress of the two women who
were *maleficiat*. Neilson was admitted to be an assizer against
Margaret Wallace, though he was brother-in-law to John
Nicol who had given information for raising the ditty, because
the ditty was not at Nicol's instance; and yet Starling was
set from being an assizer because Moore, who was alleged
to be one of the persons *maleficiat*, was his brother-in-law.
March 2. 1622. Dickson was there likewise admitted to be an
assizer, though he assisted the bailie in taking her, which was
found the office of a good citizen, and though he had deadly
feud against her husband, since it was not proved he had any
against herself.

Women are received witnesses in this crime, as is clear by
the process against Margaret Wallace, and all the processes in
August, 1661.   The not shedding of tears hath been used as
a mark and presumption of witchcraft, Sprenger, *mal. malef.*
p. 3. q. 15., because it is a mark of impenitence; and because
several witches have confessed they could not weep: but the

---

* By accomplices in the crime.

being accused of so horrid a crime may occasion a deep melancholy; and melancholy being cold and dry, hinders the shedding of tears ; and great griefs do rather astonish than make one weep.

XXV.—The punishment of this crime is with us death by the foresaid Act of Parliament, to be execute as well against the user as the seeker of any response or consultation, & *de practica.* The doom bears, to be worried at the stake, and burned.

By the civil law, consulters were punished by death l. 5. c. *de mafef.* & *mathem.* *nemo aruspicem consulat, aut mathematicum nemo ariolum, angurum et vatum prava confessio nonticescat sileat omnibus rer petuo divinandi curiositas.** In which law, fortune-tellers are also punishable ; though, with us, dumb persons who pretend to foretell future events are never punished capitally. But yet I have seen them tortured, by order from the Council, upon a representation that they were not truly dumb, but (feigning themselves to be so) abused and cheated the people. The foresaid law is renewed in the Basilicks l. 31 h. t. μηδεις ερωτατα τινα μαντικην εν αγηλλο μενον οι δε χαλδαιοι και οι μαγοι μηδε εν αυταις ταις μα.τειαις εαυτων παρεχετοσαν, αλλα δε κεφαλικη τη δα σι δηρον τιμωρια υποκεισθοσαν. † But Farin and others think that where no person is injured, death should not be inflicted; and that imprisonment and banishment is now practised by all nations in that case, lib. 1, tom. 3, quest. 20, num. 89, & *Clarus. sect. heresis num ult.* But Perezeus thinks this too favourable a punishment, except the

---

* It shall not be lawful for any one to consult a fortune-teller, or one pretending to foretell events by any mathematical rules, for all their declarations are criminal, and curiosity for divination ought to be effectually restrained.

† Let none seek advice by the art of divination, for the Chaldeans, and magicians, by no means discover the truth, wherefore they ought to be subjected to capital punishment, or public scourging.

users of these curious arts were induced thereto out of mere
simplicity, & *sine dolo malo*.* But, with us, no such distinction
can be allowed by the Justices, who must find all libels
relevant which bear consulting with witches, and, that ditty
being proved, they must condemn the panel to die,—albeit
I think the Council may alter the punishment, if it be clear
that the user of these acts had no wicked design nor
intercourse with the devil therein.

XXVI.—By the law of England, witchcraft was of old punished sometimes by death, and sometimes by exile; but 1.
Jac. this following statute was made, which I here set down,
because it is very special :—

" If any person or persons shall use, practise, or exercise in-
" vocation or conjuration of any evil and wicked spirit; or shall
" consult, covenant with, entertain, employ, feed, or reward
" any evil or wicked spirit to or for any intent or purpose ; or
" take up any dead man, woman, or child, out of his, her, or
" their grave, or any other place where the dead body resteth,
" or the skin, bone, or any part of a dead person, to be
" imployed or used in any manner of witch-cráft, sorcery,
" charme, or inchantment ; or shall use, practise, or exercise
" any witch-craft, inchantment, charm, or sorcery, whereby
" any person shall be killed, destroyed, wasted, consumed,
" pined, or lamed, in his or her body, or any part thereof :
" that, then, every such offender or offenders, their aiders,
" abbetters, and counsellors, being of any the said offence
" duely and lawfully convicted and attainted, shall suffer pains
" of death as a fellon or fellons, and shall lose the priviledge
" and benefit of Clergie and Sanctuary. If any person or
" persons take upon him or them by witch-craft, inchantment,
" charm, or sorcery, to tell or declare in what place any

* And without any evil design.

" treasure of Gold or Silver should or might be found or had
" in the earth or other secret places : Or where goods or other
" things lost or stoln, are become : Or whereby any cattell or
" goods of any person shall be destroyed, or to hurt or destroy
" any person in his or her body, albeit the same be not
" effected or done : being, therefore, lawfully convicted, shall,
" for the said offence, suffer Imprisonment by the space of a
" whole year without baile or mainprise.   Once every quarter
" of the year these Mountebanks are to mount the pillory, and
" to stand thereupon in some Mercat Toun six hours, and
" there to confesse his or her errour and offence."

OF

THE BEWITCHING

OF

SIR GEORGE MAXWELL OF POLLOK.

———

Account of SIR GEORGE MAXWELL, *and his son John.*
Taken from "Crawford's History of the Shire of Renfrew."

———

" Mr. GEORGE MAXWELL of Pollok, obtained the honour of knighthood from King Charles II. He was a gentleman of singular accomplishments, and justly esteemed a person eminent for piety, learning, and other good qualifications. Sir George deceased anno. 1677. To whom succeeded John, his son and heir; which John was raised to the dignity of baronet by King Charles IId's letters patent, bearing date, at Whitehall, the 12th of April, 1682. He was, by King William, nominated one of his Privy Council for Scotland, upon the first constitution thereof; and afterwards, in the year 1696, was appointed one of the Lords Commissioners of the Treasury of the Exchequer; and, in 1699, constituted one of the Senators of the College of Justice, and Lord Justice Clerk.

Letter which Sir John Maxwell of Pollok sent to George Sinclair, Professor of Philosophy in the College of Glasgow, along with the account of the bewitching of his father.

Pollok, 24th June, 1684.

SIR,

I send you herewith the true account my father caused me write from his own mouth, which is the surest relations I can give, either of his own trouble or what concerns Janet Douglas, first discoverer of these pictures. There fell out some less material circumstances in the family during her abode there, whereby it fully appeared that she knew what was done in distant places, and understood languages. For instance, when a chapter in the Greek New Testament was read, she made us understand by signs what the purposes were, (for at that time she was dumb, whether really or counterfeitly, it is hard to determine) and did exactly give an account to myself what we did at two miles distant from the place where she was, without any information given to her which I knew of.   I rest your affectionate friend,

JOHN MAXWELL.

[Taken from Sir George Maxwell's account of his being bewitched.]

Upon the 14th of October, 1676, my father was surprised at Glasgow, in the night-time, with a hot and fiery distemper; and, coming home the next day, he was fixed to his bed. The physician, fearing a pleuresy and a fever, opened a vein, and, the application of medicaments being made, the fiery heat was abated,—he remaining for seven weeks together under a great pain, chiefly in his right side, though not fixed to his bed. There had come to Pollok-town a young dumb girl, but from whence was not known, who had remained there for four weeks before, but seldom frequenting Sir George Maxwell's house, till at length she came to some more familiarity and converse with his two daughters. And, having observed Sir George sick and weak in his body; she signified unto them—That there was a woman, whose son had broke his fruit-yard, that did prick him in the sides.

And seeing this woman one day in the hall of Pollok amongst a great many other company, she assured his daughter that this was the woman; and the day following, she told the gentleman—That this woman (whose name was Janet Mathie, relict of John Stewart, under-miller in Shaw-mill) had formed a wax picture with pins in the side, which was to be found in her house, in a hole behind the fire, offering to bring it unto them providing she were accompanied with men to protect her from violence. At first they hardly understood her, till she went to

one of the gentlewoman's closets, and bringing thence a little
bees-wax, she plyed it before the fire, shewing the dimensions
and quantity of the picture. The gentlewomen regarded not
the information, because they thought it fabulous ; yet his two
servants, Laurence Pollok and Andrew Martin, knowing how
much the girl loved their master, and knowing that his life
was in hazard if this picture were not found, resolved at all
adventures to try whether the information were true or false ;
and therefore going along with her to the said Janet Mathie's
house, one of them planted himself on one side of the fire, and
the other on the other side, while, in the meantime, the little
girl coming quickly by Laurence Pollok, putting her hand in
the hole behind the fire, and then slips into Andrew Martin
beneath his cloak, the waxen effigy, which had two pins in it,
one in each side, but that in the right side so long as to pierce
through to the other ; that in the left was not so long, nor so
deeply thrust in. This picture being brought to Pollok, Sir
George's son, without acquainting his father, apprehended
Janet Mathie, procuring the next day the Lord Ross's order
for conveying her to prison. She being interrogated touching
the picture, after several subterfuges, alleged " it was the deed
of the dumb girl."

It was also enquired whether Sir George or his Lady had
given her at any time provocation to this malice. But it was
well known they had been courteous to her ; and, upon her
complaints, had rebuked some for spreading bad reports
upon her name, as not appearing sufficiently well founded to
a conviction. Only upon the 14th of October, above
specified, before Sir George went to Glasgow, he had called
before him a servant in Pollok-town that had broken his
orchard in harvest last, who confessed the fact, and that Hugh
Stewart, a son of Janet Mathie's, was his complice. But a
bye-stander declared that he was not now in Pollok land, but

in the Darnly. To whom Sir George replied,—" I hope my fingers may reach him in Darnly." This was all which could be thought a provocation to Mathie,—no harm being done in the meantime to her son, whom Sir George to this hour doth not so much as know by the face, but hath suffered him all the time of his sickness to live in his mother's house, even since her imprisonment. In the meantime Mathie, remaining obstinate, was searched for insensible marks before the Sheriff-Depute of Renfrew, and many famous witnesses, at Paisley, and there were very many found upon her.

After the finding of the picture of wax foresaid, there was some abatement of Sir George's sickness, but not to any observable degree, so low was he brought. But upon the 4th of January following, his sickness recurred with that violence that for four or five days his friends and relations had no great confidence of his life. But they were more amazed on the 7th of January, being the Sabbath Day, when they had an express from the dumb girl, who was at Pollok-town, but could not get over the water to the house, the river being so swelled at that time, signifying that John Stewart, Mathie's eldest son, had four days since formed an effigy of clay, for taking away Sir George's life. And when she was called for, she declared it was in his house, beneath the bolster, among the bed-straw.

The next day following, James Dunlop, of Househill, and Ludowick Stewart, of Achinhood, with some of Sir George's servants, went to Stewart's house, taking the little girl with them, resolving to make a very exact trial, that it might not be said that the dumb girl had brought anything hither. Wherefore they caused John Stewart himself to light a candle and hold it, while Ludowick Stewart and another, did, in his sight, lift the clay effigy from among the bed-straw, beneath the bolster (the little girl all the while standing at a distance from the place), but the picture having been made only three or four days before, and not sufficiently hard, did break into two pieces. In it were three pins, one in each side, and one in the breast. Stewart had nothing to say for himself, but that he knew not who had put that thing there. He was instantly apprehended, and so was a little sister of his, lately entered into the fourteenth year of her age, named Annabil Stewart, who was said to have whispered before somewhat of the waxen effigy. This poor creature proved thereafter, through God's favour, a key to the detection of making both the pictures.

At first she was very obstinate, but the next day she confessed, " That being present in her brother's house the 4th of January, while the clay picture was formed, the black gentleman being present, (which was the name she gave the devil) together with Bessie Weir, Margerey Craig, Margaret Jackson, and her brother John." But when confronted with her brother, she did not with confidence adhere to her confession. Upon the finding of this picture, Sir George did very observably recover in his health, and all the pain which was in his side, did, by degrees, wear away.

John Stewart remained, notwithstanding his sister's confession, above measure obstinate, until he was searched the next day for insensible marks, whereof he had great plenty ; at the finding whereof, he was so confounded, that immediately he confessed his paction with the devil, and almost all the other heads expressed in his judicial confession after written ; and declared, "That his accomplices who formed the effigy with him were the same his sister had named." She also came to a free and full confession of her paction with the devil, and her accession to her forming both of the waxen pictures in her mother's house, and of the clay one in her brother's house.

Upon information of the premises, the Earl of Dundonald and the Lord Ross, granted a warrant for apprehending Bessie Weir, Margaret Jackson, and Margery Craig, who had been fellow-sisters in the aforesaid sorcery.

Margaret Jackson, a woman aged about fourscore of years, after a day or two, confessed paction with the devil, and her accession to the making of both the pictures, and condescended upon the accomplices above-named. Many insensible marks were found on her body.

Upon the 17th of January last, a third portrait of clay was found under Janet Mathie's bolster, in the prison house of Paisley, which the dumb girl had given information of. But it seemed to be the picture of some woman, and probably of some of the family of Pollok. For Annabil Stewart did freely declare, " That their malice was against the whole family of Pollok." For turning to young Pollok and his Lady, she said, "And against you also." This portrait was found before four famous witnesses.

The lords of his Majesty's privy council, being informed of these pictures and effigies, the depositions of three confessing witches being sent, did grant a commission for their trial, and also for the trial of the other three that were obstinate. And in regard of the singularity of the case, they ordered the process to be very solemn, commissioning for the trial some judicious gentlemen in the country, viz. Sir Patrick Gauston of Gauston, James Brisbane of Bishopton, Sir John Shaw younger of Greenock, and John Anderson younger of Dovehill. To whom they added Mr. John Preston, advocate, (a gentleman well seen in criminals, and who exercised the office of justice-depute for several years), a *sine qua non* in the commission. And that the whole process might be the more exact, they appointed George Lord Ross assessor, with power to vote and decide. And, further, ordered Mr. Robert

Martin, Clerk of the Justice Court, to be clerk to the process, which was to be recorded in the public books of adjournal.

What follows of SIR GEORGE MAXWELL'S *affair is mostly taken out of an Authentic Copy of the Trial of the Witches, held at Paisley, Feb. 15, 1677, touching the Bewitching of* SIR GEORGE MAXWELL, *and part is taken out of* SIR GEORGF'S *Account.*

The Commissioners of Justiciary held their first Court at Paisley, the 27th of January, 1677 ; before whom Annabil Stewart, of the age of fourteen years or thereby, when brought in the presence of the Justices for the crime of witchcraft, declared that in harvest last the Devil, in the shape of a black man, came to her mother's house, and required the declarant to give herself up to him ; and that the Devil promised her she should not want any thing that was good. Declares that she, being enticed by her mother, Janet Mathie, and Bessie Weir, who was officer to their several meetings, she put her hand to the crown of her head and the other to the sole of her foot, and did give herself up to the Devil. Declares that her mother promised her a new coat for doing it.   Declares that her spirit's name was *Enippa ;* * and that the Devil took her by the hand, and nipped her arm, which continued to be sore for half-an-hour.   Declares that the Devil, in the shape of a black man, lay with her in the bed under the clothes, and that she found him cold.   Declares, thereafter, he placed her nearest himself.   And declares that she was present in her mother's house when the effigy of wax was made, and that it was made to represent Sir George Maxwell.   Declares that the black man, Janet Mathie, the

---

* Sir George Maxwell's Account says—"That the new name the Devil gave her was *Anippy.*"

G

declarant's mother (whose spirit's name was *Landlady*), Bessie Weir (whose spirit's name is *Sopha*), Margery Craige (whose spirit's name is *Rigerum*), and Margaret Jackson (whose spirit's name * is *Locas*), were all present at the making of the said effigy; and that they bound it on a spit, and turned it before the fire; and that it was turned by Bessie Weir, saying, as they turned it,—Sir George Maxwell! Sir George Maxwell! and that this was expressed by all of them, and by the declarant. Declares that the picture was made in October last. And further declares that, upon the third day of January instant, Bessie Weir came to her mother's house, and advised her to come to her brother, John Stuart's, upon the night following; and that, accordingly, she came to the place, where she found Bessie Weir, Margery Craige, Margaret Jackson, and her brother, John Stuart, and a man with black clothes, a blue band, and white handcuffs, with *hoggers*, and that his feet were cloven. And the declarant sat down by the fireside with them, when they made a picture of clay, in which they placed pins in the breast and sides. And declares that they placed one in every side, and one in the breast. Declared that the black man did put the pins in the picture of wax, but is not sure who put in the pins in the picture of clay. Declares that the effigies produced are the effigies she saw made. Declares that the black man's name is Ejoal. This declaration was emitted before James Dunlop of Househill, William Gremlaye, &c., January 27, 1677. *Ita est Robertus Park, notarius publicus*, &c.†

---

* Sir George Maxwell's Account says Janet Mathie, her mother, whose name was, from the Devil, *Lands lady;* Bessie Weir, whose name was *Sopha;* Margery Craig, whose name was *Rigeru;* Margaret Jackson, whose name was *Locas.*

† Sir George Maxwell's Account says this declaration was made before famous witnesses, subscribed by the two notaries public for her,—Robert

The second confession is of John Stuart, who, being interrogated anent the crime of witchcraft, declared that upon Wednesday, the third day of January instant, Bessie Weir in Pollok town came to the declarant late at night, who, being without doors near to his own house, the said Bessie Weir did intimate to him that there was a meeting to be at his house the next day; and that the Devil, under the shape of a black man, Margaret Jackson, Margery Craige, and the said Bessie Weir, were to be present. And that Bessie Weir required the declarant to be there, which he promised; and that the next night, after the declarant had gone to bed, the black man came in and called the declarant quietly by his name; upon which he rose from his bed, and put on his clothes, and lighted a candle. Declares, that Margaret Jackson, Bessie Weir, and Margery Craige did enter in at a window in the gavel of the declarant's house, and that the first thing that the black man required was that the declarant should renounce his baptism, and deliver himself wholly to him; which the declarant did, by putting one hand on the crown of his head, and the other on the sole of his foot. And that he was tempted to it by the Devil's promising that he should not want any pleasure, and that he should get his heart filled on all that shall do him wrong. Declares that he gave him the name of *Jonas* for his spirit's name.* Declares, that thereafter the Devil required all their consents for the making of the effigies of clay for the taking away the life of Sir George Maxwell of Pollok, to revenge the taking the declarant's mother, Janet Mathie. Declares, that every one of

---

Park, younger, Patrick Carswell in Paisley, — and subscribed by the Commissioners.

* Sir George Maxwell's Account says, "That the new name given to him by the Devil was *Jonas*."

the persons above-named gave their consent to the making of the said effigies, and that they wrought the clay; and that the black man did make the figure of the head, and face, and two arms to the said effigies. Declares, that the Devil set three pins in the same,—one in each side and one in the breast,— and that the declarant did hold the candle to them all the time the picture was making; and that he observed one of the black man's feet to be cloven; and that his apparel was black; and that he had a bluish band and handcuffs: and that he had *hoggers* on his legs without shoes : and that the black man's voice was *hough* and *goustie.* And farther declares, that after they had begun the forming of the effigies, his sister Annabil Stuart, a child of thirteen or fourteen years of age, came knocking at the door, and being let in by the declarant, she stayed with them a considerable time; but that she went away before the rest, he having opened the door to her. That the rest went out at the window at which they entered. Declares, that the effigies were placed by Bessie Weir in his bed-straw. He further declares, he himself had envy against Sir George Maxwell for apprehending Janet Mathie, his mother; and that Bessie Weir had great malice against this Sir George Maxwell; and that her quarrel was, as the declarant conceived, because the said Sir George had not entered her husband to his harvest service : and also declares, that the said effigies were made upon the fourth day of January instant; and that the Devil's name was *Ejoal.* Declares, that his spirit's name was *Jonas;* and Bessie Weir's spirit's name, who was officer, was *Sopha;* and that Margaret Jackson's spirit's name, was *Locas;* and that Annabil Stuart, the declarant's sister's, was *Enippa;* but does not remember what Margery Craige's spirit's name was. Declares, that he cannot write. This confession was emitted in the presence of the witnesses to the other confession, and on the same day.   *Ita est, Robertus Park, notarius publicus*, &c.*

The confession of Margaret Jackson, relict of Thomas Stuart, in Shaws, who, being examined by the Justices anent her being guilty of witchcraft, declares that she was present at the making of the first effigies and picture that were made in Janet Mathie's house, in October; and that the Devil in the shape of a black man, Janet Mathie, Bessie Weir, Margery Craige, and Annabil Stewart, were present at the making of the said effigies, and that they were made to represent Sir George Maxwell of Pollok, for taking away his life.   Declares, that forty years ago, or thereabout, she was at Pollokshaw-croft, with some few sticks on her back, and that the black man came to her, and that she did give up herself unto the black man, from the top of her head to the sole of her foot; and that this was after the declarant's renouncing of her baptism; and that the spirit's name which he designed her, was *Locas*.   And that about the third or fourth of January instant, or thereby, in the night time, when she awaked, she found a man to be in the bed with her, whom she supposed to be her husband, though her husband had been dead twenty years, or thereby, and that the man immediately disappeared; and declares, that this man who disappeared was the Devil.   Declares, that upon Thursday, the fourth of January instant, she was present in the house of John Stuart at night, when the effigy of clay was made, and that she saw the black man there, sometimes sitting, sometimes standing with John Stuart; and that the black man's clothes were black, and that he had white hand-cuffs; and that Bessie Weir, in Polloktoun, and Annabil Stuart, in

---

* Sir George Maxwell's Account says—"This confession had the same solemnities which the former had."

Shaws, and Margery Craige, were at the aforesaid time and place of making the said effigy of clay; and declares, that she gave her consent to the making of the same; and declares that the Devil's name, who compeared in the black man's shape, was *Ejoal.* *Sic subscribitur, ita est, Robertus Park, notarius publicus,* &c.*

One remarkable passage which is taken from Sir George Maxwell's account, runs thus: The Justice upon the 27th of January, commanded the jailor to fix Janet Mathie's feet in the stocks, that she might not do violence to her own life. The man declared, "That the next morning he had found her bolster, which the night before was laid at least six yards distant from the stocks, now placed beneath her: the stocks being so heavy, that two of the strongest men in the country could hardly have carried them six yards: he wondering, did ask her how she had win to the bolster; she answered, "That she had crept alongst the floor of the room, drawing the stocks to the same place." And before the court, she said, "She had gotten one foot free out of the hole, and with the other had drawn the stocks," a thing altogether impossible—the stocks being so weighty; nor was she able to take her foot out of the hole.

Upon the 15th of February, 1677, the Justices being convened again in court at Paisley, John Stewart, and Annabil Stewart, with Margaret Jackson, did adhere to their former judicial confession; but Janet Mathie, Bessie Weir, and Margery Craige, did obstinately deny.

---

* Sir George Maxwell's Account says,—"This confession had the same solemnities which the two former had."

*Now follow the depositions of certain persons, agreeing with the
confessions of the above-said witches.*

Andrew Martin, servitor to the lord of Pollok, of the age
of thirty years, or thereby, depones that he was present in
the house of Janet Mathie, panel, when the picture of wax
produced was found in a little hole in the wall, at the back
of the fire. Depones, that Sir George's sickness did fall upon
him about the 18th of October, or thereby. Depones, that
the picture of wax was found on the —— of December, and
that Sir George's sickness did abate and relent about the
time the picture of wax was found and discovered in Janet
Mathie's house. Depones, that the pins were placed in the
right and left sides ; and that Sir George Maxwell of Pollok's
pains, as he understood by Sir George's complaining of these
pains, lay most in his right and left sides. And depones,
that Sir George's pains did abate and relent after the finding
of the said picture of wax, and taking out of the pins, as is
said. And depones, that the panel, Janet Mathie, has been
by fame and bruit reputed a witch these several years by-past.
And this is the truth, as he shall answer to God. *Sic
subscrib., Andr. Martin.*

Laurence Pollock, secretary to the lord of Pollok, sworn
and purged of partial counsel, depones, that on the —— day
of December, he was in the panel, Janet Mathie's house, when
the picture was found ; and that he did not see it before it was
brought to the panel's door. Depones, that Sir George
Maxwell of Pollok's sickness did seize upon him about the
fourteenth of October, or thereby, and he did continue in his
sickness or distemper for six weeks or thereby. Depones, that
Sir George's sickness did abate and relent after the finding of
the said picture of wax, and taking out of the pins that were in
the effigies. Depones, that by open bruit and common fame,

Janet Mathie, and Bessie Weir, and Margery Craige, are branded to be witches. Depones, that the truth is this, as he shall answer to God. *Sic subscrib., Laurence Pollock.*

Ludowick Stuart of Auchinhood, being sworn and purged of partial counsel, depones, that Sir George's sickness fell upon him the fourteenth or fifteenth of October, or thereby. Depones that he was not present at the finding of the picture of wax; but that he had seen Sir George Maxwell of Pollok after it was found, and, having seen him in his sickness oftentimes before, he did perceive that Sir George had sensibly recovered after the time that the said picture was said to be found, which was upon the 11th or 12th of December. Depones, that Janet Mathie and Margery Craige, two of the panels, are, by report of the country, said to be witches. Depones, that he, having come to Pollok, he did see Sir George Maxwell whose pains did recur, and that his pains and torments were greatly increased in respect of what they were before the finding of the picture of wax. Depones, that upon the 8th of January, when they left the said Sir George Maxwell, of Pollok, the deponent, James Dunlop, of Househill, Allan Douglace, and several others, did go to the house of John Stuart, warlock, in Pollok-shaw, and there he found a picture of clay in the said John Stuart's bed-straw. Depones, that there were three pins in the said picture of clay, and that there was one in each side, and one in the breast. And depones, that being returned to Sir George's house, Sir George told the deponent that he found great ease of his pains, and that it was before the deponent, Househill, and the rest did reveal to him that they had found the said picture of clay; and further depones, that this is truth, as he shall answer to God. *Sic subscrib., Ludowick Stuart.*

148

What follows, is taken from SIR GEORGE'S *account.*

The justices having examined all witnesses in matters of fact, touching the effigies, Sir George's sickness, and the recovery of his health, upon the finding of the same, considering also the bad fame of those who were obstinate, and having confronted them with the confessing witches, who in their faces avowed their accession, in manner expressed in the confessions above written.   Considering, lastly, all other circumstances of their case, committed them to the trial of a judicious inquest, who, being found guilty, were condemned to the fire to be burned, and their effigies with them.   Only Annabil, in regard of her nonage, and the evidences she seemed to give of her penitency, was reprieved by order of the council, but to remain in prison.   In the meantime, both she and her brother John did seriously exhort their mother to confession; and with tears, did Annabil put her in mind of the many meetings she had with the devil in her own house; and that a summer's day would not be sufficient to relate what she had seen pass between the devil and her; but nothing could prevail with her obdured and hardened heart.

Some account of Janet Douglas, *the girl referred to in the account of the bewitching of* SIR GEORGE MAXWELL, *of Pollok.*

Sir John Maxwell, at the end of the account which he sent to Mr. George Sinclair, Professor of Philosophy, in the College of Glasgow, says,—It is to be noted, the dumb girl, whose name was Janet Douglas, doth now speak, not very distinctly, yet so as she may be understood; and is a person that most wonderfully discovers things past, and doth also understand the Latin tongue, which she never learned.

H

The following is the extract of a letter which was sent to MR. GEORGE SINCLAIR, *Professor of Philosphy in the College of Glasgow.*

"When I was at Glasgow, in summer 1677, I was desirous to see the dumb girl, (Janet Douglas.) At my first incoming she declined to entertain discourse, but my friendly expressions, and giving her some money, I gained her. I first enquired anent her parentage. ' I do not remember,' says she, ' of my parents, but only that I was called by the name of Janet Douglas by all people who knew me. I was kept when I was very young, by a poor woman who proved cruel to me, by beating and abusing me : whereupon I deserted the woman's house, and went a-begging.' I enquired next how she became dumb. She told me by reason of a sore swelling she took in her throat and tongue ; but afterwards by the application of *Album Græcum,* ' which I thought,' said she, ' was revealed to me, I recovered my speech.' I asked her, how she came to the knowledge of witches and their practices. She answered, that she had it only by a vision, and knew all things as well as if she had been personally present with them ; but had no revelation or information from the voice of any spirit ; nor had she any communication with the devil, or any spirit of that kind ; ' only,' says she, ' the devil was represented to me, when he was in company with any of the witches, in that same shape and habit he was seen by them.'—She told me, she was altogether ignorant of the principles of religion, but had some smattering knowledge of the Lord's prayer, when she had heard the witches repeat, it seems, by her vision, in presence of the Devil ; and at his desire, which she observed, they added to the word art, the letter w, which made it run, ' Our Father which wart in heaven ; ' and made the third petition thus,—' As on earth so it may in heaven ; ' by which means the Devil made the application of the prayer to himself.——I remember, that there was a woman in the town, who had the curiosity to give her a visit, who asked her, How she came to the knowledge of so many things ? But the young wench shifted her, by asking the woman's name ; says the other, ' Are there any other in Glasgow of that name ?' ' No.' says the woman. 'Then,' said the girl, ' You are a witch.' Says the other, ' Then you are a Devil.' The girl answers, ' The devil doth not reveal witches ; but I know you to be one, and I know your practices too.' Hereupon the woman ran away in great confusion, being indeed a person suspected of witchcraft, and had been sometimes imprisoned on that account. ——Another woman, whose name was Campbel, had the curiosity likewise to come and see her, and began to ask some questions at her. The wench, shifting to give her an answer, says, ' I pray you tell me where you were yesternight, and what you were doing? And withal,' says she, ' let me see your arm ; ' she refusing, the landlord laid hold upon the woman, with some others in the house, and forced her to make bare her arm, where

Janet Douglas shewed them an invisible mark, which she had gotten from the devil. The poor woman much ashamed, ran home. A little time after, she came out and told her neighbours that what Janet Douglas said of her was true ; and earnestly intreated them that they would shew so much to the magistrates, that she might be apprehended, ''otherwise the devil,'' says she, ' will make me kill myself.' But the neighbours judging her to be under a fit of distraction, carried her home to her house; but early next morning the woman was found drowned in the Clyde. ——— The girl likewise told me at Glasgow, being then under no restraint, that it was revealed to her she would be carried before the great council at Edinburgh, imprisoned there, and scourged through the town. All which came to pass, for about a year after, she was apprehended and imprisoned in the tolbooth of the Canongate, and was brought before the council, but nothing being found against her, she was dismissed ; but thereafter, for several crimes committed within the town of Edinburgh, she was taken again, and imprisoned, scourged, and sent away to some foreign plantation ; since which time I have not heard of her. There are several other remarkable passages concerning her, which I cannot inform you of, which others perhaps may do ; therefore I shall abruptly break off, and say no more, but that I am your affectionate friend." Mr. Sinclair says, "This information I have from a discreet understanding gentleman, who was one of my scholars at Glasgow several years ago."

OF

THE BEWITCHING

OF

CHRISTIAN SHAW.

THE PREFACE TO THE NARRATIVE OF CHRISTIAN SHAW.

WISE men do justly suspect, and are hardly brought to credit
the accounts of extraordinary stories; especially anent witchcraft; because the frequent impostures which the Romanists
have obtruded on the world in their miracles and legends;
the many relations of odd things as done by dæmons or
wizards, which yet, were either false or the ground of simple
natural causes; the ignorance of several Judges and Juries,
who have condemned silly creatures merely upon their
ridiculous confessions, or other slender proof; and the
difficulty of conceiving the manner or philosophy of some
operations and appearances, though undoubtedly true in fact;
are good prejudices against a sudden belief, and precautions
for an exact inquiry.   But they are men of weak souls,
destitute of distinct thoughts; who deny all, because they
have discovered error in some, or condemn as false all sects
which they are ignorant how they came to exist: by the
same rule of reasoning that there are no enthusiasts, because
the best men have been sometimes mistaken for these; nor
are there any criminals, in respect severals have suffered who
were not truly such, considering that many histories are
fabulous, therefore none is to be trusted: and all the

phænomenas in nature, whose invisible causes they cannot comprehend, are mere delusions.

The following narrative, as to the truth of fact, is the best attested piece of history of this kind that has occurred in many ages : the most of the matters therein represented having gained the assent of private sceptics : and being proven before public judges, so that it is more surprising than the strange things of witchcraft, that any should seriously deny the being thereof, and from thence discredit such useful providences at a distance, when notoriety has dispelled all objections in the places where they did exist.

Many authors have proven at large, that there are witches and witchcraft, from reason, scripture, antiquity, and experience of all nations and ages in the world, and they have solved the difficulties which might obstruct the belief of this positive proof, by possible hypothesis of philosophy : where it is to be observed, that though any such explications of the natural manner of phænomena are subject to cavil, yet the existence of a thing which hath so certain positive evidence cannot be denied in sound reasoning ; because angels and men not being made for civil converse together in this world, and all communion with devils being interdicted us, the Scripture needed to unfold little of their way of acting ; and still the next age may discover what this could not reach, as this has already unveiled what was thought inextricable in the last, unless impossibility were presently demonstrated. Therefore such a short hint, as may somewhat illustrate the events in the subsequent discourse, may suffice in the present case ; especially since providence does, by eminent occurrences, rather design our practical instruction, than a subject of national speculation.

The devil can assume a corporeal shape and bespeak man out of it : as he did to Eve, our Saviour, and in some heathen oracles: so that there is capacity for the entering into contract. Satan is willing thus to insure mortals of being enemies to heaven, earth, and their own salvation, by his indefatigable malice against all the three: as curiosity in wits, revenge, and disclosure of secrets in the great, covetousness in the worldling, or power and pleasure in all whom he thinks needful, (they being impregnable other ways), and is permitted by God, to attack in this manner, does sufficiently blind them, to be susceptible of his proposals thereanent. We see daily how criminal lusts inflamed by Satan, divert their horror, not only of eternal, but also of temporal eminent torments: perverting these instincts of nature which might fright them from surrender. But further, he does commonly facilitate his conquest on witches, by decoying them piecemeal to his lure, through the mediation of others from among mankind that are already embarked, till they be prepared, and he get an opportunity of making with them an explicit transaction.

That accordingly Satan has *de facto* prevailed in making sorcerers and witches, appears from the testimony of the wisest and best in all states and times.

The heathens, by nature and practice, discovering this truth, made laws against *maleficos and mathematicos,** (these last, though they assumed the name of an art much encouraged by the legislators, yet were known, under the cloak thereof, to consult the Devil anent the fates of men and states) which the Roman senate and people did execute; and even the Persians, in some good reigns did the same. Under the Old Testament dispensation the magicians of Egypt and Babylon were baffled by Moses and Daniel; Balaam and the witch of Endor were baffled, just judgments were inflicted on Jezebel,

---

* Witches and Mathematicians.

Manasseh, and the ten tribes for their sorceries, and witch-crafts amongst other crimes ; and the laws made against such, as distinct from other guilt under the New Testament. Simon Magus, who bewitched the people of Samaria ; Elymas the sorcerer, who was struck blind at Paul's rebuke : the Pythonisse girl who seems to have been possest of consent, because she was not tormented, but got profit thereby ; and such as confessed shewed their deeds and burned their books in Ephesus ; are undeniable instances of witchcraft. Finally, there are prophecies of false Christs with signs and wonders, able to deceive, if possible, the very elect : general councils have made canons against these wretches; and the experi-mental knowledge of injured mortals, with the public sentences which did vindicate the same, in subsequent ages, are delivered down to us by the writers thereof. Hence Guilielmus Linensis, a popish doctor, was justly put to death, even though he died penitent, he having confessed witchcraft, (whereof the written covenant was found in his pocket,) and that his share of the Devil's service was to persuade and preach that witches were only silly deluded melancholians, whereby their confessions were no proof. His success was such in this work of darkness, that the people and judge's did slack, and witches were vastly multiplied in few years, *vid. Pet. Mamorius de Lamiis*, who gives an account of the process from authentic records. Through these periods, it is observed, that Satan has oft shifted the scene, and turned himself to many shapes, as he found it most accommodating to his purposes : whereby the manner of apparition of devils has been different, according to the state of the times. So of old Satan appeared, and was worshipped as such, for deprecating his mischief, which is said to be retained in some of the most barbarous places of the Indies to this day.

In the darkness of Popery the Devil was transformed into

a more innocent spirit,* in the brounies and fairies. These were then very frequent, he having impudence thus to appear openly, proportional to the knowledge of men, over whom his reign was so universal, as it is related to continue in the more northern regions at this day. But since light has broke out in our horizon, he oftener works. externally by magicians and witches, and internally on the lusts of men, being now mostly restrained to his own sphere or subjects. Yet still he ensnares severals, partly by aping the ordinances of God ; especially as they are corrupted in the Romish Church, whence so many monks and nuns as already prepared, have been found overcome. So he keeps with them public assemblies in the night of extraordinary merit. They formally worship him by many mimical gestures ; he imprints on them a kind of sacrament ; he inflicts dreadful penances on such as have not executed the commanded mischiefs ; he teaches them odd words and signs, upon repeating of which exorcisms, he (it being his interest) effectuates the fore-pactioned operations, &c.

But though what he does of himself, or on the watch word or ensign of sorcerers or witches, may, by collection, and artful disposal of matter and form, appear surprising; yet he cannot work against nature, or so apply actives to passives, as to overturn the course thereof; since that is only competent to its author, who alone can do true miracles, or know immediately the thoughts of man. Yea, after the fall it is like, that even Satan's natural powers are come down below those of good angels; and it is certain, that he is often befooled in his designs by providence : notwithstanding whereof he retains

---

* That pretended to foretell deaths, reveal the defunct's will, discover occult murder, do other friendly offices, &c., which were subtle means of inducing to him and relying on him.

so much as (being permitted) is sufficient to bring about, by unseen natural means, most of the extraordinary appearances, that the generality of the learned have attributed to him ; and particularly those in the subsequent narrative : many of which, though they are beyond the efficiency of disease, deceit, or any visible cause ; yet may be the effects of some such unperceived means as follow.

There is no difficulty in Satan's transmitting in a short time an account of things which are past ; since it is known he goes to and fro in the earth : yea, he may have certainly foretold some future events, as Alexander's success against Persia, &c., seeing he understands and may steal the great revolutions of the world, out of the prophets, wherein they are so graphically circumscribed ; or he may discover his own resolutions whenever he is commissioned or permitted to execute a judgment ; which is the case of those, whom for seeking their horoscopes, God gives over to him to whom they do apply ; and of Saul, who got so exact an account of his own end by the Philistines. But without some such aid, Satan can only guess, like the physician by the urine, or politician by the crises of states, which is the cause that most of his oracles are ambiguous.

His transporting of witches is elsewhere explained. He can raise hurricanes, as appears in Job, which are known to carry over tracts of sea and land, very ponderous bodies ; as it is easy for him to condense a part of the vehicle, which may protect the breathing and yet cut the air, like the fence of dyvers, and beak of a sloop ; in which also he affects the magnifying of his natural powers to be no less than of good angels, who transported Ezekiel and Elijah. His covering of the witches from sight, at some times, is also cleared from the difficulties which seem to attend it, in another place, where it appears very possible that his skill in optics, reflection and

I

refraction of light, &c., to which his power and agility as a spirit subministrates materials, may effectuate all that can be proven to be true fact in the case.

But Glanvil, More, and others, lay another hypothesis in both, viz., That the soul is separable from the body in some cases without death: when by God's permission, Satan, of the parties' consent, gets power over soul and body; whereby he may carry away the one from the helm of the other, and set it back again in its seat; providing the vital spirits which make the body a fit receptacle, be well preserved by ointments, that constrict the pores till the return of its guest; but death ensues from a separation, when the organs of the body are rendered altogether unapt to obey the soul's commands in its functions. If such an opinion could be true, Satan might place this cap-. tivated spirit to actuate any shape he thinks fit. But there needs not so much metaphysics to unriddle the appearances of witches as beasts and the like, since their real persons may be covered with a vehicle, which by disposal of the rays coming therefrom, may fascinate the eyes by the same impressions that come from the true sight of such. His power of representing another thing in lieu of that which is truly present, is so certain that it is found he may make up the image of persons who are not present at all. For it is undoubted that spiritual devils may sometimes be permitted to represent by phantoms the most innocent and praise-worthy men, as devils incarnate do traduce them. He that accuseth the brethern and imitates an angel of light, may likewise personate the children of light by his delusions: yet the antecedents, concomitants, and consequents of such providences, do readily propale the falsehood, so as the just man, for the most part, shall not perish in his righteousness, and God, in his ordinary providence, will not laugh at the trial of the innocent, though sometimes it fall out that the sons of Belial may swear away the life of an innocent Naboth.

158

There are several other things of less difficult explication. Particularly, the devil or witches might have been heard in converse by the maid, and not by others, the same way as a sound directed through a speaking-trumpet does reach the ears to which it is aimed, without dispersing towards the intermediate that are not in a straight line betwixt. The confederated devil, may, upon the witches' desire, infuse poisonous humours, extracted from herbs of the same invisible operation with the steam of mad dogs, or the pestilence, which being joined to the rapidous course of the patient's own spirits, humours, and blood, that Satan, by ingyring himself thereunto, may, through the natural means of pulsion, set in career, can very well produce these extraordinary motions which are mentioned in the following account. They delight much in the torture or destruction of young children, in envy of Christ, who is tender of such little ones ; and because the crime is the greater the less the patient has offended, or can resist. They use, or make others to repeat scripture words for gaining credit, or alleviating the terror, or to disgrace the Word, by such a mock use, as they did in the time of our Saviour, and therefore their testimony was rebuted. It is observable from many passages, that he hastens sometimes, and effects their discovery, by his malice against their present temporal enjoyments, uncertainty of their continuance, and insatiable desire for their full wreck. Yet some of them, who are most maliciously bent, he thinks fit to keep here, as useful instruments ; and providence permits others to live, that they, wilfully filling up their measure, under means, may be finally inexcusable.

As to those whom, in secret judgment, the devil is permitted to torment, but, in mercy, not to overcome, he may be carried thereunto from his design of perverting them by terror, whereof he is at last disappointed. And however the defacing of God's image, and especially in despight of Jesus Christ, who honoured that nature by assuming it, is his chief delight; or he is constrained to make such stupendous appearances against his will (because he is most successful when he is least known) for a visible testimony superadded to, the greater gospel proofs, in gross times, that there are spirits and a devil to torment them, as it is observable that this was denied by Mr. Aikenhead (though he died in full conviction thereof) at the time when these things fell out in the country. Or providence may tolerate such sufferings, that they, though intended by the devil for an instance of malice, may, by their notoriety, be a means of moving the discovery, and bringing to justice these miscreants, whom he made use of as his instruments in them, and who may have lived long in rebellion against heaven, and destruction of mankind, by malefices of the same sort which fell out in this case. Finally, the abundant and efficacious grace of God is conspicuous in enabling a young girl to resist to the utmost the best laid assaults of the evil one, as it is certain that he shews the greatest malice in countries where he is hated and hateth most, and the nearer his reign be to an end.

There are many other profitable instructions which arise from this wonderful providence, for such dispensations have their own language, and the man of wisdom shall see God's name.

The usages of charms for men or beasts, certain characters, words, verses, and spells; the observation of times and seasons as lucky or unlucky; the belief of having success by carrying about some herbs, plants, or branches of trees, and many the like superstitions, which can have no natural casualty on the effects desired, are the very rudiments of witchcraft, and an implicit application to the devil for virtues which God has denied to things; whence they are to be abhorred as sinful in themselves and introductory to explicit engagement. So gross ignorance, profane looseness, stupid forgetfulness of God, and neglect of his worship in closets and families; malice, envy, revenge, discontent, oppressive fear of want, and distrustful anxiety of spirit; finally, a libidinous temper, curses, imprecations, and sinful curiosity, are to be evited as paving the way to the same mischief.

Let none inveigh against a profession of religion, because some under that specious covert have been found in league with the devil. It is because of the glorious lustre and excellency of our holy faith, that these miscreants paint themselves with it, whereby likewise they may be less suspected, and more able subtily to gain on others, and do their master's work. So it was no stain on the apostles that one of their number had a devil, was a traitor and cheat; nor that Satan transforms himself into an angel of light, of design that the good ways of the Lord may be evil spoken of. Neither let us be under a slavish fear and terror of that hellish tribe, in truckling to their humour, least they should do harm, which savours of worshipping and paying homage to the devil; whereas we ought only to make the Lord of hosts our fear and our dread.

There is no just ground to reflect on particular persons or families, upon account of such troubles. For no man knoweth either love or hatred by all that's before them. All things come alike to all. And suppose ye that these were sinners above all the Galileans, or above all that dwelt in Jerusalem ? The infinite wise God may thus try faith, patience, and Christian fortitude. Job and our Saviour were assaulted; and seven devils cast out of Mary Magdalene, a chosen vessel unto the Lord. A daughter of Abraham's was bound by Satan eighteen years; and his messenger was sent to buffet the great apostle of the Gentiles. The woman of Canaan, Matth.

xv. 22. and the godly man, Mark ix. 24. had their nearest relations vexed in this manner; and blessed be the Lord that has left such instances on record for prevention of stumbling. Though it must be confessed that the same charity which judges well of all things cannot but alter its remark, when its proof is sufficiently clear from the way in which the person affected did formerly walk, since presumptions do always cede to truth, and lawyers have a maxim, that *in re clara non est locus conjecturis.**

These things may meet with a very different reception, especially in this unhappy age and place of the world, where Britain may be termed the unfortunate island,—Afric never having been more fertile in the production of monsters,—since 'tis observed that through all the successions of men, there was never before any society or collective body of atheists till these dregs of time, though there might have been here and there some misshapen births. But wisdom is justified of her children, and 'tis the season of Samson to awake when Delilah gives the alarm that the Philistines are upon him. What, peace! so long as the whoredoms of Jezebel and her witchcrafts are so many? But good things are hoped of our magistrates, who have already so happily begun.

The apostle said of Job's trials, ye have heard of the patience of Job, and have seen the end of the Lord. So in this narrative you have a deplorable scheme of this maid's formidable fits, and of the powers of darkness that combined, not only for ruining her body, but also for murdering her soul. In the meantime, the hearts of many were bleeding for her, and much application was made to God in her behalf. Divers solemn fasts were observed, both in her father's family, in the parish, and throughout the bounds of the presbytery and elsewhere;

---

* In this case it is evident the thing is not a conjecture.

her case was expressly minded in public addresses to the throne of grace ; till at length there was a general fast religiously kept in most parts of the synod, that God might give an effectual check to Satan's rage and dominion in the country. Boasting of prayers is to be abhorred, yet it is our duty with all gratitude, to acknowledge God the hearer, and to proclaim to the world the excellency of them upon this very occasion : For he hath not turned away his ear from us, it being the comfortable result of this history, that the girl hath been perfectly well for many months : and is not this a brand plucked out of the fire ; and have not the splinters wherewith the witches thought to have destroyed her, recoiled back upon some of themselves, and we wait execution of justice on the rest.

The devil could not enter the herd of swine, nor touch one hair of Job's head, without permission from Him whose kingdom ruleth over all : whence though our enemies be very indefatigable and invisible, yet we are under the conduct of the watchman who neither slumbers nor sleeps ; to whom darkness and light are both alike ; and greater is he that is in us, than he that is in the world. So that unless we wilfully forfeit our privileges, there is no fear of counterpoising the wicked ones, throwing down the gauntlet to all their projects or machinations, since neither angels, principalities, nor powers, shall be able to separate us from the love which is in Christ Jesus our Lord ; and though no argument can be drawn from any merit in us, yet we'll carry the day against all the militia of hell under the captain of our salvation, since he will rest in his own love. Is this the manner of man, O Lord God ? yet a little while the devil and his accomplices will be cast into the bottomless pit, and we transported into Immanuel's land.

It will not be a natural sturdiness of temper, nor a lifeless mentioning of the name of God or Christ, that can shelter us from those devourers, as appears in the seven sons of Sceva, Acts xix., but if the Lord be God, then follow Him; for who is he that will harm you if ye be followers of that which is good; He will give His angels charge of thee to keep thee in all thy ways. Great peace have they that love Thy law, and nothing shall offend them. And they wrestle most successfully against principalities and powers who fight upon their knees, as resisting of the devil is the way to make him flee from us.

Yet whom Satan cannot obtain to be tortured hereafter he will (when permitted) torment in this side of time : hence, if possessions of bodies be so great a plague, how much worse is it to have him reign master of our souls? Wherefore let us watch and pray against every sin, the least of which is more pleasing to him and worse to us than the being so corporally tormented.

If Satan, as a spirit, may insinuate himself into our humours, no wonder that by having such advantage in the temper, he can influence the phlegmatic to sloth, the choleric to anger, the sanguine to lust and sinful pleasure, the melancholic to despair, &c. So they who think that they stand have need to take heed lest they fall, and to pray that the Watchman of Israel may make an hedge about them and their house, and about all that they have on every side.

Let this not only rouse our diligence and stir up our gratitude for not being affected alike; but let it recall our admiration and love of Jesus Christ, who hath freed our souls and bodies from the power and slavery of Satan; and finding ourselves too weak for him, in awarding these deluding pleasures which procure our being deserted by God, and are Satan's baits to this fearful thraldom; let us run to the Rock of Ages for protection and support, our sufficiency being only of God.

Seeing there are witches and devils, there are also immortal souls of the first, since the last do contract for them, and take such pains to retain them; so that the Sadducees, though they have a judicial blindness in their reason, are hereby rendered inexcusable by very sense. Evil books which stir up and ensnare curious fancies that are seldom accompanied with accurate judgments, (the soul's looking outward diverting it from diving into the depths of truth) are to be restrained; and also such ridiculous pamphlets, as no doubt, by the instigation of Satan, have lately been sent abroad, of design to frustrate any good use which might be made of such rare providences, as are contained in the ensuing narrative, by forging others, or disguising this.

This has been delayed so long to be published, partly that there might be the more narrow scrutiny made into the matters of fact; and partly, by some accidents which did retard it In it the reader is not to expect any accuracy of style, because the designed shortness did occasion the wrapping up of much matter in small bounds, and the punctual exactness of truth in every circumstance was the chief aim, so that other defects ought to be the less quarrelled.

The first edition of this Preface, Narrative, &c., was printed at Edinburgh, by James Watson in 1698, and entitled, "True Narrative of the sufferings and relief of a Young Girl, who was strangely molested by evil spirits and their instruments in the west. Collected from authentic testimonies, with a preface and postscript.

Containing reflections on what is most material or curious, either in the history or trial of the Seven Witches who were condemned and burnt in the Gallowgreen of Paisley.

K

JOB ii. 6. *And the Lord said unto Satan, behold, he is in thine hand ; but save his life.*

MATTH. xv. 22. *Have mercy upon me, O Lord, thou son of David; my daughter is grievously vexed with a devil.*

ROM. xv. 20. *And the God of peace shall bruise Satan under your feet shortly."*

TRUE NARRATIVE

OF THE

Sufferings and Relief of a Young Girl.

IT was about the end of August, 1696, when the first rise and occasion was given, (so far as can be known) to these strange things that befel the child, who is the subject of this narrative, and the manner was thus :—

Christian Shaw, daughter to a gentleman of good account, called John Shaw, laird of Bargarran,* in the parish of Erskine, within the shire of Renfrew, a smart lively girl, and of good inclinations, about eleven years of age, perceiving one of the maids of the house, named Katherine Campbell, to steal and drink some milk, she told her mother of it; whereupon the maid Campbell (being a young woman of a proud and revengeful temper, and much addicted to cursing and swearing upon any like occasion, and otherwise given to purloining) did, in a most hideous rage, thrice imprecate the curse of God upon the child; and at the same time did thrice utter these horrid

---

* "A little towards the south from the castle of Erskine, stands the house of Bargarran, the seat of John Shaw of Bargarran, whose ancestors, for nigh three hundred years, have possessed these lands, and derive their descent from a younger brother of the family of Sauchie, now represented by Sir John Shaw of Greenock (anno 1697) The intermarriages of this house have been with some of the most considerable gentry of this country ; as the families of Kelsoeland, Mains, Raiss, Woodhead, Glorat, Livingstone of Haining, Craigends, and Northbar."—*Crawfurd's History of the Shire of Renfrew.*

167

words, "The devil harle (that is, drag) your soul through hell."
This passed upon Monday, August 17th, in presence of several
witnesses, who afterwards made evidence of it.

Upon the Friday following, being August 21st, about sun-
rising, one Agnes Naesmith, an old widow woman, ignorant,
and of a malicious disposition, addicted to threatnings, (which
sometimes were observed to be followed with fatal events),
who lived in the neighbourhood, came to Bargarran's house;
where, finding the child Christian in the court with her
younger sister, she asked how the lady and young child did,
and how old the young sucking child was; to which Christian
replied, what do I know? Then Agnes asked, how herself
did, and how old she was; to which she answered, that she
was well, and in the eleventh year of her age.

On the Saturday night thereafter, being Aug. 22, the child
went to bed in good health; but so soon as she fell asleep,
began to struggle and cry Help, help! and then suddenly got
up, and did fly over the top of a resting bed, where she was
lying (her father, mother, and others being in the room, and
to their great astonishment and admiration) with such violence,
that probably her brains had been dashed out, if a woman,
providentially standing by, and supported by a door at her
back, had not broke the force of the child's motion; who,
being laid in another bed, remained stiff and insensible as if
she had been dead for the space of half an hour; but for
forty-eight hours thereafter could not sleep, crying out of
violent pains through her whole body, and no sooner began to
sleep or turn drowsy but seemed greatly affrighted, crying still,
Help, help.

After this the pain fixed in her left side, and her body was
often so bent and rigid, as she stood like a bow on her feet
and neck at once, and continued without power of speech,
except in some short intervals, for eight days; during which

time she had scarce half an hour's intermission together, the fits taking her suddenly, and both coming on and going off by a swerff or short deliquium, but appeared perfectly well and sensible in the intervals.

But about the middle of September, her fits returned in a manner differing from the former, wherein she seemed to fight and struggle with something that was invisible to spectators, and her action appeared as if she had been defending herself from some who were assaulting or attempting to hurt her, and this with such force that four strong men were scarcely able to hold her; and when any of the people touched any part of her body she did cry and screech with such vehemence, as if they had been killing her, but could not speak.

Before this time, as she was seized with the trouble, her parents had called for physicians from Paisley, viz.: John White, apothecary, a near relation, and afterwards Dr. Johnstone, who took blood, and applied several things, both at first, and afterwards, without any discernable effect upon the patient, either to the better or worse; and she all the while of these latter fits being afflicted with extraordinary risings and fallings of her belly, like the motion of a pair of bellows, and such strange movings of her body, as made the whole bed she lay on shake, to the great consternation of spectators.

Some days thereafter was an alteration in her fits, so far, that she got speaking during the time of them ; and while she was in the fits, fell a crying that Katherine Campbell and Agnes Naesmith were cutting her side and other parts of her body ; which parts were in that time violently tormented. And when the fit was over she still averred that she had seen the same persons doing the same things which she complained of while under the fit, (it being remarkable that in the intervals she was still as well and sensible as ever) and would not believe but that others present saw them as well as she ! In this condition she continued with some, but not very considerable variation, either as to the fits or intervals, for the space of a month.

After which time she was conveyed to Glasgow, where Dr. Brisbane,* a physician deservedly famed for skill and experience, did by Mr. Henry Marshall, apothecary, apply medicine to her ; after which, having staid in Glasgow about ten days, and being brought home to the country, she had near a fortnight's intermission. But then her fits returned, with this difference, that she knew when they were coming, by a pain in her left side, which she felt before they came ; and in these fits her throat was prodigiously drawn down toward her breast, and her tongue back into her throat : her whole body becoming stiff and extended, as a dead corpse, without sense or motion ; and sometimes her tongue was drawn out of her mouth over her chin to a wonderful length, her teeth setting together so fast upon it, that those present were forced to thrust something betwixt her teeth, for saving her tongue ; and it was oft observed that her tongue was thus tortured when she essayed to pray. And in this condition she was for some time, with sensible intervals wherein she had perfect health, and could give a full account of what she was heard to utter while in the fit.

For several days these fits continuing with some variation, her parents resolved to return her to Glasgow, that she might there have the more conveniency of being under the doctor's oversight and care, for further discerning the nature of her trouble, and making use of the most probable natural re-

---

* The Son of the Reverend Divine, Mr. Matthew Brisbane, Parson of Erskine, who was descended from the Brisbanes of Bishopton.—*Vide Crawfurd's History of the Shire of Renfrew.*

medies. But being on her way to her grandmother's house at Northbar, she did thrust or spit out of her mouth parcels of hair, some curled, some plaited, some knotted, of different colours, and in large quantities; and thus she continued to do in several swooning fits every quarter of an hour, both in her passage to Glasgow, which was by boat on Thursday, Nov. 12th, and when she was in Glasgow; for the space of three days ensuing she put frequently hair out of her mouth, and in as great quantities as the first day, her former swerffing or swooning fits recurring as often throughout the days as before; and thereafter from Monday to Thursday following she put out of her mouth coal cinders about the bigness of chesnuts, some whereof were so hot that they could scarcely be handled, one of which, Dr. Brisbane being by her when she took it out of her mouth, felt to be hotter than the heat of any one's body could make it. Then for the space of two days in these swooning fits, as formerly, there was put, or taken out of her mouth, straw in great quantities, though but one straw at once folded up together, which, when put out, returned to its length, was found to be both long and broad, and it was remarkable that in one of them there was a little small pin found. Thereafter were put out of her mouth, bones of various sorts and sizes, as bones of fowls, and small bones of the heads of kine, and then some small sticks of candle fir, (a sort of fir in the country, that burns like candle), one of which was about three or four inches long; which, when any upon sight of either bones or sticks took hold of to pull out, they found them either held by her teeth set together upon them, or forcibly drawn back into her throat; particularly Archibald Bannatyne of Kellie, younger, observing a bone in her mouth like a duck shank or leg bone, and essaying to pull it out, he declared he found something drawing it back into her throat, so that it took a deal of force to get it pulled out. It is to be

noticed, that she never knew how these things were brought
into her mouth, and when they were got out of it, she immediately recovered of her fit for that time.

After this, she put out of her mouth some quantity of unclean hay intermixed with dung, as if it had been taken out
of a dunghill, which was so stinking that the damsel could
not endure the nauseating taste and vile relish those things
produced in her mouth, which did necessitate her still to rinse
her mouth with water, after the putting of that sort of matter
out of it. Then for more than a day's space, she put out of
her mouth a number of wild fowls feathers; after that a
gravel-stone, which, in the judgment of beholders, had been
passed by some persons in a gravel fit, with some small white
stones, and a whole nut gall, (wherewith they use to dye and
to make ink), together with lumps of candle grease and egg
shells; during which time she continued as formerly in her
recurring swooning fits, with some intervals wherein she was
in perfect health : of all which there were many famous witnesses, who, in that city, (besides those who were continually
with her) came frequently to visit her.

It is to be noticed, that the damsel at the time of the putting out of her mouth the sticks above-mentioned, being in
bed about eight o'clock at night, told she was to be greviously
tormented with sore fits at night, which accordingly fell out.
For a little thereafter, she fell into a long swoon, wherein she
had no use of any sense, either of hearing, seeing, or feeling;
so as though oftimes the beholders called to her with a loud
voice, moving, also, and tossing her body, all was to no purpose; and when the Laird of Kellie, younger, above-named, to
try the truth, gave her a very sore pinch in the arm, she had
no sense of it in the time. After recovering from the swoon,
but yet continuing in the fit, she fell a reasoning with
Katherine Campbell after this manner: "Thou sittest there

172

with a stick in thy hand to put in my mouth, but through God's strength thou shalt not get leave : thou art permitted to torment me, but I trust in God thou shalt never get my life, though it is my life thou designest." (And at that time calling for a Bible and candle), said, "Come near me Katie, and I'll let thee see where a godly man was given up to Satan to be tormented, but God kept his life in his own hand; and so I trust in God thou shalt never get my life, and all that thou shalt be permitted to do unto me, I hope through God's mercy shall turn to my advantage. This man was robbed of all, and tormented in body, and had nothing left him but an ill wife. Come near me, Katie, and I'll read it to thee." And reading that passage of Job, when she came to the place where his wife said to him, "Curse God and die!" the damsel considering these words a little, said,—"O ! what a wife has this been, that bids her goodman curse God and die? she who should have been a comfort to him in his trouble, turned a cross to him?" Then, after reading of the chapter to the end, she looks towards the foot of the bed and said,—"Now, Katie, what thinkest thou of that? thou seest for all the power the Devil got over Job, he gained no ground on him ; and I hope he shall gain as little on me. Thy master the Devil deceives thee ; he is a bad master whom thou servest, and thou shalt find it to thy smart, except thou repent before thou die. There is no repentance to be had after death. I'll let thee see, Katie, there is no repentance in hell." And turning over the book, citing Luke, Chap. xvi., near the latter end thereof, and reading the same over, said,—"Katie, thou seest there is no repentance in hell for this rich man besought Abraham to testify to his five brethren, that they come not to the place of torment, where he was, but repent and turn to the Lord, for there is no winning out, if once they come there ; now, Katie, thou heard this, what thinkest thou of it ?

L

I'll let thee hear another place which should pierce thy very heart, and turning over the Book, said she would read about Adam and Eve. Thou knowest, Katie, the serpent the Devil, thy master, thought to have ruined mankind at the beginning, his malice was so great at that blessed state wherein they were then, seeing himself cast down from all hopes of mercy, used all means possible for him to subvert their happiness, by suggesting to them fair promises, and a prospect of advantage to them before their eyes, in causing them eat that forbidden fruit, whereby they and their posterity fell from that estate wherein they were, and were made subject to God's curse for ever. But God did not suffer them to be at this stance, but of his infinite mercy shewed them a better way, whereby they might have life eternal by revealing to them that blessed promise,—' The seed of the woman shall bruise the head of the serpent.'   Now, Katie, what thinkest thou of that promise ? But have mind of this, thou'lt get no advantage by it ; 'tis not made to thee, who hast renounced God's service, and taken on with the Devil,—thou art his slave; thou deniedst this, but I know thou art a hypocrite ; for I remember, when thou wast in my mother's house, thou bought a Catechism upon a pretence to learn to read, to cloak thy sin.   Wilt thou hear me, knowest thou the reward of the hypocrite ? I'll let thee hear it ; remember Mr. William Gillies was lecturing the other day upon the xxiii. of Matthew, where many a woe is pronounced against the hypocrite, eight dreadful woes here, Katie, and some of them belong to thee ; but I'll tell thee more.   Knowest thou the reward of the hypocrite ? they shall be cast into the lake that burns for ever, that's their portion. Dost thou hear this now ? thou turnest thy back to me, when I am telling the truth ; if I were reading a story-book, or telling a tale to thee, thou wouldst hear that.   Remember it will be thy portion, too, if thou do not repent, and confess, and seek mercy." Again, turning over the book, she read about Pilate, saying,—" Pilate he made a shew of cleansing himself of Christ's blood,—he washed his hands and declared himself innocent; but for all his washing, he had a foul heart,—he would not lose his office for the saving of Christ's life. He knew well enough that Christ was an innocent person; but he preferred his honour before Christ: therefore to please the Jews, and to quench the struggling in his conscience, he washed his hands, and then delivered Christ to be crucified by them." Thus she continued for more than two hours' space, reasoning at this rate, and exhorting her to repent, quoting many places of Scripture through the Revelation and Evangelists. And when any offered to pull her Bible from her, she uttered horrid screeches and outcries, saying,—" She would never part with her Bible as long as she lived,--she would keep it in spite of all the devils."

Before we pass from this, it will be needful to give the reader advertisement of some things. 1. That while she called for her Bible and a candle, she neither heard nor saw any of those persons who were then actually and discernably present in the room with her, and that Katherine Campbell, to whom she directed her speech, was not discernably present to any other body but herself. And the pinch she got in her insensible fit, she found and complained of the pain of it in that part afterward, but knew not how she came by it, nor blamed any of her tormentors for it. 2. That these words set down as spoken by her were the very same both for words and order as nearly as they could be gathered and remembered by the hearers without any addition of their own. 3. That although she was a girl of a pregnant spirit above her age, and had much of the Scriptures, and withal had a pretty good understanding, above what might be expected of one of her years, of the fundamental principles of religion taught in the Catechisms; yet we doubt not in so strong a combat, the Lord did, by His good spirit, graciously afford her a more than ordinary measure of assistance, both now and at other times in the like debates.

Sometime after the putting out of her mouth the trash above-mentioned, she fell into extremely violent fits, with lamentable crying,—four persons being hardly able to withhold her from climbing up the walls of the chamber, or from otherways doing herself hurt, meantime having no power of speech while in the fit, but her back and the rest of her body grievously pained, in which condition she continued four or five days, with the usual sensible intervals, in which she declared that four men, Alexander and James Andersons, and other two, of whom she gave particular and exact marks, but knew not their names, were tormenting her. It was observed that many of these she named were known to be persons of ill fame, as these two persons last named were. It is also remarkable that for some time she knew not the name of the said Alexander Henderson, till one day he came a-begging to the door of the house, where the damsel was, whom she seeing, immediately cried out, "that was he whom she had seen among the crew."

After this she fell into other fits, wherein she saw the forenamed persons with some others, and heard and saw several things that passed among them. Particularly, she sometimes told when she was to take the fits, how often she would take them, (which fell out accordingly), with some discourse that were among them relating to herself and others.

About the eighth of December, being brought home again from Glasgow, and having had six or seven days respite from her fits, she afterwards fell into frightful and terrifying fits; the occasion whereof she declared to be, her seeing the devil in prodigious and horrid shapes, threatening to devour her, and

then she would fall dead and stiff with all the parts of her
body distended and stretched out as a corpse, without sense or
motion, which fits as they came suddenly on without her
knowledge, so she did as suddenly recover and grew perfectly
well; and they usually came on when she essayed to pray.
In which time also other fits took her more sensibly, she
knowing when they were a-coming, how long they would continue, and when they would return; in which fits her eyes
strangely altered, and turned in her head to the admiration of
spectators, with a continual painful working about her heart;
sometimes her joints were complicate and drawn together, and
her forehead drawn forcibly about toward her shoulders; which
fits she took by first falling into a swoon, and after her violent
fits, instantly recovered after the same manner. During this
time, the fits altered again as to their times of coming and
continuance; in which she sometimes endeavoured to bite her
own fingers, or anything else that came in her way; also when
she saw the persons before-mentioned, one or two of them
about her, pointing them out to the persons present with her,
though by them unseen, and sometimes declaring that she had
hold of them by their clothes, particularly, December 17. She
being in a sore fit, she cried out of several persons that were
tormenting her; and being in the bed, grasped with her hands
towards the foot of it, and cried out that she had got a grip of
the sleeves of one J. P's. jerkin (or jacket) which was, as she
said, duddie (that is ragged or tattered) at the elbows; and at
that very instant, the damsel's mother and aunt heard the
sound of the rending or tearing of a cloth, but saw or felt
nothing, only found in each of the damsel's hands—which were
fast closed—when they got them opened, a bit of red cloth,
looking as torn off a garment; of which kind of cloth there
had been none in the room at that time, nor in the whole
house, nor near it that any knew of. Another particular she

told was, that there was such an one among the crew going to prick her tongue, which thereupon was instantly pulled back into her throat, she lying dumb for a considerable space. Sometimes upon her recovery from her fits, she told that she heard several things spoken and communed among her afflictors, but durst not make them known; because they threatened to torment her after this, or the other manner, if she should make them known; and accordingly, when, by her mother or others, she was prevailed with to begin to tell them, instantly the torment fell out as was threatened. She told further, that her tormentors appeared to her usually with lights and strange sorts of candles, which were frightful for her to look to them.

Thus she continued till the first of January, 1697, not only in the fits fore-mentioned with some alterations, but fell likewise by swooning, into light fits, wherein she continued about two or three hours together, sometimes more, sometimes less, with very short intervals, in which fits she did not much complain of pain; but had a great palpitation in her breast, and sometimes in other parts of her body, strange and unaccountable motions, which continued in a greater or lesser degree during the whole time of the fit, wherein she was somewhat light, and not so solid in her mind as at other times, though in the intervals of these, as of all other fits, she was sufficiently composed; which fits as all the rest, came suddenly on, and went as suddenly off by a swoon or swerf.

Before we proceed further in the relation, let it be noticed, first, that the foresaid Agnes Naesmith, being brought by the parents a second time to see the damsel, did (though not desired) pray for her, viz., " That the Lord of heaven and earth might send the damsel her health, and try out the verity : " After which the damsel declared that though the said Agnes had formerly been very troublesome to her, yet, from that time forth, she did no more appear to her as her tormentor, but, on the contrary, as she apprehended, defending her from the fury of the rest. Second, it is further here to be noticed, that the forenamed Katherine Campbell could by no means be prevailed with to pray for the damsel, but upon the contrary, when desired by some, cursed them, and all the family of Bargarran, and in particular the damsel and all that belonged to her, withal adding this grievous imprecation, " The devil let her never grow better, nor any concerned in her, be in a better condition than she was in, for what they had done to her." Which words she spoke before several famous witnesses. 3. That Bargarran having prevailed with the sheriff depute of the shire, to imprison the said Katherine Campbell, she from the time of her imprisonment, never appeared to the damsel; (though formerly she had ordinarily appeared as one of her most violent tormentors) except once or twice, at which times, it was found upon after enquiry, that she was not in the Tolbooth, but either in the jailor's house, or had liberty granted her to go out to church. 4. That at the time when the damsel did put out of her mouth the hair and other trash, as above related, Katherine Campbell being taken into custody, there was found in her pocket a ball of hair of several colours, which was afterwards thrown into the fire, after which time the damsel put no more hair out of her mouth. And it is to be further noticed, that she said she heard among the crew, when tormenting her, that Katherine Campbell made that ball of hair found in her pocket, of the hair of the damsel's head which had been cut when her trouble began, and which did agree in colour, &c., when compared.

Upon the first day of January, about ten o'clock at night, she fell by swoonings into fits differing from the former, in that, after the swooning fit was over, she lay quiet, as if she had been dead, making no motion at all with her body in the bed; yet, at the same time, those present heard her mournful talking, but with a low and hardly audible voice, and repeating several stories in metre, which they thought to be expressions of the rise and progress of her own trouble; and thus, she continued, (still, withal, naming some of the forementioned persons) till her parents and others offered to rouse her, by touching and moving her body: whereupon, instantly, she uttered horrid screeches, and cried as if she had been pierced through with swords, and assaulted for her life; after which she fell a singing, leaping, and dancing for a long time, laughing with a loud voice, in an unusual manner, tearing down the hangings of the bed, and pulling off her head-clothes and neck-clothes; in which extravagancies she was acted with such a force and strength, that her father and minister, though joining their whole strength together, could not get her dancing and leaping hindered.   But after prayer, the minister finding her composed, inquired if she remembered what she had done in time of the fit; to which she replied, "That she distinctly remembered her miscarriages, and, in special, her singing and dancing, saying, withal, that the witches inclosing her in a ring (or circle), and dancing and singing about her, was the occasion of her dancing, which she then gladly performed with the rest.   For some days after she had fits after this manner, with some variation; in one of which fits, as she was tearing off her head-dress clothes, her parents resolving to see what would be the event, did make no hinderance to her; whereupon she striped herself of all her clothes that were upon her, not leaving so much as her smock upon her body, if that had been permitted.

After this, toward or about the 11th Jan., she fell into fits different from the former, in which she was suddenly carried away from her parents and others that were about her, with a sudden flight, and in the first of these (to their great amazement) through the chamber and hall, down a long winding stair toward the tower-gate, with such a swift and unaccountable motion, that it was not in the power of any to prevent her,—her feet not touching the ground, so far as any of the beholders could discern, being heard in her motion to laugh in an unusual manner; but, by divine providence, the gate being shut, her motion was stopped till such time as some of the family could overtake her, who, endeavouring to carry her back, found her instantly fall as one dead, and become stiff; in which posture, being brought back to the chamber, she lay for a considerable space. And being recovered, she did declare that there were about the number of nine or ten persons who had carried her away in a shue (as she termed it, that is, as one swinging upon a rope) wherein she then took pleasure, her feet not at all touching the ground, to her apprehension.

The night following, she was suddenly carried away, as before, from her parents and others who were about her, through the chamber and hall, and sixteen large steps of a winding stair, up toward the top of the house! where she met with apparitions of strange and unaccountable things; but was carried down again, as she thought, in a shue or swing, asserting, after her recovery, that she met upon the stair the number of six women and four men, and by them was carried toward the gate again, where accordingly she was found, and was carried up as formerly, all the parts of her body distended and stiff as one dead; in which posture she lay for some time, and when recovering, declared, that both now and formerly, she had endeavoured to open the gate, and that those she saw about her were helping her, with a design to get her to the court, to drown her in the well, which she said she heard them saying among themselves they intended to do, and that then the world would believe she had destroyed

M

herself. It is observable that (these kind of fits continuing with her for some few days) in one of them she was stopped at the gate, and found in the fore-mentioned posture, which was neither locked nor barred; yet could they not get it opened, though both she and her tormentors endeavoured it.

Before we proceed in the relation, it is not to be omitted that as soon as the damsel's affliction was observed to be extraordinary and preternatural, there were (besides times formerly set apart in a more private way) at the desire of the parents and minister, and by the presbytery's special order, a minister or two appointed to meet every week, at the house of Bargarran, to join with the family, the minister of the parish, and other good christians of the neighbourhood, in fasting and praying, which usually fell to be on the Tuesday. And upon Jan. 12th, it being the turn of Mr. Patrick Simpson, a neighbour minister, to be there, when he came to the house he found both the minister of the parish, and the brother who was to join with him had been necessarily withdrawn; yet resolved to carry on the work with assistance of three elders, some other good people being present. When he first saw the damsel after he came to the house, he found her under some lesser fits which came and went off quickly, and when prayer began she was quiet and sober during the same, but in time of singing the xciii. Psalm, she fell into a sore fit, of greater continuance, first laughing, then making some sound like singing, after that pulling her head clothes down over her face, and lastly, turning so outrageous in her motions that her father could scarce get her holden with his whole strength, but behoved to lie over upon the bed with her in his arms until the fit abated. After her recovery from which, she was quiet and composed all the time of prayer; and while the minister lectured on Mark ix., from 14 to 30 v., was very attentive, carefully looking in her Bible the

Scriptures quoted, so all along both in time of prayer and singing, until the whole religious exercise was ended, and some refreshment after the same taken, at the end of which she told the company, she had something to tell, which she had heard some among her tormentors saying, which she durst not reveal ; but the minister and her mother urging her to be free and not to obey the Devil, she said she would tell it her mother in her ear. Then coming from the other side of the table, and placing herself betwixt her mother and aunt, she began to whisper in her mother's ear ; but before she got a sentence fully pronounced, she fell into a violent fit, so as her mother and those next her could scarcely hold her till the violence thereof began to abate, and then her mother told that she was speaking of a meeting and a feast they had spoke of in the orchard of Bargarran, but was able to say no more, and after recovery, her mother desiring her to tell the rest of it, and she beginning to whisper in her ear, as before, could not get one word uttered till she was seized again of a fit as violent as the former. Whereupon the minister perceiving her torment, desired them to forbear any further troubling of her. Notice, that accordingly there was a feast and meeting in that orchard about that time of the crew, acknowledged and declared afterwards by three of them, that confessed themselves to have been there, viz. :—Elizabeth Anderson, James and Thomas Lindsays, they not knowing what either the damsel had spoken, or one of them what another had confessed relating thereunto. *See No. A. of the Appendix.*

About or within a little after this time, she was again suddenly carried from them in the former manner down a stair, which goes off from a corner of the chamber to a cellar just below it, where her brother and sister were providentially gone down a little before, to bring some

drink from the cellar, and already near the stair foot, with a
lighted candle, which she soon put out; but they crying and
holding her by the head-clothes, quickly discovered to the rest
where she was.   Upon which Mr. Alexander King, minister
at Bonhill, (being then in the chamber) made haste down stairs
where he found her, but her brother and sister had lost hold
of her, she having loosed her head-clothes and let them go;
yet Mr. King having caught hold of her, kept her in his arms
till a lighted candle was brought; and endeavouring to bring
her up stairs, did declare that he found something forcibly
drawing her downwards, but he still keeping his hold, she fell
stiff, as one dead upon the stair, and was in this posture
carried up and laid in bed, where she lay a considerable space.
And when recovered of the fit, she declared that the occasion
of her going down stairs with such force, was, that the crew
had suggested to her while she was in the light fits, that the
devil was in the meal chest in the cellar, and that if she would
go down and put out the candle, she might force him out of
it.   Notice here, first, that when some fits of this kind were
ready to seize her, she sometimes gave advertisement thereof
to those present with her, giving signs of her earnest desire of
their help to prevent her motion, which usually proved to be
of good effect, wherein the divine mercy toward her is much
to be observed.   2. It is also to be noticed, that about the
time when she was in these flying fits, she used to utter horrid
shrieks and outcries, not like those of rational creatures; in
which time there were heard for three nights together when
the damsel was asleep in bed, shrieks and outcries of the
same kind in the court, when none of the family was without
doors, to the great affrightment of those who heard them, being that they exactly resembled the cries of, and shrieks the
damsel used to utter in the fits; who afterwards in one of her
intervals hearing some of the family talking of these cries and

shrieks, and alledging they had been utttered by some wild beast or other, said to them they were mistaken, for it was Margaret. And two others of the name of Margaret, called by the crew their Maggies, had uttered these shrieks, the devil having promised to them at that time to carry her out of the house to them, that they might drown her in the well, where there were eighteen more waiting for her.

After this she fell into fretting and angry fits (as she termed them) in which her humour was cross to all that those about her could say or do, nothing proving to her satisfaction, but everything displeasing, (her former fits withal now and then seizing her,) but when restored to a right composure of mind, she declared that her tormentors about her, did still suggest to her and advise her, to go to such and such remote places of the house alone, and bring with her a snood (which is a head-lace, such as women tie up their hair with) or a cravat or some such thing, promising her rough almonds or some kinds of sweetmeats which they named to her, and for that end, to bring her apron with her to hold them in, and accordingly when seized again with fits of this nature, did resolutely endeavour to repair to these places, having a snood or cravat and her apron with her, and would suffer none to be in her company, which put her parents and others to a necessity of detaining her by force, and she being thus prevented uttered hideous screeches and outcries, of which in this sort of fits she was seldom free.

Thursday, January 14th, at night, a young lass or girl appeared to her with a scabbed face amongst the rest of her tormentors, telling her she was to come to the house to-morrow about ten o'clock, and forbidding her to reveal it.

The next day being January 15th, in the afternoon, the damsel earnestly enquired at her mother and the rest of the family what beggars had come to the gate that day, and of

what countenance and visage they were? but the family not
knowing her design in such a question, gave no heed unto
it; yet, she still insisting, and being in company with her
mother and another gentlewoman, about four o'clock at
night, said to them, she thought she might tell them somewhat (the time being now past) she was forbidden to reveal it; but beginning to tell, she presently fell a crying,
that she was tormented and pricked through her whole body,
yet recovering from the fit, went on and told it. The thing
she had to reveal was, that a scabbed faced lass appeared
to her yesternight, and was to be at the gate this day at ten
o'clock. Whereupon the servants being enquired at, what
sort of beggars had been there that day, did declare among
others, there had been a beggar wife at the door, and a young
woman or lass with her who had scabs on her face, and received their alms.

Jan. 16th and 17th, when recovered of her swooning fits,
she put out of her mouth a great number of pins, which she
declared J—— P—— had forced into her mouth, and a
gentlewoman who had been one of her most violent tormentors.

Jan. 21. Her fits altered again, after this manner: she would
fall in them with heavy sighs and groans, and hideous outcries, telling those about her that cats, ravens, owls, and
horses were destroying and pressing her down in the bed;
and, at the same time, her mother and another gentlewoman
being in the room with her, did declare that immediately
after they had taken the girl out of her bed in this condition,
they did see something moving under the bed-clothes as big
as a cat.

The same morning, in the interval of her fits, she said she
heard her tormentors whispering among themselves, and
suggest to one another, (naming J—— P—— the
Andersons and other) that the Devil had promised and en-

gaged to them to carry her over the hall window to the end they might drown her in the well which was in the court, and then they said the world would believe she had destroyed herself ; and the same day, and several days thereafter, when seized with her grievous fits, did attempt with such force to get herself over that window, that spectators could scarce, with their whole strength, prevent her.

About this time, nothing in the world would so discompose her as religious exercises. If there were any discourses of God or Christ, or any of the things which are not seen and are eternal, she would be cast into grievous agonies; and when she essayed in her light fits, to read any portion of the scriptures, repeat any of the Psalms, or answer any questions of our catechisms (which she could do exactly at other times) she was suddenly struck dumb, and lay as one stiff dead, her mouth opened to such a wideness that her jaw appeared to be out of joint, and anon would clap together again with incredible force. The same happened to her shoulder blade, her elbow, and hand wrists. She would at other times lie in a benumbed condition, and be drawn together as if she had been tied neck and heels with ropes ; yet on a sudden would with such force and violence be pulled up and tear all about her, that it was as much as one or two could do, to hold her fast in their arms ; but when ministers and other good christians (seeing her in such intolerable anguishes) made serious application by prayer to God, on her behalf, she got respite from her grievous fits of this kind, and was ordinarily free of them during the time of prayer, though seized of them before ; and albeit, usually, when ministers began to pray, she made great disturbance by idle loud talking, whistling, singing and roaring, to drown the voice of the person praying.

Particularly, Jan. 22., she was more turbulent than at other times she used to be, and continued some space after the minister began to pray, singing and making hideous noise, fetching furious blows with her fist, and kicks with her feet at the minister, uttering reproachful talk of him, and calling him dog, &c. Yet, she being composed, and her fits being over before prayer was ended, and the minister, when he had done, finding her sober and in a right composure of mind, enquired why she made such disturbance? To which she replied, she was forced to do it by the hellish crew about her; and that she thought they were none of her own words that she uttered.

Jan. 24th. She said some things relating both to herself and others had been suggested to her by her troublers; but that they had threatened to torment her, if she should offer to make them known. And accordingly in essaying to express her mind, she was cast into two grievous fits, in which she cried out of violent pains; all the parts of her body becoming rigid and extended like a corpse, her head was twisted round, and, if any offered by force to obstruct such dangerous motion she seemed to be upon, she would roar exceedingly. Sometimes her neck bone seemed to be dissolved, and yet on a sudden became so stiff that there was no moving of it; and when these grievous agonies were over, she again assayed to express her mind by write, but to no purpose, for instantly she was cast into other two very grievous fits, wherein she was struck dumb, deaf, and blind, and her tongue drawn a prodigious length over her chin. And when the fits were over, declared, the Andersons, J—— P—— the gentlewoman, and I—— D—— with the rest of the hellish crew, some of whom she could not name, had been tormenting her in the fits, and that there had been fifteen of them about the house all the last night, but were now all gone save one, who was to stay about the house till her fits were over. And, accordingly, her brother and sister did declare they saw that morning a woman in the garden, with a red coat about her head, sitting at the root of an apple tree; but Bargarran, with most of the servants, being abroad, the matter was not further searched.

The same day, about six at night, she was seized with variety of grievous fits again, in which sometimes she lay wholly senseless and breathless with her belly swelled like a drum, as like a woman with child,—her eyes were pulled into her head so far that spectators thought she should never have used them more. Sometimes, when she was tying her own neck-clothes, her enchanted hand would tie them so strait about her neck that she had strangled herself if spectators had not given some relief unto her. Sometimes she was in hazard of burning herself in the fire, offering, with violence, to throw herself into the same. Divers times she did strike furious blows at her near relations in her fits. She would maintain discourse with her tormentors, and, asking questions concerning herself and others, received answer from them, which, indeed, none but herself perceived, reasoning with one of them after this manner :—

"O, what ailed thee to be a witch? Thou sayest it is but three nights since thou wast a witch. O, if thou wouldest repent, it may be God might give thee repentance. If thou wouldest seek it and confess. If thou would desire me I would do what I could, for the Devil is an ill master to serve. He is a liar from the beginning. He promises what he cannot perform." Then, calling for her Bible, she said—"I will let thee see where he promised to our first parents that they should not die;" and reading the passage, said—"Now, thou seest he is a liar, for, by breaking the commandment, they were made liable to death here and death everlasting. O, that is an uncouth word. Long eternity never to have an end,—never, never to have an end; had not God, of his infinite mercy, ordained some to eternal

N

life through Jesus Christ. The Devil makes thee believe thou wilt get great riches by serving him; but come near." And having uttered this word, she lost power of her speech, her tongue being drawn back into her throat; yet, beckoning with her hand to the spectre to come near her, and turning over the book, kept her eye upon that passage of Holy Scripture,—Job xxvii. 18,—and pointing with her finger at the place, and shaking her head, turned over the book again, and, recovering her speech, said—"I'll let thee see where God bids us seek, and we shall find." And reading over the place, said—"It is God that gives us every good gift. We have nothing of our own. I submit to His will, though I never be better, for God can make all my trouble turn to my advantage, according to His Word, Romans viii. 28,"—which place she then read, and thus continued reasoning for the space of an hour.

Sometimes she cried out of violent pain, by reason of furious blows and strokes she had received from the hands of her tormentors,—the noise of which strokes bystanders distinctly heard, though they perceived not the hands that gave them.

One night, the girl, sitting with her parents and others, cried out something was wounding her thigh, upon which, instantly, her mother, putting her hand in the damsel's pocket, found her folding knife opened, which had been folded when put in her pocket; but her uncle, not trusting the thing, did again put up the knife, and leaving it folded in her pocket, on a sudden she cried out, as before, the knife was cutting her thigh, being unfolded by means of J. P. and others, as she said; upon which, her uncle, searching her pocket again, found the knife opened as formerly. This happened twice or thrice, to the admiration of the beholders, though they took special notice that she nor any other visible hand opened it.

Jan. 25th. She was again seized with her swooning stiff fits, with this remarkable variation—her throat was sometimes most prodigiously extended, and sometimes as strangely contracted, so that she appeared in palpable danger of being choked, and through the violence of pain in her throat, and difficulty of breathing, struggled with feet and hands, as if some had been actually strangling her, and could speak or cry none, with which kind of fits she was frequently seized for several days, and in the intervals did declare that the fore-mentioned persons and others (whom she could not get then named) were strangling her; and that the occasion of her not having power to speak or cry in the fit was a ball in her throat, which also was visible to spectators, for they did clearly discern a bunch in her throat while in the fit as big as a pullet's egg, which had almost choked her.

Sometimes she was kept from eating her meat, having her teeth set when she carried any food to her mouth. Divers times, also, she was kept from drinking when at meat; for no sooner could she taste the drink but she was in hazard of being choked thereby, and herself sometimes would have held the cup so hard betwixt her teeth that it was not in the power of those with her to unloose it. And when any thing had fallen out amiss in the place where she was,—as the falling and breaking of a cup, anybody's receiving harm, and such like,—she would fall a-laughing and rejoice extremely, which kind of jollity was far from the girl's temper when at herself.

Feb. 1st. She essaying to tell some things she had been forbidden by her tormentors to make known, was handled with intolerable torments. At the beginning of her fits, usually she would be kept oddly looking, sometimes towards the chimney, sometimes towards other particular places in the room, but could not always tell what she saw; yet, for ordinary, she would name such and such persons, who, she said, were then come to cast her into fits. And when any desired her to cry to the Lord Jesus for help, her teeth were instantly set close, her eyes twisted almost round in her head, and she was thrown upon the floor with the stiffness and posture of one that had been some days laid for dead; and on a sudden recovered again, and would weep bitterly to remember what had befallen her. The same day, when her fits were over, she said she now perceived it was by the means of a charm that such restraints were laid upon her; that she could not tell what the witches had forbidden her to make known; but the charm might be found out (as she said) by searching for it beneath the bed where she lay; and she having quickly done this herself, found (to the apprehension of spectators) beneath the foresaid bed, an entire egg-shell open in the end, which being instantly thrown into the fire, did melt away after the manner of wax, without any noise as egg-shells use to make when burning in the fire. After this, the girl said she would not now be handled so severely, upon essaying to make known what the witches had forbidden her to tell, only her tongue would be drawn back into her throat, which accordingly happened. She did likewise inform her friends of many things she had not liberty to do, before the charm was found out particularly, that her tormentors had frequently solicited her to become a witch herself, and promised her great riches and perfect health also, to induce her thereunto. Which temptation, she, through the mercy of God, still resisted, reasoning with them after this manner :—"The Devil promises what he cannot perform; and granting he could fulfil his promises, yet I am sure from the Scriptures, hell and the wrath of God will be the final reward of all such as yield to this wickedness." To which she received this reply, (which, indeed, none but herself perceived) that hell and the wrath of God so much talked of, was not so formidable as was represented. She also said, the witches had importunately urged her to give them her consent, to take away the life of her young sister, who was at that time upon her mother's breast; which temptation also, she was enabled through the grace of God to resist. She told her parents likewise, there had been a charm laid upon the top of the house, where her young sister was (the child having been sent out a nursing, by reason of the continued affliction of the family) and that the charm had been placed upon the top of the house by pinched Maggy, who thereby did design the taking away of her sister's life; and that this was the cause why she had so often, for some weeks before, desired her mother to bring home her sister, constantly affirming, that the child would daily decay as long as she staid there. Whereupon her parents observing the daily decay of the infant, even to skin and bone, brought her home, where she recovered. The girl being asked how she came to the knowledge of these things? replied, something speaking distinctly as it were above her head, had suggested these, and other things of that nature to her.

Feb. 2nd. The girl being in the chamber with her mother and others, was on a sudden struck with great fear and consternation, and fell a-trembling upon the sight of John Lindsay, in Barloch, talking with her father in the hall. She said to her mother the foresaid Lindsay had been always one of her most violent tormentors, and that she had been threatened with extreme tortures, if she should offer to name him; whereupon she was desired to go towards the place where he was, and touch some part of his body in a way unknown to him, which having done with some aversion, was instantly seized with extreme tortures in all the parts of her body. After which Lindsay was put to it, and interrogated thereupon; but he giving no satisfying answer, was

desired to take the damsel by the hand, which he being
unwillingly induced to do, she was immediately upon the
touch cast into tolerable anguishes, her eyes being almost
twisted round in her head, and all the parts of her body
becoming rigid and stiff, fell down in the posture of one
that had been laid for some days dead, and afterwards got
up in a sudden, and tearing her clothes, threw herself with
violence upon him and when her fit was over, spectators
did also take the damsel by the hand, yet no such effect
followed.

About six at night there came an old Highland fellow to
Bargarran, who, calling himself a weary traveller, said, he behoved to lodge there that night; but the servants refusing him
lodging, gave him something by way of alms. At this time
the damsel being in the chamber with her mother and another
gentlewoman, said to the best of her apprehension ; there was
one of the wicked crew in or about the house at that time :
whereupon her mother made haste with her daughter down
stairs towards the kitchen. And finding there unexpectedly
the Highland fellow, whom the girl then accused as one of her
tormentors, she desired the Highland fellow to take her
daughter by the hand, which he being urged to do, the girl
immediately upon his touch was grievously tormented in all the
parts of her body. And this falling out in divine providence,
Bargarran caused secure him.

The next morning, the minister having come to Bargarran
to visit the damsel, and the matter being imparted to him,
called for the Highland fellow, and having questioned him to
and again about this matter, without any satisfying answer,
brought the child out of the chamber, covering her face, and
almost her whole body, with his cloak, and giving signs to the
Highland fellow to touch her in this posture, as he had ordered
him before, without the damsel's knowledge, which he having

194

done with great aversion, the girl not knowing of his touch, was instantly cast into intolerable agonies as formerly; yet others afterwards touching her, no such event followed. And when her fits were over, she besought the Highland fellow, to allow her the liberty for to discover and tell persons that haunted and molested her, whom he had forbidden her to make known. Upon which the old fellow looking at her with an angry countenance, her mouth was instantly stopped, and her teeth set; and being desired by those present to speak her mind freely, whether he would or not, at length replied, she feared to do it. And when, through the importunity of John Maxwell of Dargavel, and Porterfield of Fulwood, and some other gentlemen there present, she essayed to declare her mind, she was seized with her fits again.

Before this time the lamentable case of the afflicted damsel and family had been represented to His Majesty's most honourable privy council, who, upon serious application made to them, worthily and piously granted a commission to a noble lord and some worthy gentlemen to make inquiry into the same. By virtue of this commission some suspected persons were seized; particularly, Feb. 4, Alexander Anderson, an ignorant, irreligious fellow, who had been always of evil fame, and accused by the afflicted damsel, by a special order from the commissioners for inquiry, was apprehended and committed to prison, as was also Elizabeth Anderson, his daughter, upon flagrant presumptions of witchcraft; for the other year, Jean Fulton, her grandmother, an old scandalous woman, being cited before the kirk-session, and accused for hideous cursing, and imprecating mischief upon several persons, which had been followed with fatal events, the forementioned Elizabeth Anderson, her grandchild, who lived in the house with her, did declare before the session she had frequently seen the devil in company with her grandmother, in

the likeness of a small black man, who usually did vanish on
a sudden within the walls of the house when anybody came
to the door.   Upon this presumption was the said Elizabeth
Anderson seized with her father, and committed to custody;
but at first most obstinately denied accession any manner of
way to the sin of witchcraft, until afterwards, when seriously
importuned and dealt with in the prison by two gentlemen,
did, before she came to Bargarran's house, confess her guilt
without Bargarran's knowledge at that time.   And that she
had been at several meetings with the devil and witches, and,
amongst others, she did declare her own father, and the forementioned Highland fellow to have been active instruments of
the girl's trouble; and gave, before she was confronted with
him, exact marks of this Highland body, and though she declared she knew not his name, yet, when confronted with him,
did accuse him, and affirm he was the person she spoke of.
See No. A of the Appendix.

February 5th, a quorum of the commissioners being met at
Bargarran, and the persons then delated by Elizabeth Anderson to have been at meetings with the devil, and active
instruments of the damsel's trouble, viz., Alexander Anderson, her father, Agnes Naesmith, Margaret Fultoun,
James Lindsay *alias* Curat, John Lindsay *alias* Bishop,
Katherine Campbell were all of them (excepting John
Lindsay *alias* Bishop, who was not then apprehended),
confronted with Katherine Shaw before the Lord
Blantyre, and the rest of the commissioners at Bargarran, and
several other gentlemen of note, and ministers then present,
and accused by her as her tormentors.   And they having
all severally touched her in presence of the commissioners,
she was at each of their touches seized with grievous fits,
and cast into intolerable anguishes, others then present also
touching her in the same way, but no such effect followed.

196

And it is remarkable, when Katherine Campbell touched the girl, she was immediately upon her touch seized with more grievous fits, and cast into more intolerable torments than what followed upon the touch of the other accused persons, whereat Campbell herself being damped and confounded, though she had formerly declined to bless her, uttered these words—"The Lord God of heaven and earth bless thee, and save thee both soul and body." After which the damsel, when the fits were over, in which she had been a most pitiful spectacle, did declare she was now loosed, and that she might freely touch any of the accused persons, or they her after this, without trouble, which accordingly upon trial fell so out; and being inquired how she came to the knowledge of that, answered as formerly in the like case,— That something speaking distinctly as it were above her head, suggested this to her; and likewise usually gave her the knowledge of the names of her tormentors, and places in which they lived.

February 6. The girl being seized with sore fits, something was seen in her mouth, to the judgment of spectators like pieces of orange pills invisibly conveyed into her mouth, which she seemed in her agonies to be chewing, and having got down her throat, as those present apprehended, she did fall down dead and stiff, as if she had been choked, struggling with her feet and hands, as if at the last gasp, her throat swelling in a prodigious manner, to the affrightment of spectators; and when recovered, but yet in the light fit, she would say,—O it was a very sweet orange pill which I got from the gentlewoman, and did constantly affirm the same, declaring also that there had been others there present with the gentlewoman, particularly Margaret L——— or pinched Maggy, whose surname she had neither power nor liberty to express, neither durst she offer to do it, lest she

O

should be tormented as was threatened, and always fell out when she essayed to do it either by speaking or writing, which had appeared the day before in the presence of the commissioners.

About this time Thomas Lindsay, a young boy, not yet twelve years of age, was seized, upon flagrant presumptions of witchcraft. He had said before several credible persons the devil was his father, and, if he pleased, he could fly in the likeness of a crow upon the mast of a ship. He sometimes caused a plough to stand, and the horse break the yoke upon the pronouncing of some words, and turning himself about wider-shins, that is, turning himself round from the right hand to the left, contrary to the natural course of the sun. This he would do upon the desire of any body who gave him a halfpenny. Upon these and the like flagrant presumptions he was apprehended, who, at first, though he continued most obstinate in denial, yet afterwards confessed to the minister in his own house, before famous witnesses, compact with the devil, and that he had received the insensible mark from the devil, which is visible upon his body ; as also that he had been at several meetings with the devil and witches, where he said were present his brother James, with others, and particularly those who had been delated by Anderson. This he confessed, with some other wickedness of this kind, before he was committed to custody in Bargarran house.

After this Bargarran made diligent search for James Lindsay, elder brother to Thomas, having been all along accused by the afflicted damsel as one of her troublers, whom she called the gley'd or squint-eyed elf (as he was indeed) for that was the name the crew about her gave him, who, when he was brought upon the place, though he did at first most obstinately deny his guilt, yet at length, through the endeavours of Mr. Patrick Simpson, a neighbour minister, ingeni-

ously confessed the guilt he was charged with, and in his confession did agree in every material circumstance with the
other two, though he knew not what they had confessed, he
having not seen them before his confession, nor had he any
occasion of information in conference with others thereanent,
being immediately brought to the place from the tolbooth of
Glasgow, where he had been some weeks before that time in
prison as a vagabond beggar, upon a design to have sent him
to foreign plantations.

A more particular account of what they freely confessed
and acknowledged before the commissioners, for inquiry, we
have for the satisfaction of the reader subjoined to the
narrative, with an abstract of the report made by the
commissioners to the lords of his Majesty's most honourable
privy council, concerning the whole affair.

February 11. There was by the presbytery's appointment
a public fast kept upon the damsel's account in the church of
Erskine, in which Mr. Turner, minister of the place, began the
work with prayer, expounding Rev. xii. from verse 7 to verse
13. Mr. James Hutchison, minister at Kilellan, took the next
turn of prayer, and did preach upon 1 Pet. v. 8.; and Mr.
Simpson concluded the work, preaching upon Matthew xvii.
20. 21, where the girl was present all day; but before she
came to church that morning, she told that, while she was in
one of her fits the night before, she heard the Devil speaking
of that public fast, and what ministers were to be there, and
that old man Mr. James Hutchison should stumble, and his
peruke fall off as he went up to the pulpit, and all the people
should laugh at him, and he should break his neck in going
home. And when she came out of the church after the forenoon's work, she said the Devil was a liar; for no such thing
fell out as he had threatened. She was all day very quiet in
church, although, being in some of her light fits, some spectres

appeared in time of the public work, which she told of there after.

About six at night there were present in the chamber with the damsel Mr. Simpson with his wife, Lady Northbar, and others, discoursing and conferring about her case; and while they were conferring together she told them she would gladly make some things known if she durst for her tormentors; and afterwards essaying to do it, was instantly seized with a violent fit, in which she leapt straight up, and appeared as if she had been choked, so it was as much as one or two could do to hold her fast in their arms; and when the fit was over, Mr. Simpson going about family worship, did expound Psalm cx., and speaking of the limited power of the adversaries of our Lord Jesus Christ, from the latter part of verse 1., she was on a sudden seized with another grevious fit, in which she put out of her mouth some blood, which raised grounds of fear and jealousy in the minds of spectators, that something in her mouth hurting her had been the occasion of it; yet they could not get her mouth opened, though they used means to open the same, her teeth being close set. And in the interval of the fit, she being asked if she found anything in her mouth that had been the occasion of her putting out of blood; she replied she found nothing, nor knew the cause thereof; but opening her mouth, those present found one of her double teeth newly drawn out, but knew not what became of the tooth; for though search was made for the same, it could not be found. After which the minister proceeded upon the same subject, but was again interrupted by her renewed fits, yet closed the exercise with prayer, after which, without more trouble, she was taken to her bed.

February 12. Margaret Lang and her daughter, Martha Semple, being delated by the three confessants, and accused by the girl to have been active instruments in her trouble, came of their own accord to Bargarran's house, and, before they came up stairs, the girl said she was now bound up, and could not accuse Margaret Lang to her face; and accordingly the girl's mother having desired some of those who were sitting by her to feel some parts of her body, and they having done it, found her body so stiff and inflexible, that there was no moving of it, and immediately again, found some parts of her body so contracted and drawn hard together, as if by cords. After this, Margaret Lang and her daughter, having gone to the chamber to the girl, did in presence of the ministers and others, desire the damsel to come to her, for she would do her no harm; and laying her arms about her, spake very fairly to her, and questioned her if ever she had seen her or her daughter amongst her tormentors, to which the girl did positively reply, she had frequently seen her daughter; but declined through fear to accuse herself, saying faintly, No. After which Margaret and her daughter returning into the hall, and the minister enquiring at her why she said No, seeing she had accused her before, she answered, take me contrary, upon which she was seized with a grievous fit; yet after her recovery, being urged again by those present, to tell her mind freely, whether or not Margaret Lang was one of her tormentors, the child thereupon essaying to say Yes, and having half pronounced the word, was cast into inexpressible anguishes; and again, in the interval of the fit, she essayed to express the same thing, and saying the word, Tint (that is lost) was on a sudden struck with another fit; and when the fit was over, and the child returned to the chamber, Margaret Lang, who was sitting near the hall door, spoke these words after her, "The Lord bless thee, and ding (that is beat or drive) the devil out of thee." A little after which words, Margaret going down stairs, the damsel came to the hall, and said, her bonds were now loosed, and that now she could accuse Margaret

Lang to her face, and declared the occasion of her being so restrained and bound up while Margaret was present, was her letting fall a parcel of hair at the hall door as she came in; being a charm made by her for that end, which also had been the occasion of her uttering the word tint, in the former fit; and accordingly a parcel of hair had been found at the hall door, after Margaret Lang had gone straight from the hall to the chamber, which immediately was cast into the fire and burned. And it is remarkable that it could be attested, that there was no hair, or any other thing else in that place before Margaret Lang came in; and the girl being inquired what way she knew Margaret Lang had laid the forementioned charm upon her, replied, something speaking distinctly to her as it were above her head had suggested that to her.

About eight at night she was severely handled in her fits, much after the former manner, and while she was in her swooning fits, there was seen in her mouth a pin, wherewith she seemed almost choked, but by divine providence it was with great difficulty got out. After this she was somewhat composed, and did not much complain of pain; but was distinctly heard to entertain discourse with some invisible creature about her, and the replies given by her, and heard by those who took care of her, gave them ground to conclude she was tempted to set her hand to a paper then presented to her, with promises that upon her yielding thereunto, she should never be troubled any more; as also that she should get sweetmeats, a drink of sack, a bonny handsome coat with silver lace. She was also distinctly heard say, resisting the tempter, "Thou art a filthy sow, should I obey thee; this was not the end of my creation, but to glorify God and enjoy Him for ever; and thou promiseth what thou cannot perform. Art thou angry at me for saying thou sow? what could I call thee, but thou filthy sow? Art thou not the filthy devil; for as brave as thou art with thy silver and gold lace, wouldst thou have me renounce my baptism? Dost thou promise to give me brave men in marriage, and fine clothes, and perfect health, if I should consent thereunto? Dost thou say my baptism will do me no good, because thou allegest he was not a sufficient minister that baptized me? Thou art a liar; I will be content to die, before I renounce my baptism—O through the grace of God I will never do it." And thus she continued reasoning, being both blind and deaf, for the space of two hours; and when she came to herself, did declare it was the Devil who first presented himself, tempting her in the shape of a sow, to renounce her baptism, as is hinted; and that he did chide her when she called him thou sow, and immediately appeared to her again in the shape of a brave gentleman, as having gold and silver lace on his clothes, still urging her to renounce her baptism, which temptation she, through the special assistance of the grace of God, effectually resisted. She also said, that it had been suggested to her by the spirit, speaking to her, as it were above her head, after the combat with the tempter was over, that one of her tormentors would be at the house the morrow.

February 13. She was seized with a sore fit about twelve o'clock of the day, in which she continued for more than two hours space, both deaf and blind. Those in the room with her, crying to her with a loud voice, and pinching her hands and other parts of her body; but all to no purpose. And in this posture was hurried to and fro with violence through the room; and when anybody by force offered to hinder the dangerous and violent motion she seemed to be upon, she would roar exceedingly; sometimes she desired her father and mother and others to come and take her home, (supposing herself not to be in her father's house). When the girl was in this deplorable condition Margaret Roger, who lived in the neighbourhood, came to the house of Bargarran, enquiring for the lady ; and having come up stairs, the parents of the damsel remembering what the girl had said the night before, that one of her tormentors was to come that day to the house, brought Margaret Roger to the chamber where the girl was, and so soon as she entered the door, the damsel, though she could discern none of those who were present with her, nor answer them when they cried to her ; yet presently saw her, and ran towards her crying,— " Maggy, Maggy, where hast thou been ? wilt thou take me with thee, for my father and mother have left me." Where- upon spectators being astonished, caused Margaret speak to the child, which she having done, the girl distinctly heard and answered her every word.   After this, the three con- fessants were also brought up to the chamber where the damsel was, and so soon as they entered the door, she ran also to them laughing as if she had been overjoyed, answering them when they spoke to her ; and Margaret Roger there present, being confronted with the confessants, they did declare that she had been at meetings with the Devil and witches in Bargarran orchard, consulting and contriving Christian Shaw's ruin.

The Lord's day following, being February 14, after some short intervals she was again seized with her fits, in which she said, " Margaret Lang and her daughter Martha Semple, were tormenting her and cutting her throat," which words, through violence of pain, and difficulty of breathing, she uttered with a low and hardly audible voice ; and upon the naming of Margaret Lang and her daughter she was tossed and dreadfully tormented in all the parts of her body, being made sometimes to stand upon her head and feet at once, sometimes her belly swelling like a drum and falling again in a sudden, and sometimes her head and other parts of her body were like to be shaken in pieces, so that spectators feared she would never speak more. And when the fit was over she declared Margaret Lang said to her, when in the fit, "That she would give her a tosty" (which imports hot and severe handling), for naming her.

At this time she was seldom free of her light fits, which for most part were all the respite and ease she had from the unexpressible agonies she endured in her more grievous fits, unless when asleep; and while she was in these fits nobody could persuade her to pray; yet when in a right composure of mind and perfectly at herself, she would weep bitterly to remember this, expressing her fears lest that might be any evidence God would forsake her.

February 18. About two in the afternoon she being in the light fit, said, "the Devil now appeared to her in the shape of a man;" whereupon, being struck with great fear and consternation, was desired to pray with an audible voice, "The Lord rebuke thee, Satan," which she essaying to do, instantly lost power of speech, her teeth being set, and her tongue drawn back into her throat; and she essaying again, was immediately seized with another grievous fit, in which her eyes being twisted almost round in her head, she fell down as one dead, struggling with her feet and hands, and again getting up on a sudden, was hurried with violence to and fro through the room deaf and blind; yet was speaking with some invisible creatures about her, saying, "with the Lord's strength thou shalt neither put straw nor stick into my mouth." After this she cried in a pitiful manner "the bumbee has stinged me," then presently sitting down and loosing her stockings, put her hand to that part which had been nipped or pinched, whereupon spectators did visibly discern the lively marks of nails of fingers deeply imprinted on that same part of her leg. And when she came to

P

205

herself, she did declare "that something speaking to her, as it were above her head," told her it was M. M. in a neighbouring parish, (naming the place) "that had appeared to her, and pinched her leg in the likeness of a bumbee." She likewise did declare that the fore-mentioned M. M. "instantly after this had been suggested to her, appeared to her in her own shape, and likeness as she used to be at other times." Shortly after this, being still seized with her light fit, she whispered in her mother's ear, "the Devil was now appearing to her again in the shape of a gentleman;" and being instantly seized with her fits, in which she was both blind and deaf, was distinctly heard arguing after this manner:—"thou thinkest to tempt me to be a witch; but through God's strength thou shalt never be the better. I charge thee, in the name of God, to be gone, and thy papers too. In the Lord's strength I will not fear thee. I will stand here and see if thou can come one step nearer me; I think thou fearest me more than I fear thee." Then turning herself again, she was hurried to and fro with violence through the room, as formerly, saying,—"She was bitten or pinched very sore in the hand with teeth, and nipped with fingers about twenty-four times;" which constrained her to horrid screeches and outcries at every time she received them, shewing and pointing with her finger to these parts of her arm and leg which had been pinched and bitten, but neither saw nor heard any about her. And accordingly spectators did visibly discern the evident marks of teeth and nails of fingers upon her arms and legs. In this posture the girl continued from two till five in the afternoon, and when her misery was over, she said, "M. M. told her in the fit, that Margaret Lang, then in custody, had ordered her to handle her after that manner; and that Margaret Lang had a commanding power over her."

Friday and Saturday thereafter, being February 19th and 20th, she was frequently seized with the forementioned fits, and being violently bitten, pinched, and nipped in her hands, neck, and other parts of her body, so that the clear marks of the nails of fingers and steads of teeth, both upper and lower, with the spittle and slaver of a mouth thereupon, was evidently seen by spectators. About this time, when seized with her blind and deaf fits, a crooked fellow appeared to her, having his feet deformed, his two heels wrying inward toward one another, and the foreparts of his feet outward from one another, so that the broadside of his feet moved foremost; and upon the appearing of this fellow her feet were put in the very same posture, during the time he tormented her. It is to be noticed that there is a fellow in one of the neighbouring parishes, whose feet are exactly in that manner deformed, who has been a long time of ill fame, and given up by the confessants to have been at meetings with the Devil and the rest of the crew in Bargarran orchard.

Saturday, being Feb. 20th, the whole family being gone to bed, they had left a great quantity of peats or turf, beside the hall chimney, which the next morning they saw them burnt to ashes, though there had been no fire in the chimney nor near them, so that the plaister and stones of the wall, where the peats or turf lay, were in a great part turned to rubbish through the violence of the fire, but no other damage followed, the hall floor being laid with stones, and the peats lying within the bosom of a large chimney brace.

Feb. 27th. The chamber fire having been covered with ashes in the chimney, when the family went to bed, the next morning, though a good quantity of ashes had been left, yet they found all clean swept away, and no appearance of ashes nor fire there at all; albeit none in the family that night nor next morning had been there after the fire was gathered, before this was observed.

207

In fits of this kind she continued for several days thereafter, naming the forementioned crooked fellow, J. R. and M. A. living in the neighbouring parishes, which two women were delated by the three confessants to be amongst her tormentors; and particularly upon the Lord's day, being Feb. 21st, and the Monday following, the said J. R. appearing to her, grievously vexed her, withal telling her she was commissioned so to do, the gentlewoman, M. M., having a pain in her head at the time, and so not able to come forth, concerning which, it is worthy of remark, that the damsel declared M. M. to have appeared to her about two days thereafter, with her head bound up with a napkin, or handkerchief, in which like habit or posture she did not formerly appear.

Upon Thursday thereafter, being Feb. 25th, she continued in the former fits, weeping bitterly and complaining of pain in both her sides : she also told in the interval of her fits that she was that night to be in very grievous and sore fits, her tormentors being resolved to choke her by putting pins in her mouth, which (though she emptied herself of all that were in her clothes) yet accordingly came to pass; in which she was both blind and deaf, leaping up and down in an extraordinary manner, pulling down whatever came to her hand; and thus continued for some days, putting out of her mouth a great quantity of small broken pins, which she declared J. R. had forced in the same.

Upon the Lord's day, being the last of Feb., about five o'clock in the afternoon, she fell into grievous fits, accompanied with hideous or loud laughing, leaping, and running with violence to and fro, and thereafter wept sore, crying out of pain, that a little Highlandman (whom she knew to be such by his habit and speech) was now breaking her leg; which (because of pain) she scarce could get told in the fit,

and putting her hand to the part of her leg affected, spectators untying her stocking, distinctly observed a sore bruise
in her shin bone, which, when touched, did so pain her,
that she uttered horrid screeches and cries; and when
recovered, did declare that the little Highland fellow had
given her that bruise. After this, she put out of her mouth
a crooked pin, by which she told the foresaid Highland
fellow having forced it into her mouth, designed to choke
her.

The first eight days of March she continued in her former
fits with little variation, putting out of her mouth a great
number of small pins, often fainting and falling as dead upon
the ground on a sudden, again struggling with feet and hands,
by all which, her natural spirits were much weakened and ex-
hausted; sometimes also she essayed to go into the fire.
About this time, when ministers and other Christians met in
the family for prayer, she used at the beginning of the work
to make great disturbance, particularly March 2d, which day,
being set apart for fasting and prayer in the family, prayer
begun, she was for some time very composed, until of a
sudden, a strong blast of wind forced open the windows of
the room, upon which she was instantly seized with a violent
fit, the minister in the very same time supplicating God that
she might be delivered from Satan's bonds; in which fit she being both blind and deaf as to all, except her tormentors, was
hurried with violence to and fro in the room, sometimes falling down as one dead, sometimes singing and making a hideous loud noise; sometimes naming M. M. and others, who,
she said, were there present, afflicting and tormenting her
withal, naming the particular places of the room where she saw
them standing and sitting. After all which, when recovered
out of the fit, she told that a gentlewoman and a little Highland fellow came in with the blast of wind which forced open

the windows. This falling out upon the Tuesday, she continued in the light fit without any intermission till the Sabbath thereafter, not being seized with any of her sore fits; and having gone to church the Lord's day following, was perfectly well for the most part of the day; yet affirmed she saw Janet Waugh and others, in one of the windows of the church, though invisible to all others.

Tuesday, being March 9th, her mother and Margaret Campbell, her cousin, took the damsel to walk with them in the orchard; and returning back to the house, her mother entering the tower gate first, the damsel being at her back and Margaret Campbell tarrying a little while at the gate, her mother going into the kitchen supposed they had been with her, whereas the damsel was of a sudden carried away in a flight up stairs with so swift and unaccountable a motion that her absence was not in the least suspected. Her mother turning and missing her, cried, whither is Christian and Margaret Campbell? and instantly running up stairs to look for the damsel heard a noise, and, following the same, found the damsel leaping and dancing upon one of the stairs, being seized with fits, out of which, when she had recovered, she told that J. P. had carried her away from her mother's back as she entered the kitchen door (her not touching the ground to her apprehension), and that with a design to strangle her in an high wardrobe with ropes, on which the linen used to dry, but that the said J. P. could carry her no further than the place where she was found, and did therefore leave her in such a violent fit.

Upon the Lord's day thereafter, being March 14th, her fits again altered, in that her mouth and nose were prodigiously distorted and turning about while in the fit, her face being thereby strangely and horribly deformed. The same day she being in church in the forenoon, her glove falling from her,

210

the same was again put into her hand by some invisible agent, to the amazement of beholders. To which we add here, as that which is worthy of remark, that all this while an invisible being haunted her on all occasions, suggesting many things to her both concerning herself and others, but yet never heard by any but herself.

The same day betwixt sermons, she told that she was to be violently tormented in the afternoon, which accordingly came to pass; and when in her fits she named one J. K., a woman living in the neighbouring bounds, of whom she said, that she had seen her in the church, as also that she was master of these kind of fits she was afflicted with; withal asserting that if the said J. K. were not sent for, she would grow worse and worse, which her parents finding to be true, sent in the evening for the said J. K., threatening her, if the damsel was any further troubled with her, that she should be apprehended as others had been; after which, the damsel being in the meantime in a very sore fit, the forementioned J. K. prayed (though not desired) that God might send the damsel her health, whereupon the damsel was no more troubled with these kind of fits, but did instantly recover, by falling into a swoon as she used to do before recovery out of any of her fits.

Tuesday, being March 16th, she was again seized with her other kind of fits, all the parts of her body being stiff and rigid; and sometimes in them was heard conversing with the gentlewoman (as she called her), vindicating herself of what the gentlewoman alleged against her, viz., that she had accused some innocent persons as her tormentors. To which the damsel distinctly replied that she was a liar, saying, it was you yourself and none other ever mentioned any such thing.

Thus she continued until the Friday thereafter, being never free of the light fits, now and then also falling into swoons, and appeared to be almost choked by the means of some

charms and enchantments invisibly conveyed into her mouth;
which, to the apprehension of spectators, were as if it had
been pieces of chesnuts, orange pills, whites of eggs, or such
like, all which were distinctly observed, when occasionally in
the fit she opened her mouth; and when spectators essayed
to get them out, she kept her mouth and teeth so close, that
no strength could open the same. When recovered out of the
fit, she told L. M., a woman living in the neighbouring bounds,
had put them in her mouth.

Upon Friday, being March 19th, she was violently tormented with sore fits, in which her neck was distorted and bended
back like a bow towards her heels, struggling with feet and
hands, sometimes stiff, blind, and deaf, putting out of her
mouth a great number of small pins, which she said the forementioned L. M. had put into her mouth. And about six
o'clock that same night, being violently tormented, fell a-cry-
ing, that if the gentlewoman was not apprehended that night,
it would be in vain to apprehend her to-morrow: for, said she,
I have much to suffer at her hands betwixt twelve and one
o'clock in the morning. After this the damsel lifting up her
eyelids with her hands, and looking upwards, said, what art
thou that tells me that the sheriff and my father are coming
here this night? After which the sheriff, her father, and
James Guthrie, macer to the justiciary court, instantly came
up stairs, to the amazement of those who remembered what
the damsel just now had said. The damsel continuing all
this while blind and deaf; yet was heard (the foresaid persons
being present) distinctly to discourse with some invisible being
near to her, saying, is the sheriff come,—is he near me? and
stretching out her hand to feel if any were about her, the
sheriff put his hand in hers, notwithstanding of which, she
said to the invisible being discoursing with her, "I cannot
feel the sheriff; how can he be present here? or how can I

have him by the hand as thou sayest, seeing I feel it not? Thou sayest he hath brown coloured clothes, red plush breeches with black stripes, flowered muslin cravat, and an embroidered sword-belt. Thou sayest there is an old grey haired man with him, having a ring upon his hand; but I can neither see nor feel any of them. What, are they come to apprehend the gentlewoman? is that their errand indeed?" And the girl being enquired how she came to the knowledge of these strange things, replied as formerly in the like case, something speaking distinctly as above her head suggested them to her. It is very observable here, that the foresaid persons had that same afternoon got an order from the commissioners of justiciary to apprehend the same gentlewoman, and were so far on their way to put it in execution against the next morning; but being witnesses to the damsel's trouble, and hearing what she had told, viz., that a delay in that matter would prove to her exceeding dangerous, they went straight on in their journey that same night to the gentlewoman's habitation, and put their warrant to execution.

As the damsel still continued to be violently tormented, sometimes lying with her neck and other parts of her body upon the ground, as if they had been disjointed; sometimes, also, essaying to throw herself into the fire. About ten o'clock the same night, she continuing in the fit, her father (who had not gone with the sheriff) beginning to read a part of the Word of God, she repeated the words after him, though blind and deaf in the meantime, which made spectators apprehend that the damsel had the sense of hearing in these sort of fits, at least when the Word of God was read; to find out the truth of which, her father did cease from reading, which, though he did, yet the damsel continued to repeat the following verses of the chapter, while none in the room were reading, and she herself had no book; withal being

Q

heard say to some invisible being about her,—"Wilt thou teach me a part of the Old Testament as well as the New."

The damsel still continuing in the forementioned fits, said unto the persons present, that "now it was twelve of the clock; oh! it is now past twelve," sometimes lying as one dead, through the violence of pain and decay of her natural spirits, sometimes again recovering, essayed to express somewhat, but could not; withal putting out of her mouth a great quantity of crooked pins, and the parts of her body being prodigiously distorted, she complained of great pain. Thus she continued until half-an-hour after twelve o'clock at night; when on a sudden she recovered, to the admiration of beholders, telling them she might now go to bed, being told by some invisible informer that the sheriff and the other gentleman, to wit, the macer, had now entered the gentlewoman's house, and accordingly going to bed, was no further troubled that night. It is worthy of remark here, that the sheriff and macer, at their return, did declare that it was just about that time they entered the gentlewoman's house, which the damsel condescended upon.

Saturday, being March 20th, about ten o'clock in the forenoon, she was of a sudden seized with fits, falling down as one dead, her eyes quite closed, sometimes again opening and turning in her head, she saw nor heard none about her, but was hurried with violence to and fro through the room, crying with a loud voice when any by force would hinder her motion. She being in this posture, and deprived thus of her senses, James Lindsay, one of the three confessants, was brought into the room, who no sooner had entered the door, but was perceived by her, and she, smiling, ran towards him, saying,—"Jamie, where hast thou been this long time—how is it with thee?" and answered him distinctly to every word he spake, though at the same time she neither heard nor saw any other in the room, nor could converse with them, albeit, tried by several experiments for that purpose, particularly a tobacco box being held before her eyes by a person present in the room, she did not see it; but as soon as it was put in the hand of James Lindsay, she inquired at him where he had got that box? She, continuing in this posture, the sheriff and her father being present, thought it fit to confront M. M., who was now come, thereby to try if the damsel would hear or see her, as she had done James Lindsay, which accordingly they did. And as soon as M. M. entered the door, the damsel (though still in the fit) presently smiled and said,—" I see the gentlewoman now," though formerly she had never seen her personally, but only her spectre in the fits. She likewise heard her, when she spoke to her, answering distinctly some questions proposed by M. M., such as, when it was she had seen her tormenting her? to which she answered, she had seen her the other night in her fits, and further challenged her, why she had restrained her from making known the Highland wife's name, as also saying unto her, thou pretends thou knowest not what I say—thou knowest well enough. Upon all which, the gentlewoman on a sudden (without being desired) prayed that the Lord might send the damsel her health, saying,—" Lord help thee, poor daft child, and rebuke the Devil." Which words were no sooner uttered than the damsel fell down as dead, and being in this posture carried to another room, instantly recovered of the blind, deaf, and also of the light fit, becoming perfectly well, and continued so for some time; and being thus recovered, and M. M. removed into another room, the damsel was enquired at, whom she had seen in the last fit? to which she replied, she had seen the gentlewoman, though in the meantime she was ignorant of the gentlewoman's ever being personally present in the room with her.

The same day the commissioners of justiciary having come to Bargarran, M. M. and the damsel were again confronted, upon which the damsel (being in the light fit), upon the first look of the forementioned M. M. was suddenly seized with sore fits, out of which, when she recovered, she accused her as being one of her most violent tormentors, particularly mentioning such and such times, in which she had in an extraordinary manner afflicted her, as also what words she spoke in her hearing while in the fit; and which is yet more remarkable, did question the gentlewoman if she did not sometime in December last, when she was tormenting her, remember how she went away from her in great haste, saying she could stay no longer, being obliged to attend a child's burial at home. In confirmation of which, we are very credibly informed, that W. R., a near neighbour of her's, had a child buried that same day, and that the gentlewoman came not in due time to attend the corpse to the burial place but the corpse being near to the churchyard ere she reached the house from whence they came, she returned again to her own lodging, and so did not accompany the burial at all.

The Lord's day following, being March 21st, she fell into swooning fits, complaining of no pain, except near to her heart, falling down as dead, not only when the fits seized her, but also when she recovered, sometimes singing after an unusual manner, withal informing spectators that J. G. constrained her to that kind of music, her own lips not at all moving in the meantime, which beholders saw to be true, only her tongue, for preventing of which she frequently put her hand into her mouth. And at this time, when either she herself, or those about her, offered to read any part of the Scripture, she was violently tormented, declaring if she did but so much as hear the word of God read that day, she would certainly be extremely tortured; in confirmation of which, when some essayed to read Heb. xi. 2, 4, 6, Isa. xl., Psal. iii. she uttered horrid screeches and outcries, complaining that she was pinched, in evidence of which, the prints or marks of the nails of fingers were distinctly seen on her arms; and being thus pinched or bitten for several times with great violence and pain, the skin itself was seen to be torn from off those parts of her arms and fingers, where the prints of the teeth and nails were observed; so that, from the deepness of the wounds, the foresaid parts affected fell a-bleeding, which blood was both seen and handled by spectators. Moreover, the damsel, while in this sad and lamentable condition, seemed to be extremely affected and oppressed with sore sickness, as one in a fever, crying sometimes to remove these dead children out of her sight; which she frequently repeated from six to nine in the morning, and she still continuing the rest of the day, it was observed that some charms and enchantments were put in her mouth as formerly, of which the damsel being very sensible, fell down on a sudden on the ground, putting her hand to some spittle which she had put out of her mouth, and lifted some trash which she again cast down to the ground, it making some noise, but yet neither seen in her spittle nor elsewhere by spectators, though while in her mouth, they observed something like orange pills, whites of eggs, and pieces of chesnuts.

Monday, being March 22d, the forementioned L. M. or J. G. came to Bargarran's house, and being confronted with the damsel, questioned her if ever she had seen her in any of her fits, withal alleging that she, viz., L. M. or J. G., could be none of her tormentors, because the damsel was not now seized with a fit, though looking upon her as she used to be, when she looked upon any of her other tormentors when confronted

with them ; upon which, the damsel being for some time silent, L. M. or J. G. did again propose the same question to
her, to which the damsel distinctly replied—Yes ; upon which
L. M. replied, "perhaps you have seen the Devil in my
shape."

As to the conference, there are several things exceeding remarkable ; as first, that the damsel, upon her answering yes,
was immediately seized with a fit ; secondly, that however, after Katherine Campbell had touched the damsel in
presence of the Commissioners, upon the 5th of Feb. last,
she had ever since that time freedom to touch any of her
tormentors without being seized with her fits, as has been
hinted ; yet true it is, that in the room of that charm a
new one took place, viz., when any time she looked upon her
tormentors in the face, at the very first look she was seized
with her fits ; which charm she declared was laid by means of
the forementioned L. M. or J. G., and also taken off again by
her that very morning before she came to visit the damsel ;
and this, she said, was suggested to her by some invisible
being, speaking distinctly as it were above her head, and that
therefore the damsel now had freedom to look L. M. in the
face without being seized with fits, which for a considerable
time before she could not do when confronted with any of her
tormentors ; thirdly, it is yet more observable that in the same
morning, before ever L. M. came to visit the damsel, it was
told by the damsel to several persons in the family that L. M.
had taken off that charm of her being seized with fits when
looking any of her tormentors in the face ; but, withal, that
she had laid on another in its room, viz., that as soon as the
damsel should by words confer with any of her tormentors, so
soon should she be seized with a fit, which accordingly was
verified when she spoke to L. M. or J. G.

Tuesday, being March 23d, the damsel being asleep in the

bed with her mother, about three o'clock in the morning, was on a sudden awakened (having for some time struggled in her sleep) in great fear and consternation, and being seized with her blind and deaf fits, took fast hold of her mother, declaring to her father and her, that the Devil was standing near to the bed assaulting her, upon which she cried suddenly: "God Almighty keep me from thy meetings. I will die rather than go to them. I will never, through the grace of God, renounce my baptism; for I will certainly go to hell if I do it. Thou says I will go to hell, however, because I am a great sinner; but I believe what the word of God saith,—though I have many sins, yet the blood of Christ cleanseth from all sin; and I will not add that great wickedness to my other sins, which thou art tempting me to do. It is no wonder thou lie to me, seeing thou wast bold to lie in God's face. I know thou art a liar from the beginning; and the red coat thou promises me, I know thou canst not perform it. And although I should never recover, I am resolved never to renounce my baptism. It is God that hath kept me all this time from being a witch, and I trust he will yet by his grace keep me, not because of any thing in me, but of his own mercy; and that he who hath kept me hitherto from being devoured by thee I hope will yet keep me." This conference continued near the space of an hour, her father, mother, and others being ear witnesses to the same. And after recovery the damsel declared that it was the Devil, who (in the shape of a naked man with a shirt, having much hair upon his hands, and his face like swine's bristles), had appeared to her tempting her as aforesaid.

Until Sabbath following she continued in the light fit, but withal every morning and evening was still seized with her sore fits, continuing still to name M. M. (who was at this time set at liberty), the forementioned L. M., E. T., an Highland wife, and others as being her tormentors. It is more than remarkable here, that M. M. being set at liberty upon bail, the very day after she went home, she appeared again to the damsel tormenting her in her fits, and continued so to do several days thereafter, particularly upon the Saturday, being March 27, after she was set at liberty; the which day, the damsel was heard name her in the fits, and say to her: "Wilt thou say, God help me, poor mad or foolish child, as thou said the other day before the judges: art thou wishing the devil to take me; where is the habit thou was clothed in the other day?"

On Sabbath morning, being March 28th, the damsel through God's great mercy towards her, was perfectly recovered, both of all her sore and light fits; becoming as well, sensible, and composed as ever.

End of the Narrative of Christian Shaw.

*The Editors of the first Edition of the Narrative, which was
printed in 1698, have subjoined the following information,
&c., to the Narrative :—*

IF it shall be questioned how the truth of all these strange
things is attested? there is none of those particulars mentioned in the Narrative, but had, in the first draught, the witnesses inserted at the end of every particular paragraph, and
attested before the commissioners for enquiry at Renfrew, by
the subscriptions of the respective witnesses. But seeing the
placing of them so now would have occasioned the repetition
of several persons names over and over again, and would
have made this Narrative swell too much in bulk, therefore
we judged it fittest now to set down the names altogether at
the end of the Narrative ; and the rather that, seeing these
things fell not out in a private corner, but thousands in this
country have been eye and ear witnesses thereof, to their admiration and raising of their sympathy, and been fully convinced beyond all debate of a diabolical influence upon
the affliction of the damsel ; we shall now make mention of
a few, viz., beside the father, mother, grandmother, and nearest relations of the damsel, and servants of the family, who
were always present with her in her fits, such as the commissioners for enquiry and of justiciary as had occasion to be on
the place of the events, particularly the Lord Blantyre, Mr.
Francis Montgomery of Giffen, Sir John Maxwell of Pollok,
Sir John Houstoun of that ilk, the Laird of Blackhall younger,
the Laird of Glanderstone, the Laird of Craigends, Porterfield
of Fulwood, John Alexander of Blackhouse, Mr. Robert
Semple, sheriff-depute of Renfrew, and several other honourable persons of good sense and prying wits, such as the noble
Earl of Marshall, the Laird of Orbistone, the Laird of Kil-
marnock, the Laird of Meldrum, the Laird of Bishopton,
elder and younger, Gavin Cochrane of Craigmure, William

R

Denniston of Colgrain, Dr. Matthew Brisbane, &c., and many
ministers, who kept days of humiliation and prayer weekly to
the family, and sometimes in the parish church with the congregation, viz., Mr. James Hutchison, minister of the gospel
at Kilellan, Mr. Patrick Simpson at Renfrew, Mr. James Stirling at Kilbarchan, Mr. Thomas Blackwell * at Paisley, Mr.
James Brisbane at Kilmacolm, Mr. Robert Taylor at
Houston, and of neighbouring presbyteries, Mr. Neil
Gillies, Mr. James Brown, Mr. John Gray, minister of
the Gospel at Glasgow, while the damsel was there ; Mr.
John Ritchie, minister at Old Kilpatrick ; Mr. Alexander
King, at Bonhill ; Mr. Archibald Wallace, at Car-
dross ; Mr. John Anderson, at Drymmon ; Mr. Andrew
Turner, minister of the place, who was frequently there ; besides Mr. Menzies of Cammo, and Mr. Grant of Cullen, advocates, who were eye and ear witnesses to several important
passages of the damsel's affliction, and the convincing evidences of its flowing from the operation of the Devil and his
instruments.   The truth whereof is further adminiculat by the
progress and issue of the trial, at which were present at
several occasions not only Sir John Shaw of Greenock, Com-
missar Smollet, at Bonhill, Mr. John Stewart, advocate, who
were concerned in the commission, with these others before-
mentioned ; but also great confluence of several nobility and
gentry out of the country, such as the Earl of Glencairn, the
Lord Kilmaurs, the Lord Semple, &c.

And now we are sure that after all the pregnant evidences
of the truth of this relation, as to matter of fact, they must be
persons very hard of belief that can allow themselves to deny
credit thereunto ; and must need conclude that there is

---

* Author of the *Schema Sacrum* and *Ratio Sacra*, and afterwards Professor
of Divinity in the University of Aberdeen.

nothing credible in the world that ever hath been delivered to mankind or posterity, and that they resolve to believe nothing though never so fully attested which they do not see with their own eyes, and perhaps there are some hardened in their pre-judicate conceits that will not believe even these so far as they may have influence to convince them of their errors; but wisdom is, and will be justified of all her children. Among all ingenuous persons, we are hopeful this Narrative, (which plainly relates things as they fell out without any kind of dis-guise), will obtain such entertainment as it is truly designed for, viz. :—That we be hereby more and more confirmed in the faith of the being of God and invisible spirits, and admire and adore the wonderful works of God in the depths of His judg-ments, and that there is really a hellish hierarchy and combi-nation of infernal spirits, enemies to God, and working all the mischief they can to men; whereby also, there is an evident testimony given to the truth of what is related in the Scriptures concerning the same, and withal, to lament, that through the just displeasure of our holy and righteous God, those devils get leave to break forth with so much rage and fury, and gets so many among professed christians into a hellish confederacy with them-selves, to be the instruments of their malice, and the actors of so many tragedies in the christian world ; to stir us up also to bless and magnify our God, that those devils and their instruments are chained and limited, that they cannot work all the evil they would, and as long as they will ; and therefore to join in thanksgiving to God for His deliverance to that afflicted family and damsel. Finally, as we are to submit to such afflictions as the Lord may think fit to measure out unto us, by whatsoever instruments, as in the case of Job ; so we are called to watch and pray that we enter not into temptation, while we have such adversaries going about still seeking to devour us ; and to rejoice that we have a strong protector,—

the blessed Captain of our salvation, the Lord Jesus Christ,—
who hath obtained the victory over all the devils in hell, and
hath promised all His saints a share in His victory, which
they begin to have in time. 1 Epistle John, iv. 4,—" And He
hath given us hope, even through grace of a speedy and
certain accomplishment thereof." Luke xxi. 22,—" Let us
lift up our heads, because our redemption draweth nigh."

APPENDIX, No. A.

THE subscribed attestations of Dr. Matthew Brisbane, physician, and Mr. Henry Marshall, apothecary in Glasgow, did influence the belief of an extraordinary cause of these events.

The doctor, on the 31st December 1696, tells, that at first sight, when he was brought to the girl she appeared so brisk in motion, so florid in colour, so cheerful, and, in a word, every way healthful, that he could hardly be persuaded she had need of a physician; but within ten minutes he found himself obliged to alter his thoughts, for she rose from her seat, and advertised she was instantly to be seized with a fit, according whereunto he observed a considerable distention in her left hypochondre, which in a trace falling, she was forthwith taken with horrid convulsive motions and heavy groans at first; which afterwards as soon as she was able to frame words, turned into exposulatory mourning against some women, particularly Campbell and Naesmith. Yet he thought these symptoms were reducible to the freaks of hypochondriac melancholy, and therefore put her in such a course proper against that kind of malady. Upon which, being freed for some time, he was alarmed that the child was returned to town worse than ever for having his assistance. He then was frequently with her, and observed her narrowly, so that he was confident she had no visible correspondent to subminister hair, straw, coal cinders, hay, and such like trash unto her; all which upon several occasions he saw her put out of her mouth without being wet; nay, rather as they had been dried with artifice, and actually hot above the natural warmth of the body, sometimes after severe fits, and other times without trouble when discoursing with him. When she had only light convulsive motions, but to a high degree, such rigidity of the whole body, as we call τιτινο, she did not fancy, as at other times, she saw these persons already named about her; but the upcasting of the trash above-mentioned did no sooner cease, than in all her fits, when she was able to speak any, she always cried out they were pricking or pinching her. He saw her also when free of fits, suddenly seized with dumbness, &c. And this he solemnly declares himself to have seen and handled; and were it not for the hay, straw, &c., he should not despair to reduce the other symptoms to their proper classes, in the catalogue of human diseases.

Mr. Marshall, the apothecary, concurs with the doctor, and gives some particular instances of his own observation; and among the rest, that the girl having fallen headlong upon the ground, as she had been thrown down with violence, fell a reasoning very distinctly, thus:—"Katie, what ails thee at me; I am sure I never did thee wrong; come let us gree; let there be no more difference betwixt us; let us shake hands together;" (putting forth her hand said,) "well, Katie, I cannot help it, ye will not gree with me." And immediately she cried, fell into a swoon, and out of that into a rage, wherein she continued without intermission for about half an hour; and perfectly recovered. Then she told him that she saw Katie Campbell, Nancy Naesmith, &c., and many more. Camp- was going to thrust a sword into her side, which made her so desirous to be agreed with her; and when the girl told him this, she instantly fell into another fit as formerly, in which she continued another half hour, &c. Dated 1st Jan., 1697.

"The lamentable case of the afflicted damsel and family, had been represented to his Majesty's most honourable Privy Council," * and on the 19th of Jan., 1697, a warrant of Privy Council was issued, † which set forth that there were

---

* Page 91.   † *Vide* Records of Privy Council, 19th Jan., 1697.

pregnant grounds of suspicion of Witchcraft in the Shire of Renfrew, especially from the afflicted and extraordinary condition of Christian Shaw, daughter of John Shaw, of Bargarran. It therefore granted permission to Alexander, Lord Blantyre, Sir John Maxwell of Pollok, Sir John Shaw of Greenock, William Cunnyngham of Craigens, Alexander Porterfield of Duchall, ———— Caldwall of Glanderstoun, Gavin Cochrane of Thornly-muir, Alexander Porterfield of Fulwood, and Robert Semple, sheriff-depute of Renfrew, or any five of them, to interrogate and imprison persons suspected of Witchcraft, to examine witnesses, &c., but not upon oath, and to transmit their report before the 10th of March, 1697. The Act of Privy Council is subscribed thus :—" Polwarth, *Cancellar*, Argyle, Leven, Forfar, Raith, Belhaven, Ja. Stewart, J. Hope, W. Anstruther, J. Maxwell, Ro. Sinclair."

———

An Abbreviate of the Precognition and Report made by the Commissioners appointed by his Majesty's Privy Council for enquiry: and the confessions of Elizabeth Anderson, James and Thomas Lindsay, transmitted by these Commissioners, and presented to the Privy Council on the 9th of March, 1697.

The Commissioners for enquiry, having met at Bargarran in February, 1697, did choose the Lord Blantyre, Preses., and took the confession of Elizabeth Anderson, aged about seventeen years, as follows :—Declares " that about seven years ago she staid with Jean Fulton, her grandmother, and playing about the door she saw a black grim man go into her grandmother's house ; after which, her grandmother came to the door, called her in, and desired her to take the gentleman (as she named him) by the hand, and which she did, but finding it very cold, became afraid, and immediately he vanished.

About a month thereafter, her grandmother and she being in the house together, the said gentleman (whom she then suspected to be the Devil) appeared to them, and fell a talking with her grandmother, by rounding in one anothers ears; upon which the grandmother desired her to take him by the hand, being a friend of hers; but Elizabeth refusing, the grandmother threatened that she would get none of the clothes promised to her unless she should obey; yet Elizabeth withstood, saying, "the Lord be between me and him," whereupon he went away in a flight, but she knew not how. Elizabeth was not troubled for a long time thereafter, till her father desiring her to go with him a begging through the country, and she saying that she needed not to seek her meat, seeing she might have work; her father pressed her to go alongst, and took her to a moor in Kilmalcolm, where were gathered together, at that and other subsequent meetings, Katherine Campbell, Margaret Fulton (her grandaunt), Margaret Lang, John Reid, smith, Margaret and Janet Rodgers, the three Lindsays (besides the two confessant ones), &c., and several whom she did not know, and the foresaid gentleman with them. He came to Elizabeth, bidding her to renounce her baptism, promising that if she would consent thereunto, she should get better meat and clothes, and not need to beg. But (as she declared) she would not consent. Then he enquired what brought her hither; she answered, that she came with her father; whereupon the devil and her father went and talked together apart, but she knew not where about. Declares, that in that meeting was concerted the tormenting of Mr. William Fleming, minister at Innerkip, his child. Elizabeth confesses she was at another meeting with that crew above the town of Kilpatrick, with the foresaid gentleman, whom they called their lord; and that she went with her father to the ferry boat of Erskine, where the Devil, with the rest of the band, overturned the boat, and drowned the Laird of Brighouse, and the ferrier of Erskine, with several special circumstances thereanent; particularly that some of the crew would have saved the ferrier, but one of them, viz., his mother-in-law, gain-stood it, in regard he had expelled her out of his house a little while before the meeting. Acknowledges she was present with them at the destroying of William Montgomerie's child, by strangling it with a sea napkin; where they, having entered the house, lighted a candle, which was somewhat bluish, and Agnes Naesmith saying, "what if the people awake?" Margaret Fulton replied, "ye need not fear;" as also declares, that about five weeks before the date, her father brought her on foot to Bargarran orchard, into which they entered by a slap in the dyke, and where were present the persons before-named, &c., and the Devil, who told that nobody would see them, at which they laughed. At this meeting they, with their lord, contrived the destruction of Christian Shaw; some being for stabbing her with a touck, others for hanging her with a cord, a third sort for choking her, and some intended to have her out of the house to destroy her; but fearing they might be taken before the next meeting to that effect, their lord (as they called him), gave them a piece of an unchristened child's liver to eat (but the declarant and the other two con-fessants slipped the eating of it), telling them that though they were apprehended they should never confess, which would prevent an effectual discovery; and further, several of them being afraid that the declarant would confess, and tell of them as she had done formerly on her grandmother, they threatened to tear her all in pieces if she did so; and particularly, Margaret Lang threatened her most. After two hours or thereby, they disappeared in a flight, except the declarant, who went home on her foot. Confesses like-

S

wise, that one night her father raised her out of her bed, and they having gone to the water side, took her on his back, and carried her over the river in a flight; from whence they went on foot to Dumbarton, and in Mr. John Hardy, minister, his yard, the crew and their lord being met, they formed the picture of Mr. Hardy, and dabbed it full of pins, and having put it amongst water and ale mixed, roasted it on a spit at a fire, &c. After which her father and herself returned in the same manner as they went. Declares the particular persons that were employed, and most industrious in the several facts before mentioned, &c."

James Lindsay, aged 14 years, declares, "That one day he met with the deceased Jean Fulton, his grandmother, at her own house, where she took from him a little round cape and a plack; but being grieved, he required them from her again, and she refusing, he called her an old witch and ran away, upon which she followed him and cried that she should meet him with an ill turn. About three days thereafter, he being a begging in the country, he met his grandmother with a black grim man, &c., whom she desired him to take by the hand, which James did, but found it exceeding cold, and was straitly griped; whereupon the said gentleman (as she termed him) asked the declarant if he would serve him, and obey him, and he should have a coat, hat, and several other things, to which James answered, "yes, I'll do it." And after this the foresaid gentleman (whom the declarant knew thereafter to be the Devil), and his grandmother went away, but knows not how. Acknowledges he was frequently thereafter at meetings with the Devil and witches, particularly these mentioned in Elizabeth Anderson's confession: that their lord came to James at the first public meeting, took him by the hand, and forbade him to tell: that they contrived beforehand at the said meeting, the drowning of Brighouse, and concurs with Elizabeth Anderson anent the design of saving the ferrier, which his mother-in-law did divert. He being interrogate, declared he did not see J. K. and J. W. at committing of the foresaid fact, (and indeed they were then in prison) : that they with a cord strangled Matthew Park's child : and that the person who waited on the child, finding it stiffled cried out, 'Matthew! Matthew! the bairn is dead.' Elizabeth Anderson concurs in this particular, and tells, that when they had done, they took the cord with them. Declares, that he was present at strangling William Montgomerie's child with a sea napkin, and heard Agnes Naesmith say, 'draw the loup,' &c. That about five weeks since, he was carried to them in Bargarran's orchard, and concurs with Elizabeth Anderson in what was treated there, anent destroying Christian Shaw, and the charm against confessing. Likewise the meeting in Dumbarton, anent Mr. Hardy, is acknowledged by him ; and that he has several times appeared to Christian Shaw, both in Glasgow and Bargarran, with the others that did torment her, and put in her mouth coal cinders, bones, hay, hair, sticks, &c., intending thereby to choke her : that he and they did oftentimes prick and stab her in this manner, viz., he had a needle which, if he put in his clothes, her body would be pricked and stabbed in that place where he fixed the needle, and if he put in his hair, that part of her head would be tormented : that he saw her put out the pins they had put in, at which time he cried these words, ' Help, J. D.' who was also then present : that when the ministers began to pray in Bargarran's house at several occasions, the Devil and they immediately went away," &c.

Thomas Lindsay, being below pupilarity, declares, " The same Jean Fulton, his grandmother, awaked him one night out of his bed, and caused him take a black grim gentleman (as he called him) by the hand ; which he felt to be cold ;

and who having enquired if Thomas would serve him and be his man, and he would give him a red coat, the declarant consented ; and the gentleman (whom he knew thereafter to be the Devil) gave him a nip in the neck, which continued sore for ten days.   Thereafter, one day after his grand-mother's decease, coming by her house, he thought she appeared to him clapping his head, and desiring him to be a good servant to the gentleman to whom she had gifted him, and forbidding him to reveal it.   Declares, that one night lying in bed in the house of one Robert Shaw, he was awakened out of his sleep and carried in a flight to Matthew Park's house, where were present the particular persons named by him, and concurs to the manner of strangling of the child with James Lindsay his brother ; and that another night, being in the house of Walter Alexander, he was brought to the strangling of William Montgomerie's child, and agrees likewise in the manner of it with his brother, only, he says the sea napkin with which they committed the fact was speckled.   He likewise concurs as to the meeting in Bargarran's orchard about five weeks ago, and what was acted therein : as also anent Mr. Hardy ; with this addition, that himself turned the spit whereon the picture was roasted," &c.

It is to be noticed that the three confessants were separately apprehended upon several occasions, so they (after the obstinacy to discover was abated) did emit these confessions in several distinct places, without communication with, or knowledge of, another's confession in manner mentioned in the preceding narrative.   The commissioners did examine them upon other trying questions that were new, thereby to make experiment of their consonancy or disagreement, but still found them strangely to accord.   The facts did fall out in the manner declared by them, particularly the strangling of the children, death of the minister, drowning of those in the boat, and torture of Bargarran's daughter mentioned in the confessions before expressed.   Further, the commissioners did confront them both with Christian Shaw, the afflicted girl, and the persons declared (whom they caused apprehend), and both the girl and confessants did accuse these to their faces, and bind them in circumstances with great steadiness and congruity, though separately brought in.   The commissioners did also try some experiments anent the girl, her falling in fits on approach of the accused, as is expressed in the Narrative, and examined her with those who staid commonly about her upon the particulars of her sufferings.   They tried to cause her write (since she could not say out), the name of a person whom she first called Margaret or pinched Maggie, and asserted to be one of her chief bourriers, yet upon writing Margaret, and the letter L of her surname, the girl was presently taken with a fearful convulsion, the pen being struck out of her hand, and herself falling as dead, with groans heavier and sorer than ordinary.   After some recovery, whereof some ministers pointed to her a passage of the Bible, but upon essaying to cast her eyes on it, she fell into vehement pangs, till one of the commissioners desired the book might be closed, and that being done, she immediately came to herself, &c.   Lastly, the commissioners called before them those persons who had signed the passages of the several days in the written journal of the girl's sufferings ; and having examined them thereupon, transmitted the same, with the declarations of the three confessants and several of the passages that occur in the precognition, to His Majesty's Privy Council, by whom they were appointed for that effect.

The Commissioners represented that there were twenty-four persons, male and female, suspected and accused of

Witchcraft, and that further enquiry ought to be made into this crime.*

Agreeable to this report, a new warrant was issued by the Privy Council on the 5th April, 1697, † to most of the Commissioners formerly named, with the addition of Lord Hallcraig, Mr. Francis Montgomery, of Giffen ; Sir John Houston of that Ilk ; Mr. John Kincaid of Corsbasket, advocate ; and Mr. John Stewart, younger, of Blackhall, advocate, or any five of them to meet at Renfrew, Paisley, or Glasgow, to take trial of, judge, and do justice upon the foresaid persons; and to sentence the guilty to be burned, or otherwise executed to death, as the commissioners should incline. It further ordained the commissioners to transmit to the Court of Justiciary an authentic extract of their proceedings, to be entered upon its records ; and contained a recommendation to the Lords of the Treasury to defray the expenses of the trial. The Act of Privy Council is subscribed thus : " Polwarth, *Cancellar*, Douglas, Lauderdale, Annandale, Yester, Kintore, Carmichael, W. Anstruther, Archd. Mure."

Hugo Arnot, Esq., author of a collection of celebrated Criminal Trials in Scotland, from which I have taken the copy of the warrants, dated 19th Jan., 1697, and 5th April, 1697, says, " The commissioners, thus empowered, were not remiss in acting under the authority delegated to them. After twenty hours were spent in the examination of witnesses, who gave testimony that the malefices libelled could not have proceeded from natural causes, and that the prisoners were the authors of these malefices—after five of the unhappy prisoners confessed their own guilt, and criminated their alleged associates —after counsel had been heard on both sides, and the counsel

---

* *Vide* Records of Privy Council, 9th March, 1697.
† *Vide* Records of Privy Council, 5th April, 1697.

for the prosecution had declared that ' he would not press the jury with the ordinary severity of threatening an assize of error,'* but recommended to them to proceed according to the evidence ; and loudly declared to them, that although they ought to beware of condemning the innocent, yet if they should acquit the prisoners, in opposition to legal evidence, ' they would be accessory to all the blasphemies, apostacies, murders, tortures, and seductions, whereof these enemies of heaven and earth should hereafter be guilty.' After the jury had spent six hours in deliberation, seven of those miserable persons were condemned to the flames."

Mr. Arnot further says, " The order of Privy Council for recording the commissioners' proceedings in the books of justiciary was not complied with. I am therefore unable to give any further particulars of the catastrophe of these miserable persons, or of the criminal absurdity of those who committed them to the flames."

Mr. Arnot further says, " These instances afford a sufficient specimen of the mode of prosecution against the multitude of miserable persons who were sacrificed at the altar of the fatal sisters,—Ignorance, Superstition, and Cruelty. But it is impossible to form an estimate of the number of the victims. For not only the Lords of Justiciary, but bailies of regalities, sheriffs of counties, and the endless tribe of commissioners appointed by the Privy Council, and sometimes by Parliament, officiated as the priests who dragged the victims to the altar."

Mr. Arnot further says, " The last person who was prosecut- before the Lords of Justiciary for Witchcraft, was Elspeth Rule, who was tried at Dumfries, in 1709. The last person who was brought to the stake in Scotland for the crime of

---

* *Vide* the Advocate's speech to the inquest.

235

Witchcraft was condemned by Captain David Ross of Little Daan, Sheriff-depute of Sutherland, A.D. 1722."

Doctor Brisbane being adduced upon oath in the trial, he adheres to his former subscribed attestation, and in respect of what is mentioned in that attestation, and some other specialities, the Doctor depones, that in his opinion the things mentioned in his attestation, did not proceed from natural causes arising from the patient's body.

The sum of the confessions of Margaret and Janet Rodger, who confessed during the trial of the rest beyond expectation.

During the dependence of the trial, Janet and Margaret Rodgers confessed in this manner: The commissioners had adjourned for two several diets, and though they were to meet on the third, yet it was not expected that they would proceed till providence might clear the prisoners' guilt by further testimonies of those who might come to confess. The very morning of the third term, the Rodgers did confess, which was a surprise to every one that came up to attend the court, since these, as they were women, and were not formerly noticed as others were: so they confessed of free motion, without any persons desiring it of them at the time; they had not such means of instruction as were administered to others: and the conjuncture of many circumstances were altogether singular. Their confessions did coincide as to the meetings and things acted therein, with the three former confessants, and the other evidences of the visible matters of fact: only they were so pointed as to condescend upon some of the panels whom they did not see at these rendezvouses; and great care was taken, to compare their testimonies which had been already discovered, and to expiscate their certain knowledge, by new interrogators, when they were separate from one another, &c. The whole crisis had such an evidence, that now the commissioners, with the general approbation of the most intelligent of the country, who came in to attend the court, allowed the going on of the process to debate of the relevancy, and putting seven of the best known criminals, for whom an advocate appeared, to the knowledge of an inquest : according whereunto there were some days allowed for the panels giving in their informations upon the relevancy ; and at the term, there was a great time spent in adducing the probation, an account whereof is referred to Appendix No. B.

APPENDIX No. B.

An account of Two Letters which were written after the persons were condemned, and before they were executed, which contain a Summary of what appeared most Material or Curious, in the Trial of the Seven Witches, who were condemned to be burned on the Gallowgreen of Paisley.

THE truth of the strange things mentioned in the preceding Narrative was at first carefully searched into only by private persons, but at last became so notour that, upon application founded on a journal of these extraordinary events, attested by many of the gentry in the country, the council gave a commission for enquiring thereanent.

,The honourable persons to whom this was recommended did, with great impartiality and exactness, make a report which, in providence, proved a means of moving the Government to notice the execution of justice on some of these witches, who otherwise might have lurked without being discovered.

For, hereupon, the Council directed a second commission, for trial of those who appeared to them to be most loaded

T

by the preliminary probation adduced on the first. Several
of these judges were not only persons of honour, but also
of singular knowledge and experience; conform whereunto
they did proceed with singular caution, and were so far from
precipitancy in the affair, that, after several diets of Court,
they adjourned to a longer term, that, in the meantime, the
prisoners might be provided of advocates.

Accordingly an advocate compeared for them, and
managed their defence with all the accuracy that could be
expected. There were about twenty hours employed at one
diet in examination of witnesses; and the inquest being en-
closed, did consume about six hours in comparing the probation. Whereupon seven of the most notorious criminals were
convicted and condemned.

The crimes libelled and found proven against them, were
not mere spectral imaginations, but open and obvious facts,
viz.:—The murders of some children and persons of age,
and the torturing of several persons, particularly Bargarran's
daughter; and both these, not at a distance, but contiguously,
by natural means of cords, pins, and the like, besides the
other ordinary works of Witchcraft, such as renouncing
baptism, entering in contract with, and adoring the Devil
under a corporeal shape, &c., which could not but be
sustained relevant in Scotland, since there is an express
statute, Parl. 9th, Act 73, Queen Mary, appointing the pain
of death to such.

To make the probation the more convincing, it was
adduced orderly in three periods. The first consisted of
unsuspected witnesses, who proved facts. From whence it
was necessarily inferred that there was Witchcraft in the case.
The second did include also unexceptional witnesses, who
deponed upon facts; which made it probable if not necessary, that the panels were the Witches. The third did

comprehend six positive testimonies of these who did see and hear these Witches committing the malefices libelled.

The only valuable subject of debate, was anent the import of these last testimonies; five whereof were by confessants who had been at the meetings in which were committed the crimes libelled; and the sixth of Bargarran's daughter, who was one of the persons maleficiat. The antecedent part of the probation was by witnesses beyond exception; and the judges upon a long debate did sustain four of these six only *cum nota*, and two of them to be examined without oath, so nice were they in favour of the panels' lives, since some of these witnesses might have been admitted in such a crime without any quality by the most scrupulous judicatory in Europe. But all things were carried on in this procedure with tenderness and moderation, for even the advocates, who were sent to prosecute the indictment by his majesty's council and advocate, did not act with the bias of parties; but, on the contrary shewed an equal concern to have the panels assoilized, if it could be found compatible with justice.

This is the reason for which the publisher doubts not, but the two following Letters (the one whereof gives a compend of the advocate's speech to the jury, and the other of their answers to the objections against the confessant witnesses) will afford a satisfying view of the chiefest part of the trial, since the objections which were or might have been made, are therein stated and answered, or anticipate and prevented; and the intended brevity would not permit to print at this time the whole process, which being extant upon record, any who are curious may have easy access thereunto.

There is scarcely need to take notice of a late scurrilous pamphlet that had been printed in England, and pretends to give an account of those proceedings; for any who reads it may easily find that the author has been either fool, knave, or both, there being neither good language, sense, nor truth, in the most part of it.

The above Preface to the Letters was printed in 1698.

LETTER I.

SIR,—You having told me, that the odd passages which occur in the west, have put many of your neighbours and yourself upon reading all the books you can get treating of Witchcraft; and therefore desired me to transmit to you my observations at the court. I shall not pre-occupy your opinion by giving them in my own form, but herein I send to you the exactest duplicate of the advocate's speech to the inquest that I could obtain; and by the next post you shall have something more curious, viz., A collection of their answers to the objections against the six last witnesses, that were adduced for concluding the proof: having these, you will want little that could be agreeable to such an accurate gust as yours is.

The Advocate's Speech to the inquest was of this import:—

GOOD MEN OF INQUEST,—You having sitten above twenty hours in overhearing the probation; and being inclosed, where, it is like, you will take no small time to reconsider and compare it, we shall not detain you with summing up the same in particular; but shall only suggest some things, whereof it is fit you take special notice in your perusal of it, viz., 1st, The nature of your own power, and the management thereof; 2dly, The object of this power which lies before you, wherein you are to consider in the first place, whether or not there has been Witchcraft in the malefices libelled? and in the next place, whether or not these panels are the Witches?

As to your power, it is certain that you are both judges and witnesses, by the opinion of our lawyers and custom; therefore you are called out of the neighbourhood, as presumed best to know the quality of the panels, and the notoriety of their guilt or innocence. Your oath is, that you shall all truth tell, and no truth conceal; which does plainly imply, that you are to condemn or assoil, conform to your proper conviction. Such is the excellent constitution of juries in England, and ought to hold more specially in this circumstantiate case, where there is such a chain of different kinds of probation concurring against the same panels, as will appear by the review thereof in its proper place.

We are not to press you with the ordinary severity of threatening an assize of error, in case you should absolve; but wholly leave you to the conduct of God and your own conscience, and desire that you proceed with all the care of the panels' lives that is possible for you; as the honourable judges have set to you a desirable pattern, in their great caution thereanent.

As to the probation itself, you see that it is divided in three parts, viz. :—The extraordinariness of the malefices; the probability of the concurring adminicles; and the clearness of the positive probation.

As to the first part, the malefices, or *corpora delicti*, are proven by unexceptionable witnesses, to have fallen out in such an odd and extraordinary a manner, that it points out some other causes than the ordinary course of nature to have produced these effects.

For clearing of this, particularly in relation to the torments of Bargarran's daughter, you may consider not only the extraordinary things that could not proceed from a natural disease, which lie proven before you; but also several other matters of fact, which is notour, have been seen by some of yourselves, and lie here in a journal of her sufferings ; every article whereof is attested by the subscriptions of persons of entire credit, before the honourable commissioners appointed by his Majesty's Privy Council for making enquiry there-anent.

This girl's throwing out of hairs, pins, and coals of greater heat than that of her body or blood ; as also so dry that they appeared not to have come out of her stomach ; nor had she any press of vomiting at the time ; that she declared the same to have been put in her mouth by her tormentors, is deponed by Dr. Brisbane, in his opinion, not to proceed from a natural cause.

She was not tormented by any of the panels after their imprisonment, except two nights by Katherine Campbell ; which being a surprise, it was thereafter discovered, that these two nights the jailor's wife had got out Katherine Campbell to spin in her house.

She having been speaking to one of her tormentors as present (though invisible to the bye-standers), and asking how her tormentors had got these coloured red sleeves ; she suddenly gets up, takes hold of them, the company hears a shried, and she pulls away two pieces of red cloth, which all the bye-standers beheld with amazement, in her hand ; nor was there any other piece of this kind of cloth to be found in the room at that occasion.

She told that her tormentors were giving her a glass of sack, an orange pill, &c. (thereby ensnaring her to accept of a favour from them), and, accordingly, she was seen to move her lips, and to have an orange pill betwixt her teeth ; though there was no visible hand that could have done it.

She advertised beforehand that one of her tormentors was to be at the door at a particular hour, and that another of them was in the kitchen before any did tell her thereof ;

which accordingly fell out. And these being brought to her presence, became obnoxious to the ordinary means of discovery.

When her glove fell down from her, at a time when several persons were about her; it was lifted again by a hand invisible to them.

She was not only transported through the hall and down stairs without perceiving her feet to touch the ground; but also was hurried in a flight up stairs: and when a minister endeavoured to retain her, he found a sensible weight, besides her own strength, drawing her from him.

When she complained that her tormentors had bitten and scratched her, the steads of the nails and teeth were seen upon her skin, with blood and spittle about the wounds, which were above twenty-four; while neither her own, or any other teeth that were visible, could have done it.

She was most vehemently distorted upon attempting to tell or even write the names of her tormentors; yet that ceased as to any of them how soon the person was delated; and particularly she had liberty, after many painful attempts, to accuse Margaret Lang, how soon a charm of hair to restrain her, which Margaret had left behind the door, was found and burned; the girl having told it to have been tint, in manner mentioned in the deposition.

She did throw out no more hair after the finding the ball of hair, of the same colour and kind with that thrown out by the girl, in Katherine Campbell's pocket, with pins in it, and the burning of it.

After Agnes Naesmith had prayed for her, she did appear to her, but not torment her.

She foretold that her tormentors had concerted to throw her in a fit (whereof they did premonish, of design to fright her to renounce her baptism by the terror) at a certain hour, and had left one of their number to execute it; according whereunto, there was a woman with a red coat seen under a tree in the orchard, and the torment was brought on at the time appointed.

When she told there was something tormenting her under the clothes, the spectators saw the bed clothes move in an extraordinary manner, after the girl had been raised out of them.

When she complained she was beaten, the bye-standers heard the noise of the strokes.

She cried out at a time, that her thigh was hurt; and one of the company having searched her pocket, found a knife, but unfolded: however, having folded up the same, and put it in a second time, she cries of new; and upon the second search, (it, though secured by the spring) is found open, to the great wonder of beholders; since they did watch, that no visible thing could have possibly opened it.

She told of a charm under the bed; and accordingly it was found in the shape of an egg, which melted away being put in the fire: she told also that her sister, who was boarded abroad, had charms put above her in the house, and would not recover of the decaying sickness till she was brought out of it. According whereunto, the child being brought home, she straightway recovered.

She told of their meeting in the yard of Bargarran, for consulting anent the destroying of her; and accordingly the confessants have deponed that they did meet and consult her ruin in that place.

The story anent her telling that the commissioners, though at three miles distance, had granted a warrant to the sheriff to apprehend one of her tormentors; her telling so perfect an account of the sheriff and of Mr. Guthrie who was with him, while her eyes were tied and fast; her being in excessive torments, (as she foretold) till that person was apprehended, and immediately thereupon, though at many miles distance, her telling that her tormentors were now taken, betwixt twelve and one o'clock in the morning, and the sheriff, when he returned, did declare the seizure to have been about that time, is so notour, and so well attested, that we need only to put you in mind thereof.

Her falling in fits upon the sight or touch of her tormentors, was no effect of imagination; for she was fully hood-winked with a cloak, so as she saw nobody whatsoever; yet upon the approach of her tormentor, she immediately fell down as dead : whereas she remained no ways startled upon the touch of any other; which experiments were tried for ascertaining this means of discovery.

Finally, she is naturally sagacious and observant, and discovered her integrity in face of court; for when the president asked, whether or not she knew one of the panel's name that was to be pricked? she answered, that though she knew her well enough of herself, yet one had told her the name of this panel when she was sent for to be confronted with her. So far did this girl discover her aversion from any thing that might seem intended to aid unfairly the natural evidence of truth, and her firmness to the outmost against temptations of becoming a witch, particularly against the last assault of Satan, wherein he persuaded her at least to go to their meetings; and she answered, that she would not follow such a base fallen creature; and he rejoining, that she would go to hell, however, for her other sins; and she answering, that he was a liar from the beginning; and the blood of Jesus would cleanse her from all iniquity : whereupon he disappeared, and she perfectly recovered upon the Sabbath thereafter; was an happy end put this fearful tragedy of Witchcraft, and confirms to conviction the reality of it.

As to the murdering of the children, and the minister

U

libelled; you may observe several extraordinary things appearing in them; particularly, the witnesses depone the minister to have been in excessive torments, and of an unusual colour, to have been of sound judgment; and yet he did tell of several women being about him, and that he heard the noise of the door opening, when none else did hear it. The children were well at night, and found dead in the morning, with a little blood on their noses, and blaes at the roots of their ears; which were obvious symptoms of stranglings: besides, that it is testified that the keeper of one of them cried out, "Matthew! Matthew! the child is dead." And the house of the other was whitened within, with sifting of meal the night before; both which particulars were told and discovered by the confessants, before the witnesses which now concur with them in it were examined.

The second part of the probation consists of several adminicles, proven by unsuspected witnesses, which lead us to suspect those panels to be Witches, as so many lines drawn from a circumference to a centre, and as an avenue to the positive probation thereafter adduced; and these either strike at the whole panels in general, or some of them in particular. In general, we need not enumerate all these adminicles, but remit you to the probation, which is so full thereanent; only you will be pleased to notice, that it is clearly proven that all the panels have insensible marks, and some of them in an extraordinary manner; that most of them have been long reputed witches, and some of them delated in 1687, by a confessing witch, whose subscribed confession has been produced. You see that none of them doth shed tears; nor were they ever discovered to do it since their imprisonment, notwithstanding of their frequent howlings; so that it is not a sudden grief or surprise. And finally, that the girl fell into fits of torment upon the panels approach to her, and that she did name them all frequently, either out or in her fits.

In particular, you see how Katherine Campbell was provoked by this girl's discovering her theft; whereupon she has brought in the rest of her confederates to act the following mischiefs. How, thereupon, Campbell did curse and imprecate in a terrible manner; how she staid out of her bed at night, and was frequently drousy in the morning; how she was named by the girl, particularly the two nights that she was out of prison. The ball of hair was taken out of her pocket and burned; whereupon the girl's throwing out of hair did cease; she could not express one word, even when on her knees, of prayer for the girl's recovery; and the insensible marks on her were remarkable.

Agnes Naesmith did not torment the girl after she had prayed for her. She was reputed a witch and hath the marks. She came early in the morning to Bargarran's close, when, by refusing to go in, it appeared she had no business; yea, it is plain that she had a resentment for her not getting a greater alms the last time she was there. The girl declared, *ex incontinenti*, that Naesmith asked her health and age, which, in these circumstances, was a shrewd presumption of her evil design; and she acknowledged herself to have done this when she asked the age of another child, wherein by Providence she was befooled, since that which she thought would have been an excuse, tended to discover her guilt. And lastly, after this appearance of Agnes Naesmith, the girl did take her first fit, and nominate her among her first tormentors.

Margaret Lang, that great imposter, has been a great master-piece of the Devil. She has confessed unnatural lust, which is known to some of your number; she sat near the door where the charm of hair was found, which the girl declared did keep up her tongue; and upon burning thereof, it

was loosed. The girl fell in fits upon her approach; she has notable marks, particularly one which the confessant declared she lately received; and, by inspection, it appears to be recent. When she came from her private conversation (no doubt with the Devil) she raged as if she had been possessed, and could not but declare that she expected a violent death. She looked in the face of James Millar's child and asked her age, whereupon that child sickened.the same night, and named Margaret Lang on her death-bed. It appears she was ready to show to Janet Laird a sight of her mother, who had been three years dead. And finally, she has been taken in several lies and gross prevarications; particularly you may remember how six hours ago, when the witnesses were examined on the ball of hair found with Katherine Campbell, a gentleman, (Mr. Stewart of ——) heard her say to Katherine in the ear, "This is well waird on you, because you would not put it away when I desired you," &c. Which the said Mr. Stewart did openly testify in court upon oath; notwithstanding whereof, this impudent wretch had the confidence to deny it, though Katherine Campbell also confessed that she pulled at her, and had spoke somewhat to her, to which she did not advert. This was no wonder, the witnesses deponing at the same time, being close against Katherine.

Margaret Fulton was reputed a Witch, has the mark of it, and acknowledged, in presence of her husband, that she made use of a charm, which appeared full of small stones and blood; that her husband had brought her back from the fairies; and her repute of being a Witch is of an old date, besides her being often named by the maleficiate girl.

As to the Lindsays, they all have the mark, and were all of a long time reputed to be Witches. John Lindsay, in Barlock, was accidentally discovered by the girl's taking a fit upon his coming to the house. John and James Lindsay were delated

by a confessing Witch in anno 1687, which confession is publicly read before you, and there was money given to the Sheriff-
depute for delaying of the pursuit. James Lindsay appeared
to William Semple suddenly, and flew about like a fowl, for an
opportunity to strike him, in revenge of the quarrel mentioned
in the deposition, and at last prevailed to strike him dead
over a dyke: And finally, which is a remarkable indication
both to truth and providence, the very witnesses adduced in
the exculpation for the Lindsays, deponed so clearly against
them, even beyond the pursuer's witnesses, that their advocate
was stunned thereat, and thereupon desisted from craving any
more witnesses to be examined on the exculpation.

It is true some of these indications may be in one, and
others of them in another, either from nature or accident, and
yet that person not be a Witch; but it was never heard nor
read, that all these indications, which are so many discoveries
by providence of a crime that might otherwise remain in the
dark, did ever concur in one and the same individual
person that was innocent; yea, on the contrary, they, by the
wisdom and experience of all nations, do also convincingly
discover a Witch, as the symptoms of a leprosy concerted by
all physicians do unfold the person affected with the same to
be leperous, but *esto*, they are not sufficient of themselves; yet
their tendency and meaning, being cleared and applied to
their proper cause, by a liquid and positive probation, there
wants no more to determine you anent the panel's guilt, and
therefore,

Thirdly,—As to the third part of the probation, we remit
the positive depositions of the confessants, and against whom
they do concur, wholly to your own perusal or examination;
only you would be pleased to notice, 1st, Something which
do very much sustain the credibility of their testimonies
arising from their examination in court; 2dly, We shall ex-

plain to you the import of the word *Nota*, which is added to the interlocutor of the judges admitting these last witnesses.

First, Elizabeth Anderson is of sufficient age, being seventeen; but so young and pointed, {that her deposition appears no effect of melancholy; she accused her father to his face when he was a-dying in the prison, as now there are two of her aunts in the panel, which certainly must proceed from the strength of truth, since even Dives retained a natural affection to his relations; she went on foot to the meetings with her father, except only that the Devil transported them over the water Clyde, which was easy to the prince of the air, who does far greater things by his hurricanes; she tells that Montgomerie's house was meally when his child was strangled; and declares, that she never renounced her baptism, but was carried along by the concussion of the parent, so that nothing can be objected against her testimony in any judgment, much less an excepted crime.

James Lindsay, it is true, is of less import; yet by his weeping when he came in and was admonished of the greatness of his guilt, it appears that he had a sense of it. He hath a natural precipitancy in what he speaks, yet that is commonly the concomitant of ingenuity, as importing his expressions not to be forethought. He concurs in most things with the others, and yet he has declared, that he saw not Margaret Fulton at Dumbarton, &c., which implies that he does not file the panels all at random, but tells what occurred to his senses, &c.

Janet and Margaret Rodgers are instances of a singular providence; for they did confess the same morning that the court did last sit, of their own proper motive, there being neither ministers nor judges beside them at the time. Agnes Naesmith is Janet's relation, and she tells that she never saw Katherine Campbell, as Margaret declares that she did not see John Lindsay in Barloch; which plainly demonstrates that they tell only the dictates of their natural conscience, arising from discretion and knowledge of the true matters of fact: they both professed their repentance last Sabbath in the church, and do persist with great firmness, as you see their deportment, in deponing to the congruous and exact.

Thomas Lindsay and Christian Shaw being under pupilarity, we did not press their being put to an oath; yet you saw that they did declare in court againt those panels in such an harmony with the rest of the deponents, and gave such a cause of their knowledge, that it is certain their own youngness in years adds extremely to the credit of their testimony; because thereby it is incredible that they could have contrived or executed the acting of concert.

As to the second, since these witnesses are admitted by the judges, it necessarily implies that they meant them to be probative; only they adjected the words *cum nota*, that is, you must notice, or *notandum est*, that there must something else concur to prove the guilt of the panels, by and atour the depositions of any two such witnesses; but so it is that all the adminicles on which you have seen probation led, for more than sixteen hours of your time, are strengthening evidences of those witnesses' credibility, and cannot but have been noticed by you, as illative of the same things which they depone. Whereby the *nota* is fully taken off by the concurrence of four other positive testimonies, agreeing with that of two of these witnesses; by the extraordinariness of the *corpora delicti;* by the probability of the adminicles; and, finally, by the whole chain of this affair, and the sparkles of an infernal fire which in every place hath broken out of it.

It is true, there are some few of the adminicles that are proven only by one witness, but as to this you may consider, 1st, That a witness deponing *de facto proprio*, is in law more credited than any other single witness, and this is the present case as to some of the adminicles ; 2dly, The antecedent concomitant and subsequent circumstances of fact, do sustain the testimony and make the *semi plenary* probation to become full ; but 3dly, The other adminicles undoubtedly proven by concurring witnesses, are *per se*, sufficient ; and therefore you saw us, at the desire of the Judges, forbear to call the far greatest part of our witnesses, because the time had already run to so great a length, and it was thought that there was already enough proven of presumptions ; for it may also reasonably be imagined, that the most regular and curious scheme had emerged from the fortuitous concourse of atoms, roving without rule, as that so many indications should concenter against each of these panels, and yet they remain innocent of Witchcraft.

Now upon the whole, you will take notice that presumptions, being vehement, make a more certain probation than witnesses ; because presumptions are natural emanations of the thing itself, which cannot be bribed ; whereas witnesses are obnoxious ; so in our law there was one condemned for theft, another for falsehood, and a third for murdering of a child, merely upon presumptions, as is related by M'Kenzie in his Criminal Treatise, much more may presumptions abstract the faith of, and take off the *nota* from positive witnesses ; for it is a gross mistake that several proofs which have each of them some import may not be joined to make a full evidence, the same way as two small candles in a dark room will not suffice, yet several others being added to them will make a sufficient light to discover the murderer ; two boys will be able to carry a weight which one of them would not be able to sustain, as two units make a full number : one witness of whatsoever dignity proves nothing ; yet out of the mouth of two or three witnesses every truth shall be established. And finally, though one coal make not a fire that can do the work, yet several coals added to it, increase the flame, which is hoped will be sufficient for the operation.

We shall, therefore, leave you with this conclusion, that as you ought to beware of condemning the innocent, and ought to incline to the safest side; so if these panels be proven legally guilty, then *quad* bygones, your eye ought not to spare them, nor ought you to suffer a Witch to live; and as to the future, you, in doing otherwise, would be accessory to all the blasphemies, apostasies, murders, torture, and seductions, &c., whereof these enemies of heaven and earth shall thereafter be guilty when they have got out. So that· the question seems simply to come to this, whether upon your oath *de fideli*, you can swear that the panels, notwithstanding of all that is proven against them, are not guilty of Witchcraft; in the determination whereof, we pray God may direct you to the right course.

The inquest being inclosed near six hours, brought in their verdict to Court that they found the libel proven.

LETTER II.

Sir,—I have collected, according to my promise, what appeared to me most specious in the reasonings, either in Court or private conversation, anent receiving of the confessants as witnesses. You are not to imagine that the panels were condemned on the faith of these; for I do believe the probation by unexceptionable witnesses, led antecedent to this last, was so pregnant that the panels might have been condemned on it, though these last had not been adduced.

I may have misled the energy of the argument sometimes, in a case which in itself is abtruse; however, you have it in

v

such a manner as I was able to penetrate thereunto, as follows:—

In order to the more satisfactory answering of the objections made against these last witnesses, we shall first lay before you the state of the case, and then clear up the determination of it.

As to the first, the question is not whether partners in the crime, or others mentioned in the objections, can be a concluding proof of themselves, though two of them would concur as to the same act of witchcraft; but whether the *corpora delicti* appearing already to imply witchcraft, and the extrinsic adminicles being so pregnant, to infer that these panels are the Witches; their concurring such characters, as by observance of all nations and ages, are the symptoms of a Witch; particularly the marks, fame, not shedding of tears, &c., which are discoveries of providence of such a crime, that like avenues lead us to the secret of it. And finally, when six persons of different ages and stations, five confessants, and the girl, do, when separately examined, agree in their answers to every material question that is put to them, even though it be new, so that it could not be concerted: we say, whether or not in such a case, may witnesses be received to put the copestone on the evidence by a positive probation, of a matter of fact, which is the object of sense, though otherwise they may be liable to exception, if such extraordinariness of the *corpora delicti*, clearness of the adminicles, and of the diagnostics of Witches, did not precede them as you have seen proven before you that they do.

The cases are not, whether these witnesses would be habile in an ordinary crime, which commonly falls to be exposed to other witnesses than those concerned in it; but whether they can be received in this extraordinary, occult, and excepted crime of Witchcraft, wherein there are two special cases to be noticed, viz. : sometimes the acts thereof are open and admit the choice of witnesses, such as charms used in the day time, when the actor is visible. But that part of Witchcraft, whereby Witches meet in the night time, adore their lord, contrive their malefices, and accordingly thereafter execute them when other witnesses are asleep, or the Witches themselves are covered from sight, we say this can be no otherwise proven than by these that are intimate to it, joined to the positive proof and adminicles before mentioned.

We do not allege that persons altogether destitute of knowledge and natural conscience are not to be admitted in any case, such as infants, furious, fatuous, &c. Neither do we contend that Thomas Lindsay and Christian Shaw, who are under pupilarity, should be put to an oath; for they are only to be examined separately before the court, upon interrogators, by which it may appear, whether or not they coincede with the four other confessants that are to depone before them; and this is the panels' advantage in case of disagreement. But we insist, that any person above pupilarity, giving evidences of considerable knowledge and natural conscience (which is a sufficient fund for all the credit that we need in this case, that is already almost fully proven) it is to be received as a witness.

As to the second, we shall make this as clear as noon. 1st. From reason and the nature of the thing; 2dly, Our own customs and decisions; and 3dly, The singularity of the circumstantiate case.

As to the first, the going to and coming from meetings, especially on foot; the falling down and worshipping the Devil there, under a corporeal shape (which he had when he tempted our Saviour to do it). The actual murdering of children by a cord and napkin; and the tormenting of others by pins, &c., are plain objects of sense; and therefore the senses are to be believed anent them. For as reason hath things intelligible, and faith things supernatural; so the senses have things corporal for their objects, whereanent they are to be trusted, aye, and while it be proven that the appearance is impossible, or that the witness of it is an impostor. It is a part of the Witches' purchase from the Devil, that they cannot be seen at some occasions; so that the abominations committed then would remain unpunished if such witnesses were not admitted. It cannot be thought that Witches (who of all criminals are the most obstinate to confess) would venture the loss of their own lives by deponing against others, against whom they have no special pique; yea, for whom they have particular affection, as several of the panels are some of the witnesses' relations. Nor has the Devil any peculiar interest to instigate them thereunto; for several of the panels have confessed other execrable crimes; whereby it cannot be supposed that Satan would be divided against himself. God, in his ordinary providence, has taken such care of public judgments that the enemy of justice, his special power ceases thereabout, as appears by the Witches not being able either to do more harm, or escape after God's ministers being to counteract Satan's instruments by imprisonment. And finally, the oddness of the malefices, the concurrence of the adminicles, and the existence of matters of fact wherein these confessants (though not knowing the same otherwise) do agree with other unexceptionable witnesses, &c., do sufficiently abstruct their credibility. For as falsehood being a crime is ever presumed, so a person found true in many things is still presumed to continue such till the contrary be evinced.

As to the second, we have the testimony of our famous K[ing] J[ames], 6th, Demon. lib. 2. C. ult., telling us that it is our law that boys, girls, infamous persons, &c., are not to be rejected any more in Witchcraft than in human lese majesty, even though they assert others to have been present at imaginary meetings; because this supposes their having entered into a precontract. He says that Satan's mark and the want of tears are pregnant aids to the discovery. He gives an instance of a girl who, having named Witches in her fits, they were all condemned upon other concurring adminicles. This not a common author, but a man who as curious, was exact; as prudent, did not publish such things without the approbation of the best divines and lawyers; as a prince, is to be credited anent the law of his own country; and as a king, has determined any dubiety that might have remained in this point as far as the law of our government will permit.

But further, our judges and lawyers have followed his Majesty; for in all the processes in the journals, fame and delation, and the mark, are still sustained as most pregnant presumptions; whereupon, and a very small probation besides, Witches have been frequently condemned. So in the processes against the bewitchers of Sir George Maxwell of Pollok, and Hamilton of Barnes, Anno 1677, *socius criminis*, though under age, is sustained to be a witness; and witnesses are adduced before the inquest for proving that the mark was found upon some of the Witches. Women and minors have been received by multitudes of decisions cited by M'Kenzie, Tit. prob. by witnesses, and Tit. Witchcraft. And he also cites decision, where in parallel cases, *socii criminis*, and others inhabile, were admitted, particularly in treason and in falsehood; and all lawyers conclude that Witchcraft is as much an excepted crime as these.

As to the third, whatever inhability these witnesses might be under, it is fully made up, and they rendered unexceptionably habile by the chain of this whole business. It is true one man, through the concurrence of corrosive humours, may have an insensible mark ; another be enviously defamed; a third may, through sudden grief or melancholy, not be able to weep, &c. ; a fourth may be loaded with suspicious circumstances, when extraordinary things fall out in the country ; a fifth may be deponed against by two false witnesses, though neither of these separately be truly Witches ; but by the known observation and experience of mankind, none except Witches have had the unhappy medley and concourse of all or most of these *indicia*, and ordinarily, and for the greater part, Witches have them ; so that since the rules of judgment are established upon that *quod plerumque sit*, which does obtain till an exception be apparent in a special case, the conjunction of these in one person does as plainly give his character, as the most certain symptoms of the plainest disease being universally concerted in all parts of the world, points out to us that the haver of them is a person truly affected with that disease, whereof he hath the concurrent diagnostics.   In a word, one or other of these may concur in the innocent ; but no writers do attest that all of them have concentred in any other person in the world but a Witch ; and on the other hand, they, taking place in Witches through all parts in the world, must proceed from a common, and not from a peculiar humour or cause.

The specific aptitude of some of the nicest of the *indicia*, which appeared from the probation already led to discover a Witch, do serve to clear the ground of the world's observation anent them.   Particularly the devil as aping God, imprints a sacrament of his covenant ; besides that, commonly this mark being given at the first meeting, does, by its intolerable pain, force the Witch to a second rendezvous for curing it, at which the poor wretch, being under this furious necessity, fixes the paction by renewing it with deliberation, having been diverted in the meantime from considering the horridness of the first engagement by the pain. The inhability to shed tears may be characteristic of hardening, though not always in the case of Christians; yet in those who have ceased to be such, least the Devil giving them such words of Scripture and prayer as many have, it should be impossible to discover their hypocrisy; and that is not Satan's own interest, since by this discovery, occasion is given to buffoon the profession of holiness. A report often arises without ground, but a constant repute that keeps footing, implies for the most part a surer cause, especially when it is of persons below envy, and by persons above calumny. The girl falling in fits at approach of the panels might proceed from antipathy, arising from the poisonous steams of the Witch accustomed to produce that effect through a virtue affixed thereto by the Devil, by conjunction of natural causes (the same way as the invisible pestilence does operate) or his promise of casting the girl in fits at the Witch's presence, might have been general; whereby the Witch was eventually befooled and discovered, as it often falls out : for Satan envies even their temporal felicity, and fears, lest by continuing here, they should be reft out of his hands by conversion, when they come to perceive the delusion of his promises to make them rich, &c.

There was one thing further which was tried before your lordships, viz. :—None of the panels that were tried (though most sagacious and knowing, and perfect in memory, so that it could not proceed from ignorance or forgetfulness) could make out the attempt of saying the Lord's prayer; which may either be a secret judgment for renouncing their first Lord, after whom it is peculiarly denominate, or by restraint of their new lord, who may think that too special an homage to his adversary. But we have hindered you too long with that which is not necessary; for this being incontrovertible law and custom, there needs no philosophy to support it;

since legislators do reason, but subjects must obey : and both the fool and lazy (who have neither read nor thought enough to understand this subject) are to be left to their own chimeras ; yet lest they should insult, we shall answer in their fashion such of the objections as the panels' advocate thought anywise worthy to be repeated in this place.

Whereas it is objected that Delrio, sect. 5. § 4. says, that *socii* are not to be admitted witnesses *ad condemnandum*, especially considering that the probation ought to be *luce meridiana clarior*.

It is answered, that the place itself confutes this inference in the present case ; for it says, *ex his solis non est procedendum ad condemnationem scio contrarium communius teneri & in praxi obtinere, &c.*, so it is evident, 1st, The common opinion and custom is in the contrary, even where there is no other probation, but by the partners of the crime ; yet, 2dly, We are not so straitened, but subsume in his very words, *ex his solu*, we do not desire the panels should be condemned ; but your lordships see these witnesses we are to adduce are not *soli* or alone ; for the probation led these last sixteen hours, are so many concomitants and discoveries of providence, which abstruct and make up any defect in their credit that can be desiderate ; 3dly, Hence the meaning of that maxim (which is metaphorical, as appears by the words *clarior luce meridiana*, an equal clearness being sufficient) is fully answered, and takes place in the present case ; for the extraordinariness of the *corpora delicti*, pregnancy of the adminicles and pointedness of the positive probation, being conjoined, there is not a clearer proof upon record in any nation, than that to which it is hoped these will amount.

Whereas this allegance is enforced, by pretending it were of dangerous consequence to allow such witnesses to prove meeting with the Devil, since Satan might have represented others by their false shapes.

It is answered,—1st. That we are not straitened in this, because there are many other articles proven which could not have been falsified; but if we give some scope to reasoning, even in this point, it is to be considered that the rules of judgment are established upon that which, for the most part, does still obtain,—and rules are to be followed till an exception be proven in a particular circumstantiate case. But so it is by the experience and observation of the wisest divines, lawyers, philosophers, physicians, statesmen, judges, and historians, at home and abroad (that are too wise to be imposed upon, and too ingenuous to deceive us when they all concur in the same matter of fact), besides the testimony of Witches themselves everywhere, make the apparitions of Witches to be commonly and mostly real; and, therefore, the testimony of the senses is always to be credited anent them, aye and while it be canvelled. For single or few instances of false representations to the senses, esteeming them to be true, or a possibility of appearances being false, can nowise invalidate the rule established upon experience, which is common, and, for the most part, whereby no exception is to be presumed till it is proven in a special case; since a wonder does not subvert the proof drawn from a common course of nature; logic admits not to argue a *particulari*, or from possibility to existence; law puts the burden of proving simulation on the affirmer, and that which seldom occurs is not considered by the legislators.

For illustrating of which, it is further to be considered that for the most part and ordinarily, the Witches are personally existant in the places where they appear, because it is more easy for the Prince of the Air to transport them in his hurricanes which he can raise, as is plain in the instance of Job (who was put in his power, *i. e.* his natural power without

w

delegation) forming a fence upon their face, whereby the violence of the air may be diverted from choking them, then to form the curious miniature of such various transactions on their brain : the difficulty whereof is the greater, that all their fancies are not disposed at all times the same way, and they have not the seeds of this work, unless they had once acted it in reality. It is both the greater crime and pleasure to act in truth ; which therefore the Devil and Witches do rather choose (unless the place be far distant, or the party indisposed) and this *de facto* is attested to be so by the writers and Witches in all nations and ages, as said is.

2dly. Notwithstanding that the rule must hold till an exception of exculpation be evinced, *quoad* a particular person, by evidencing that the real appearance was in that special case a true mistake ; yet this exception is sufficient for safety of the misrepresented, since the same providence which permitted the affliction will order the outgate and exculpation, either by the ærial bodies not biding the touch, or some other distinction, as providence commonly allows the Devil to personate only with a cloven foot ; or that the apparition was folly to one single witness who cannot be a proof; or that the innocent can prove *alibi;* or finally, the notour character of a Samuel will purge and dispel the aspersions of Satan, contrived of purpose to discredit the evidence of sense, by which alone his instruments can be discovered. Especially this character being joined to the other circumstances of the providence, such as, when good men are disguised, they are mostly passive in the scene and outwith thereof: whereas Witches are personally active in their common life by such words and deeds as (in conjunction with these appearances) conspire to make us know and distinguish them from the truly good ; since these Witches' open profanity, naughtiness, or unveiled hypocrisy, being cleared by fame, sealed by the mark, and confirmed by the other discoveries of the adminicles that lie proven before you, do still make a land mark betwixt the children of darkness and light. So Delrio, lib. 5. sect. 16. N. 5. tells of Athanasius and St. Germanus, against whom probation was adduced for sorcery, but providence did canvel it. It is a famous instance of Susanna, represented by the elders, which, though not in the case of spectre, yet agrees in the rational. The representation of Pharoah's magicians had concomitants, by which they were discovered and confounded. But lastly, suppose that God, in the depths of his wisdom (to convince the error of nimious self-confidence) should permit all necessary probation to concur against an innocent; yet the judge, following the faith of proofs established by divine and human laws, is altogether innoxious. Since this case being very rare, the evil is less than the establishing a principle, by which most of all these monsters could not be cut off.

Upon the whole, it is certain that as though oft-times false witnesses set on by the Devil have taken away a harmless life, by accusing it of other crimes, yet the testimony of witnesses must still be credited till they be redargued; so these appearances of Witches with the other specialities before expressed, being proven, ought to be esteemed real till the fallacy be established. Especially seeing there are examples in ancient and modern history of Satan's representing the best of men, committing murder, buggery, &c., in effigy, so Delrio, lib. 5. sect. 16. N. 5. relates that St. Silvanus was represented by the Devil, as committing a common capital crime; and the like of a monk; whereof there are several modern parallel instances; yet this cannot enervate the rule and faith of public judicatures, founded on no more but upon the sight of the like appearances; and any argument against the probation in Witchcraft will equally hold against the probation of any other crime whatsomever;

wherefore the rules of them both must be common, as to
believing the senses fortified *ut supra*, till their error be
individually discovered.

Finally, the certainty is noways diminished by the extraordinariness of the appearance to the senses ; for in law and
nature reality, and not simulation, is presumed, till the contrary be made appear that it is actually false.　This is answer
enough to those who place a great part of their small wit in
nonsensical arguing against all divine authority ; but writers
further illustrate that the extraordinariness of a matter of
fact does not exclude its realities being the subject of the
testimony of witnesses in our Saviour's miracles, transfigura-
tion, walking on the waters, standing in the midst of the
disciples while the doors were shut, and arguing assurance
by their senses, that a spirit had not flesh and bones, though
indeed the surer word of prophecy did put these beyond
doubt.

Nor could it be alleged for the panels (though they had
the last word, as perhaps they have not, in objections against
witnesses, since therein *rei fiunt actores* by attacking the
witnesses' presumed hability) that it is not conceiveable, how
the girl or witnesses could see what the by-standers could not
behold ; beside the impossibility of the real bodies entering
at close doors and windows, or not intercepting the sight of
what is at its back.

For this it would be answered,—1st, Proven facts must not
be denied, though philosophers have not yet certainly reached
the invisible manner of their existence ; so in nature the loadstone draws the iron, the compass turns always to the poles,
&c.　In Scripture the angel (and the Devil was once such,
retaining as yet his natural powers) smote the Sodomites, that
they could not see the door, though they saw the house.　.
Balaam's ass perceived the angel that stood undiscovered to

himself; and the rod thrown down by the magicians of Egypt, was no doubt seen by themselves, though invisible to the by-standers, which holding of their eyes, interpreters explain to have been done by natural means; and yet the manner thereof is certainly difficult.

However, it is also certain, that if a possible way can be proposed, the reality of a proved fact is not to be contradicted; and this can be done in the present case.

For, 2dly, Satan's natural knowledge and acquired experience, makes him perfect in the optics and limning; besides that, as a spirit, he excels in strength and agility, whereby he may easily bewitch the eyes of others, to whom he intends that his instruments should not be seen in this manner as was formerly hinted, viz., he constricts the pores of the Witches' vehicle, which intercepts a part of the rays reflecting from her body; he condenses the interjacent air with grosser meteors blown into it, or otherwise does violently agitate it, which drowns another part of the rays; and lastly, he obstructs the optic nerves with humours stirred toward them; all which joined together, may easily intercept the whole rays reflecting from these bodies, so as to make no impression upon the common sense: and yet at the same time, by the refraction of the rays gliding alongst the fitted sides of the volatile couch, wherein Satan transports them, and thereby meeting and coming to the eye, as if there were nothing interjacent, the wall or chair behind the same bodies may be seen; as a piece of money lying out of sight in a cup becomes visible, how soon the medium is altered by pouring in some water on it. Several of your number do know, that the girl declared that she saw and heard the doors and windows open at the Witches' entry, when, no doubt, the Devil had precondensed a soft postage on the eyes and ears of others, to whom that was unperceived.

So Apolonius escaped Domitian's flight, and Giges became invisible by his magical ring. John of Sarisberrie tells us of a Witch that could make anything not to be seen; and Mejerus relates another that had the like power. Some Italian Witches of greater than ordinary wit, confessed to Grilandus the Devil opening doors and windows for them, though the more ignorant, by a fascination, think themselves actors of this; whence it ought not to be doubted by any reasonable man, what in all times and places is so incontestible fact.

Finally, the panels could not insist that these confessants are to depone only on their imagination, which can prove no more against themselves or others than a dream.

For still it is to be minded that there are other proofs to which this is only necessary as a consonant adminicle. But further, *Arg. causa*, it is answered that the allegiance is a mistake, seeing they are plain matters of fact, obvious not only to one, but several of their senses, viz.—some of them went the greatest part of the way to these meetings on foot; they there saw and touched their confederates; they heard their combinations to destroy and torture the infants, girl, and ministers: they returned on foot again, and even when they were carried fore or back, they knew on the next day that it was no dream, the same way as all other mortals discover the difference. But, moreover, this is adminiculate by some real effects of a personal presence, as you have seen in the probation: and yet it is further cleared by the journal of Bargarran's daughter's sufferings, which was attested before the former commissioners, and is notour in the country, particularly the glass of sack and orange pill, the pieces of the clouted sleeves, the words expressed by the keeper on the sudden murder of the child, which are constantly told by some of the confessants; as also the house being meally that night; the girl, though hoodwinked at the time, her falling in fits at their ap-

266

proach, &c., and others which shall be pointed at to the assize, conjoined together, can be ascribed to no other cause than the real existence of the Witches' persons in the place, unless it be said that Satan might possibly have foisted and suborned all these; and thence it be concluded that the Devil did actually so, in which case the objectors are the persons that bottom their opinion on imagination, without any positive ground of the reality of what they fancy; yea, against positive grounds of belief in the contrary, which, arguing from possibility to existence, is already sufficiently exploded.

Whereas for sustaining the objection, it is likewise alleged that the confessants having been in the Devil's service, and renounced Christ, they are not capable of the religion of an oath.

1st, In the rules of charity, &c., the confessants, though once Witches, yet now they, at least the majority of them, have ceased to be such, having had the use of means by the ministers and word, and actually declared their repentance, and the Devil ceasing to molest them ; particularly Elizabeth Anderson was only carried alongst violently by her father, and stood out to the last against her renouncing of her baptism, or consenting to these crimes which were contrived in their meetings. Janet and Margaret Rodgers do testify a great remorse, and avowed the same last Sabbath, in the face of the congregation. So those three are sufficient, whatsoever it might be said against the other two, especially if we join the improbability either of hazarding their own lives, or the Devil's sending them out against the panels, of their destroying their own relations as was remarked before.

But, 2dly, Whether they remain Witches or not, it is certain, by reason and experience, that the Devil's peculiar influence ceaseth in and about judgment by the common course of providence; and, therefore, the authors before cited admit Witches whether penitent or not.

3dly, All the defects of their hability is supplied, and the entireness thereof completed, by their testimonies being so wonderful adminiculate; particularly the confessants are constant from the first discovery; uniform in so various circumstances, not only with themselves, but with the girl; they declare nothing but what is probable, most of the panels have been reputed Witches, all of them having the mark; and one or other of them (to whom the associates delighted in mischief, never missed to join,) having had particular irritation to take revenge by the torture and deaths libelled; besides the other adminicles of guilt already proven before you. The confessants were threatened to retract by the panels themselves and their friends; besides the bad usage from others in the country. They concur with the maleficiat's testimony, and amongst themselves, even when interrogate singly; and upon new things, as several of your number have tried the experiment; the reiteration of the acts which they declare anent some persons whom they never saw except in these congresses; yet whom they know now on the first sight, is unaccountable if they were falsaries. And that they are not such, is further abstructed by some of the panels being delated by a confessing Witch in anno 1687. And you know that others delated by these confessants were lately brought in guilty by the verdict of a former inquest, &c., which are so many joint proofs of these witnesses' integrity, and makes a chain of evidence and moral demonstration, both against error in themselves, and delusion in relation to others, &c.

There were some things objected out of the law of Scotland, of which I shall give you some touch.

Whereas it was alleged, that *irretiti criminibus capitalibus,* and so under the pursuer's power cannot be admitted to be witnesses, conform to a statute in *Regiam Majestatem.*

To this it was answered, that we need not say that these statutes have not the force of law, except in so far as they are received by custom, unless conform thereto. A laik [layman] cannot witness against a clerk, or *e contra*, &c. Nor need we make use of that which is obvious, viz., that these statutes are only common rules in the ordinary crimes, such as Withchcraft, &c. *Nam omnu regula subverti potest*, and particularly this rule, is actually so restricted in the case of Witchcraft, by the opinion of lawyers and customs before-mentioned, which are the best interpreters of laws; for if this application should hold, *socius criminus* could never be admitted; but we positively deny that those confessants are under our power or influence, seeing Elizabeth Anderson is not guilty of Witchcraft for anything that doth appear, the Lindsays were never indicted for it, and the diet was deserted against the Rodgers. As the whole commission is to expire against the first of June, betwixt and which time they are to proceed no further than this particular trial. So that this objection vanishes to smoke.

Whereas it is pretended that the Rogers cannot be received, because not given out in the list of witnesses, conform to the regulations whereby the panels might have proven their objections by their exculpation.

It was answered,—1st, This objection ought to be repelled, because, besides that the act speaks only of criminal libels, and not indictments, which with the list of witnesses, may be given in far shorter time than the additional list has been given to the panels, being prisoners; this act is interpreted by the common custom of the justice court; of giving additional lists after the first, upon shorter time than this has been given; as it is particularly attested by James Gutherie,

x

macer, who has given them, and, who being a person in office, his testimony is to be credited in what relates to his office; so that the old custom, confirmed by a decision, August 3d, 1661, where Alexander Forrester was cited *apud acta* against a Witch, continues *quoad* this point, as is related by M'Kenzie, page 529; but, 2dly, Any objection that the panels pretend against these witnesses, is *in jure*, or may instantly appear; 3dly, the case is altogether extraordinary and circumstantiate, for the witnesses had not confessed, and so were not existent under that redublication when the principal list was given out, whereby the Act of Parliament can only be understood of witnesses that were then existent; and finally, the panels got a general warrant of exculpation for citing of any witnesses they pleased, and they have had several days since they got this additional list, so that they might have cited witnesses to prove their objections, were it not, the truth is, they have none besides these that are common and before answered.

Thus I have given you hints that your own reasoning (which I know to be refined) may improve and apply, so as to dissolve the quibbles which the petty wits, who have not soul enough to penetrate into the true light of what is recondite, may raise against it; it being their common talent either to skip over the surface of mines, or otherwise to tear asunder some apurtenances of a scheme, and then presently pronounce it mortally maimed.

I must confess that none could be more sceptical anent the truth of such odd things as I have heard, nor inquisitive for canvasing the reality and explications of them, than I was before my attendances on Bargarran's house, and the several diets of court, and my conversation with some of those concerned thereanent. But now, after all I have seen, reasoned, and heard, I do acknowledge myself entirely captivate by the dictates of natural understanding and common sense, into a sound mind and persuasion that, as there is such a thing as Witchcraft, so it was eminent in its forementioned effect; and the seven panels were some of the Witches.

I have troubled you little with my proper observations; yet lest you should think me either too lazy or peevish, I shall make one, and it is, that I do not think the greater part of the condemned prisoners will ever fully confess; of which conjecture I have two chief grounds, viz.,—that they are neither ignorant nor melancholic; but on the contrary, some of them would seem to have been once enlightened before they fell away; so that, if this be a sin unto death, there is no appearance that they will glorify God by acknowledgement.

Several of them are of singular knowledge and acuteness beyond the common level of their station; particularly, Margaret Lang did make harangues in her own defence, which neither divine nor lawyer could reasonably mend; yet I thought that when they spoke in a matter of any concern, their eyes stood squint and fixed, as if they had been turning their ears and attentive to a dictator. Their answers to the trying interrogatories put to them, were surprisingly subtile and cautious; though, indeed, by the industry of some of the Judges and lawyers, they were at occasions involved in lies, prevarications, and contradictions, which might have proceeded either from natural or preternatural causes. Some of them were esteemed in the country very sagacious and exact in their business,—Margaret Lang having been a midwife, and one of the Lindsays having acquired a considerable fortune by his tillage and trade; yet it was noticed, something odd either of iniquity or affectation; and Lindsay did finely get off from the sheriff when he was formerly accused in 1687.

Melancholians are lovers of solitude; Witches of society

and feasts; those are commonly pale and heavy; many of these corpulent and voluptuous. Witches are hard to confess as knowing their guilt; melancholians delight to discover their horridest damps, because they think them no crime;— the one's confessions everywhere are uniform, the others' phantasms are as various as their humours. Finally, Witches teach their trade; whereas conceits would die with them, and could be no more conveyed than the humour which is the specific cause thereof. As these distinguishing characters do hold in general, so it is already manifest, that the real effects in several passages of Bargarran's daughter, were not possibly producible by any imagination or humour; and it is special in this case, that neither the panels nor confessants were distempered by being kept from sleep, tortured, or the like, which were too usual in former times; but all the measures were strictly observed that are the requisites of a truly impartial judgment.

Indeed, not to have sent unto you the doubles of the depositions themselves; because it is not denied that the depositions are such as they are represented in the pleadings; the chief question being anent the hability of the last deponents. Neither was you to expect the defenders' part of the debate, separately by itself, in respect that what was dispersed here and there for them, is faithfully repeated and implied in what you have, as to those points which I thought worthy the notice.

Upon the whole, I do believe that there is scarcely a more rare providence of this nature in any true history,—a more exact caution in any enquiry or trial of this kind,—a more clear probation without confession of the panels themselves,—or a more just sentence, putting together all circumstances upon record.

APPENDIX No. C.

An Account of the Confession and Death of JOHN REID, *Smith
in Inchinnan, who made a discovery conform to the former
witnesses after the trial was over.*

Upon the 21st of May, 1697, after the trial of the seven
Witches, there is an attestation subscribed by Mr. Patrick
Simpson, Minister at Renfrew, Walter Scott, Bailie there,
&c., of this import:—John Reid, Smith in Inchinnan, prisoner,
did, in the presence of the said persons and some others,
declare that about a year ago the Devil (whom he knew to
be such thereafter) appeared to him when he was travelling
in the night-time, but spoke none to him at the first encounter. At the second appearance, he gave him a bite or a nip
in his loin, which he found painful for a fortnight. That the
third time he appeared to him as a black man, &c., desired him to engage in his service, upon assurance of
getting gear and comfort in the world, since he should
not want anything that he would ask in the Devil's name ;
and then he renounced his baptism, putting the one hand
to the crown of his head, and the other to the sole of his
foot, thereby giving himself up to Satan's service ; after which
the pain of the bite or nip ceased. He told that hitherto
there were no others present ; but thereafter he was at several
meetings, particularly that in Bargarran's yard, about the time
when there was a fast for Christian Shaw, where the Devil
appeared in the same kind of garb as he first appeared to him,
and they consulted Christian's death, either by worrying or
drowning her in the well ; and the Devil said he should
warrant them that they should neither be heard, seen, nor
confess ; to which end he gave every one of them a bit of
flesh, that the declarant got, but let it fall and did not eat

it. Thereafter, in the presence of the Laird of Jordanhill, the Minister, Mr. Andrew Cochran, Town Clerk, and Bailie Paterson, he owned his former confessions; and being enquired of Jordanhill how they were advertised of their meetings, he said that ordinarily at their meetings the time of the next was appointed; but for particular warning there appeared a black dog with a chain about his neck, who, tinkling it, they were to follow, &c. And being enquired by the minister, if he did now wholly renounce the Devil (for he had formerly told how Satan had not performed his promise) and give himself to Jesus Christ, and desire to find mercy of God through him, he assented thereunto. It is to be observed that John Reid, after his confession, had called out of the prison window, desiring Bailie Scott to keep that old body Angus Forrester, who had been his fellow prisoner, close and secure; whereupon the company asked John when they were leaving him, on Friday's night the 21st of May, whether he desired company or would be afraid alone; he said he had no fear of any thing. So being left till Saturday's forenoon, he was found in this posture, viz. :—Sitting upon a stool, which was on the hearth of the chimney, with his feet on the floor and his body straight upward, his shoulders touching the lintel of the chimney, but his neck tied with his own neckcloth (whereof the knot was behind) to a small stick thrust into a clift above the lintel of the chimney; upon which the company, especially John Campbell, a surgeon who was called, thought at first in respect of his being in an ordinary posture of sitting, and the neckcloth not having any run loup, but an ordinary knot, which was not very straight, and the stick not having the strength to bear the weight of his body or the struggle, that he had not been quite dead; but finding it otherwise, and that he was in such a situation that he could not have been

274

the actor thereof himself, concluded that some extraordinary cause had done it, especially considering that the door of the room was secured, and that there was a board set over the window, which was not there the night before when they left him.

APPENDIX No. D.

I am much obliged to John Stewart, near Neilston, for favouring me with the curious old manuscript volume, from which the following Sermon is extracted. I understand that this curious old manuscript volume came into Mr. Stewart's possession from his forefather's. This book was originally the property of A. Mathie, who, probably, was a Student in the University of Glasgow between the years 1707 and 1709, for these dates are written on it.

In this Sermon, besides such ancient orthography, as, *ane* for *an* and *one*, *doe* for *do*, *hes* for *has*, *hiest* for *highest*, &c., a great number of contractions also occur, as, *J*. X for *Jesus Christ*, *qch.* and *wc*, for *which*, *qm.* for *whom*, *qn.* for *when*, *qo.* for *who*, *qr.* for *where*, *wt.* for *with*, *ye.* for *the*, *ym.* for *them*, *yn.* for *then* and *than*, *yr.* for *their* and *there*, *ys.* for *this*, *yse.* for *these*, and *yt.* for *that*.

A SERMON,

Preached by Mr. David Brown,* at Paisley, on Wednesday the 9th of June 1697 years, being the day before the execution of several persons condemned for witchcraft.

1. Timothy i. Chap. 16. v.—"Howbeit, for this cause I obtained mercy, that in me first Jesus Christ might shew forth all long suffering, for a pattern to them that should hereafter believe in him to life everlasting."

MAN by nature, since the fall, is a guilty creature, and being guilty is ready to be jealous of God, as if all his designs were designs of wrath against him; yea, oftentimes so suspicious is man of God, that he is jealous of the hardness of his design in that which is one of the greatest instances of his love in the world, and that is in sending his Son Jesus Christ into the world to save sinners. To obviate this, the Apostle tells us, John iii. 17., *God sent not his Son to condemn the world, but that the world might be saved through him.* Even Luther himself, as is reported of him, was so suspicious of God this way, mistaking that place of Scripture, Rom. iii. 25, 26., *Whom God hath set forth to be a propitiation, and through faith in his blood to declare his righteousness,* he understood it as if the words, *to declare his righteousness,* had been that God sent forth his Son to the world, to set forth his judgments upon the world. I say, sometimes man comes so great a length in this, that he thinks it impossible God can find in his heart to forgive, and therefore the Apostle shews, in

---

* It is probable that this Minister was the David Brown who was Minister of Neilston between 1689 and 1693, and was afterwards translated to another Parish, and who was an elder brother of Thomas Brown, Mr. Blackwell's colleague at Paisley.

opposition to this, that Christ had put him in the ministry, in the 12th verse, and that, notwithstanding of the bad life he had lived before his conversion, in the 13th verse, *and that the grace of our Lord was exceeding abundant*, in the 14th verse, which was the matter of his joy and rejoicing, 15th verse. And here he gives account why God was pleased to call and justify him, and that is, that he might set him forth as an instance of the glory of God, and be an encouragement to others, who were great sinners, to believe in Christ to life everlasting.

In the words ye have two things considerable. (1.) The great mercy conferred upon this Apostle Paul, in this expression, *Howbeit, I obtained mercy;* and no doubt he speaks here of pardoning mercy; for mercy supposes misery on the sinner's part, and free favour on God's part, and here it supposes sense of the one and the other too in Paul's case.

(2.) Ye have the reason of this dispensation of mercy in these words, *that in me first Jesus Christ might shew forth all long-suffering, for a pattern to them that should hereafter believe on Him to life everlasting;* in which ye have three things. First, the author of this pardoning mercy, *Jesus Christ.* Second, the end for which he obtained mercy, and that is, *that in me he might shew forth all long suffering for a pattern.* Third, the end for whom, and that is, *for a pattern to them that should hereafter believe on him to life everlasting.*

I return to the first of these. The author of this pardoning mercy *Jesus Christ.* Ye know Jesus Christ is not only the meritorious cause of pardoning mercy, but the author also of eternal salvation to as many as believe on Him. John xvii 2., *that he should give everlasting life,* by his death, *to as many as thou has given him:* so that he hath promised everlasting life by his death; yet he hath also power to give everlasting life, and to forgive sin.

Y

Again, secondly, ye have the end for which he obtained mercy; *that in me first he might shew forth all long-suffering for a pattern*, where ye have three things. 1. That he might shew forth all long-suffering. 2. That he might shew it forth for a pattern. 3. That he might shew it forth in me first. First, That he might shew forth all long suffering, ye have three things. 1. That he might shew forth, that is, that he might make manifest. There are some sovereign steps of his grace and mercy hid, and out of the common observation of men, and therefore he says that he might shew forth all long-suffering. 2. That he might shew forth long-suffering, that is, that he might shew forth patience to me that had sinned so long. 3. That he might shew forth all long suffering, that is, that he might shew forth patience to me, in a great and eminent degree; a patience becoming, and like unto God.

2. Ye have in this part of the verse, "That he might shew it forth for a pattern," that is, for a copy, that others might take me for an example of God's patience,—that they might take me for a copy to encourage them that will believe on Christ to life everlasting.

Again, that in me first, that is, in me the chief of sinners, as in the 13th verse; or me, that is among the first rank of sinners; or, in me first, that is, that having put me into the ministry, he might make of me a special instance of grace, who was a gross sinner; therefore he pitched on such an one as me to send among the Gentiles who were gross sinners.

Again, ye have the end for whom the Apostle was made an instance of grace, and that is, *for them that should hereafter believe on Christ to life everlasting;* where ye have something implied, and something expressed. That which is implied is in these two things. 1. That there are some who shall believe, that do not yet believe on Christ Jesus. 2. That everlasting life is attainable by them that believe on him. That which is expressed is, that the reason of making him an instance of grace, was to be a pattern for the encouragement of great sinners to believe on Christ Jesus to life everlasting.

The observation I make on the verse, That God is pleased to give some rare instances of his mercy, for the encouragement of the worst of sinners to believe on Christ Jesus to obtain life everlasting. This ye see exhausts the substance of this verse, that the Lord is pleased to give some rare instances of his grace and superabundant mercy for the encouragement of the worst of sinners to believe in Christ Jesus to obtain life everlasting. In clearing of this doctrine, I would, 1. Give you some instances of the great riches of his grace. 2. What way these instances of grace may have influence upon the greatest of sinners to believe on Jesus Christ to life everlasting. 3. I would shew you why God is pleased to give such instances of grace for the encouragement of the greatest of sinners to believe on Jesus Christ to life everlasting. 4. I would shew you what it is to believe on Christ Jesus, which these instances of grace calls sinners to do in order to obtain life everlasting. 5. What everlasting life is, which is the consequent of believing on Jesus Christ.

Now for the first of these. To shew you some instances of the great riches of his grace, I shall begin with the same Apostle, and lead you to one place where he gives a full accompt of himself, Acts xxvi. 10, 11, in which ye have seven or eight sad aggravations of his own case. There he tells you, that he gave his voice against them that were put to death; that he compelled the saints to blaspheme; that he persecuted them to strange cities; and that he had authority from the high priest against them; and that he persecuted them in a constant track, and yet he obtained mercy, because he did it ignorantly; but all that this will say is, that therefore his sin was pardonable, because he had not sinned wilfully against the knowledge of the truth ; but certainly this made him a great instance of the grace of God, that yet he obtained mercy.

2. Another instance you have in Acts xix. 18, 19. Ye see there, that many of them that believed came and confessed their deeds, and many of these were such as used curious arts,—devilish magical arts,—and yet the grace of God brake in upon them. There is a great instance of the grace of God.

3. Another instance you have in Luke vii. 37, where you see a woman who was a sinner comes to Christ. Now a sinner in the New Testament sense is a grievous sinner, a vile strumpet and whore, and yet Christ himself tells us, *her sins which are many are forgiven her.* Because she loved much, The Lord forgave her.

4. Ye have the instance of Manasseh, which is very suitable to the case of these I am now speaking to.* 2. Chren. xxxiii. 2., where ye find he did evil in the sight of the Lord, like the abominations of the heathen, whom the Lord cast out before the children of Israel. Ye will find he built high places, made groves, and set up altars in the house of the Lord, and caused his children to pass through the fire to Moloch, and used inchantments, and consulted with them that had familiar spirits ; and yet behold an instance of the sovereign grace of God,—that he yet made Israel to sin above the abomination of the heathen, that he greatly humbled himself, and the Lord pardoned him, and was intreated of him. Here is a great instance of the grace of God, which is a great encouragement for all such sinners to close with Christ in order to life everlasting. I might give you more

---

* It is evident from this, and other places of this Sermon, that the seven persons condemned for witchcraft, were present during Mr. Brown's discourse.

instances,—as the instance of the prodigal, and these, 1 Corinth. vi. 10, where the Apostle, speaking of these that shall not inherit the kingdom of God, Idolators, Fornicators, Adulterers, Drunkards, &c. says he, " and such were some of you, but ye are washed, but ye are sanctified, but ye are justified in the name of the Lord Jesus." One instance more, Acts ii. 36, 37, the Apostle Peter says, *He whom ye crucified is both Lord and Christ;* as if he had said, ye are the folks that have crucified the Son of God, and yet there came a work of grace on their hearts, that made them cry out, *Men and brethren, what shall we do to be saved?* If ever Christ would have stood upon it and not forgiven, it would have been such as were guilty of such an atrocious crime; and yet behold the riches of the grace of God, in that they obtained mercy. Certainly this is a great instance now, I tell you; the Lord hath set up such instances for the encouragement of the worst of sinners to believe on Christ to life everlasting.

In the second place, I come to shew you what way these instances of grace ought to have influence upon great sinners, to encourage them to believe on Christ to life everlasting.

And first, from these instances ye may draw this conclusion, that sure it is not from any inherent worth that God pardons, which may have influence on you to believe. If it had been intrinsic worth, would he ever have forgiven them that crucified him? would he ever have forgiven Paul or Manasseh? What excellency or worth was in them? Should we not therefore reason thus with ourselves, " Thou that forgives, because thou will forgive, wilt thou not have pity upon us?"

Second, ye may from these instances draw this conclusion, that he hath no reason out of himself to forgive, and this is a great foundation to close with Christ; there is no worth in us, therefore all the goodness must be in himself. He hath mercy, because he will have mercy ; he sheweth compassion, because he will shew compassion ; and if it had not been something in his own bosom, none had ever obtained mercy.

A third conclusion is, that sure there is not ground to think that God cannot find in his heart to forgive.   For Christ says, Mat. xii. 31, *All manner of sin and blasphemy shall be forgiven to you.* No sin is unpardonable except the sin against the Holy Ghost.   I cannot determine whether any of you be guilty of the sin against the Holy Ghost, but except it be that, all manner of sin may be forgiven, and this may have influence on us to make us haste unto Jesus Christ.

A fourth conclusion is, that the Lord here acts as God,—he acts like himself.   When ye read such instances of grace as I have been naming to you, you may draw this conclusion, that he acts like himself.   Isaiah xliii. 24.—*Thou hast bought me no sweet cane with money, neither hast thou filled me with the fat of thy sacrifices ; but thou hast made me to serve with thy sins, thou hast wearied me with thine iniquities. I, even I, am he that blotteth out thy transgressions for my own sake, and will not remember thy sins.*   I am, says he, like myself ; I am he, and as he says elsewhere, beside me there is none.   So much for the second thing.

In the third place, I shall show you why the Lord is pleased to give such instances of grace for the encouragement of the greatest of sinners to believe in Christ to life everlasting. And the first reason is, because greater sinners have often-times a secret despair, and Satan is ready to suggest that prayers, exhortations, and means are needless, and that now their case is past cure and remedy, and this is ready to occasion either desperation or obduration, that they think God cannot find in his heart to forgive them.

Second, because though there be not a secret despair, yet

282

at least there is some extraordinary jealousy, and kind of suspicion, and likening God to themselves; thinking they could never forgive others, if others had done to them what they have done to God, and that therefore God will not forgive them. But let such consider, John vi. 37, *He that cometh to me I will in nowise cast out;* and this is very significant with respect to the doubt of poor sinners; and the doubt lies here, if I would come he would shut the door upon me. No, says he, *him that cometh I will in nowise cast out:* that is, I will receive him, I will open the door and let him in and make him welcome.

Third, the Lord gives such instances of his grace for the encouragement of great sinners to believe on Christ to life everlasting, because that oftentimes when sense of sin and fear of wrath lights upon the conscience, and when there is a sight of the holiness and justice of God, they are extraordinarily damped; and this doth so seize upon them that it renders them incapable for any duty, and therefore the Lord has set out such instances of his grace: and the Apostle Paul says expressly, God hath set me up as a pattern to them that should hereafter believe on Christ to life everlasting. God hath set me up as a monument of grace, that to whomsoever the sound of this gospel comes, after me never one needs to despair, for God hath shewed mercy to me, and has set me up as a beacon of mercy, that never one needs question God's good will to pardon them after myself.

In the fourth place, I come to shew you what this believing in Christ is, which these instances of grace do encourage great sinners to; and there are four things in this believing,—1. Knowledge; 2. Assent to the truth of the gospel; 3. Consent to take Christ Jesus, and, 4. Recumbency and resting upon him.

1. I say knowledge. And though knowledge be true, yet

it may be without faith; but there can be no faith without
knowledge, and sometimes faith is expressed by knowledge.
John xvii.—3. *It is life eternal to know thee, the only true God
and Jesus Christ whom thou hast sent.* This believing
supposes the knowledge of a man's self, the knowledge of his
sin, the knowledge of Jesus Christ in his natures and offices.
Take heed to this, for I tell you what it supposeth, that ye
may not think it the easiest thing in the world to believe.
For the Apostle tells us that no less is requisite to it than the
mighty power that raised Christ from the dead. The sinner
must know the abominableness of his own heart, know his lost
state and condition, know how matters stand betwixt God and
him, he must know these peculiar evils to which he is subject,
he must know Christ Jesus in his fulness—in his willingness to
save sinners, he must know him in what he hath done for
sinners, he must know him in his excellency, in his answer-
ableness to him, and all the wants he can be trysted with.

2. Again, in this faith there is an assent to the truths of the
gospel, and neither is this saving; for there may be an assent
where there is not grace. *The Devils*, it is said, *believe and
tremble*, and this is a great evidence of many folks' stupidity
then, that they have less faith than the devils themselves have;
but there must be an assent to the truths of the gospel, because
of the authority of God interposed. Thus a man must believe
the Bible and the records God hath given of his Son, and that
these things that he presses are absolutely necessary in point
of obedience.

3. Again, there is a consent, and this is the heart of this
faith. A man must be content to take Jesus Christ. Isaiah
xliv. 5.—*One shall say, I am the Lord's, and another shall
subscribe with his hand to the Lord, and surname himself by the
name of Israel.* And in that consent, there is this, to take
him for our portion, that we shall not place our happiness in

the world, that Christ shall get our hearts, that we shall take his law for our rule, and consent to the strictness of holiness, and that he shall rule our life and conversation. In a word, to take Christ for all, and to take all for Christ, and to take him for ever ; and to make an everlasting covenant with him never to be forgotten. This is, indeed, the nature of faith, and ye that have given your consent to be the Devil's, must be no more his, but consent to be Christ's.

4. In this believing, there is also a recumbency and resting upon him. The man, when he hath declared his consent to take Christ, when he hath considered the offers of the gospel, he is content with the whole device, and rests there, and there he casts all his burden ; now he answers all his challenges in Jesus Christ, now he flies from his own righteousness, and rests in the righteousness of Christ by faith ; he renounceth his own righteousness, and therefore the Psalmist says, *Enter not into judgment with thy servant, for in thy sight no flesh can be justified.* Thus, I have told you what this believing takes in, the consequent of which is life everlasting. I might consider it as opposed to eternal death, and as it includes the highest happiness, and the eternity of it. Everlasting life is a freedom from the wrath to come. Ye will never be able to dwell with everlasting fire and devouring burnings ; and seeing ye may have Christ and His fulness, will ye, to please the Devil, forego your inheritance. What will you be able to say, when you are brought before the tribunal, ere the general judgment come, if you refuse to take Christ for your pattern, and believe on him to life everlasting.

But I come to one use of this doctrine. If it be so that the Lord hath been pleased to give such instances of grace, for the encouragement of the worst of sinners to close with Christ, in order to life everlasting, then you may see that instances of grace are not given you to encourage you in sin ; it is that it

z

may be a pattern to them that believe. The reason is not that ye should continue hard and secure, and delay your confession, but that you may believe; for I assure you, the riches of the grace of God has no tendency at all to make folk secure, if you consider these three things :—1. That it is the sweetest cord in the world to draw folk from sin. Some have such undaunted spirits, that nothing but the greatest revelation of wrath can have influence upon them ; but if there be any true generosity in a soul, there is no greater encouragement to close with Christ than the riches of His grace and mercy. 2. If anything be able to break a rocky heart, it is the riches of His grace ; and when I come to tell you before you go to eternity, of the riches of His grace, will ye remain so hard that your hearts cannot be broken so far as to come to Jesus Christ for life everlasting. 3. If ye consider that we offer Christ and salvation upon honourable terms. Christ is as a noble prince, that such as are content to subject themselves to Him, He is willing to save them. The lion of the tribe of Judah is willing to make peace, but He will make peace upon honourable terms. You must forsake sin and Satan, and have no correspondence with them, and we can offer you Christ upon no other terms than these, that you lay down the weapons of rebellion against Jesus Christ indeed.

A second use of this doctrine. Is it so, indeed, that the Lord hath been pleased to give such instances of His grace for encouragement of the worst of sinners to believe on Christ to life everlasting? Then how sad must their case be that cannot be brought to Christ ; and I am come to tell you this day that the offers of the grace of God will be amongst the heaviest of their aggravations at that day. I shall first let you see what great sinners you are, that you may see your need of closing with Christ to obtain life everlasting ;

2. let you see your dangerous condition if you believe not on Christ to life everlasting.

And first, to let you see something of the greatness of your sin. And now consider I am speaking to you that are under the sentence of death for the sin of Witchcraft, and not in suspense as if you were not guilty ; for since ye are found guilty by sound evidence, we do not question it to let you see then the great evil of Witchcraft, that ye may see the great need ye have to believe or close with Christ to life everlasting. 2. It is the highest act of rebellion against the God of heaven and earth, you have drawn up with God's greatest enemy, who is the head of the rebellion of the whole world, and therefore called rebellion. *Rebellion is as the sin of Witchcraft.* Besides, it is a great apostacy from God. Ye were given away to God in baptism, and possibly some of you have given away yourself to Him, and now you declare you rue it, and all the deed of gift in baptism you declare you rue it ; and, besides, your sin hath in it an eminent trampling under foot the blood of Christ, *and if he that sinned under Moses' law died without mercy, of how much sorer punishment must he be worthy that hath trampled under foot the blood of the covenant.* You have sinned under the gospel many a day ; you have sitten in the house of God and put on a mask of religion, and have been deep dissemblers with God and man. And is not this an eminently grevious trampling under foot the blood of the covenant. Again, in your sin there is a renouncing of Christ, heaven, and glory. And you have declared by your practice, and keeping company with the Devil, and being his servants, that you care not for Christ, heaven, or glory. There is your sin ! and have ye not need to close with Christ in order to life everlasting. Again, you have waged war against Christ, against the saints, and against the world, and stated yourselves enemies to

287

Christ, heaven and the world ; for where you had access, you have wrought mischief upon children, ministers, and others,* so that ye may be looked upon as enemies to the whole creation except the Devil, with whom ye have associated yourselves; and now, by your obstinacy, you declare you are content to dwell with the Devil and everlasting burnings ; and since you are in the Devil's service, what can ye expect but the Devil's reward, as long as your hearts are hardened from God's fear.

Second, I come to let you see your danger. Will it not be sad that your heart should be hardened now when ye are come to your extremity, and when it might be expected that messengers of grace should be acceptable to you. We are come to you, when ye are within a few hours of eternity, to intreat you, before ye perish for ever, to embrace the offers of Christ. For, first, ye go aback from the remedy if ye close not with Christ; for though now conscience be secure, yet it will rise like a roaring lion at the last ; and though ministers would weep over you, as if we were seeking from you some great thing for ourselves, yet ye will stand it out. What will conscience say when the Devil will be at the gallows † foot ready to harle you down to hell ? and no sooner in hell, but conscience will say, when God sent his ministers to you, ye believed the Devil and would not yield to Jesus Christ ; and what will ye say to conscience then ? When conscience will say, Now, this is your lodging for ever ; now, eternity ! eternity ! what will ye do through eternity ?—ye are laying a foundation of challenges through eternity. Another thing that makes your case dangerous, ye declare you will not be in Christ's reverence for mercy. I will tell how so, if you will be

---

* *Vide* Narrative, Confessions, &c.

† This shows that the witches were first hanged and then burned.

in His reverence, why will ye not confess your sin, and renounce the deed of gift to the Devil? Ye declared your denial in the face of courts, and frequently since ye have done. O how dreadful will your condition be if you die in such a case!

I come to the third use of this doctrine. If it be so that the Lord is pleased to give such instances of his grace, then the exhortation runs, that ye should come this day and embrace Jesus Christ. As long as ye are impenitent I can but threaten heavy judgments to you, but if you will confess and repent, and come unto Christ, I come to you with the best news ever were heard. The Apostle Paul, 1 Tim. i. 15, was much taken with these news, " *This is a faithful saying, and worthy of all acceptation*," says he, " *that Jesus Christ came to save sinners.*" This should be the best news to you. The offer of Christ is come to you this day before the execution. And I will tell you two or three things to confirm you that there is mercy for you if ye improve it aright.

First, God hath proclaimed His name to be merciful and gracious, if you will come to Christ, ye will find that He is merciful. Again, Christ was called a friend of publicans and sinners, when He was in the world, because He showed mercy to all, and never put away any that came to Him; and though He be now in heaven, yet He retains His bowels of mercy still. Again, His name is *Saviour*, and He left His Father's glory and came to the world in the likeness of sinful flesh, to save sinners. Sure then, if He had done great things, He will not refuse any thing to those that come to Him. Again, to let you see He is merciful, He commands His disciples to preach remission of sins in His name, beginning at Jerusalem, the very place where He was crucified; and further, the last words He said, are, " He that believeth shall be saved;" so that ye see there is mercy for you, if ye believe to life everlasting.

I would speak to two things here; 1. Offer you some

motives to close with Christ. 2. Give you some directions.
And, I. For the motives to close with Christ. There are two
notions of faith suitable to your case, the first is a flying to the
city of refuge ; and there are two things suitable for you. 1.
You are guilty of blood, you have murdered your own souls
and others, therefore run to the city of refuge. 2. You have
little time, your time is nigh a close, your glass is nigh run,
therefore make haste unto Jesus Christ; it is a pity you should
put it off to the last. If ye had confessed in time ye might
have had the prayers of many of the godly. II. Another
notion of faith suitable to you is coming to the market of grace
and buying. " *Ho ! every one that thirsteth, come ye to the waters
and buy.*" Now this is suitable to you, for it is said buy without
money, but ye have spent your money for that which is not
bread, Isaiah lv. 2. " *Wherefore do ye spend money for that
which is not bread, and your labour for that which satisfieth not.*"
What fruit have ye now of those things whereof ye may be
ashamed. How aged are some of you, and now what comfort
have ye in the meetings ye had with Satan, or in your corres-
pondings and actings with him. When ye go to eternity you
will say, alas ! what satisfaction have I now in Satan's service !
Another part of this notion is coming, and that supposeth a
term from which, and a term to which ye come : Away then
with sin and Satan, and come to Christ and remember Him.

A second thing is, to show ye the necessity ye have of
closing with Christ. It is most necessary for you to embrace
the Son of God, or ye are undone. It is most necessary for
you, for you will never be able to endure the wrath of God.
Who can dwell with devouring fire ? O sins ! can ye hold out
against the Almighty? Are ye resolved to fight it with the
Lord? Can ye be able to encounter with the wrath of God,
and enter into the sea of wrath? Can ye endure the wrath of
God world without end? O ! therefore, come and close with

Christ. Observe the providence of God that has brought to your hand a discovery of your case, and in telling you ye are in the snare of the Devil, and that hath trysted you with a discovery of the remedy, and now ye are inexcusable; and if ye perish, ye perish justly. I come now to the directions, and intreat you to look upon them as the last directions ye will have in public in this world for anything we know.

What would ye have us to do? I say that ye ought to confess your sin. Acts xix. 18,—Many of them that had used magical art came and confessed their deeds. It is impossible ye can give a convincing evidence of your repentance, if ye do not confess. But say ye, What need we confess our deeds to men, if we repent between God and us? What needs us trouble the world with confession? we will but lose our name and put a stain upon our posterity and friends. But I answer, when folk have stumbled the Church of God, they have confessed their deeds; even David himself confessed his sins. Again, it is all the folly in the world not to confess your deeds, because they will be brought out before angels and men; and even in point of policy ye ought to confess your deeds, for ye are captives in Satan's snare, and ye have lost your wills. Ye should confess, therefore, that God's people may pray for you. If ye would be out of the claws of the Devil, it will take all the prayers you can get.

The second direction is,—To be deeply humbled for your sin. Ye remember what is said of Manasseh, 2 Chron. xxxiii. Chap.,—Manasseh humbled himself greatly. And though your heart were like to break, and your sorrow like to bring you to the grave, it were little wonder; great sin must have great humiliation: and sure if ever God grant you repentance unto life, and show you mercy, there must be deep humiliation with you.

The third direction is,—You must have more than ordinary

prayer, ye must have more frequent and fervent prayer, ye must be more importunate with God; and if ye ask, what should we pray for? I answer, a discovery of the sinfulness of this sin of Witchcraft. For if ye saw it, it would be in hazard to distract you. Pray for brokenness of heart, and that these hard and rocky hearts of yours may be made hearts of flesh. Pray for pardon of sin. *Blessed is the man that hath his iniquities pardoned and his sins forgiven.* Woe to you! if ye get not your sin pardoned. Pray for a sight of your lost estate, that ye may see yourselves under the sentence of the wrath of God, as well as under the sentence of men. Pray for a discovery of Jesus Christ in His fulness, in His suitableness to you, in His offices, and in His glory; that ye may think shame that ever you thought so little of Him. Pray that ye may not go to the grave with a lie in your right hand. Be importunate, then, since your work is so great, the time so short, and eternity so long: be not asleep or unconcerned, for if ye would put off never so confidently, you will have the colour of hell upon you in that day when ye appear before the tribunal of Christ.

The fourth direction is this,—Renounce your deed of gift to the Devil, and if ye should satisfy the people of God, give a declaration that you are grieved for giving yourself to Satan, and give away yourself to the Son of God from head to foot. This is certainly most suitable for you.

But further, another direction is,—That though ye do renounce your deed of gift to the Devil, and give yourself to Christ, yet do not give yourself to Him only in a formal manner, saying,—I give myself to Jesus Christ; but try the sincerity of your hearts in it, and consider ye must have indignation at yourself for your sin as long as ye live. 2 Cor. ii. 11.,—*Lest Satan should get an advantage of us: for we are not ignorant of his devices.* There will be such indignation in your bosom, if ye be sincere, that ye will be in danger to take amends of yourselves. Ye will wonder that ye are not sent down to the pit ere now. There will be an uncouth fight between hope and fear in your bosoms.

One word further, and that is,—Delay no longer. Ye have put it off before and since the sentence ; ye have been much dealt with, and now it comes within a day of your stepping into eternity, and we are come to you the day before your death entreating you to put it off no longer. O be serious ! God hath exercised a great deal of longsuffering towards you, and ye have hardened your hearts ; and now we are come to you in your adversity, at last to desire you to take Jesus Christ, and now we take God to record that we have offered you Jesus Christ, and if ye will not take him we are free of your blood, and Jesus Christ is free of your blood ; and if ye should endure a thousand hells, ye yourselves are only to be blamed for the slighting the great salvation.

The End of the Sermon.

APPENDIX No. E.

Some passages which fell out before and at the execution of the seven persons who were condemned and burned for Witchcraft on the Gallowgreen of Paisley.

First printed at Edinburgh in the year 1698.

There shall be little added anent what passed at the execution of the seven witches (on Thursday, the 10th of June, 1697 *), because there is no subscribed attestation thereanent ; and the design of the publishers has been to advance

---

* *Vide* Semple's " History of Renfrewshire," and Mr. David Brown's Sermon, Appendix No. D.

A 2

nothing but what stands warranted by testimonies of known credit beyond contradiction. Yet this much is notour, that when they were going to the stake one of the Lindsays was overheard to say to the other, "Now, brother, it is time that we confess since our keeping it up will serve us no purpose," or the like expression; to which the other answered, "that they should never do that," &c. And Margaret Lang, before and about execution, let drop at minutes of the Devil's inadvertence—That when the Devil first appeared she knew him not to be such till afterwards; that he gave her the insensible marks found on her body; she yielded to engage herself in his service by a covenant; and besides public meetings, she had been about eighty times in private conferences with him. Being enquired by a near relation of her own anent her being in Bargarran's house tormenting Christian Shaw, she answered in these words, "The Devil having an absolute power and dominion over me, carried my shape whither he would;" and it is known how she confessed unnatural lust and profound hypocrisy, &c., though, truly, it did appear from her concurring mien and circumstances that these things fell from her at seasons, when unnatural ingenuity and the vigour of truth got the start of Satan's manacles. So Agnes Naesmith, &c., frequently told the minister that their heart and tongue were bound up in such a manner that they could not express what they would; and sometimes it appeared by ocular inspection of their visages that convulsive damps did seize their heads upon getting out the initial words of any such attempt.

There are two remarkable instances in the case of Katherine Campbell, who was chief instrument and author of the girl's trouble, viz., an eminent minister discoursing before famous witnesses to Katharine, and enquiring if she did not distinctly remember the godly counsels and gracious admonitions which

294

Christian Shaw, while in a fit, mentioned in the Narrative pages 76, 77, 78, gave her a certain time, and instancing some particulars thereof. Her answer was with heavy groans, " Yes, I remember." But being urged wherefore she would not confess the rest as well as that passage, and finding herself to be gravelled, she began to retract and seemed damped, not being able to extricate herself, answered before-mentioned. This occurred while she was in prison before the trial; and after it she, in presence of several witnesses, did get out these words, " That the doom pronounced on her was just, and that she could not free herself of witchcraft." But upon such attempts she fell down dead, strangely distended, and that six or seven times successively, with a suddenness that was both surprising and convincing to the spectators; at which occasion it was observed that immediately before her falling into these fits, and upon her essaying to speak when there were charges laid home on her natural conscience, her mouth seemed to contract, and she uttered heavy moans; whereupon did follow her convulsions, but after rising out of them she turned to be obstinate and inflexible: and whenever there was any appearance of her being more pliant, the foresaid fits did overtake her.

There is one thing further which does abstruct the credibility of what these confessants averred, viz. :—That there are some others, both men and women in the country, who had confessed, and told the same things before some of the best gentry and others, whose case could proceed no further for. want of authority, which in due time will, no doubt, not suffer these Witches to live, whom divine and human laws have so justly ordained to be cut off. Wherefore, till the event of a further discovery, there shall only be added some passages which were omitted in the Narrative, though they be attested by some of the same persons that were witnesses to the other matters that were mentioned therein.

Particularly, the girl declares that in one of her conflicts with the Devil, he told her how a certain minister (for whom she had a special respect) did compile his sermons through the week, what books he chiefly made use of, and several other matters anent his method of study in his closet, that no mortal, could know by ordinary means; by which, no doubt, Satan did partly design (though by a very false argument) to raise the esteem of books above sermons collected out of of them; concealing in the meantime, both the gift of improving helps, and the blessing promised to the hearer of the Word preached. When the Lady Bargarran received the two pieces of red cloth the girl had torn from one of the Witches' sleeves, as is above narrated, she locked up the same and kept the key; notwithstanding of which caution, some friends having come to visit the girl, and being desirous to see the foresaid pieces of cloth, she being in one of her fits, laughed, and told that her mother needed not to seek for them in the place where they were locked up—the' Witches having taken them away, and laid them in a corner of the cellar; and accordingly being searched for, they were found in the particular place condescended on. There was another like passage which occurred to a friend, who came in with Bargarran, for soliciting a commission from the council: for he having brought alongst with him those pieces of cloth, and buttoned his pocket on them at night, and put it in security as he thought; behold they are a-missing in the morning! But after search, are 'found in a good distance from the pocket, though none visible had been in the room to open it and carry them off. Finally, this girl did, in discourse, discover a great sagacity, yet accompanied with extraordinary modesty; and among other instances, she did observe the

doors and windows open and shut again, upon the Witches'
entry thereat. There was at no time such a number of them
about her as the room might not very well contain, with the
visible persons that were present therein. She observed them
to shift their place with great agility, when any other came
into it, or attacked upon her pointing to them. And she
often averred from the instance of the spirit that spoke to
her above her head, told their names, and gave her other means
of discovering of them, &c. That Satan does often contrive
their ruin, by the most undiscernable methods he can, because
an open deed would scar others to undertake with so faithless
a master, &c.

APPENDIX No. F.

Hugo Arnot, Esq., Advocate, author of a Collection and
Abridgement of Celebrated Criminal Trials in Scotland, from
A.D. 1536 to 1784, calls the title of this trial in 1697,
Impostor of Bargarran.* As he takes the opposite side of
the subject, I think it fair to give it a place here.

He says, " An impostor appeared in the character of a person tormented by Witches, Christian Shaw, daughter of John
Shaw of Bargarran, a gentleman of some note in the county of
Renfrew. She is said to have been but eleven years of age :
and although it is probable that hysterical affections may in

---

* I think it is proper to apprise the reader from what sources Mr. Arnot
got his information concerning Christian Shaw. This I am enabled to do
very easy, for Mr. Arnot always gives his authorities in notes at the foot of
the page, and the authorities he quotes for the account of this trial are,—
" True narrative of the sufferings and relief of a young girl. Edinburgh,
printed by James Watson, 1698," and " Records of Privy Council, January
19th, March 9th, and April 5th, 1697."

part have occasioned her rhapsodies to proceed from real illusion, as well as accounted for the contortions which agitated her body, yet she seems to have displayed an artifice above her years, an address superior to her situation, and to have been aided by accomplices, which dulness of apprehension, or violence of prejudice, forbade the bystanders to discover.

" This actress was abundantly pert and lively; and her challenging one of the house-maids for drinking, perhaps for stealing, a little milk, which drew on her an angry retort, was the simple prelude to a complicated and wonderful scene of artifice and delusion,—of fanaticism and barbarity.

" In the month of August, 1696,* within a few days after her quarrel with the house-maid, the girl was seized with hysterical convulsions, which in repeated fits displayed that variety of symptoms which characterise this capricious disease. To these, other appearances were speedily added, which could only be attributed to supernatural influence, or to fraud and imposition. She put out of her mouth quantities of egg-shells, or orange-pill, feathers of wild, and bones of tame fowl, hair of various colours, hot coal cinders, straws, crooked pins, &c.†

" Having by these sensible objects impressed the public with the most complete and fearful conviction of her being grievously vexed with a devil,‡ she found herself capable to command the implicit assent of the spectators in matters that were repugnant to the evidence of their own senses. For this purpose she fell upon the device of seeming to possess the faculties of seeing and hearing, in a manner opposite to that of the rest of mankind. She would address some invisible beings as if actually present; at other times, in her conversation with those invisible beings, she would rail at them for telling her

---

* Page 71.　　　† Pages 73, 74, &c.　　　‡ Mat. xv. 22.

that persons actually present were in the room; protesting that she did not see them, yet at the same time minutely describing their dress. For instance, she spoke as follows to the chief of her alledged tormentors, Katharine Campbell, with whom she had the quarrel, and who, to use the language of those times, was not discernibly present: 'Thou sittest with a stick in thy hand to put into my mouth, but through God's strength thou shalt not get leave. Thou art permitted to torment me, but I trust in God thou shalt never get my life.* I'll let thee see, Katie, there is no repentance in hell. O what ailed thee to be a witch! Thou sayest it is but three nights since thou wast a witch. O, if thou wouldest repent, it may be God might give thee repentance, if thou wouldest seek it and confess: if thou would desire me, I would do what I could, for the Devil is an ill master to serve,' &c., &c.† After that she took up her Bible, read passages and expounded them, and, upon one's offering to take it from her, she shrieked horridly, exclaiming, 'She would keep her Bible in spite of all the devils in hell!'‡ Then she fought, and knocked, and writhed herself, as if struggling with some invisible tormentor. When the sheriff depute of the county, accompanied by a macer of justiciary, came to apprehend some of the persons whom her diabolical malice had accused, and were actually in her presence, she addressed an imaginary and invisible correspondent thus: 'Is the sheriff come? Is he near me?' (Then stretching forth her hand, as if to grope, and the sheriff putting his hand into hers, she proceeded) 'I cannot feel the sheriff. How can he be present here? or how can I have him by the hand, as thou sayest, seeing I feel it not? Thou sayest he has brown coloured clothes, and red plush breeches with black

---

* Pages 76 and 77.   † Page 93.   ‡ Page 79.

stripes, flowered muslin cravat, and an embroidered sword
belt.   Thou sayest there is an old grey haired man with him,
having a ring upon his hand; but I can neither see nor feel
any of them.   What, are they come to apprehend the gentlewoman?   Is this their errand indeed?'*

"These reiterated and awful exercises of the dominion of
Satan (for such they were universally deemed), impressed all
ranks with amazement and terror.   The clergy, as was their
duty, were the foremost to embrace the cause of a disciple
that was engaged in more than spiritual warfare with the
grand enemy.   Clergymen, by rotation, attended the afflicted
damsel to assist the minister of the parish, the family of
Bargarran, and other pious Christians in the expiatory offices
of fasting and prayer.   A public fast was ordained by authority of the presbytery.   Three popular clergymen successively harangued the trembling audience; and one of them
chose for his theme this awful text, 'Woe to the inhabitants
of the earth and sea, for the Devil is come down unto you,
having great wrath, because he knoweth that he hath but a
short time.   And when the dragon saw that he was cast down
unto the earth, he persecuted the woman.'   And the prayers
and exhortations of the Church were speedily seconded with
the weight of the secular arm."

* Pages 116 and 117.

APPENDIX No. G.

Written by DR. WALTER YOUNG, *Minister of Erskine,
M.A., F.R.S., Edinburgh, in* 1792, *extracted from his
Statistical Account of the Parish of Erskine.*

"One of the last trials for Witchcraft which happened in
Scotland, had its origin in this parish in 1696-7. The person
supposed to have been bewitched, or tormented by the agency
of evil spirits, or of those who were in compact with them,
was Christian Shaw, daughter of John Shaw of Bargarran,
then about 11 years of age. A short account of this trial may
be seen in Arnot's Collection of Criminal Trials. *

"Three men and four women were condemned to death,
as guilty of the crime of Witchcraft, and were executed at
Paisley. † A particular account or journal of the extraordinary circumstances of this case was drawn up at the time when
it happened; every paragraph of which is affirmed to have
been originally subscribed by witnesses, among whom we
find the names of almost all the noblemen and gentlemen,
and many of the ministers of the neighbourhood. The narrative was afterwards printed ‡ without these subscriptions,
along with a very pious and decently written preface, by the
publisher. There were subjoined to it the attestations of a
physician and surgeon, the judicial confessions of some of the
persons accused of Witchcraft, and an abstract of the pleadings
of the advocates on the part of the crown, and of their charge

---

* All that Mr. Arnot says about this trial is printed in this volume.

† They were first hanged for a few minutes, and then cut down and put into
a fire prepared for them, into which a barrel of tar was put in order to consume them more quickly.

‡ In the year 1698, by James Watson, Edinburgh, and entitled, "True
Narrative of the sufferings and relief of a young girl, &c."

B 2

to the jury. These last, in their reasonings upon the nature of the evidence, and the credibility of the facts, and in the answers to objections, discover much learning and ability. A few copies of the original publication are still extant, and a new edition of it was, a few years ago, printed in Paisley. * It may furnish ample matter of speculation to those whose object it is to trace the progress and variation of manners and opinions among men. The subsequent history of this lady is, however, more interesting to the political inquirer.

" Having acquired a remarkable dexterity in spinning fine yarn, she conceived the idea of manufacturing it into thread. Her first attempts in this way were necessarily on a small scale. She executed almost every part of the process with her own hands, and bleached her materials on a large slate placed in one of the windows of the house. She succeeded, however, so well in these essays as to have sufficient encouragement to go on, and to take the assistance of her younger sisters and neighbours. The then Lady Blantyre carried a parcel of her thread to Bath, and disposed of it advantageously to some manufacturers of lace ; and this was, probably, the first thread made in Scotland that had crossed the Tweed. About this time, a person who was connected with the family, happening to be in Holland, found means to learn the secrets of the thread manufacture, which was then carried on to great extent in that country, particularly the art of sorting and numbering the threads of different sizes, and packing them up for sale, and the construction and management of the twisting and twining machines. This knowledge he communicated on his return to his friends in ' Bargarran, and by means of it, they were enabled to conduct their manufacture with more regularity

---

* By Alexander Weir in 1775.

and to a greater extent. The young women in the neighbourhood were taught to spin fine yarn, twining mills were erected,
correspondencies were established, and a profitable business
was carried on. Bargarran thread became extensively known,
and, being ascertained by a stamp, bore a good price. From
the instructions of the family of Bargarran, a few families in
the neighbourhood engaged in the same business, and continued in it for a number of years. It was not to be expected,
however, that a manufacture of that kind could be confined to
so small a district, or would be allowed to remain in so few
hands for a great length of time. The secrets of the business
were gradually divulged by apprentices and assistants. A Mr.
Pollock in Paisley availed himself of these communications,
and laid the foundation of the well established manufacture of
thread, which has ever since been carried on in that town.
From that time the women in this neighbourhood have continued to practise the spinning of fine yarn, which they
disposed of to the Paisley manufacturers."

APPENDIX No. H.

Christian Shaw was married to a Mr. Miller, the parish
minister of Kilmaurs, about the year 1718. The following
quotation from Mr. Alex. Millar's statistical account of the
Parish of Kilmaurs, speaks of Christian Shaw's husband. "A
disposition to secede from the established church hath long
subsisted among the Inhabitants of Kilmaurs: and this
disposition was first excited by the following circumstance.
About the year 1712, Mr. Hugh Thomson, then minister of
this parish, demitted upon the expectation of being called to
Stewarton, but was somehow disappointed; and either his

pride would not permit him to solicit a re-admission, or a majority of the people, disobliged with his giving them up, refused it. He retired to a small property of his own in the parish, and on Sabbaths preached sometimes at his own fireside, and sometimes from a tent in the fields, to as many of his friends as would hear him. Five or six years elapsed before another minister was elected ; during which time Mr. Thomson had frequent opportunities of reconciling himself to many of his former congregation. After Mr. Miller was chosen and ordained, Mr. Thomson still continued to preach in his own barn, or in the fields, to as many as were willing to hear him. Inconstancy, which always attends the multitude, disposed some to go one way and some another ; directed by humour, local convenience, or the influence of one upon another, they attended sometimes Mr. Miller, at other times Mr. Thomson.

Christian Shaw's husband came to pay his friends a visit at Bargarran, sometime before the year 1725, when he took badly and died there, and was buried in Erskine Church. He was universally lamented by his parishioners, great numbers of whom attended his funeral. After his death Christian Shaw and her family came and resided in Bargarran. Mr. Semple in his History of Renfrew, says,— " About the year 1725, the making of white stitching thread was introduced into the west country by Mrs. Millar of Bargarran, who, very much to her own honour, imported a twist or thread miln, and other necessary utensils from Holland, and carried on a small manufacture in her own family." The Editor saw on the 10th May, 1809, a William Jamieson, an old man, who told him that he had wrought three years and a half on the original thread miln at Bargarran, that he came to Bargarran in the year 1743, and at that time none of the family of Bargarran was alive but Mrs. Shaw, Jean Shaw, (the old sister,) and Mr. Fergusson her husband, who was factor to Lord Blantyre.

APPENDIX No. I.

Mr. Robert Wodrow, Minister at Eastwood, in his History of the Sufferings of the Church of Scotland, from the Restoration to the Revolution, vol. 1, Appendix to Book 2nd No. 11th, in William Sutherland's Declaration and Examination, there is mention made of a person being executed for a Witch about the year 1661. William Sutherland says,—" I being come of poor parents in Strathnaver, (the wildest part of the north Highlands) who were not able to keep me, I was hired with a master who sent me to bring back a horse that Colonel Morgan's party had taken from him ; which party I followed till the enemy fell betwixt me and home, and being afraid to go back, and having a desire to learn the Lowland tongue, I came alongst in a sad condition with the said party, till I came to Spey-side, where I herded cattle for a year in the Parish of Boharm, at a place called the New Kirk ; from thence I came to the Parish of Fyvie in Buchan, where I herded cattle for another year ; from that place I came to the Bridge of Stirling, where I followed the same employment for a third year, which was the year the King came home, (1660) ; and from thence I came to Paisley, where, after herding cattle a fourth year, I fell in extreme want, and that by the reason, the master whom I served being owing to one of the Bailies, called John Weres, the Bailie seized upon my master's goods, so that he ran away, and I lost my fee, and was engaged by the counsel of some honest men, from that scripture,—*Suffer not a Witch to live*, to execute a Witch, and to cleanse chimney-heads, whereby I gained somewhat for livelihood; and having a mind to learn to read, I bought a question book, but finding the people there to fear at my company, so that none would give me a lesson, I came from Paisley to Irvine, about five years since," &c., that is five years before 1666, which makes it to be 1661 the time he was in Paisley.

Mr. Burns, in the Chronological part of his English Dictionary, under the article Paisley, says,—" That five women were burned there for Witchcraft, anno 1667." I suppose this a mistake, as I can find no historical account for this. Hugo Arnot, Esq., says,—" For some time after the Restoration, the records of Privy Council are in a manner engrossed with commissions to take trial of Witches. There is an instance of the Council, at one sederunt, granting fourteen separate commissions to take trial of Witches. Records of Privy Council, November 7, 1661, January 23, 1662." I intend at some future period to notice this of Mr. Burns, and what Mr. Semple says concerning the burning of the Witches on the Gallowgreen of Paisley, in his History of Renfrewshire.

APPENDIX No. K.

Having shewn how the laws and practice of this country, concerning Witchcraft, stood before A. D. 1736, it is certainly necessary to let the Public see what the law is at present on Witchcraft.

ANNO NONO.

GEORGII II. Regis. 1736.

CAP. V..

An Act to repeal the statute made in the first year of the Reign of King James the first, intituled, *An Act against Conjuration, Witchcraft, and dealing with evil and wicked Spirits*, except so much thereof as repeals an Act of the fifth year of the Reign of Queen Elizabeth, *Against Conjurations, Inchantments, and Witchcrafts*, and to repeal an Act passed in the Parliament of Scotland in the ninth Parliament of Queen Mary, intituled, *Anentis Witchcrafts*, and for punishing such persons as pretend to exercise or use any kind of Witchcraft, Sorcery, Inchantment, or Conjuration.

Be it enacted by the King's most Excellent Majesty, by and with the advice and consent of the Lords, spiritual and temporal, and Commons, in this present Parliament assembled, and by the authority of the same, that the statute made in the first year of the Reign of King James the first, intituled, *An Act against Conjuration, Witchcraft, and dealing with evil and wicked Spirits*, shall, from the twenty-fourth day of June next, be repealed and utterly void and of none effect (except so much thereof as repeals the statute made in the fifth year of the Reign of Queen Elizabeth, intituled, *An Act against Conjurations, Inchantments, and Witchcrafts.*)

II. And be it further enacted by the authority foresaid, that from and after the said twenty-fourth day of June, the Act passed in the Parliament of Scotland in the ninth Parliament of Queen Mary, intituled, *Anentis Witchcrafts*, shall be and is hereby repealed.

III. And be it further enacted, that from and after the said twenty-fourth day of June, no Prosecution, Suit, or Proceeding, shall be commenced or carried on against any person or persons for Witchcraft, Sorcery, Inchantments, or Conjuration, or for charging another with any such offence, in any Court whatsoever in *Great Britain.*

IV. And for the more effectual preventing and punishing any pretences to such arts or powers as are beforementioned, whereby ignorant persons are frequently deluded and defrauded; be it further enacted by the anthority aforesaid, that if any person shall, from and after the said twenty-fourth day of June, pretend to exercise or use any kind of Witchcraft, Sorcery, Inchantment, or Conjuration, or undertake to tell fortunes, or pretend from his or her skill or knowledge in any ocult or crafty science to discover where or in what manner any Goods or Chattels, supposed to have been stolen or lost, may be found; every person so offending, being thereof lawfully convicted on indictment or information in that part of *Great Britain* called *England,* or on indictment or libel in that part of *Great Britain* called *Scotland,* shall for every such offence suffer imprisonment by the space of one whole year without Bail or Main-prize, and once in every quarter of the said year, in some market Town of the proper County, upon the market day, there stand openly on the Pillory for the space of one hour, and also shall (if the Court by which such judgment shall be given, shall think fit) be obliged to give sureties for his or her good behaviour, in such sum, and for such time, as the said Court shall judge proper, according to the circum-

308

stances of the offence, and in such case shall be further imprisoned until such sureties be given.

APPENDIX No. L.

Hugo Arnot, Esq., in his collection of celebrated Criminal Trials in Scotland, when speaking of the above Act, says,— "Locke had written upon government, Fletcher had been a patriot statesman, Bolingbroke had been a minister in the augustan age of Queen Anne, ere this system of legal murder and torture was abolished. This was an honour which the tardy humanity of their countrymen reserved, almost to the middle of the present century,* for Mr. Conduit, Alderman Heathcote, and Mr. Crosse. These gentlemen brought a bill into the House of Commons, which was passed into a law, repealing the former statutes against witchcraft, Scots as well as English, and discharging prosecutions for that crime, or for accusing others of that offence. On the enactment of this statute vanished all those imaginary powers, so absurdly attributed to women oppressed with age and poverty.

"While we reflect upon the blind and barbarous superstition of our ancestors,—while we bestow the tribute of applause on those humane and liberal senators who introduced this law, we cannot help lamenting that a sect among us looks upon the abolition of the penal statutes against witchcraft not only as an evil, but a sin. The seceders published an act of their associate presbytery at Edinburgh, A.D. 1743. This act† was reprinted at Glasgow so late as the year 1766. In it there

---

* Eighteenth Century.
† Act for renewing the Covenants, p. 26, 27, 34.

C 2

is contained *the annual confession of sins,* which to this day they read from the pulpit.‡ Among the sins national and personal there confessed, are the Act of Queen Anne's Parliament for tolerating the Episcopal religion in Scotland, the Act for adjourning the Court of Session during the Christmas holidays ; as also the penal statutes against Witches have been repealed by parliament, contrary to the express law of God.—(Exod. xxii. 18.) The seceders comprehend a very large body of the populace in Scotland."

APPENDIX No. M.

Having got my hands on an old folio volume of acts of the General Assembly of the Kirk of Scotland, which were passed between the years 1639, and 1649. The following extracts are curious.

I see in the year 1640, the General Assembly passed an Act against Witches and Charmers, as follows: "The Assembly ordaines all Ministers within the kingdome, carefully to take notice of Charmers, Witches, and all such abusers of the people, and to urge the Acts of Parliament to be executed against them ; and that the Commissioners from the Assembly to the Parliament, shall recommend to the said supreme judicatory, the care of the execution of the lawes against such persons in the most behoovefull way." Also, 5th Aug. 1642, " The Assembly doe therefore ordain all Presbyteries to give to the Justice, the names of the Adulterers, incestuous persons, Witches, and Sorcerers, and others, guilty of such grosse and fearfull sins within their bounds, that they may be processed and punished according to the Laws of this kingdome : and

---

‡ Printed in 1785.

that the Presbyteries and Synods be carefull herein, as they will answer to the General Assemblies," &c. Also Sess. ult. Aug. 19, 1643. I find overtures anent Witchcraft, and Charming, &c., which occupy a page and a half, and beginning with, "the abundance and increase of the sin of Witchcraft, in all the sorts and degrees of it in this time of Reformation, is to be taken to heart by this reverend Assembly, who would to that end consider," &c., and ending with, "The sins aforesaid of Witchcraft, Charming, and consulting with Witches, or Charmers, or such like wickedness, may be tried, restrained, and condignely censured and punished ecclesiastically and civally;" and in the year 1649 there is a "Commission for a conference of Ministers, Lawyers, and Physitians, concerning the tryal and punishment of Witchcraft, Charming, and Consulting," and runs thus :—"The General Assembly taking to their serious consideration the growth of the sins of Witchcraft, Charming, and Consulting, notwithstanding the frequent recommendations for restraining thereof ; and remembering that the General Assembly, 1647, did propose a good way for the tryal and punishment of these sinnes, by appointing conferances with some Ministers, Lawyers, and Physitians, in that matter which hath never yet taken effect ; therefore the Assembly doth appoint Masters Robert Dowglas, Robert Blair, Mungo Law, James Hamilton, John Smith, Robert Traill, George Leslie, John Hamilton, John Duncan, Samuel Rutherfoord, James Wood, John Leviston, James Guthrie, Andro Cant, David Calderwood, John Moncrieff, Frederick Carmichael, James Durhame, Patrick Gillespie, Robert Ker, Ephraim Melville, Ministers ; * to consider seriously of that matter, and to

---

* See the Scots Worthies for an account of these Ministers.

consult and advise therein amongst themselves, as also with Sir Archibald Johnston of Wariston, Clerk Register; Mr. Thomas Nicolson, His Majesties Advocate; Mr. Alex. Peirson, one of the ordinary Lords of Session; Sir Lewes Stewart, Mr. Alex. Colvill, and Mr. James Robertson, Justice Deputes; Messrs. Rodger Mowet, John Gilmoir, and John Nisbet, Lawyers; and with Doctors Sibbald, Cunninghame, and Purves, Physitians; severally or together as occasion shall offer, and the Assembly earnestly requests and confidently expects from these learned and judicious Lawyers and Physitians before-named, their best endeavours and concurrence with their brethren of the Ministrie for advise and counsell herein, and for conference in said matter; and Ordaine the said brethren to make report of the result of their consultations and conferences from time to time as they make any considerable progresse to the Commission for publick affaires, and the said Commission shall make report to the next Generall Assembly."

APPENDIX No. N.

Upon Sunday the 28th of March, 1697, after Sermon, intimation was made by Mr. THOMAS BLACKWELL, *the Minister, of a fast to be kept by the Congregation of Paisley the ensuing Wednesday, the Causes whereof are below.*

My friends, we have been preaching of Christ to you, we are now about to speak of the Devil to you,—the greatest enemy that our Lord and His kingdom hath in the world. The thing I am about to intimate to you is this,—The members of the Presbytery having taken to their consideration how much Satan doth rage in these bounds, and which

is indeed very lamentable in our bounds, and in ours only.
They have thought fit to appoint a day of fasting and
humiliation, that so He who is the lion of the tribe of Judah,
may appear with power against him who is the angel of the
bottomless pit, and throw him down, who is now come
out in great wrath ; O ! that it may be because his time
is short.

As to the causes of the fast, I shall but hint a few things
to you, the thing being so well known in the bounds, the
Presbytery did not think it needful to be any way large or
formal in drawing up of causes ; however, I may say in the
first place, the causes of our preceding fast * remain yet not
sufficiently mourned over, so that though we had no other
causes but 'these, we have ground to observe more fasts
than one or two.

But yet a little more close to the purpose. First, Satan
is greatly raging in our bounds ; he hath in all probability
enjoyed a long and old stock of subjects, even among the
hearers of the Gospel ; it may be, some of them are hearing
me just now, conscience being best judge in that matter,
and now he hath come that length, no doubt, being permitted of God, that his power is not only to be perceived
in keeping many hearts from closing with Christ, but also in
tormenting a family extraordinary in our bounds, so that it
is known to be the Devil and his instruments, and none
else, therefore, Satan who is raging, and who hath gotten
many in all probability to devote themselves soul and body
to him.

*   *   *   *   *

Again, 2dly, There is the impenitency and obstinacy of

---

* This was at least the second fast kept on Christian Shaw's account.

persons supposed upon many accounts truly to be guilty,
their continuing obstinate and impenitent, and refusing to
confess guilt in that matter, that God who hath the power
of conscience, by the power of His Spirit, in the use of other
lawful means for the finding out of the truth, may make
these means effectual, and may win in upon their consciences
to make them confess guilt.

3dly, The great affliction of that poor child (Christian
Shaw,) and that family in whom she is so nearly interested,
none of us knows her affliction, and her father's, so as it is
in itself. It is easy to look upon one so tormented as she is,
be what it would be if we were so tormented ourselves, or
yet any one in our family. We would remember them that
are in bonds as bound with them, and therefore our petitions
have a special respect to them of that family, that is
set up as a beacon on the top of a mountain for all to take
warning.

Again, in the fourth place, Another reason is, the mysteri-
ousness and difficulty of the process of Witchcraft, so that it
is the process of all others, that requires most prudence,
solidity, and several other things, to name which, many of
you would not understand me ; but in a word, it requires
much of the presence of the Spirit of God to guide the
Judges, and work upon the consciences of the panels, that
so the truth may be found out, and judgment accordingly
execute ; thus we offer several reasons why it is necessary
for us to observe a day of fasting and humiliation before
God.

And now, my friends, all I add is this;—in the first place,
I am sure ministers, and I am sure the godly are called to
be very importunate with God in this matter. Would ye
know, my friends, why we preach in vain to them that have

devoted themselves to the Devil; it is that that makes the Gospel so barren, and who knows but in this congregation there be many who have these many years hence been under vows to Satan, and as for you that are the people of God, ye pray in vain for the success of the Gospel to them, for till once they be brought to see the evil of their sin, and to be convinced of the evil thereof, and to lothe themselves upon account of the same, neither will the Gospel, nor your prayers do them any good; so it is the ministers' and the people of God's duty, and interest, not only to pray that God would find out the guilty among these that are apprehended, but that God would discover all others that are guilty, and who are not apprehended, that the kingdom of Christ may run and be glorified, and the kingdom of Satan destroyed.

FINIS.

315

APPENDIX.

BY DAVID SEMPLE, F.S.A.

THE names of the persons accused, convicted, and afterwards
"worrit" and burnt for the crime of witchcraft on the Gallowgreen of Paisley on 10th June, 1697, are not very distinctly
stated. Three men and four women were convicted, and two
of these men and the four women were executed, and the
other man committed suicide in Renfrew Prison on 21st May
previously. The greater number of the names mentioned in
the foregoing pages will be found in the Poll Tax Rolls for
Renfrewshire for the year 1695,* which corroborate and confirm the authenticity of both records. The names of the seven
convicted persons would seem from the foregoing history to
have been,—1st, John Lindsay; 2nd, James Lindsay; 3rd,
John Reid; 4th, Catherine Campbell; 5th, Margaret Lang;
6th, Margaret Fulton, Dumbarton; and, 7th, Agnes Naismith.
From the Poll Tax Rolls it would appear that John Lindsay
was a cottar in Barloch of Bargarren; James Lindsay a
cottar in Billboe, in Orbistoune's lands of Erskine; Margaret
Lang, the wife of William Semple, cottar in Cartympen,
also in Orbistoune's lands, all in the parish of Erskine;
John Reid was a smith in the Laird of Hapland's lands,

---

* [These Poll Tax Rolls were published in the Glasgow *Herald* on several dates
during 1864. They contain the names of all male persons in the county in 1695, with
their calling and residence, the maiden names of their wives, children, and servants,
&c. These Records, which the compiler sent to several libraries in Scotland, are exceedingly interesting and valuable.—*Ed.*]

in the parish of Inchinnan; Catherine Campbell, Margaret
Fulton, and Agnes Naismith are not to be found in
these Rolls, from the first probably having become a servant
to the Laird of Bargarren at Whitsunday 1696, the second
being resident in Dumbarton, and the third perhaps in
the parish of Kilpatrick, on the opposite side of the River
Clyde from Bargarren. A few excerpts from these authentic
Poll Rolls made up a year before the trial are here given to
show the status of the persons who were brought before the
Commission for a crime that really could not have any existence.

ERSKINE PARISH.

John Shaw and Christian Shaw, page 71 ; *Jean Shaw, page*
209.

Poll Tax Rolls, page 99.

John Shaw, of Barrgarrane, 300lib val., 9lib 6sh;
Christian M'Gilchrist, spouse, 6sh; Jo., James,
Christian,* Elez., and Jean, childreine, each 6sh;
John Bartholemew and Robert Mountgomrie,
servants, each 20lib fie, 10sh; Ro. Blackwood,
herd, 7lib fie, 3sh 6d; Elez. Orr, Cat. Dean, and
Agnas M'Cashlane, servants, each 20mks. fie,
6s 8d,   -   -   -   -   -   -   -   -15   1   6

John Lindsay, page 97.

Poll Tax Rolls, page 99.

John Lindsay,† in Barloch, 40mks. val., 5sh 4d;
Margaret Patiesoune, spouse, 6sh; Margt. M'Inlay,
servant, 8lib fie, 4sh; Sara Clerk, in hervest 5lib
fie, 2sh 6d,   :   -   -   -   -   -   - 1   9   10

---

* Christian Shaw. The impostor of Bargarran, who pretended she was bewitched,
and made credulous ministers believe her rhapsodies.

† John Lindsay, a cottar on the lands of Bargarran, who must have been seen every
other day by Christian Shaw.

Pinched Moggy, page 97; *Margaret L———, page* 101: *Margt. Lang,* 104; *Martha Semple,* 104.

Poll Tax Rolls, page 103.

William Semple, in Cartympen, cottar, 6sh; * Margt. Lang, spouse, 6sh; Mertha, his daur., 6sh; Elspe Glasfoord, sert., 8lib fie, 4sh, - - - - 1 8 0

INCHINNAN PARISH.

" Grandmother's house at Northbar," page 75; *Lady Northbar, page* 104.

Poll Tax Rolls, page 95.

Aikine, Lady Northbarr,† 4lib 6sh as her pole, the third pt. of her husband's pole, being 500lib val.

Alexander Anderson, page 78.

Poll Tax Rolls, page 94.

Alexander Andersoune, cotter,‡ - - - - 0 6 0

Margaret Fulton, page 100.

Poll Tax Rolls, page 95.

John Gemmell, cordoner, 12sh trade and pole; Margaret Fulltoune, spouse, 6sh,§ - - - 0 18 0

John Reid, Smith, page 132.

Poll Tax Rolls, page 97.

John Reid,‖ smith, 12sh; Jennet Hendersoune, spouse, 6sh, - - - - - - 0 18 0

---

* Margaret Lang was the spouse of a cottar in Cartympen, which was situated a little to the south of the present parochial school of Erskine, and on the north side of the new road leading to Greenock. She was a midwife, an intelligent woman, endowed with abilities at least equal, if not surpassing, those of her superstitious accusers and judges.

† Mrs. M'Gilchrist, maternal grandmother of Christian Shaw.

‡ Residing on the lands of Southbar, in the immediate vicinity of Bargarren.

§ A shoemaker residing on the lands of Northbar, in the neighbourhood of Bargarren.

‖ This unfortunate person committed suicide in Renfrew prison on 21st May, 1697.

PAISLEY PARISH.

John White, apothecary, page 73.
Poll Tax Rolls, page 59.

John Whyte,* apothecarie, 12lib 6sh Jean Johnstoun,
his spouse, 6sh ; Robert, John, and Agnes Whytes,
his children, each 6sh ; Jean Young, sert., 2lib fee,
1sh, and 6sh general pole, -   -   -   -   -13 17   6

Dr. Johnstone, page 73.
Poll Tax Rolls, page 60.

Doctor John Johnstoune,† 12lib 6sh ; Helen Little,
spouse, 6sh ; John, Christian, Helen, and Elizabeth Johnstounes, children, each 6sh ; Elizabeth
McKie and Margaret Johnstoune, servants, each
16lib 6sh 8d fee, 6sh 8d,   -   :   -   -   -15   1   4

John Campbell, Surgeon.
Poll Tax Rolls, page 61.

John Campbell,‡ appothecarie, 12lib 6sh ; Margaret
Walkinshaw, spouse, 6sh; Mary Houstoune, servt.,
20 merks fie 6sh 8d; Petter Pettersoune and Wm.
Park, prentices, each 9sh ; Jennet Campbell, his
daughter, 6sh,   -   -   -   -   -   -   14   2   8

---

* John Whyte was a near relation of the Shaws, and resided on the west side of
St. Mirin Wynd, Paisley, where the Old Bank of Scotland had since been erected. His
house was burned in 1733 in the great fire of that year. The bank has now been taken
down.

† He resided in Smithhills Street, Paisley, and had a good medical practice.

‡ He resided and carried on business in the house that had been erected by Sir James
Sempill of Belltrees, Sheriff of Renfrewshire, at the north east angle of High Street
and St. Mirin Wynd in which Robert Sempill, born in 1599, author of "Habbie
Simpson," had been brought up. John Campbell was afterwards elected a bailie of
Paisley in 1703 and 1706. A fire occurred in the laboratory in 1733, and burned
both sides of St. Mirin Wynd, and parts of High Street, the Cross, and Causeyside.

Ministers in the County of Renfrew mentioned in the foregoing history.

William Fleming, Innerkip, page 132.

Poll Tax Roll, page 195.

Mr. William Fleming, minister of Innerkippe, his own pole, 3lib 6sh ; Agnas Aird, his wife, 6sh ; John M'Latchie, servand, 16 merks fie, 11sh 4d ; Jennet Miller, 20 mks. fie, 12sh 8d ; Anna Tam, 6lib fie, and bounties, 9sh, - ; - - - 5 5 0

James Hutchison, Kilalan, page 103.

Poll Tax Rolls, page 114.

Mr. James Hutchesoune, minister, 3lib 6sh; Margt. Gillhugie, spouse, 6sh ; Christian, his daur., 6sh ; Wm. King, sert., 16lib fie, 8sh ; Ann Reid, sert., 12lib fie, 12sh ; Jean Hendersoune, sert., 12lib fie, 12sh, - - - - - - - - 5 16 0

James Stirling, Kilbarchan, page 126.

Poll Tax Rolls, page 126.

Mr. James Stirling, minister, 3lib. 6sh ; Margt. Dunloap, his spouse, 6sh; Jean and Bessie Stirlings, childreine, each 6sh ; James Wayllie, servant, 8lib fie, 4sh ; Jennet Murdoch, sert., 14lib fie, 7sh, - - - - - - - - 5 7 0

James Brisbane, Kilmalcolm, page 126.

Poll Tax Rolls, page 155.

Mr. James Birsbane, minr., 3lib. 6sh ; Chr. Sheirhun his wife, 6sh; Mar. Chambers and Marion Daviesoune, each 16lib fie, 8sh. each, and 6sh gnall. pole ; and   Lang, sert., 10lib fie, 5sh, and gnall. pole 6sh, - - - - - 5 1 0

A Brief and True Narrative Of some Remarkable Passages Relating to sundry Persons Afflicted by Witchcraft, at Salem Village Which happened from the Nineteenth of March, to the Fifth of April, 1692.

This is the earliest known published account of the outbreak of witchcraft accusation and prosecution at Salem. It was written by the Rev. Deodat Lawson, who had been a minister at Salem Village between 1684 and 1688. It was published in Boston with remarkable speed by Benjamin Harris in 1692. It was reprinted by John Dunton in London, 1693.

Deodat Lawson was a highly educated and scholarly Englishman who had emigrated to New England. He returned to England in 1696. Perhaps because of his association with the case, even although he was not a prominent actor in it, his subsequent life was one of destitution and penury.

H.V.McL

On the Nineteenth day of March last I went to Salem Village, and lodged at Nathaniel Ingersols near to the Minister Mr. P's. house, and presently after I came into my Lodging Capt. Walcuts Daughter Mary came to Lieut. Ingersols and spake to me, but, suddenly after as she stood by the door, was bitten, so that she cried out of her Wrist, and looking on it with a Candle, we saw apparently the marks of Teeth both upper and lower set, on each side of her wrist.

In the beginning of the Evening, I went to give Mr. P. a

visit. When I was there, his Kins-woman, Abigail Williams, (about 12 years of age,) had a grievous fit; she was at first hurryed with Violence to and fro in the room, (though Mrs. Ingersol endeavoured to hold her,) sometimes makeing as if she would fly, stretching up her arms as high as she could, and crying "Whish, Whish, Whish!" several times; Presently after she said there was Goodw.N. and said, "Do you not see her? Why there she stands!" And the said Goodw. N. offered her The Book, but she was resolved she would not take it, saying Often, "I wont, I wont, I wont, take it, I do not know what Book it is: I am sure it is none of Gods Book, it is the Divels Book, for ought I know." After that, she run to the Fire, and begun to throw Fire Brands, about the house; and run against the Back, as if she would run up Chimney, and, as they said, she had attempted to go into the Fire in other Fits.

On Lords Day, the Twentieth of March, there were sundry of the afflicted Persons at Meeting, as, Mrs. Pope, and Goodwife Bibber, Abigail Williams, Mary Walcut, Mary Lewes, and Docter Griggs' Maid. There was also at Meeting, Goodwife C.(who was afterward Examined on suspicion of being a Witch). They had several Sore Fits, in the time of Publick Worship, which did something interrupt me in my First Prayer; being so unusual. After Psalm was Sung, Abigail Williams said to me, "Now stand up, and Name your Text": And after it was read, she said, "It is a long Text." In the beginning of Sermon, Mrs. Pope, a Woman afflicted, said to me, "Now there is enough of that." And in the afternoon, Abigail Williams upon my referring to my Doctrine said to me, "I know no Doctrine you had, If you did name one, I have forgot it."

In Sermon time when Goodw. C was present in the Meetinghouse Ab. W. called out, "Look where Goodw. C sits on the Beam suckling her Yellow bird betwixt her fingers"! Anne Putnam another Girle afflicted said there was a Yellow-bird sat on my hat as it hung on the Pin in the Pulpit: but those that were by, restrained her from speaking loud about it.

On Monday the 21st of March, The Magistrates of Salem appointed to come to Examination of Goodw C. And about twelve of the Clock, they went into the Meeting-House, which was Thronged with Spectators: Mr. Noyes began with a very pertinent and pathetic Prayer; and Goodwife C. being called to answer to what was Alledged against her, she desired to go to Prayer, which was much wondred at, in the presence of so many hundred people: The Magistrates told her, they would not admit it; they came not there to hear her Pray, but to Examine her, in what was Alledged against her. The Worshipful Mr. Hathorne asked her, Why she Afflicted those Children? she said, she did not Afflict them. He asked her, who did then? she said, "I do not know; How should I know?" The Number of the Afflicted Persons were about that time Ten, *viz.* Four Married Women, Mrs. Pope, Mrs. Putman, Goodw. Bibber, and an Ancient Woman, named Goodall, three Maids, Mary Walcut, Mercy Lewes, at Thomas Putman's, and a Maid at Dr. Griggs's, there were three Girls from 9 to 12 Years of Age, each of them, or thereabouts, *viz.* Elizabeth Parris, Abigail Williams and Ann Putman; these were most of them at G. C's Examination, and did vehemently accuse her in the Assembly of afflicting them, by Biting, Pinching, Strangling, etc. And that they did in their Fit see her Likeness coming to them, and bringing a Book to them, she said, she had no Book; they affirmed, she had a Yellow-Bird, that used to suck betwixt her Fingers, and being asked about it, if she had any Familiar Spirit, that attended her, she said, She had no Familiarity with any such thing. She was a Gospel Woman: which Title she called her self by; and the Afflicted Persons told her, ah! She was, A Gospel Witch. Ann Putman did there affirm, that one day when Lieutenant Fuller was at Prayer at her Fathers House, she saw the shape of Goodw. C. and she thought Goodw. N. Praying at the same time to the Devil, she was not sure it was Goodw. N. she thought it was; but very sure she saw the Shape of G. C. The said C. said, they were poor, distracted Children, and no heed to be given to what they said. Mr. Hathorne and Mr. Noyes replyed, it was the judgment of all that were present, they were Bewitched, and only she, the Accused Person said, they were Distracted. It was observed several times, that if she did but bite her Under lip in time of Examination the persons afflicted were bitten on their armes and wrists and produced the Marks before the Magistrates, Ministers and others. And being watched for that, if she did but Pinch her Fingers, or Graspe one hand hard in another, they were Pinched and produced the Marks before the Magistrates, and Spectators. After that, it was observed, that if she did but lean her Breast against the Seat, in the Meeting House, (being the Barr at which she stood,) they were afflicted. Particularly Mrs. Pope complained of grievous torment in her Bowels as if they were torn out. She vehemently accused said C. as the instrument, and first threw her Muff at her; but that flying not home, she got off her Shoe, and hit Goodwife

C. on the head with it. After these postures were watched, if said C. did but stir her feet, they were afflicted in their Feet, and stamped fearfully. The afflicted persons asked her why she did not go to the company of Witches which were before the Meeting house mustering? Did she not hear the Drum beat? They accused her of having Familiarity with the Devil, in the time of Examination, in the shape of a Black man whispering in her ear; they affirmed, that her Yellow-Bird sucked betwixt her Fingers in the Assembly; and order being given to see if there were any sign, the Girl that saw it said, it was too late now; she had removed a Pin, and put it on her head; which was found there sticking upright.

They told her, she had Covenanted with the Devil for ten years, six of them were gone, and four more to come. She was required by the Magistrates to answer that Question in the Catechism, "How many persons be there in the God-Head?" she answered it but oddly, yet was there no great thing to be gathered from it; she denied all that was charged upon her, and said, They could not prove a Witch; she was that Afternoon Committed to Salem-Prison; and after she was in Custody, she did not so appear to them, and afflict them as before.

On Wednesday the 23 of March, I went to Thomas Putmans, on purpose to see his Wife: I found her lying on the Bed, having had a sore fit a little before. She spake to me, and said, she was glad to see me; her Husband and she both desired me to pray with her, while she was sensible; which I did, though the Apparition said, I should not go to Prayer. At the first beginning she attended; but after a little time, was taken with a fit: yet continued silent, and seemed to be Asleep: when Prayer was done, her Husband going to her, found her in a Fit; he took her off the Bed, to set her on his Knees; but at first she was so stiff, she could not be bended; but she afterwards set down; but quickly began to strive violently with her Arms and Leggs; she then began to Complain of, and as it were to Converse personally with, Goodw. N., saying, "Goodw. N. Be gone! Be gone! Be gone! are you not ashamed, a Woman of your Profession, to afflict a poor Creature so? what hurt did I ever do you in my life! you have but two years to live, and then the Devil will torment your Soul, for this your Name is blotted out of Gods Book, and it shall never be put in Gods Book again, be gone for shame, are you not afraid of that which is coming upon you? I Know, I know, what will make you afraid; the wrath of an Angry God, I am sure that will make you afraid; be gone, do not tourment me, I know what you would have (we judged she meant, her Soul) but it is out of your reach; it is Clothed with the white Robes of Christs Righteousness." After this, she seemed to dispute with the Apparition about a particular Text of Scripture. The Apparition seemed to deny it, (the Womans eyes being fast closed all this time); she said, She was sure there was such a Text; and she would tell it; and then the Shape would be gone, for said she, "I am sure you cannot stand before that Text!" then she was sorely Afflicted; her mouth drawn on one side, and her body strained for about a minute, and then said, "I will tell, I will tell; it is, it is, it is!" three or four times, and then was afflicted to hinder her from telling, at last she broke forth and said, "It is the third Chapter of the Revelations." I did something scruple the reading it, and did let my scruple appear, lest Satan should make any Superstitious lie to improve the Word of the Eternal God. However, tho' not versed in these things, I judged I might do it this once for an Experiment. I began to read, and before I had near read through the first verse, she opened her eyes, and was well; this fit continued near half an hour. Her Husband and the Spectators told me, she had often been so relieved by reading Texts that she named, something pertinent to her Case; as Isa. 40. 1, Isa. 49. 1, Isa. 50. 1, and several others.

On Thursday the Twenty fourth of march, (being in course the Lecture Day, at the Village,) Goodwife N. was brought before the Magistrates Mr. Hathorne and Mr. Corwin, about Ten of [the] Clock, in the Fore Noon, to be Examined in the Meeting House; the Reverend Mr. Hale begun with Prayer, and the Warrant being read, she was required to give answer, Why she aflicted those persons? she pleaded her owne innocency with earnestness. Thomas Putman's Wife, Abigail Williams and Thomas Putmans daughter accused her that she appeared to them, and afflicted them in their fitts: but some of the other said, that they had seen her, but knew not that ever she had hurt them; amongst which was Mary Walcut, who was presently after she had so declared bitten, and cryed out of her in the meeting-house; producing the Marks of teeth on her wrist. It was so disposed, that I had not leisure to attend the whole time of Examination, but both Magistrates and Ministers told me, that the things alledged by the afflicted, and defences made by her, were much after the same manner, as the former was. And her Motions did produce like effects as to Biteing, Pinching, Bruising, Tormenting, at their Breasts, by her Leaning, and when, bended Back, were as if their Backs was broken. The afflicted persons said, the Black Man whispered to her in the Assembly, and therefore she could not hear what the Magistrates said unto her. They said also that she did then ride by the Meeting-house, behind the Black Man. Thomas Putman's wife had a grievous Fit, in the time of Examination, to the very great Impairing of her strength, and wasting of her spirits, insomuch as she could hardly move hand, or foot, when she was carryed out. Others also were there grievously afflicted, so that there was once such an hideous scrietch and noise, (which I heard as I walked, at a little distance from the Meeting house,) as did amaze me, and some that were within told me the whole assembly was struck with consternation, and they were afraid, that those that sate next to them, were under the influence of Witchcraft. This woman also was that day committed to Salem Prison. The Magistrates and Ministers also did informe me, that they apprehended a child of Sarah G. and Examined it, being between 4 and 5 years of Age, And as to matter of Fact, they did Unanimously affirm, that when this Child did but cast its eye upon the afflicted persons, they were tormented, and they held her Head, and yet so many as her eye could fix upon were afflicted. Which they did several times make careful observation of: the afflicted complained, they had often been Bitten by this child, and produced the marks of a small set of teeth, accordingly, this was also committed to Salem Prison; the child looked hail, and well as other Children. I saw it at Lieut.Ingersols. After the commitment of Goodw. N., Tho: Putmans wife was much better, and had no violent fits at all from that 24th of March to the 5th of April. Some others also said they had not seen her so frequently appear to them, to hurt them.

On the 25th of March, (as Capt. Stephen Sewal, of Salem, did afterwards inform me) Eliza. Paris had sore Fits, at his house, which much troubled himself, and his wife, so as he told me they were almost discouraged. She related, that the great Black Man came to her, and told her, if she would be ruled by him, she should have whatsoever she desired, and go to a Golden City. She relating this to Mrs. Sewall, she told the child, it was the Divel, and he was a Lyar from the Beginning, and bid her tell him so, if he came again: which she did accordingly, at the next coming to her, in her fits.

On the 26th of March, Mr. Hathorne, Mr. Corwin, and Mr. Higison were at the Prison-Keepers House, to Examine the Child, and it told them there, it had a little Snake that used to Suck on the lowest Joynt of it[s] Fore-Finger; and when they inquired where, pointing to other places, it told them, not there, but there, pointing on the Lowest point of Fore-Finger; where they Observed a deep Red Spot, about the Bigness of a Flea-bite, they asked who gave it that Snake? whether the great Black man, it said no, its Mother gave it.

The 31 of March there was a Publick Fast kept at Salem on account of these Afflicted Persons. And Abigail Williams said, that the Witches had a Sacrament that day at an house in the Village, and that they had Red Bread and Red Drink. The first of April, Mercy Lewis, Thomas Putman's Maid, in her fitt, said, they did eat Red Bread like Mans Flesh, and would have had her eat some: but she would not; but turned away her head, and Spit at them, and said, "I will not Eat, I will not Drink, it is Blood," etc. She said, "That is not the Bread of Life, that is not the Water of Life; Christ gives the Bread of Life, I will have none of it!" This first of April also Marcy Lewis aforesaid saw in her fitt a White man and was with him in a Glorious Place, which had no Candles nor Sun, yet was full of Light and Brightness; where was a great Multitude in White glittering Robes, and they Sung the Song in the fifth of Revelation the Ninth verse, and the 110 Psalm, and the 149 Psalm; and said with her self, "How long shall I stay here? let me be along with you": She was loth to leave this place, and grieved that she could tarry no longer. This White man hath appeared several times to some of them, and given them notice how long it should be before they had another Fit, which was sometimes a day, or day and half, or more or less: it hath fallen out accordingly.

The third of April, the Lords-Day, being Sacrament-day, at the Village, Goodw. C. upon Mr. Parris's naming his Text, John 6, 70, *One of them is a Devil*, the said Goodw. C. went immediately out of the Meeting-House, and flung the door after her violently, to the amazement of the Congregation: She was afterward seen by some in their Fits, who said, "O Goodw. C., I did not think to see you here!" (and being at their Red bread and drink) said to her, "Is this a time to receive the Sacrament, you ran-away on the Lords-Day, and scorned to receive it in the Meeting-House, and, Is this a time to receive it? I wonder at you!" This is the summ of what I either saw my self, or did receive Information from persons of undoubted Reputation and Credit.

Remarks of things more than ordinary about the Afflicted Persons.

1. They are in their Fits tempted to be Witches, are shewed the List of the Names of others, and are tortured, because they will not yield to Subscribe, or meddle with, or touch the Book, and are promised to have present Relief if they would do it.

2. They did in the Assembly mutually Cure each other, even with a Touch of their Hand, when Strangled, and otherwise Tortured; and would endeavour to get to their Afflicted, to Relieve them.

3. They did also foretel when anothers Fit was a-coming, and would say, "Look to her! she will have a Fit presently," which fell out accordingly, as many can bear witness, that heard and saw it.

4. That at the same time, when the Accused Person was present, the Afflicted Persons saw her Likeness in other places of the Meeting-House, suckling her Familiar, sometimes in one place and posture, and sometimes in another.

5. That their Motions in their Fits are Preternatural, both as to the manner, which is so strange as a well person could not Screw their Body into; and as to the violence also it is preternatural, being much beyond the Ordinary force of the same person when they are in their right mind.

6. The eyes of some of them in their fits are exceeding fast closed, and if you ask a question they can give no answer, and I do believe they cannot hear at that time, yet do they plainly converse with the Appearances, as if they did discourse with real persons.

7. They are utterly pressed against any persons Praying with them, and told by the appearances, they shall not go to Prayer, so Tho. Putmans wife was told, I should not Pray;

but she said, I should: and after I had done, reasoned with the Appearance, "Did not I say he should go to Prayer?"

8. The forementioned Mary W. being a little better at ease, the Afflicted persons said, she had signed the book; and that was the reason she was better. Told me by Edward Putman.

Remarks concerning the Accused.

1. For introduction to the discovery of those that afflicted them, It is reported Mr. Parris's Indian Man and Woman made a Cake of Rye Meal, and the Childrens water, baked it in the Ashes, and gave it to a Dogge, since which they have discovered, and seen particular persons hurting of them.

2. In Time of Examination, they seemed little affected, though all the Spectators were much grieved to see it.

3. Natural Actions in them produced Preternatural actions in the Afflicted, so that they are their own Image without any Poppits of Wax or otherwise.

4. That they are accused to have a Company about 23 or 24 and they did Muster in Armes, as it seemed to the Afflicted Persons.

5. Since they were confined, the Persons have not been so much Afflicted with their appearing to them, Biteing or Pinching of them, etc.

6. They are reported by the Afflicted Persons to keep dayes of Fast and dayes of Thanksgiving, and Sacraments;. Satan endeavours toTransforme himself to an Angel of Light, and to make his Kingdom and Administrations to resemble those of our Lord Jesus Christ.

7. Satan Rages Principally amongst the Visible Subjects of Christ's Kingdom and makes use (at least in appearance) of some of them to Afflict others; that Christ's Kingdom may be divided against it self, and so be weakened.

8. Several things used in England at Tryal of Witches, to the Number of 14 or 15, which are wont to pass instead of or in Concurrence with Witnesses, at least 6 or 7 of them are found in these accused: see Keebles Statutes.

9. Some of the most solid Afflicted Persons do affirme the same things concerning seeing the accused out of their Fitts as well as in them.

10. The Witches had a Fast, and told one of the Afflicted Girles, she must not Eat, because it was Fast Day, she said, she would: they told her they would Choake her then; which when she did eat, was endeavoured.

Finis.

National Archives of Scotland, Manuscript JC/26/81/D9. Glasgow May 1699.

This previously unpublished document shows that, with regard to witchcraft accusation and prosecution in Renfrewshire, Christian Shaw had a far smaller part on a far larger stage than has commonly been imagined. This is a record of suggested evidence against twenty five people who were charged with witchcraft. They were required to 'compear before their Lordships within the Tollbooth of Glasgow on 19th of May, 1700'. The case was 'deserted' i.e. dropped. Not all those who were accused of being witches were charged with witchcraft. Not all those who were charged were tried. It was more complex and, as I have suggested before, far more interesting than witchcraft cases of old are generally thought to have been. Notice that there is no punctuation of any sort in this long document.

H.V.McL.

My Lords Commissioners of Justiciary Unto Your [Manuscript torn] and complainers Sir James Stewart of Glasgow his Majestys advocat and Sir patrick [illegible] persuer for his Highness aacting in the matter undertaken upon Jean Haldron relict of   Baxter in the brigend of Kilmacolme Bessie Cochran relict of John Lylle in Rochbuss Jannet Laing spouse to John Mathey elder in Penitorsone John Paterson in Geillis Elspeth Wood relict of   Miller in Overgourock Annabell Reid spouse to John Stewart in Inchinan Bessie Miller spouse to Gavin Parks in Kellilan Jean Drummond spouse to William Gardiner in Kilbarchan Issobell Houston spouse to George Wilson in Houston John Dougall in Grenock Margaret

Alexander in Paisley Jean Ross there Alexander Lyle there Jean Whythill spouse to James Peacock in   Mary Morrison spouse to Francis Duncan skipper in Greenock Margaret Duncan relict of the merchant there Jannet Gentleman spouse to George Craigend late beadle of Agner[illegible] in Port Glasgow Jannet Robinsone spouse to James Hill smith in Govan Anna Hill her daughter Jean Gilmore spouse to Hector Jamison beadle ther Jannet Boyd late servitrix to Craigtone and Elspeth Taylor spouse to William Scot Shoemaker in Newark THAT WHERAS by the law of god the common law and laws of all weill governed nations and the laws and acts of parleiment of this kingdom the Crymes of witchcraft sorcery and charming are punishable by death and particularly by the 73 act parl[iamen]t   Queen Mary it is stated that no manner of person or persons take upon hand any tyme there after use any manner of witchcraft sorcery or Nigromancy or give themselves forth to have any such craft or knowledge thereof therthrough abusing the people nor that no man seek any like response or Consultation at any such users or abusers foresaid of witchcraft sorceries or Nigromancy under the pain of death YET NOTWITHSTANDING the said Jean Haldron Bessie Cochrane Bessie Laing John Petersone Elspeth Wood Annabell Reid Bessie Miller and the haill remnant persons above complained upon shaking off all fear of god and regard to the laws has presumed to committ and are guilty of the fores[ai]d most horrid and abominable crymes of witchcraft sorcery and charming IN So FARR AS the said Jean Haldron is commonly repute to be a witch and she has the insensible mark and was named by Margrat Laird as

one of her tormentors And that the said Margaret Laird fell
in fits of torment when the s[ai]d Jean Haldrons name was
named to her And in the month of March and April May
June Jully or Agust 1695 one or oth[e]r of the days of the
months of the said year 1695 The said Jean Haldron having
sought almes from David Miller at the bridgend Miln which
he having refused when she went away muttering some
words upon which the Miln stopt upon a sudent and took
fyre and was like to burn and albeit the neighbours about
used all the endeavours they could to make the mill to go
yet they could not do it nor did they know wher the stop
lay and having lifted up the hoops they asayed to turn the
stone but it would not turn and they endevoured to
[illegible] the stone by the lefter [illegible] on the syde of
the [illegible] stone lifted and the other stack [illegible] to
the Northern miln   times fell out and the said David
Millers corn being taken out of the hopper and an other
mans corn putt in [illegible] immediately [was] weill as ever
without any help   and   when they offered again to grind
the said David Millers corn the miln fell a wrong and would
not go through there was no [illegible] and when they took
out David Millers Corn and putt in another mans corn the
[illegible] went without any help as also in January 1698 on
on[e] or other of the days of the months of the s[ai]d year
1698 Patrick Fleming in [illegible]bank having disharged
his wife to give the s[ai]d Jean Haldron any almes because
she was of ill fame she went away in great rage scolding and
blaspheming and in a fortnight thereaft[e]r or thereby the
s[ai]d Patrick Fleming fell into strnage kinds of fitts of
trembling and chocking in his throat as if he had been
strangled or his breath stopt and continued so for [illegible]

days and the s[ai]d Jean Haldron being chalanged and threatened by the minister of the parish for laying such a disease thereupon the s[ai]d Patrick Fleming she sayd The Lord God send him his health and after that the said Patrick Fleming recovered AS Also In the month of November or December 1694 or January or February 1694 Jannet Scot in [illegible] having [illegible] the s[ai]d Jean Haldron carreing away peats and challenged her for it and witch wife are ye steilling peittes the said Jean Hadron threatened to make the said Jannet Scot reu it and w[i]thin four days thereafter Jannet Scots cows milk went from her and she gave nothing and blood [illegible] before she would have given a pynt of milk at a [illegible] and about five weeks therafter five of her [illegible] and a horse pined away and died and all her other bestial   and goods   and banished away and she could never gett a good use of her milknes LYKEAS the said Bessy Cochran relict of John Lylle in Rockhous has presumed to comitt and is guilty of the fors[ai]d most horrid and abominable crymes of witchcraft sorcery and charming In SO FAR AS she is commonly repute to be a witch and was fyled and delated to be a witch by other confessing witches and she was named by Margrat Laird as one of her tormentors And that the said Margaret Laird fell in fitts of torment when the said Bessy Cochranes name was named to her And in the monthes of May or June that y[ea]r nynty eight on on[e] or other of the dayes of the monthes of the said year The said Bessy Cochrane having desyred Alex[and]er Hallrig to lend her his horse which he having refused she went away muttering some words and shortly thereafter the said Alex[and]er Hallrigs [horse]took ane extraordinar decease of trembling and [illegible] and could not goe And that trouble having left the horse for ane hour the same trouble during that space was upon Mathew [illegible] in [illegible] cow and when it left the cow they did fall again upon Alex[and]er Halllrigs horse of which the horse dyed also the said Bessie Cochran did lay   [illegible]   befor John Lairds in Bruntbraes kine and blew candles in the door and on [one] of the said John Lairds kye and the milk was taken from another LYKAS The said Jannet Laing spouse to John Mathey elder in penilersen has presumed to comit and is guilty of the fors[ai]d most horrid and abominable crimes of witchcraft sorcery and charming IN SO FAR AS SHE is commonly repute to be a witch and was fyled and delated to be a witch by other confessing witches and was named by Margrat Laird as on[e] of the tormentors and the said Margrat Laird fell in fitts of torment when the said Jannet Laings name was named her and when without Margrat Lairds knowledge or any of the bystanders the said Jannet Laing looked in at the door wher Margrat Laird was the said Margrat fell into a violent fitt and when she was brought under cover to the midle of the floor the said Maragrat fell into another fitt and when under cover she was asayed to touch the said Margrat Laird when her hand was drawing near her the said Margrat Laird fell into another fitt and when she fell into one insensible fitt she saw and spoke with Jannet Laing when she did not see nor could speak to any of the bystanders As also Margrat Orr spouse to farmer Sclatter in dougalshill having said to on[e] of the said Jannet Laings bairnes that ther mother was the occasion of the death of her nephews horse which being told to Jannet Laing she caim and scolded Margrat Orr and said she had gotten on an [illegible] and may be it should not be long befor she gott an other but befor this tyme the said Margrat Orr had on[e] chyld dead and the same day of the scolding she had another chyld that fell in a deep tub of water as also upon the   day of   or ane other of the days of the s[ai]d month the said Margrat Orr having bought a cow and one calfe in the mercat and brought them home to her house the cow would not eat nor the calfe suck And Margrat Orr having accidentally mett with the said Jannet Laing he told [s]he told her of it and Jannet Laing said I shall learn the[e] how to help [illegible] take the rope that binds the cow and tyed about her neck and the rope that bindes the calfe and ty it about its neck and drive them home to the mein door from whom ye bought them and let them stand ther a litil by me and bring the[m] back again And I shall warrand them which the said Margrat Orr having done accordingly and the cow and the calfe being brought back the cow did eat and the calfe sucked and no more damages followed LYKAS the said John Paterson in Geillie has presumed to committ and is guilty of the forsaid most horrid and abominabe crymes of witchcraft sorcery and charming IN SO FAR AS the said John Patersone is commonly repute to be a warlock and was fyled and delated to be a warlock by other confessing witches and he has ane insensible mark and was named by Christian Shaw daughter to Bargarran and by Margrat Laird as on[e] of their tormentors and when Margrat Laird was in her insensible fits her foot did stand away as his did and she walked like him upon a staff LYKEAS Elspet Wood relict of   Miller in Overgourock has presumed to commit and is guilty of the forsaid most horrid and abominable crimes of witchraft sorcery and charming IN SO FAR AS the said Elspet Wood is commonly repute to be a witch and was fyled and delated to be a witch by other confessing witches and was named by Margrat Laird to be on[e] of her tormentors And when Elspet Wood was tormenting Margrat Laird with other witches she said to the other tormentors her accomplices [illegible] upon you all that ye can doe no more to Margrat Laird for I my self alone hath keeped on in greater torment than ye hath done her or some such expression to that purpose As also upon a feist night which was keeped for Christian Shawes affliction The said Elspet Wood came to Mr James Brisbane Minister at Kilmacolme immediately as he came out of the kirk and [illegible] conferred with him and repeated a pairt of the first prayer in the morning and the [illegible] and for and after noons sermones and yet that same day she or some in her shape was seen sitting in Kililan kirk the whole day [illegible] Elisabeth Anderson a confessing witch declared that the s[ai]d Elspet Wood maid a pictur wax for tormenting Mr William Fleming Minister at Innerkips as also Margrat Wood the said Elizabeth Woods neice being in some company wher the said Elspet was blamed for a witch and the said Margrat being much concerned at it said that if her ant were a witch she would dyshonour god and be a disgrace to her relations and the said Elspet having heard of this she came to Margrat Wood her neice and scolded her for her and expressions and [illegible] tymes with cursing and swearing uttered these words I shall think upon it or words to that purpose and within a few days thereafter the said Margrat Wood fell into horrible fitts of torments and was extraordinarily pained and had excessive struggling beating her selfe with her hand

342

and tearing her flesh with teeth and nailles and sometymes her tongue would be drawn back and down her throat and sometymes she would fall into hideous fits of laughter and was tormented after that manner for the space of twenty three weeks and when she was in these fitts of torment she frequently saw the said Elspet Wood tormenting her tho for a long tyme she concealed it out of respect for her during which tyme the said Elspet Wood came never to see her but once and then she had these expressiones to the said Margrat Wood will thou not trust my god with they soull will thou not trust my god w[i]they body and it shall be wiell with the[e] And Sir William Stewart Castlemilk upon whose ground both the s[ai]d Margrat and Elspet Wood lived getting notice how the said Margrat was tormented came to the place where she was and having seen her in several of her tormenting fitts and [illigible] condition he sent for Elspet and chalanged her as having occasion to Margrat Woods torment and the said Margrat for a long tyme denying and [illegible] sent expressione to Sir William upon which he having peremtorly told her that he would use his uttmost endeavour to get her burnt if she would not break the charme she had layed upon Margrat had these expressions The god that took the[e] out of thy mothers belly The god of Abrahame make the[e] better and send the[e] release and after this Margrat Wood recovered and had no more fitts of that nature Lyke As the said Annibeill Reid spouse to John Stewart in Inchinan has presumed to commit and is guilty of the fors[ai]d most horrid and abominable crimes of witchraft sorcery and charming In So Farr As The said Annibe[ll] Reid is commonly reput to be a witch and was named by Margrat Laird to be on[e] of

her tormentors and   in the months of   the year
or on[e] or other of the days of the months of the said year
The said Anniball Reid having touched Margrat Lairds
hand she said who is this and Aniball answered it is a lass
like thy selfle and immediately Margrat Laird fell in a
tormenting fitt then in a deaf fit and her hands swelled and
turned blackish and some of the persones present having
said that Anibeill Reid was on[e] of her tormentors she
presently went away but being brought back and Mr James
Brisbane Minister having challanged her that she had layed
a charme upon Margrat Lairds hand and having caused
[illegible] by the said Anniballs hand and threatened that
she should [illegible] ther befor the charme were taken off
for which Anniball said the Lord Jesus Christ take it off for
I cannot And immediately Margrat Lairds hand return[ed]
to its colour And the swelling fell and Margrat Laird had
ease of her pain And Maragrat Laird was in use to fall in
fitts of torment upon naming of the said Anniball wher
LYKEAS the said Bessie Millar spouse to Gavin Park in
Kelelan has presumed to comitt and is guilty of the fors[ai]d
most horrid and abominable crime of witchcraft sorcerie
and charming IN SO FARR AS the said Bessie Millar is
commonly reputt to be a witch and was named by Margrat
Laird to be one of her tormentors and in the month of June
or Jully 1698 on one[e] or other of the days of the month
of the s[ai]d year She having come into the roume when
Margrat Laird was to be confronted with her the said
Margrat fell into violent fitts of torment as also in the
months of March Apryl May or June 1694 on on[e] or other
of the days of the said months The said Bessie Millar having
cursed John King in poghall by many excreble imprecations

that he and his might never doe well the night after the said
John King had a very good and sound mair which took a
trouble and lost the power of her hind parts of which she
recovered but upon a second outcast about a year thereafter
the same mair within twenty four hours after the outcast
took fits of trouble that in a night tyme she sweat to death
And that same year the said John King had six or seven
beasts which dyed within ten or twenty days on[e] after
another And about a month after the said Bessie Miller
cursed John King he became sikly and tender and could
not work and within ane quarter of ane year after he fell
into great trouble and sickness and was exceedingly
tormented with paines through his body that he was many
tymes in hazard of deceasing and gott no releife by anything
that the doctor prescribed for him and so continued under
this great trouble and torment for the space of two years
and having grownen worse every day he dyed and may times
in his sickness he said that he had gotten skaith by Bessie
Miller Lykas the said Jean Drummond spouse to W[illia]m
Garner in Kilbarchan has presumed to comitt and is guilty
of the foresaid most horid and abominable crymes of
witchcraft sorcery and charming IN SO FARR AS the said
Jean Drummon is commonly repute to be a witch and was
named by Margrat Laird to be on[e] of her tormentors and
the s[ai]d Margrat Laird was in use to fall in her fitts when
the said Jean Drummonds name was named to her AS also
Christian Shaw daughter to Ba[r]garran did like wise delate
the said Jean Drummond to be on[e] of her tormentors and
in the month of   16   year on on[e] or other of the days
of the months of the s[ai]d year the s[ai]d Jean Drummond
having fallen out with Jean Houstone spouse to John Young

in Glenlyan she did curse the said Jean Houstone and did imprecat that the divill make swell her as great as the tour of Kinill or the kirk of Kilbarchine and clasped her hand and spate in the said Jean Houstones face and within a quarter a year therafter the said Jean Houstone contracted a great sickness and swelled prodigiously so that he skin was like to rive and still she grew bigar and biggar until she dyed and all the neighbours about blamed the s[ai]d Jean Drummond for having witched the s[ai]d Jean Houstone lykas Issobell Houstone spouse to George Wilson in Houstone has presumed to comitt and is guilty of the fors[ai]d most horrid and abominable crymes of witchcraft sorcery and charming IN SO FARR AS the said Isobell Houstone is commonly reput to be a witch and was fyled and delated to be a witch by other confessing witches and was named by Margaret Laird and Christian Shaw daughter of the Laird of Bargarran to be ane of the tormentors and Margrat Laird was in use to fall in her fits when the said Issobell Houstones name was named wher [illegible] the said Issobell Houstone having upon the

day   of 16   year come to the house wher Margrat Laird was she did imediately cry out of a great pain in her shoulder which continued with her for some weeks the cause of which pain Margrat Laird said was a charme that Issobel Houstone had laid upon her when she same to see her and Issobell Houstone being brought back and challanged for it she had these expressions to Margrat Laird the Lord god help the[e] and from that tyme Margrat Laird was no more troubled with the pain in her shoulder and when without Margrat Lairds knowledge or any of the bystanders the s[ai]d Issobell Houstone looked in at the

door wher Margrat Laird was the said Margrat fell into a
violent fitt and when she was brought in under cover to the
midle of the floor the s[ai]d Margrat fell into an other fitt
and when under cover she asayed to tutch the said Margrat
Laird when her hand was drawing near her the said Margrat
fell into an other fit and when she fell into ane insensibe
fit she saw and spoke to the said Issobel Houstone when
she did not see nor could speak to any of the bystanders
and when the s[ai]d Margrat Laird was in her fitts she saw
the said Issobell Houstone in the roume and spoke to her
and challanged her for tormenting her but the said Issobell
Houstone was invisible to any other person in the roume
as also the said Issobel Houstone tormented a chyld of
Mr James Brisbane Minister at Kilmacomes by a pictur of
wax untill the chyld dyed and in the month of   the
year   on on[e] of the days of the months of he s[ai]d
year James Kackson in Houstone being in his bed the s[ai]d
Isobell Houstone appeared to him on[e] morning at his
bed syde although the door was lockt and imediately he
fell in a great feaver and [illegible] disease as also in Apryle
May June 1696 on on[e] or other of the days of the s[ai]d
months about three years since John Herriot officer to the
Laird of Houstone having come in to the s[aid] Issobell
Houstones byre he found a leather rolled round about a
cow and over the back of the byre and the said Issobell
Houstone was drawing at the leather with her hands going
up and down upon it as a woman used to doe with cow paps
when milking them and just besyde the leather and cow he
saw a boul of fresh [illegible] milk about four or five pints
which more than that cow or any ordinur cow in that place
was used to give at a tyme and albeit the said Issobel Houst

kept but on[e] cow and that she was never known to buy any milk yet she had every year more butter and cheese of her own making than her neighbours had of thers five or six kindes milk albeit every on[e] of her neighbours cows in all likelyhood was as good as hers as also some person having told the said Issobell Houstone this Patrick Bar in [illegible] had said of her that she had drawn milk out of a leather the said Issobell Houstone upon the

day of the month of   the year   did curse the said Patrick Barr by many excerable imprecations and [illegible] that the divill make draw him through hell and that he nor nothing that he had might thryve and within fyve days therafter on[e] of his horses took an extraordinary disease and sweat to death LYKEAS John Dougall in Greenock has presumed to Comitt and is guilty of the forsaid crymes of witchcraft and charming and is commonly repute to be a warlock and charmer and [illegible] James Orr at the park of old Govan being afflicted with trouble of mynd the said John Dougall came to him in the year of 169[4?] and offered cure him and in order therto he made a Rounytree or woodbon belt and desired the s[ai]d James Orr to keep it about his waisline nightly and if he did not wear it about his waist all the [illegible] to be sure to keep it ane at night and then burn it in the fire but the said James Orr only keeped it about him ane quarter of ane hour he threw it away and the same day or the nixt the said John Dougall maid a cross of rouny tree and said as it if had been agreed to it in the Irish tongue and desyred James Orr to wear it beneath his coat and John Dougall putt it there which when the said James Orr perceived he threwed it away as also in the year 1672 about twenty years since the beasts of

relict of   Hunter in Hawick having taken the disease called the sturdy John Dougall came and offered to cure them upon which the said   gave him a quey that had the sturdy to make what use of it he pleased with a load of peet and the said John Dougall promised that ther should never more of her beasts take the sturdy and accordingly it did fall our that none of her beasts therafter was troubled with that disease and he advised John Hunter to sow sour milk amongst his corn on Bellan day to make the corn crow weill and for curring of the convulsion fitts he had prescrived deseased persons the pairing of the desease[d] pairties naills and the pulling out some haires of ther eye brows and crown of ther head and appoynted them to be bound up in a clout with a halfe penny and laid down in another mans land and the s[ai]d John Dougall maid use of that cure as also for curing of John Hunters beasts and others of the sturdy he did advyse to cutt of a picke head and boyll it and burn the bones to ashes and bury the ashes in another mans land and he actually himself practised that cure and

having complained to him that he had not gotten many fishes he bid him take the [illegible] pin out of his neighbours boat and he would gett abundance of fish LY[K]E AS Margrat Alex[ande]r in pasley has presumed to comitt and is guilty of the forsaid most horrid and abominable crymes of witchcraft sorcery and charming IN SO FARR AS the said Margrat Alex[ande]r is commonly reputt to be a witch as also in the monthes of August September October November or December 1696 year on on[e] or other of the days of the said monthes Margrat Slater servant to William Baird meeson in pasley having refused the said Margrat Alex[ande]r ane alms she said to Margrat Slater I shall cause you rue it ere it be long and imediately went to the door and Margrat Slater was taken with horrible convullsive fitts of heat sweat and   trembling and lost the power of her speech and when she recovered a litil she said that Margrat Alex[ande]r was pulling the tongue out of her head and continued in the distemper for the space of twenty four houres and during the tyme that she was in her fitts she thought she saw Margrat Alex[ande]r coming in at the bed foot upon her and she cryed out to take her away AS also in the months of June Jully August or September 1691 on on[e] or other of the days of the said months the said Margrat Alex[ande]r having asked a peece of loaf from Maargrat Cuming spouce to James Arthur in Pasley which she having refused to give the said Margrate Alex[ande]r went away muttering some words to herselfe and saying she has as good had given it me and William Arthur the said Margrat Cumings son being sitting in the door as Margrat Alex[ande]r went away she stood looking at him with strange looks near a quarter of ane hour and within a fourtnight therafter the said William Arthur fell in a great distemper and several times by heyes arms and foot would have been burled and threwen about and his tongue putt down his throat out of sight and his bowells and belly would rise up [illegible] and some tymes the boy would have been stiff lyke a table and his face turned to his neck and some tymes he neither saw nor heard and all the tyme he did eat not but they only dropped a litil milk down the throat and he was oft bended backward like a bow in his bed so as three or four men could not hold him and continued in these torments for the space of a month or

therby and all that tyme he could not speak but was sensible
that he was tormented by Margrat Alex[ande]r and others
tho the s[ai]d Margrat being the Chief tormentor and tho
he could have spoken he durst not tell of them for they
tormented him with pines needles and awles and some
tymes his armes would have been so straightened up that
no men could pull them down and the said Margrat
Alex[ande]r being sent for she promised to cure him for a
dollar and Margrat Cumming his mother having given her
a peck of [illegible] the said Margrat Alex[ande]r crossed the
chylds brow with a [illegible] that Margrat Cumming had
made herself for anointing him and said three tymes Lord
Jesus Christ send him his health and they saw her lips going
as if she had been speaking to herselfe and the same night
they saw the chylds tongue which they had not seen for a
month before and when the said Margrat Alex[ande]r did
cross the chylds brow with the [illegible] she said that the
woman that Margrat Cumming had refused the alms to
had wronged the chyld and Margrat Cuming not knowing
that Margaret Alex[ande]r was the person whom she
refused the loaf to at that tyme as also said that the chyld
would speak the next day by two of the tyme and as furder
evidence that the said William Arthur distemper was
proternaturall all proper midicaments were maid use off by
the direction of Doctor Johnstone and John Whyte
appothecary in Paisley but tended nothing to his cure as
also in Marche or Aprylle 1698 on on[e] or other of the
days of the s[ai]d months James Hage weaver in Caneran
being at a [illegible] walk when the said Margrat Alex[ande]r
was and he having thrown a piece of peet at her she said
she should cause him rue it and the next day therafter the

said James Hage was seased with ane unusaull sickness for the space of ane month and had great pains through his whole body and was waisted with extraordinary sickness as also in the month of April or May 1698 Margrat Graham spouse to John Alex[ande]r in Mossyde of Anoran having desyred Margrat Alex[ande]r to goe to the kirk on a fast day befor the comunion but she refused to doe and the same night Margrat Alex[ander]r the said Margrat Grahams daughter a chyld of ten years of aig took ane extraordinary sickness and lost her speech and seemed as if she had been worried [i.e. strangled] in the throat and the chyld having continued so for two hours then suspecting that Margrat Alex[ande]r had witched her they sent for the said Margrat Alex[ande]r to come and immediately the chyld became better and spake to them and recovered perfectly within three days and when the chyld began to recover Margrat Wallace the servant maid became verry sick and the s[ai]d Margrat Graham having told it Margrat Alex[ande]r she said the servant maid would grow better as also some debate having fallen out betwixt Marion Whyte spouse to James Alex[ande]r in Cameron and the said Margaret Alex[ande]r in May or June 1698 upon the [illegible] that she would not sell the said Margrat Alex[ande]r a house the said Marion Whyte therafter fell sick and in her sickness she said that she thought Margrat Alex[ande]r was worrying her by the throat and she being much spent by her sickness she said to her husband that she feared she had gotten wrong from Margrat Alex[ande]r and desyred that he would send for her which at first he refused telling her that she should seek help from god and not from the Devil but the said Marion Whyte still continuing ill she said that now she was sure

Margrat Alex[ande]r was wronging her and if she were not
sent for she would be cutt short whereupon the said James
Alex[ande]r allowed his wife to send for Margrat Alex[ande]r
and when she came the said Marion Whyte spake to her
face and gave her meat and drink and though she was so
ill before that she would have been halfe ane quarter of ane
hour or therby between words yet she was then able to
speak to Margrat Alex[ande]r freely but the said Marion
Whyte died of the desease two days therafter as also in
January February or March 1691 on ane or other of the
days of the said monthes the said Margrat Alex[ande]r
desyred from Robert Patersone in Brigend of Johnstone
some shilling which he having refused her she said weil weil
keep to your selfe it may be ye shall be litill richer of it
before this tyme twelve months and that same night he
ryding by a door of a house wher she was standing before
he rode halfe a myle his horse which was then perfectly weill
in a sudden lost the power of his [illegible] and hind legs
and could not stand and swelled from his hips upward to
his ears and on[e] of his ears turned as big as a mans shoe
and continued so for eighteen days then the said Margrat
Alex[ande]r sent word to Robert Patersone to get a litil salt
which they used to gett for two shillings [illegible] beasts
and make it in [illegible] belly and put it in the reidest kail
bladder he could get and tye it to the horse['s] neck and not
tutch his teeth and the horse would recover which
accordingly being done the horse presently and the said
Robert Patersone having therafter occasionaly mete with
the said Margrat Alex[ande]r she told him she had sent him
word to use that cure and farder said she would warrand
he would [illegible] the horse and he went and sold him at

Glasgow but the horse died within twenty days therafter as
also in the months of Jully or August 1696 on on[e] or
o[the]r of the days of the said months Margrat Alex[ande]r
having come begging to the Abey of P[ai]sley Jannet Parkhill
spouse William Clyde Gairdner ther having desyred her
husband to give her something for she was not cany to
which Margrat Alex[ande]r an[swer]ed that she heard what
she said of her and she went way muttering some words
[illegible] that she should cause [illegible] and within eight
days therafter William Clydes sone having met with the
said Margrat Alex[ande]r as he was going to buy a sheet of
paper in the town [of] pasley she hung out her tongue and
followed him to the yard of pasley and when he was
climbing up a tree she came up the tree and gaped upon
him an hung out her tongue again upon [wh]ich he fell
down off the tree and wanted the power of his whole body
and was not able to goe into the house but was carried an
immediately he fell into a great distemper hanging out his
tongue an his   were drawn back which he thought
Maegrat Alex[ande]r did to him for he saw her all of the
tyme he was ill gaping and hanging out her tongue to him
and when he could in his tongue he cried out O Margrat
Alex[ande]r telling in what posture he mete her and desyred
his Mother to hold fast his [illegible] for they would be riven
sundry and the s[ai]d William Clyde continued under [tha]t
distemper for the space of two days LYKEAS the said Jean
Ross in pasley has presumed to comitt and is guilty of the
fors[ai]d most horrid and abominable crymes of witchcraft
sorcery and charming IN SO FAR AS the said Jean Ross is
Commonly reputt to be a witch and she having much
frequented the house of Jannet Stewart spouse to W[illia]m

354

Baird meason in pasley and in the monthes of March Apryl or May 1697 about two years since the s[ai]d Jean Ross having very often desyred drink from Jannet Stewart the s[ai]d Jannet told her on[e] day not to trouble her any farder for she would not an[sw]er her in her desyred [way] upon which the said Jean Ross ràn away murmuring and that same night the said Jannet Stewarts Chyld was taken with extraordinary paines which always began with horrible convultious motions and ane extraordinary stiffnes about twelve oclock at night and continued till five in the morning every night and morning for the space of ten days and the chyld was black and blue after the fitts were over as if he had been pinched and bruised and the rest of the day the chyld sleeped and was for the most pairt pretty weill untill the paines returned him about twelve oclock at night and all persones looked upon it as one extraordinary distemper and phusitians and o[the]r skilled persones could assigne no cause for it and the chyld died of the s[ai]d torment within ten or twelve dayes [th]erafter As also in the month of Apryl March May or Jun 1688 year about eleven years Since Alex[ande]r Mure [illegible]in paisley having a daughter at the said Jean Roses school and some quarreling having fallen out betwixt him and the said Jean Ross concerning the chyld Jean Ross went away muttering some words and within six or seven days [th]erafter the chyld was troubled with a strange and extraordinary sickness as one distempered and out of her witts for she did climb up the walls with her feet and dashed her selfe to the bed so that he could hardly hold her with all his strength and some tymes she would have gone out of his hands as souple as a willow wand and the chyld continued under this distemper

for three days then she dyed and two or three nights befor
the chyld fell sick the house was infested by a multitude of
cats [whi]ch maid ane extraordinary noise othyer than ever
he observed catts to make and to his aprehention the house
did shake as also in the months of April May or June 1698
year the said Jean Ross having inquired at Marion Kirley
spouse to W[illia]m Scot shoemaker in Glasgow hou many
children she had and [whi]ch of them she had at the school
Marion Kirly ansored that she had but on[e] at Alex[ande]r
parks school and Jean Ross having sayed that he was not a
good scholar Marion Kirly replied that he pleased her and
as she was going away Jean Ross urged her to stay and speak
with her but she refusing she spake something roughly to
Jean Ross and so left her and about a month therafter a
son of the said Marion Kirleys about three years and ane
halfe old contracted such a horrible distemper and used
strong cryes and would not be held on the bed and was
sometyme so stiffe [tha]t he could not be bound no more
than he had been a tree and did leap upon the wall and
bedstack w[it]h his hand and did [illegible] as it were upon
the crown of his head and the chyld continued in these
torments from the Sunday night till Tuesday morning and
then dyed and all medicines was used to help to give him
ease yet they had no effect and the chyld in the tyme of his
sickness had strange looks and was always as if he had been
afrighted LYKAs the said Alex[ande]r Lyle in [illegible] has
presumed to committ and is guilty of the forsaid most
horrid and abominable cryme of witchcraft sorcery and
charming IN SO FAR AS the said Alex[ande]r Lyle is
commonly repute to be a warlock and was delated by
Margrat Laird as one of her tormentors and has confessed

356

he was a warlock and that Bessie Cochran his mother
caused him putt the on[e] hand to the crown of the head
and the o[ther]r to the sole of his foot and give himself over
to a blackman and the blackman came sometymes and took
him away and he declared to Bessy Kelso daughter to
George Kelso in Burnbank a[nd] John Llairds wife in
Barnbrae that the Devill gave [illegible] Mulk [illegible]
[whi]ch took effect and [tha]t they lighted blue candles in
Jon Lairds house which hindred the peuple to wacken And
when the said Alex[ande]r Lyle his hands were tyed beneath
his haughs Ane he throwen in a deep pole of water to see
if he would sink he did not sink but cocked up and sat there
upon the water And when some persones that wer
beholding the experiment indeavored to putt his head
under the water he fell cocked up again [whe]ras the
persones who were standing by having throwen another boy
int[o] the same pooll of water he imediately sunk to the
bottom and would certainly have been drowned if he had
not been presently pulled out by a rope that was tyed about
his west LYKAS the said Jean Whythill spouse to James
Peacock in   has presumed to committ and is guilty of
the fors[ai]d crymes of witchcraft sorcery and charming IN
SO FAR AS the said Jean Whythill is commonly repute to
be a witch and hath the insensible mark and was delated
by Margrat Laird as on[e] of her tormentors And at the
naming of the said Jean Whythill Margrat Laird was in use
to fall into her fits of torment LYKAS the said Mary Morison
spouse to Francis Cuncan skypper in Greenock has
presumed to committ and is guilty of the fors[ai]d most
horrid and abominable crymes of witchcraft sorcery and
charming IN SO FARR As she is commonly repute to be a

witch and was fyled and delated to be a witch by o[ther]r
confessing witches and was named by the said Margrat
Laird and Margrat Murdock daughter to John Murdoch of
Craigtown and Christian Shaw daughter to Bargarran to
be on[e] of her tormentors And upon the naming of the
said Mary Morison Margarter Laird was in use to fal into
her fitts of torment And in the month of   16   year
on on[e] or o[th]er of the dayes of the said months Jean
Morisone servitrix to Agnes Stephen Having Margrat
Murdock the tormented person in her arms she became so
heavy that she was not able to bear her and said to the said
Margrat Murdock O but you be very heavy and Margrat
Murdoch answered it was no wonder for Mary Morison was
holding them both down L[Y]Kas the said Margrat Duncan
relict of the deceast John Bell mer[chan]t in Glasgow
Marion Ure relict of George Rae mer[chan]t ther and
Jannet Gentleman spouse to George Craigend late beddall
ther have presumed to committ and are guilty of the
fors[ai]d most horrid and abominable crymes of witchcraft
sorcery and charming IN SO FAR As they are commonly
repute to be witches and were named by Margrat Murdock
to be of her tormentors As also upon the twenty eight day
of March 1697 being sabath day William Scot Couper in
Glasgow lyig in his bed in the fornoon sorely tormented
w[it]h sickness the said Margrat Duncan Marion Ure and
Jannet Gentleman came all into the Chamber wher he was
lying and spoke to him as followeth the s[ai[d Margrat
Duncan who had conceived a prejudice ag[ains]t him upon
the accompt he would not marry her daughter came
straight forward to the bedstack and leaned her elbou upon
the end of the bedd and sayed hou are ye W[illia]m And

358

he answered Not weill mistress and she replyed if ye had
married the on[e] [tha]t I thought ye would have married
ye would not been lying as ye are this day and farder
W[illia]m did ye not see me when ye was going to the
session house in the laigh Church that I crossed your track
and my daughter Anna Kelso w[it]h me an he sayed yes
mistress I saw you and farder sayed to him did ye not mete
an old woman he he sayed yes mistress I mett her and she
replyed I am sorry for onthing that is committed and this
the said Margrat Duncan sayed when W[illia]m Scot was
going to Mr Grayes chamber to be marrayed And [Janere]
Gentleman stood at the foot of the bed and girned fearfully
on the s[ai]d William Scots face and sayed to him were it
not for [illegible] her daughter and for me he should be
tormented ten tymes worse that he was And the said
Marion Ure sayed to him with t[h]reatening words if ever
he devulged or revealed any of ther names he should be
tormented to death And they requyred ane oath of him
that he should not reveal nor repeat to any what they sayed
which he refused And upon the Monday following being
the 29 of the said month they all three appeared in the
chamber wher the said William Scot was lying in the bedd
betwixt two and three hours in the morning in the likeness
of ane sow a catt and and ape and danced in the rome
before his bed he being waking at the tyme and verry
sensible of ther being present And after a litil tyme they all
three vanished LYKAS the said Agnes Snype in Port
Glasgow has presumed to comitt and is guilty of the
for[sai]d most horrid and abominable crymes of witchcraft
sorcery and charming In SO FARR AS the said Agnes
Snype is commonly repute to be a witch and was delated

by Margrat Murdock daughter to   Murdock of
Craigtown and the said Margrat Laird to be on[e] of their
tormentors and also ther having some discord fallen out
betwixt the said Agnes Snype and Margrat Scot servitrix to
John Fyfe the said Margrat Scot was afected w[it]h a waisting
desease and pin away and became like ane [illegible] And
that it was the common report of the countrey that Agnes
Snype was the occasion of the said sickness LYKEAS the
said Jannet Robertsone spouse to James Hill smith in
Govan whom the Devill [illegible] Blackface Anna Hill her
daughter Jean Gilmour spouse to Walter Jamesone beddall
ther and Jannet Boyde lait servitrix to Craigtoun have
presumed to comitt and are guilty of the fors[ai]d crymes
of witchcraft And In So Farr as the s[ai]d Jannet Robertsone
and Anna Hill her daughter Jean Gilmore and Jannet Boyd
are all commonly repute to be witches and are delated by
Margrat Murdoch as her tormentors And in the month of
March Apryl May or Jully 1696 on ane or o[the]r of the
dayes of the said months the s[ai]d Margrat Murdoch having
taken a [illegible] or litill peece of bread from Jannet
Robertsones daughter the s[ai]d Jannet Robertsone
threatened that she should garre repent it that had the year
the Devil having come to the s[ai]d Margrat Murdoch w[it]h
se[ver]all witches and Jannet Rob[er]tsone amongst the rest
And the Devil having a piece of silver in the one side of his
mouth and a piece of paper in the o[the]r Jannet Rob[er]tsone
desyred the said Margrat Murdoch to subscrive the paper
[wh]ich she having refused the s[ai]d Jannet sayed to the
divill will not we gett leave to torment her more seeing she
refuses to subscrive the paper and the Devil said they should
gett more power the morrow and the next day the s[ai]d

Margrat Murdochs torments to the observation of all persones present were greater And the s[ai]d Margrat Murdock was heard in her torments to say ye are more afraid of me than I am of you ye dare not come one hair breadth nerer me I will lick now of your muges And it was observed that at this tyme some oyly substance had been rubed upon Margrat Murdoc[h]s hands and at ane o[th]er tyme when the said Margrat Murray was in her fitts she was heard say that Jannet Robertsone had taken her by the throat and at the same tyme it was observed by persones that were in the rume that Margrat Murdoch seemed to be as if she had been worrieing [i.e. choking] as also in the months of   16   year the said Margrat Murdo[ch] being in on[e] of her fitts she was boued back lyke a bow and her neck leges and armes styff like a tree and her head took a shaking and if it was holden it turned about in her neck and she blamed Jannet Robertsone for it as on[e] of her tormentors at that tyme And sayed to Agnes Stephen relict of the deceast Walter Brock Maltman in Glasgow [tha]t Jannet Robertsone had beat her from the laigh kirk of Glasgow to the s[ai]d agnes Stephenes house which was opposite to the flesh market And the said Margrat Murdoch having called for a key of the yeard to go ther to pray Jannet Robertsone came ther to her And desyred her put her on[e] hand to the Crown of her head and the o[the]r to the sole of her foor And give herselfe over to a brave man and she should gett all the floures in the yeard and many brave things which the said Margrat Murdoch refused to do saying [tha]t was the way the witches did And she having fallen aweeping and being exceedingly afryghted she would not goe home alone upon [wh]ich the s[ai]d Agnes Stephen

sent her daughter w[it]h her and as they were going home
they having cast off ther shoos and stockines and go[ne] in
to the water of Clyde to wash ther feet they were like to sink
down through the sand And Agnes Stephens daughter
having prayed the Lord to guid them they came out of the
water and then Margrat Murdoch who could not speak
when she was in the water told Agnes Stephens daughter
[the]r[e]after [th]e s[ai]d Jannet Rob[er]tsone was then
indeavouring to drown them And the o[th]er witches were
in use to call the divill ther lord but Jannet Rob[er]tson
called hym her Joy And in the months of   16
year Margrat Murdock being sitting upon W[illia]m Roan
of dumbrockes knee And the s[ai]d Jean Gilmair having
come into the roume and taken Margrat Murdock by the
hand she imediately cryed out of a pain [in] her arm And
the s[ai]d W[illia]m Rouan and o[the]rs [tha]t were in the
rume did see nipes on the back of the s[ai]d Margrat
Murdocks hand and the marks of bites upon the endes of
her finger and of pricks of pins betwixt her shoulders and
on her neck And the s[ai]d Margrat Gilmair having gone
away W[illia]m Rowan followed her and desyred her to lift
[tha]t charme which she refused and all [tha]t day Margrat
Murdock was tormented w[it]h biting and pricking and has
been so ever since and was not known to be tormented
w[it]h any torment by byting nipping or pricking befor
[tha]t day As also after [tha]t tyme ther was black [illegible]
rubbed upon Margrat Murdochs arm by an invisible power
[whi]ch did most violently torment her befor it was washed
way w[i]th warm water Likeas Elspeth Tailor Spouse to
William Scot Shoemaker in Newark has presumed to
commit and is guilty of the fors[ai]d crymes of witchcraft

sorcerie and charming In So Far As the s[ai]d Elspeth Taylor
is commonly repute to be a witch and she has the insensible
mark off all which crymes or one or other of them the said
Jean Hadron Bessie Cochran Janet Layng and the haill
remnant peresones above complained upon are guilty as
[illegible] art and part And ought to be punished by the
pains of death

Christ's Fidelity the Only Shield against Satan's Malignity

by

DEODAT LAWSON

This is said by the Rev Mr Lawson in his preface, the rest of which is reprinted below, to have been a sermon 'Deliver'd at SALEM-VILLAGE the 24th of March, 1692. Being Lecture-day there, and a time of Publick Examination, of some Suspected for WITCHCRAFT'. It is, no doubt, based on it but it is far too long to have been that sermon. It has been rewritten, polished and enlarged by Lawson. It is best thought of as a treatise on witchcraft. At such, it is sophisticated and well written no matter how bizarre some of his beliefs might appear to us to be. How many clergymen of our own age would be able to write with the flair and erudition that is shown here? Very few, I would imagine.

As an expression and exposition of a framework of thought which, to those who reasoned within it, seemed comfortably to accommodate a belief in the existence of witches, Lawson's following discourse is unsurpassed. Notice, however, that Lawson's particular brand of Christian theology does not in any sense logically compel its adherents to believe in witchcraft. One could, and I am sure that many did, believe in a theological framework similar to that presented here by Lawson and yet not believe in witchcraft. Lawson's theology might have given a particular meaning and significance to the term's 'witch' and 'witchcraft'. It left one free to believe whether or not witches and witchcraft thus conceived existed. (See McLachlan, 2006.)

Lawson is generally thought to have had the effect by his sermon of fanning the witchcraft panic and encouraging the trials. See, for instance, Morgan (1979). 'Spectral evidence', that is, testimony about the supposed spectres of the bodies of suspected witches, a sort of evidence that normally would not have been admissible, seems to have been crucial in the conviction of the suspected Salem witches. What this meant was that what people said that spectres did was used in evidence against those people of whom the alleged spectres were spectres. Lawson writes:

'...[W]e may learn that Witches make Witches, by perswading one the other to Subscribe to a Book, or Articles, &c. And the Devil, having them in his subjection, by their Consent, he will use their Bodies and Minds, Shapes, and Representations, to Affright and Afflict others, at his pleasure, for the propagation of his Infernal Kingdom...'.

However, note that Lawson's sermon, at least in its published form, is not a wild incitement to or a zealous, intemperate promotion of witchcraft prosecution. He writes that: 'Prayer is the most Proper, and Potent Antidote, against the Old Serpent's Venomous Operations'. He speaks loudly and eloquently against what you, he and I would regard as irrational and superstitious ways of providing evidence of the guilt of suspected witches. In addressing the Salem village magistrates, he says, with regard to witchcraft: '... do your utmost in the use of all Regular means to Search it out.' By 'irregular means', he means such tests as burning suspects hair, experimenting with their nails, urine and blood and other such devices which: '... I forbear to mention, least unwary Persons should be inclined to try these Diabolical Feats'. When people resort to tactics such as this, they are, he says:

'... made Witches, by endeavouring, to Defend themselves against Witchcraft, and using the Devil's Shield, against the Devil's Sword, or (as I may allude) going down to the Philistines, to have those Weapons sharpened and pointed with which we intend to Fight against them'.

Note too that Lawson's notion of a literal signature of affiliation with Satan might be thought to have had a particular resonance within the Scottish Covenanter tradition. However, in the Scottish witchcraft trials, the use of spectral evidence and reference to actual signatures was not common. One might recall, from the previously unpublished witchcraft Manuscript (JC/26/81/D9) that Elspet Wood or the shape of her was said to have been seen somewhere other than Elspet was said to have been. There is, of course, in any legal system a difference between evidence used in courts in actual trials and information gathered in the course of investigations of alleged crimes.

When Americans sometimes say that, in their form of Government, there is an impenetrable wall between the civil and the religious sphere the rest of us do not always believe them. Some Americans act as though they do not believe it themselves. What is the proper relationship between the state and religion and between the state and God? Lawson's sermon, I feel, has relevance to that question and to how it has been addressed and answered implicitly as well as explicitly in America. Why were the magistrates in Lawson's congregation thought of and addressed as magistrates rather than merely as fellow souls? Is there (in the minds of Americans) a particular relationship between the American people or state and God? If the Devil particularly loathed a particular group of people at a particular time and place, did God love them particularly? If He did, does He still do? President George W. Bush considers that America is engaged in a war against terrorism, in a war of good against evil where his country is, unequivocally, thought by him to be on the on side of the former. Does such a stark, dogmatic, doctrinaire and combative notion of right and wrong and of 'them and us' have its roots in the sort of views expressed by the Rev Mr Lawson? It should, however, be stressed, to avoid a misunderstanding which it is easy to fall into, that Lawson and his fellow New Englanders were not Americans: they were English colonists. The United States of America were not formed until 1776.

Christ's Fidelity the Only Shield Against Satan's Malignity was first published in Boston in 1693 by Harris. This is a reprint of the second edition. It was published in 1704 by Tookey in London. As far as I am aware, it has not been reprinted commercially since then.

H.V.McL.

Preface

Rev. 12. 12. Wo to the inhabitants of the Earth, and of the Sea, for the Devil is come down unto you, having Great Wrath, because he knoweth that be hath but a short time.

Rom. 16. 20. And the GOD of Peace shall Bruise Satan under your Feet shortly, &c.

This Discourse, concerning CHRISTS Prevailing Intercession, against SATAN's Malicious Operations: Being Delivered in a Congregation of that Vicinity, where most of them were present, As a Token of his Sincere Respects and Observance, Is Humbly Offered and Dedicated by

DEODAT LAWSON

Having Perused this Discourse, Entituled CHRISTS Fidelity the only Shield against SATAN'S Malignity, We do hereby signify; That we Apprehend several Weighty, Profitable, and Seasonable Truths, are therein soberly Explained; some of the Mysterious Methods, and Malicious Operations of Satan, modestly Discussed; the main Scope of this Excellent Subject, by Scripture and Argument solidly Confirmed; and the whole suitably applyed to all sorts of Persons. That the blessing of the LORD that hath Chosen Jerusalem, may accompany it, to the Spiritual Benefit, of all that shall Peruse it; and that the Author may have much of the Grace and Spirit of Christ, to assist him in his Labours, and so become an Instrument of doing much Service For, and bringing Great Glory To the Name of God, in his Day, and Generation, is the Prayer of

Your Servants for Christ's Sake,

Increase Mather, Charles Morton, James Allen, Samuel Willard;.John Bailey, Cotton Mather.

To all my Christian Friends and Acquaintance; the INHABITANTS of SALEMVILLAGE.

Christian Friends,

The Sermon here presented unto you, was Delivered in your Audience; by that Unworthy Instrument, who did formerly spend some Years among you, in the Work of the Ministry, tho' attended with manifold Sinful Failings and Infirmities, for which I do Implore the Pardoning Mercy of God in Jesus Christ, and Intreat from you the Covering of Love: As this was prepared, for that Particular Occasion, when it was delivered amongst you; so the Publication of it, is to be particularly recommended to your Service.

My Hearts Desire, and continual Prayer to God for you. ALL is, that you may be saved in the day of the Lord Jesus Christ, and accordingly that all means he is using with you, by Mercies and Afflictions, Ordinances and Providences, may be sanctified, to the building you up in Grace and Holiness, and preparing you for the Kingdom of Glory. We are told by the Apostle, *Acts* 14. 22. That through many Tribulations, we must enter into the Kingdom of God. Now since (besides your share in the common Calamities, under the Burthen whereof this poor People are groaning at this time) the Righteous and Holy God hath been pleased to permit a sore and grievous Affliction to befall you, such as can hardly be said to be common to Men viz. By giving Liberty to Satan, to range and rage amongst you, to the Torturing the Bodies, and Distracting the Minds of some of the visible Sheep and Lambs of the Lord Jesus Christ. And (which is yet more astonishing) he who is THE ACCUSER of the Brethren, endeavours to introduce as Criminal, some of the visible Subjects of Christ's Kingdom, by whose sober and godly Conversation in times past, we could draw no other Conclusions than that they were real Members of HIS mystical Body, representing them, as the Instruments of his Malice, against their Friends and Neighbours.

I thought meet thus to give you the best Assistance I could, to help you out of your Distresses. And since the Ways of the Lord, in his Permissive, as well as Effective Providence, are Unsearchable, and his Doings past finding out. And Pious Souls, are at a loss, what will be the Issue of these things. I therefore Bow my Knees unto the God and Father of our Lord Jesus Christ, that he would cause All Grace to abound To you, and In you, that your poor Place may be deliver'd from those Breaking and Ruining Calamities, which are threatned as the pernicious Consequences of Satan's malicious Operations. And that you may not be left to Bite and Devour one another in your Sacred or Civil Society, in your Relations or Families; to the destroying much Good, and promoting much Evil among you: So as in any kind, to weaken the Hands, or discourage the Heart, of your Reverend and Pious Pastor, whose Family also, being so much under the Influence of these Troubles, Spiritual Sympathy cannot but stir you up to Assist him as at all times, so Especially at such a time as this: He (as well as his Neighbours) being under such awful Circumstances. As to this Discourse; my humble Desire and Endeavour is, that it may appear to be According to the Form of sound Words, and in Expressions every was Intelligible to the meanest Capacities. It pleased GOD, of his free Grace, to give it some Acceptation, with those that heard it, and some that heard of it, desired me to transscribe it, and afterwards to give way to the Printing of it. I present it therefore to your Acceptance, and Commend it to the Divine Benediction; And that it may please the ALMIGHTY GOD, to manifest his Power, in putting an end to your Sorrows of this Nature, by Bruising Satan under your Feet shortly. Causing these and all other, YOUR and OUR troubles, to work together for our Good Now; and Salvation in the Day of the Lord; is the unfeigned Desire, and shall be the Uncessant Prayer of, Less than the Least, of all those that serve, in the Gospel of our Lord Jesus,

DEODAT LAWSON.

Christ's Fidelity the only Shield against Satan's Malignity

Zach. 3. 2. And the LORD said unto SATAN, the LORD Rebuke Thee, O SATAN; even the LORD that hath chosen Jerusalem, Rebuke Thee: Is not this a Brand pluckt out of the Fire?

It seemed good to the Great and Glorious God, the Infinite and Eternal ELOHIM in the beginning, to Create the Heavens and the Earth; and together with and in the Third Heavens, a numberless number of Glorious Angels; that were Ordained to do his Pleasure, and obey his Commands. To these he appointed (as a tryal of their obedience) a Ministration in this lower World, for the good of the Children of Men, and especially of the Heirs of Salvation. But a number of these Intelligent Spirits, being unwilling (as some Learned conceive) to yield their Service to man, of so much an inferiour nature to themselves being made of Earth: They Rebelled against the Will of their Soveraign Lord and Creator; For which their Horrid Transgression, they were by the Righteous Judgment of God, thrust down from that Glorious Place, which was once Appointed to be their own Habitation, into the Lake of Eternal Perdition, there to be Reserved in Chains of Darkness, to the Judgment of the Great Day, *Jude* 6. SATAN himself then, and all his accursed Legions being Fallen into a miserable and irrecoverable Estate, are filled with Envy at and Malice against, all Mankind; and do set themselves by all ways and means, to work their Ruin and Destruction for ever: Opposing to the utmost, all Persons and Things Appointed by the Lord Jesus Christ, as Means or Instruments of their Comfort here, or Salvation hereafter. Hence, when Joshua (the Type of JESUS) stood to Minister, as High Priest before the Lord, to make Atonement for the People of his Covenant; SATAN stands at his Right-hand to withstand and oppose him in his Ministration: which the Blessed Jesus (the Antitype of Joshua) taking notice of, he doth according to his Soveraign and Irresistable Power and Authority Command Deliverances to his Chosen Ones, by Stilling the Clamour and Suppressing the Power and Malice of SATAN, their Grand Adversary and Implacable Opposer, as in the Words now before us; And the LORD said unto SATAN, *the LORD Rebuke thee, O SATAN, &c.*

THESE Words are part of the Prophecy of Zechariah, whose Name by Interpretation, signifies the Remembrance or Memory of the Lord, and his Title agrees to the very Nature of this Prophecy; which was to put them in mind, what GOD had done for them, in delivering them from Captivity, and what they had done against him by Iniquity; that so they might be awakened unto Reformation of what was amiss. He was the Second Prophet, that came from the Lord to the People of Israel, after their Return from the Babylonish Captivity.

He was Contemporary and Colleague with Haggai, beginning to Prophecy but two Months after him, and backing what the other had said, more briefly, with more full and mysterious Testimonies; especially as to the Coming of the Messiah, &c. He warns them of the Amazing Revolutions, were coming upon them, in the Destruction of Jerusalem, and the Second Temple by the Romans, and Foretells the Rejection of the Jews, for their Sins, and

especially, for Rejecting of the MESSIAH, who was to be Born among them according to the Flesh. The Prophecy contains then, Exhortations to true Repentance, dispersed throughout the Prophecy, Predictions of many Blessings and Mercies to the Faithful, relating to the Times of the Gospel, viz. The Coming of the LORD JESUS, the Calling of the Gentiles, and the Protection of his Church to the end of the World, notwithstanding all the Rage and Fury of his and their Enemies; together with severe Comminations against the Enemies of the Jews, and against the Impenitent among themselves; Intermingling Encouragements to Joshua, and all Leaders, both in Civil and Sacred Order, to be Faithful in the Discharge of Duty incumbent on them in all respects as the matter might require. These are the principal matters in the whole Prophecy. In this Chapter, we have an account of Zechariah's Fourth Vision, concerning the Restoration and Establishment of the Priesthood, and Temple-Worship; and the Comforts Redounding to the Church from those Administrations; Typically by Joshua the Brand, Spiritually and Mystically by JESUS the Branch.

Particularly, First we have the Conflict of the Angel of the Lord, that is Christ, against SATAN on behalf of Joshua, whom, the Mischevious (yet seemingly zealous) Devil, (transforming into an Angel of Light) objected against, and despised, by reason of his filthy Garments; verse 2, 3.

Secondly, SATAN being rebuked for his Malice, the cause of his objection is removed, by taking away the filthy Garments, and giving him change of rament; verse 4. And in order to his New Inauguration, or Enstallment in the

Priesthood, there are bestowed on him, those Ornaments which might Represent him, full of Splendour, and fitly qualified for that Office, verse 5. Upon his Installment, the Angel of the Lord gives him a renewed Charge, in a Solemn Protestation of the continuance of his Office, and that he would be with him, and assist him in all Administrations, that were according to his own Institution, verse 6, 7.

Thirdly, We have GOD the FATHER, Revealing the Lord Jesus Christ, the Great and True High Priest. First, Under the Title and Metaphor of the BRANCH, Verse 8. Secondly, of a STONE with Eyes, being full of Providence and Wisdom for the Church, verse 9. Adjoyning the Special Effects, of his Coming, in Taking away Iniquity, latter end of verse 9. And in Propagation, and Enlargement of his Kingdom and Interest, under the Gospel; v. 10. Here then, in the first Verse, we have the Representation of Joshua the High-Priest, or Great Priest, as the Hebrew, who was so by Descent, a great Officer in the Church, however mean he was in his Garb, and being a Publick Person, Represented the whole Church, And as he Conducted the People out of Babylon, and Rebuilt the Temple, was a Type of Christ, both in his Name and Office. (2) We have the posture of this Joshua; Standing before the Angel of the Lord, the Angel of the Covenant, as he is elsewhere called. Now Joshua is brought in standing (1) As a Servant, to show Inferiority as sitting, denotes Dignity, and Superiority; As a Servant deriving Authority, in his Office; from his Lord; As a Servant manifesting all Readiness, and Reverence in Obedience. As a Servant to be by his Lord directed, as also under his Eye, for Support and Protection. Or,

(2) Standing, as a guilty Person; As one unworthy to

be employed, in such Eminent service; And as a Publique Person, had much to answer for the sins of the People, as well as his own.

(3) Here is the Opposition Joshua met with, And SATAN the Adversary; whose malice appears, against all good men, and good things in the World.

(4) We have the Posture, and Order of SATAN in Opposing, and accusing of Joshua; standing at his Right Hand the Right Hand is the place of the accuser that being

1 The Weapon Hand.

2 The Working Hand. Satan the accuser or opposer, there takes his advantagious station.

(5) We have the end of Satan's so standing; viz. To resist him, to oppose his Execution of the Priests Office, the words in the Hebrew signify the withstander stood to, withstand him, both to accuse, and oppose him.

In this second verse we have the LORD appearing in the vindication of Joshua, from the malicious accusation of Satan, according to his Covenant Mercy, and Special Favour shewed to him, and the People in delivering them from the Babylonish Captivity; Particularly Here we Note.

1. The Person speaking, the LORD that is Jesus Christ, set forth by a Title of Glorious Soveraignty and Power, the LORD-REDEEMER, and Restorer of Mercy, to His Covenant People. The LORD-MEDIATOR, King and Head of his Church; He before whom, Joshua but now stood, as a SOVERAIGN LORD, appears for him, as a Glorious Advocate, and Intercessor.

2. We have The Person spoken to, and that is Satan the ADVERSARY and Enemy, as the Devil ever was and the

Notation of the Title here given to him holds forth.

3. The Testimony of the Blessed Jesus, against the cursed Satan, the Enemy of Gods Covenant-People; *The Lord Rebuke thee O Satan, &c.*

Where Note we, First, The Glorious Name, and Soveraign Authority, he uses for the Repelling of Satan, and Repressing his Malice, and Opposition, viz. The Dreadful Name, of GOD the FATHER, the Great and Everlasting JEHOVAH. (2.) The Soveraign and Powerful Manner of his Checking Satan, and that is, *The Lord Rebuke thee, O Satan,* he doth not stand to dispute the matter with him, but silenceth him at once, and the reduplication of the Rebuke points out to us. (1.) Satan's Earnestness in his Opposition; he stands in need of Rebukes, again and again, before he would yield and be gone. (2.) CHRIST's Pitty, Tenderness, and Fidelity, in opposition to Satans Impudence and Importunity: Thirdly, We have the Rebuke armed and strengthned, by Arguments drawn from the Covenant of GOD, with Joshua and the People, in that Expression, The God that hath chosen Jerusalem. (4.) There is also Argument drawn, from that Special Salvation of which Joshua and the People had so lately been made partakers; (q.d.) *It is but a vain thing for thee, O Satan, to move me against them, I know their Faults, but I will now admit no further accusations, being resolved to perfect my Mercy to them, Is not this a Brand pluckt out of the Fire?* The Hebrew Word [unintelligible] rendered *Brand,* signifies Light and sparkling on Fire, so that it would have been utterly burnt up, if the Lord had not been exceeding merciful; and therefore nothing but Diabolical Cruelty, could put it into the Fire again, the like Expression we have, *Amos. 4. 11. Ye are as a Brand pluckt out of the Burning.* The Sum is here then; I have (q.d.) but now gratiously delivered them, and I will not by any of thy Malicious Clamours, be moved to Reject or Afflict them.

The Doctrine then is:

That the LORD JESUS Christ, is the only Prevalent Intercessor with GOD the FATHER, for the relief of those that are in Covenant with him, and are made partakers of his special mercy; when they are under the most threatning and amazing distresses, that by the rage and malice of Satan they can be exposed unto.

The whole Explication, and Confirmation of this Doctrine, will be dispatched, in the Illustration of these Propositions contained therein.

PROPOSITION I.

Satan is the ADVERSARY and Enemy. He is the Original, the Fountain of malice, the Instigator of all Contrariety, Malignity and Enmity; It is to be observed, this Title is here given to the Devil in our Text, and Context, on account of the Malicious Opposition, he made to Joshua as a Type of Christ, and representative of the People, for it is noted by Criticks the Hebrew word Satan signifies the most Universal Opposition both in words and deeds; and in a Radical Noun, derived from the Verb, which is in the close of the foregoing verse, rendred Resist, Oppose, or Withstand. Hence it is read frequently, Adversary, importing the same with the Greek Word [unintelligible] used 1 *Pet.* 5. 8. which signifies not barely Adversary, but Adversary in Cause, Suit or Action; The Scope then of this Proposition is couched under the

Name or Epithes here given to the Devil, which is SATAN, the Adversary, or ARCHENEMY: And this Title is given him, in two eminent cases, by our Saviour himself, as in the Parable of the good Seed and Tares; *Mat.* 13. 28. An Enemy hath done this, which our Lord himself declares, verse 39. in Opening the Parable, is the Devil. Again, *Luke* 10. 19. Over all the Power of the Enemy. Which is interpreted of the Devil, or Unclean Spirits, verse 20. In this Rejoice not, that the Spirits are subject to you, but rather, &c.

In a word, what was foretold concerning Ishmael, is in the most Absolute sense true of him, *Gen.* 16. 12. His Hand is against every Man, and every Mans Hand is (or should be) against him. Such an Universal and Implacable Adversary and Enemy is this Satan. But to Instance briefly in the Objects of his Enmity.

1. First, He is God's Enemy. He sets himself against the Infinite and Eternal GOD, All Satan's designs and Operations; do strike and level, at the very Being of God; he wou'd dethrone and Un-God him, if it were possible. He fell from Gods favour at first, by rebellion, and hence by his Righteous Judgment, was doomed to continue, under the power of Irreconcilable enmity, against him for ever. He is an Enemy to all the Divine Attributes, and most glorious Persons in all their holy designsand operations. To all the Divine Attributes, Negative, Positive, Relative, and Endeavours by Blasphemous denying them, to Eclipse the glory of them; he was a Lyar in and from the beginning, against the Truth and Holiness of GOD; *Gen.* 3. 1. Yea hath GOD said, &c. He puts them, upon scrupling the truth of the threatning; and in the fourth verse down right denies it, ye shall not surely dy, &c. Herein also he reflected

upon the Holiness of God, by which he was engaged in that threatning, to advance his own Glory; viz. The Glory of his Justice, by punishing men's transgression with Dying the Death as is denounced, Gen. 2. 17. *Thou shalt surely die, or die the Death.*

Thus the Unclean Lying Satan, set himself against these Essential, and Inseperable Attributes, of the Blessed God: And in the same manner, doth he Eclipse the rest, so far as he is permitted to do it. Again, he is an Enemy to all the most glorious Persons in the God head; FATHER, SON, and HOLY GHOST, in their joynt Determinations, and Eternal Decrees, concerning the Redemption, and Salvation of sinners; by and under the Mediator; and he is an Enemy to them in their Distinct Operations, in a way of Efficiency, for the promoting that which is Holy, and Just, and Good. To GOD the FATHER in Managing his Eternal Purposes of Grace, to Sinners by and in the New Covenant, and manifestnig his Electing Love unto them, which is primarily and properly ascribed to him, 2 *Thes.* 2. 13. As also Eph. 1. 3, 4, 5. Of these Purposes, Designs and Resolutions, Satan mightily opposeth the Execution: As in this Instance of Joshua; GOD the FATHER, had a Decree of Mercy to him, and to his Covenant People Represented by him; Satan stands in Opposition to that Gracious Resolution. He is an Enemy to GOD the SON, to God made Man, and the more, because he was made Flesh, and shewed such Favour to Mankind, as to Tabernacle among them; *John* 1. 14. And indeed, this Humiliation of the SON of GOD being made Man gave Satan advantage to shew and exercise his Enmity against him, (i.e.) as he was the Seed of the Woman, for as he was the SON of GOD, he could not any way come at him, being God over all Blessed for ever, *Rom.* 9. 5. But when once Incarnate, and become an Inhabitant of this Lower World, where Satan ranges to and fro continually; then he spits his Venemous Malice against him, to cut him off by Herods bloody Decree, *Mat.* 2. 16. To Overthrow his Obedience, and Draw him to Sin; *Mat.* 4. to 11. To Destroy him, by stirring up Judas to betray him into the Hands of his Enemies, *Luke* 22. 3. *Satan entred into Judas, &c.* Again, he is the Enemy of the HOLY GHOST, as he is the Spirit of Grace, *Heb.* 10. 29. The Spirit of Truth. *John* 14. 17. The Spirit of Holiness, or Holy Spirit, *Eph.* 4. 30. And his being so called, imports the Holiness of his Nature, and Operations, in opposition to the Unclean Spirit, and his Operations. Hence Annanias is said to Lie against the HOLY GHOST, or Spirit of Truth, *Acts* 5. 3. And indeed, this Unclean Spirit, or Grand Fomenter of Spiritual Wickedness, is ever doing all he can, to Oppose and do Despight unto the Holy Spirit of Grace, *Heb.* 10. 29. By stirring up men to Resist him, *Acts* 5. 51. Thus Satan is an Enemy to GOD CREATOR, to GOD REDEEMER, to GOD SANCTIFIER, in all their Operations, and Designs of Grace.

2. Satan is the GRAND Enemy of all mankind. He is full of Enmity, against the Woman and all her Seed, as Eve was the Mother of all living; *Gen.* 3. 15. *And I will put Enmity betwixt thee and she woman, &c.* Now Enmity denotes a Principle of irreconcilable Hatred, an innate Contrariety, which vents it self in all manner of Endeavour, to prevent the good, and promote the hurt, ruine and destruction of the Object. This Enmity of Satan, appears in the Names given him in Scripture, relating to man, as the Object of

his Malice; He is called THE Accuser, even of the Brethren, *Rev.* 12. 10. THE Tempter, *Mat.* 4. 3. The Devourer, 1 *Pet.* 5. 8. The Destroyer,hence the Eastern Antichrist, is so named in two Languages, Abaddon in the Hebrew, and Apollyon in the Greek *Rev.* 9. 11. because he acts in his horrible Destructions and Devastations of People and Kingdoms as the inspired Instrument substitute and representative of Satan the Grand Destroyer. It appears also, by Allusions made in the Sacred Pages, to Creatures that are a dread to man. He is called a Serpent, *Genesis* 3. 13. The Old Serpent *Rev.* 20. 2. A Dragon, *Rev.* 12. 13: A Lyon, 1 *Pet.* 5. 8. Now put all these three together, that Satan hath the subtilty of the Serpent, the malice of the Dragon, and strength of the Lion, and suppose all these to be improved to the utmost vigour, of Angelical Activity; and we must believe him to be a most Formidable Enemy. He as such, did set upon, and was too hard for our First Parents, striking at the Stock and Root of all Mankind, in order to the certain confusion of the whole Progeny and Posterity: Which Hellish Design had undoubtedly succeeded to full effect, had not the promise of the MESSIAH been Revealed to lost Man, to lay hold of for his restoring to a State of Reconciliation, and consequently to Eternal Salvation.

The Sum is, Satan being doomed to the Chains of Eternal Darkness, for his Treason against his Creator, and spight against Man, his Fellow-Creature; swells with cursed Enmity, against the Children of Men, yea, and against the adopted children of GOD, so long as they are in this world; and being a spiritual Enemy, he is the more formidable, because an UNEQUAL match, for poor mortal flesh: For though by his fall, he lost his Angelical Holyness, yet he did not loose his Angelical nature, so that his Enmity must needs be Exceeding fierce and Penetrating; and although his Powers are much debased, from what they were in his State of integrity, yet do they vastly exceed, the most Elevated Powers, of any meer mortal whatsoever. But Particularly here; First, He is the Enemy of the SOULS of Men. And indeed, this is that he drives at, in all his designs, and operations, to catch devour and destroy SOULS; hence when he draws wretched mortals, to Contract with him; he bargains with them, that after the time of his service to them, he will have their Souls, viz. To be Tormented with him for ever.

He is a Spirit, and hence strikes at the spiritual part the most Excellent (Constituent) part of man. Primarily disturbing, and interrupting the Animal and Vital Spirits, he maliciously Operates upon, the more Common Powers of the Soul, by strange and frightful Representations to the Fancy, or Imagination, and by violent Tortures of the body, often threatning to extinguish life; as hath been observ'd, in those that are afflicted amongst us. And not only so, but he vents his malice; in Diabolical Operations, on the more sublime and distinguishing faculties, of the Rational Soul, raising Mists of Darkness, and ignorance, in the Understanding. *Eph.* 4. 18. 2 *Cor.* 4.4. Stirring up, the innate Rebellion of the will, though he cannot force it unto sin. Introducing Universal Ataxy, and inordinancy, in the Passions, both Love and Hatred, the Cardinal or Radical affections, with all other that accompany or flow from them; hence we read of Hating God, who ought above All to be loved; *Rom.* 1. 30. And loving the World (i.e.) the Pleasures, Treasures, and Honours thereof, in such a degree as is inconsistent, with the love of the Chief good; 1 *John* 2. 15. *James* 4. 4. And although it must be acknowledged, that there is a Corrupt Principle in fallen Man; yet it is Satan, that frequently moves it unto act, and all he intends thereby is the Captivateing the whole Soul, and by consequence the whole Man, to Disobedience of the Command of GOD; that by his Holy, and Righteous Judgment, his Wrath might be Revealed to the utmost, against the Souls and Bodies of Impenitent Sinners, Cursing them to Everlasting burnings, prepared for the Devil and his Angels, *Mat.* 25. 41. And thus he would destroy all Souls, did not Divine Grace prevent.

Secondly, Satan is the ENEMY of the BODIES of Men. The Soul being the better part, is the principal Object of his Malice, but together with that (as an Instrument by which it Exerteth its Powers in the State of Union) the Body is often sorely afflicted by him, when he cannot obtain leave to go any further, And here

1. Sometimes he brings Distress upon the Bodies of Men, by malignant Operations in, and Diabolical Impressions on, the Spirituous Principle or Vehicle of Life and Motion. This we have set before us in the case of the Possessed, *Mark* 9. 18. *and wheresoever he taketh him, he teareth him, and he foameth, and gnasheth with his Teeth, &c.* Now although Actual Possessions, were most frequent and observable, while our SAVIOUR was on the Earth, and it seems to be so much permitted in that time, that the Eternal Power and GODHEAD, of the Lord Jesus might appear, in the subduing Satan, and suppressing his Tyranny, over, the Souls and Bodies of the Children of Men: Yet there are certainly some Lower Operations of Satan, (whereof there

are sundry Examples among us) which the Bodies of Men and Women are liable unto. And whosoever, hath carefully observed those things, must needs be Convinced, that the Motions of the Persons Afflicted, both as to the manner, and as to the violence of them, are the meer effects of Diabolical Malice and Operations, and that it cannot rationally be imagin'd, to proceed from any other cause whatsoever.

2. Sometimes by Moving and Exasperating the Corrupt Particles of the Blood, and vitiated Humours of the Body, he doth (by God's Permission) Smite the Bodies of Men, with Grievous, Pestilential and Loathsome Diseases; of this JOB was a special Instance, *Job 2. 7. So Satan went and smote Job with sore Boils, &c.* It is not expressed, what Disease it was, with which the Devil smote Job; but certainly it seized him, with the utmost degree of Malignity and Loathsomness, that natural causes, under the influence of Diabolical Malice, could produce; and we may rationally conceive that never any man, had that Disease or those Boils (as Job had them) who out-lived the Tormenting Pains, and Malignity thereof. Neither can we deny, but that Satan may (by Divine Permission) spread the Contagious Atomes of Epidemical Diseases, in the Airy Region (the Teritory assigned to him) who is Prince of the Power of the Air, *Eph.* 2 2. And make them Penetrate, so as to render them the more Afflictive and Destructive to the Bodies of such as are Infected by them. This he did by Permission (not only for Tryal as in Job's case) but also for the Punishment of Sinners; hence we read of his being employed sometimes by the Great God, as the Executioner of His just Revenges, in the Destruction of His and his People's Enemies; and thus

he was among the Egyptians when the Lord plagued them, *Psal.* 78. 49, 50. *By sending Evil Angels among them. He spared not their Souls from Death, but gave them over to the Pestilence.* Besides, I may not insist here, How Satan by wicked men his Instruments brings outward Calamities, Sorrows, Pains, and Punishments on the Bodies even of the Children of God; of whom as the Appostle declares the World was not worthy, *Heb.* 11. 37, 38. They Wandred in Sheep-skins and Goat-skins, in Dens and Caves of the Earth, &c. by reason of the malicious Persecutions of wicked Tyrants, the Instruments of Satan, and who doubtless were hurried on by his Instigations. And surely what is said concerning Casting into Prison, is likewise true of other Afflictions, as Scourgings, or any Corporal Punishments for Righteousness sake. That though men are the Actors, yet it is the Devil that shall cast some into Prison, *Rev.* 2. 10. He is the principal Instigator, in all such Designs for the hurting the Bodies of men, when not permitted to proceed further, being willing to do all the mischief that he can, when he cannot do so much as he would: But

Thirdly, Satan vents his Malice against the very LIVES of men, to cut them off and destroy them. He is the Prince of Death, that hath the Power of Death, *Heb.* 2. 14. He is the DESTROYER of all Life, both Spiritual and Corporal. All his Designs against the Souls and Bodies of men, terminate here, even in the Weakning or Extinguishing of Life, and when he touches the life of the Body, he Aims at the Life of the Soul: He it was that stirred up Cain, to Commit the first Murder in the World, when he slew Abel his Brother, for which he is said to be of the Wicked One; 1 *John* 3. 12. (i. e.) Acting from the same principle of Enmity: As if he

were his very Spawn and Offspring. He it was that Raised a
wind, that smote the House where Job's Sons and Daughters
were, and flew them all, *Job* 1. 19. Having permission so
to do, verse 12. This same Adversary it was, that stirred up
David to Murder the People, that so by displeasing GOD,
70000 men might be cut off by the Pestilence; 1 *Chron.*
21. 1. *2 Sam.* 24. 15. This Design against the Lives of Men,
the GRAND Destroyer hath been carrying on, from the
beginning, by stirring up Wars, Tumults, Insurrections,
Commotions and Confusions, amongst People, Nations
and Kingdoms, by which means multitudes of multitudes
have fallen in the valley of Destruction, and gone down
to the Congregation of the Dead; the Devil hath begotten
Pride, Pride hath Created Wars, and Wars promoted
Slaughter, and Destructions; so that it is the true Mark
and Character of Satans Kingdom, that it is Established,
Supported, and Propagated by Malice, Enmity, Wars,
Blood, Slaughter, and Destruction of Mankind.

PROPOSITION II.

*That Satan makes it his business to improve all Opportunities
and Advantages, to Exercise his malice upon the Children of
Men.*

He is an Indefatigable, as well as an Implacable Enemy:
Thus he was willing to represent himself, as appears by his
answer given to the GREAT GOD, when he inquired of
him, *Job* 2. 2. *Whence comest thou? Satan said from going to and
fro in the Earth, &c.*(i. e.) Traversing the Earth, to spie out
what mischief he could do, against the Inhabitants thereof.
This is the Argument used by the Apostle Peter, 1 *Pet.* 5. 8.
Be sober, (i.e.) be in a Holy Frame, to Attend all Duty; *Be*

vigilant, (i. e.) be careful to avoid all that Sin which might betray you, Because your Adversary the Devil goes about as a Roaring Lion, seeking whom he may Devour; here note we his strength, a Lyon; his Malice, a Roaring Lion; his Industry, he goes about; his End and Design, seeking whom he may devour: And he exerts his malice, either (1) Immediately, or (2) Mediately; Of each of these briefly.

1. Immediately and directly, Operating in and upon the object by his own power and influence. And indeed his Angelical Activity is such, as doth render him capable to Operate far beyond Humane Power of Resistance, without any Instrument whatsoever, whensoever he hath obtained the Divine Permission, and this he doth

1. Sometimes by sudden Injections, or Suggestions working upon the corrupt principle, or Original Depravity that is in Man. Thus Satan is said to have filled the Heart of Annanias to Lye against the Holy Ghost, *Acts* 5. 3.

2. Sometimes by false Representations to the Eyes, or only to the minds of men, concerning things delightful to the Senses: Of this kind was the Representation of the Kingdomes of the World, to our LORD Jesus Christ, *Mat.* 4. 8. Some think it was in a Vision, or Illusion, some by pointing at the four quarters and in words relating the glory thereof; Doctor Taylor judgeth the Devil offered the Images, and representations of them all, sensibly and actually, in a strange manner, making their Images appear to his Senses, and not by vision or Illusion, which did not so well agree to the Perfection of Christ's mind. But Christ did indeed, see the Images and most glorious Representations of the World and the Kingdoms thereof. And the better to perswade him, that he saw the things indeed, he set him on an Exceeding

High Mountain; I do the rather conceive this to be the manner, because men by art can Represent to the Senses in a Glass, the Lively Image of a Person or thing, and Satan certainly can do it much more; and besides, it seems hardly safe to believe, that the Devil was capable, to impose upon the Pure and sinless imagination of our LORD JESUS CHRIST, by any Illusion whatsoever.

3. Sometimes by Entring into, and Possessing the Soul of the Man; bringing him unto full Submission, and entire Resignation to his Hellish Designs; thus it is said, Satan Entred into Judas, *Luk.* 22. 3. that is, Totally Enslaved him to his Authority and direction. In this manner he Captivates the whole Soul in all its Faculties by Seven Spirits (i. e.) Fulness of Devils, *Luk.* 11. 26. And this may be, in those that are not Bodily Possessed, and indeed is in a sort, in all Unregenerate SINNERS, as 2 *Tim.* 2 26. Who are taken captive by him at his Will; The Greek Word [unintelligible] there used, signifies to Hunt and Catch alive. The man with all his Faculties and Powers, are at the Devil's Beck; and Devoted to his Service.

Secondly, Mediately by employing some of Mankind or other creatures, and he frequently useth other Persons or Things that his Designs may be the more undiscernable. Thus he used the Serpent in the first Temptation, *Gen.* 3. 1. Now when he useth Mankind, he seemeth to bring in what he intends, in a way of Familiar Converse with us Mortals, that he may not be suspected at the bottom of all. Hence he Contracts and Indents with Witches and Wizzards, that they shall be the Instruments by whom he may more secretly Affect, and Afflict the Bodies and Minds of others, and if he can prevail, upon those that make a Visible Profession, it may be the better Covert unto his Diabolical Enterprizes: And may the more readily pervert others to Consenting unto his subjection. Thus in Tempters to any Wickedness, but in reference to the Present occasion, especially in Witches, Sorcerers, Diviners, &c. So far as we can look into those Hellish Mysteries, and guess at the administration of that Kingdom of Darkness, we may learn that Witches make Witches, by perswading one the other to Subscribe to a Book, or Articles, &c. And the Devil, having them in his subjection, by their Consent, he will use their Bodies and Minds, Shapes, and Representations, to Affright and Afflict others, at his pleasure, for the propagation of his Infernal Kingdom, and accomplishing his Devised Mischiefs, to the Souls, Bodies and Lives of the Children of men; yea, and of the Children of GOD too, so far as permitted and is possible.

PROPOSITION III

The Covenant People of God, and those that would Devote themselves Intirely to his Service, are the special Objects of SATAN's Rage and Fury.

He is the malicious Enemy of the Church of God, and of every Member thereof; and that on account of the Kingdom of Christ that is Established, and the Ordinances of the LORD JESUS that are Celebrated there, and the Benefits that accur to the Souls of men, by those Blessed Institutions, for the Translating of them, from the Power of Satan unto the Subjection of the Lord Jesus Christ; the Redeemer of his People, and Head of his Church; hence, when the Church is resembled to a Woman, for

Beauty of Holy Profession, Cloathed with the Sun, (i.e.) adorned with all Sanctifying Gifts and Saving Graces of the Spirit of GOD, shining with utmost brightness, of the Faith and Order of the Gospel, *Rev.* 12. 1. To a Woman for Tenderness and Weakness. Yea, and to a Woman, For Fruitfulness, being with Child and ready to be Delivered, verse 2. Then do we find the Implacable Adversary of Mankind, Represented by a Great Red-Dragon, verse 3. (i.e.) most formidable, both for his Power, a Great Dragon, and for his venomous Rage and Fury, A Red Dragon; and he is set forth, pouring out his Malice against her, in a fearful manner, by a Flood out of his Mouth, verse 13. And here we may note two things.

First, That the more Solemnly, any Person or People are Devoted to God, and thence do shine with Lustre of Holiness, both of Heart and Life, the more vehemently doth Satan Oppose, Malign, and Persecute them. That which makes him so malicious against the Children of GOD is his accursed contrariety to the Image of God that is on them, and the Principle of Holiness that is in them. So that the more Beauty of Holiness, they hold forth in their Conversation, the more violently, and outragiously doth he Oppose them: A special Instance of this we have in Job, concerning whom the Searcher of Hearts, did (before his afflictions) give this Testimony, that he Feared God, and Eschewed evil, *Job* 1. 8. Upon the notice whereof, Satan set himself against him, to interrupt him in, and divert him from, that Sincerity and Universality of Obedience, by obtaining permission to bring Crosses and Afflictions upon him, in his Estate and Children, Chap. 1. And finding him to be constant in his Resolution, to Serve

GOD Uprightly, according to the Testimony of GOD himself, Chap. 2. 3. He pleads for a farther Permission, against his Person, Chap. 2. 5. And in the Management of his Designs, he did Transform himself into an Angel of Light, as the Apostle saith, 2 *Cor.* 11. 14. (i. e.) pretend to as much Holiness in outward Appearance, as the best; hence when the Sons of GOD, viz. the Angels, the Eldest Sons of GOD by Creation, came to Present themselves before the Lord, (i.e.) to pay their Homage unto, and to receive the Commands of their Soveraign LORD, Satan came also among them, *Job* 1.6. Thus also by Seducers and False Teachers; 2 *Cor.* 11. 1. [Illegible] he insinuates into the Society of the Adopted Children of GOD, in their most Solemn Approaches to him, in Sacred Ordinances; endeavouring to look so like the true Saints, and Ministers of Christ, that if it were possible, he would deceive the very Elect, *Mat.* 24. 24. by his Subtilty; for it is certain, he never works more like the Prince of Darkness, than when he looks most like an Angel of Light, and when he most pretends to Holiness, he then doth most Secretly,and by consequence most Surely undermine it, and those that most Excel in the Exercise thereof.

Secondly; *That the more eminent Service, or Office any person is employed IN, or called to the discharge OF, for the Glory of GOD, and the good of his Church, the more violently doth Satan Resist, Withstand or Oppose him.*

In this Context, we have Joshua who was ordained to be the High-Priest of GOD, a Representative of the whole People, whose Office it was, to Offer Sacrifice for their sins, and to Enter into the Holy-place once a year, with the

Blood of Attonement, *Exod.* 30. 10. (being therein also a Type of Christ, the Great High-Priest of his People). He stood before the Angel, or Messenger of the Covenant of the LORD to Attend his Duty, and Discharge his Office; and presently the Devil or Calumniator, stands up to Accuse, and Satan, or the Withstander to resist him; yea, such was the Subtilty, Impudence and Enmity of the Old Serpent, called the Devil and Satan, (all engag'd against our Lord Jesus Christ, the Antitype of Joshua,) that no sooner, was he explicitely Ordained, to the work he came into the World for, *Mat.* 3. 17. but immediately Satan sets upon him to hinder him, and (if it had been possible) to make void the whole Design, *Mat.* 4. 1. to the 11th. Thus also we find Paul, the Apostle of our Lord Jesus Christ, (who was so Laborious, and Indefatigable, in the Work of the Gospel, 1 *Cor.* 15. 10. complaining of Satan's putting Impediments or Discouragements in his way of coming to the Thessalonians, 1 *Thes.* 2. 18. Wherefore we would have come unto you (even I Paul) once and again, but Satan hindred us: Partly by Persecutions, raised against him, and the Lying in wait of the Jews, mentioned, *Acts* 20. 19. And again, Chap. 23. 16. as a Discouragement to him, partly by Raising Troubles in other Churches, and thereby finding Paul other Business, as an Impediment to his Serving them. Thus Satan still is, and will be, the Opposer of the Faithful and Fervent Officers of the Church, to the end of the World, and so I pass to the next Proposition.

PROPOSITION IV.
That in all Satan's Malicious Designs, and Operations, he is

absolutely Bounded and Limited, by the Power and Pleasure of the
Great and Everlasting GOD, the LORD JEHOVAH.

That is the Title given to God the Father in our Text,
and although many times particularly applyed to GOD the
FATHER, yet is comprehensive of all the Persons in the
Godhead, and especially, relating to the Execution of the
Eternal Purposes of Grace, and Good Will to the Elect, for
Opera Trinitatis ad Extra, sunt indivisa & indistincta. Polan.
Syn. Here then are two of the Persons in the Ever Blessed
Trinity, mentioned, each under the Title of JEHOVAH, the
LORD the SON, making use of the Soveraign Name and
Authority, of Jehovah the FATHER, *The Lord Rebuke thee O*
Satan, the Lord that hath Chosen Jerusalem Rebuke thee.

Now Election, is Primarily ascribed, to the Eternal
Purpose, and Soveraign Pleasure, of GOD the Father in
concurrence with GOD the Son and GOD the Holy Ghost,
These Glorious Divine Persons, Coequal, Coessential, and
Coeternal, do hold Satan, in the chain of their absolute
Power and Soveraignty being able at their pleasure, with
a word of rebuke, to Remand and Restrain, yea totally to
vanquish and Suppress him, in his most outragious Efforts
of malice, against the Children of Men, or Servants of
the MOST HIGH GOD. This is presented to us in that
Expression used in our Text. The LORD REBUKE thee,
the Hebrew word [unintelligible] used here, signifies to
rebuke, not only in Word but in Deed; *Cum Potestate*
Objurgare, to rebuke with Power, so as totally to Subdue,
and Suppress, thus it is used, *Ps.* 9. 6. *Thou hast rebuked*
the Heathen, (i.e.) suppressed their Power, and Rage, even
to their utter destruction, as in the next words, *thou hast*

394

Destroyed the Wicked, and put out their Name for ever, the words then, *the Lord Rebuke thee*, Import.

First, Authority of Office, to reprove and rebuke, Titus is directed, Ch. 1. 13. *Rebuke them sharply*, (i. e.) by virtue of thine Office Power, and Authority, thus their Lord and Master Rebuked the Heat and Rashness of his Disciples, *Luke* 9. 54, 55. But he turned and Rebuked them and said, *ye know not what manner of Spirit ye are of.*

Secondly, Rebuking imports, putting, to Shame, in sense of weakness in arguing, or disputing; *Jude* 9. [deletion] brought not railing accusation; but made the Grand Railer ashamed by saying, *the LORD Rebuke thee, or Confound thee in thy Argument.*

And (Thirdly) it imports Checking and putting to silence. *Luke* 19. 39. *Master Rebuke thy Disciples*, (i. e.) Put them to silence, Thus it belongs to the Soveraignty of the blessed Jehovah, One God in Three Persons, with Authority to rebuke Satan, to Shame him in his Accusations, and to Silence his Clamours against the Servants of God. And that will appear, if we consider three things.

(First) The Great God the Eternal Jehovah, did at first Create him by his Power, He made him in a glorious state of Happiness, and perfection of Holiness, in the beginning of time; when the innumerable company of Angels were made in and with the highest Heavens, to do his Pleasure *Ps.* 103. 20, 21. And although, the Apostate Angels that fell by Rebellion, are Reserved in Chains, &c. *Jude* ver. 6. Yet our Saviour tells the Devil *Mat.* 4. 10. *Thou shalt worship the Lord thy God, &c.* Therein not only testifying his own Son-like subjection to God his Father, and steadfast Resolution, to exalt his Glory, against all manner of Temptations, but also thereby, putting Satan in mind, that even He and all other Creatures, are bound to worship GOD, their Soveraign Lord and Maker, and thence that the Devil ought to worship the Lord Jesus who was truly and Essentially GOD his Creator. For surely he is even the Devil's GOD by Creation, in which he was made a Glorious Angel, but he made himself by Transgression an Horrible Devil.

(Secondly) The Soveraign Power, of the Great God to rebuke Satan, appears, In that he doth Manage and Over-rule, all his Motions and Operations, to serve his own most Holy Ends, and to advance his own Glory in the winding up. Angelical natures are very active, and as the Blessed Angels, are very diligent in serving GOD, and ministering for the good of the heirs of Salvation, Hebr. 1. 14. So the cursed Devils, are full of Subtile contrivances, Malicious designs, and Diabolical operations, for the dishonour of GOD, the ruine of Mankind, and injuring the Heirs of Promise, to the uttermost of their Permission and Ability.

But what the Wise man saith, wisely and Truly concerning the Devices of man, is every way true of the Designs of Satan, *Prov.* 19. 21. There are many devices in a man's Heart, but the Counsel of the Lord it shall stand, (i.e.) totally to Defeat the accomplishment of them, or to Over-rule the issues, effects and consequences of them to his own Glory. Thus the GREAT GOD, doth many times out-do Satan's Politicks, and over-shoots him in his own bow, making that which he designed, as a means to Prevent the good of the Church, appear to be a most proper medium to Promote the Benifit thereof, according to his Blessed will and Counsel, who can say concerning his own most Holy Designs; and be as good as his word, in despight of Men and Devils, *Isa*. 46. 10. *My counsel shall stand, And I will do all my pleasure.* This will appear, if we consider the Pernicious designs, and Malicious methods of Satan, in order to the Crucifixion of our LORD JESUS, and the End he aimed at in his being cut off; and how in a Stupendious manner; all was over-ruled, to accomplish God's Eternal Purposes, in the Salvation of his Elect.

Briefly then, The Devil finding nothing in him, (as our Saviour saith, *John* 14. 30.) on which to fix any Temptation, whereby he might Stain him in his Holiness; or Pervert him from his Obedience; but was totally overcome, and Routed, in a single Conflict with the Captain of our Salvation, *Mat*. 4. 1, to 11. He is resolved to prosecute another design, even the taking away his bodily life, in order whereunto He Entred into Judas Named Iscariot one of the Twelve. *Luke* 22. 3. Who presently went and set himself to take opportunity to betray him, v. 6. Then Satan stirred up the Envy of the people, to deliver him to the Judgment, *Mat*. 27. 18. Brought in Two false Witnesses against him; *Mat*. 26. 60. Moved Herod, and Pontius Pilate Gentiles, to condemn him, and therein gratifie the Wicked people of Israel, that were gathered together, *Acts* 4. 27. And (to compleat the Diabolical Tragedy) Instigated the People, with Wicked hands to Crucifie him. *Acts* 2. 23. And after his Burial, they endeavour to prevent his Rising again, or removal out of the Sepulcher (as they pretended) by setting a Guard about it, rolling a Great stone upon it, and sealing it, to make it unalterable; *Mat*. 27. 66, &c.

SATAN then had thus far gained the Point, and prevailed in his Hellish designs, against the Life of the Man CHRIST JESUS; yet in all this process he had neither broken the

Chain by which the GREAT GOD holds him, nor could he (in the least) overstrain one link thereof; nor yet deviate one inch from the methods determined, and traced out, by the Purpose of the Eternal God in any one step or intreague of this whole affair: But in spight of all the Malice,Power and Policy of EARTH and HELL, it came to pass in every particular passage thereof, as the Hand of GOD disposed, in the Course of his Providence: According as his Counsel Fore-determined should be done, *Acts* 4. 27. 28. As also, *Acts* 2. 23. Hitherto we may observe, how Satan's plot and project, seemed to be agreeable, (though against his Will) to the Purpose, and Eternal Counsel of the Blessed GOD: But in the Ends and Issues proposed, Behold how vastly (even *Toto Cœlo*) they differ! For Instance, Satan's Design herein was to cut off the hopes of the Sons of Men, as to Redemption and Salvation by the Man Christ Jesus, 1 *Tim.* 2. 5. That so the benefits of the New Covenant, of which he was the ONE, and Only MEDIATOR, might utterly fail, and Poor Miserable man, might again fall, Fearfully, Fatally, and Irrecoverably, into the hands of the LIVING GOD, *Heb.* 10. 31. And by the Infinite weight of his vindictive Justice be crushed down to the Nethermost Hell: But on the other hand, GOD's designs was far otherwise, even by the Deep Humiliation, and Death of the Man Christ on the Cross, to produce such Effects as these, Namely that Man's Redemption might be wrought out and Finished, *John* 19. 30. Peace made by the Blood of his Cross, betwixt an offended God, and sinful man. *Eph.* 2. 14, 16. Sinners Redeemed from the Curse of the Law, by Christ's being made a Curse for them, *Gal.* 3. 13. And be made Heirs of the Blessing, v. 14. A number of lost Souls, Bought with a

Price from the Bondage of Satan, and Power of Sin, to be Instruments of Glorifying God, in their Bodies and Spirits which are Gods, 1 *Cor.* 6. 20. In a word; that the Eternal Power and God-Head of the LORD JESUS, (the Blessed Seed of the Woman, according to his Humane Nature) might appear in a Fatal wounding and Bruising the Head of the Old Serpent, *Gen.* 3. 15. And a final Destruction of Death, and him that had the Power of Death, that is the Devil, *Heb.* 2. 14. And no less eminent, is the Soveraign Wisdom and Power of God, in over-ruling this Tragical Scene of Diabolical Malice, in the Glorious Consequences thereof, viz. Loosing the pains of Death, by which it was Impossible the LORD JESUS should be held, *Acts* 2. 24. Raising him from the Dead, v. 32. That having Conquer'd Death, Hell, and Satan; and spoiled Principalities and Powers, openly triumphing over them, *Col.* 2. 16. He might appear to be the Author of Eternal Salvation, to all them that obey him, *Heb.* 5. 9. And having Humbled himself to death, even the Death of the Cross, *Phil.* 2. 8. Might by GOD the FATHER, be highly Exalted, verse 11. And ascending on high, might Lead Captivity Captive, *Psal.* 68. 18. *Eph.* 4. 8. And set down at the Right Hand of the Majesty on high, *Col.* 3. 1. Far above all Principalities and Powers, *Eph.* 1. 21. Expecting, until all his Enemies be made his Foot-stool, *Heb.* 10. 13. Until the day be come; in which he shall appear in Power and great Glory, *Mat.* 24. 30. To judge the Quick and the Dead, at his Appearance and his Kingdom, 2 *Tim.* 4. 1. Thus, did the Ever Blessed God, Over rule the Grand Project of the Old Serpent against the Saviour and Salvation of his Elect, bringing his mischievous Devices, upon his own pate, to his utter Amazement and

Confusion for ever. And since the Salvation of us ALL, is so much concerned therein, this may excuse my so free and large dilating upon the Description thereof. Thus is Satan under the Limitations of God's Soveraignity in all his Operations which yet farther appears.

Thirdly. In that God will Judge and Sentence him at last, unto Eternal Punshment. Satan is now but God's Instrument, as all other Creatures are; and it is the Property of an Instrument, to be Absolutely subservient to the Pleasure of the principal Agent, or Efficient; when therefore the GREAT GOD hath used him for a while, to serve his own most Holy Designs, in the World, by the Trying of his People, and the Judicial Blinding, and hardening of Obstinate and Impenitent Sinners unto their Eternal Destruction: When the day is come, in which he hath Appointed to Judge the World by Jesus Christ. Acts 17. 31. Then shall that Old Serpent, called the Devil and Satan, be Judged, Sentenced, and Confined to those Everlasting Torments prepared for Him, and together with him, for all such Miserable, and accursed Souls as have here been Deluded and Ensnared by him. As appears by that dreadful Definitive Sentence, that shall then be pronounced, by the GREAT KING, in the Day of his Wrath, and Revelation of his Power, *Mat.* 25. 41. Go ye Cursed into Everlasting Burnings prepared for the Devil and his Angels. If therefore GOD Created him; Overrules all his Operations; and shall at last Judge him to Eternal Destruction, then it will follow, he is alwaies absolutely Bounded and Limited, by the same Soveraignity of GOD, which sets bounds to the Sea permitting it so far, Hither to shalt thou go, and prohibiting it from going any farther, and here shall thy proud Waves be stayed, *Job* 38. 11. The like limitations Satan had, in his permission concerning *Job*, as in Chap. 1. 12. & 2. 6. And he could in no degree, exceed the limits of God's Power and Pleasure, notwithstanding all his Malicious Inclinations thereunto.

V. PROPOSITION.

That Whensoever, God hath declared a Person or People, to be in Covenant with Him, as the Objects of his Special mercy and Favour, he will assuredly and shortly, Suppress the malice of Satan, however violently engaged against them.

To Explain this Proposition, we may consider the Arguments used in the Text, to Repress Satan's importunity and Magnify God's Mercy, which are Twofold,

First, God's Free-Love, set on them from Eternity, in that Expression, *The LORD that hath Chosen Jerusalem, &c.*

Secondly, HIS particular favour, in delivering Joshua and them from the Babylonish Captivity. *Is not this a Brand pluckt out of the Fire?*

Of each of these a few Words.

First, God's free love From Eternity, placed on his Covenant people. The Lord that hath chosen Jerusalem, &c. God at the first, chose the seed of Abraham, Isaac and Jacob, to be a People to himself, above all the Nations of the Earth, *Psal.* 105. 6. And Avouched them to be His peculiar People, *Deut.* 26. 16. He chose the land of Judea, to be the place of their abode, and there he chose the City of Jerusalem, or the Vision of Peace, as the name signifies, in which his People might enjoy Peace and Quietness; after their Travails, Toils and Troubles in the Wilderness, where the Thrones of Judgment were established, *Psal.* 122. 5.

Where also the Temple was builded, and the Worship and Ordinances of GOD, Celebrated, and the tokens of Gods presence were placed. So that Audience, and Acceptance of prayers, might be expected, when offered towards this City and House, 1 *Kings* 8. 44. Hence by a Metonymie of the City, put for the inhabitants, it notes the People of Jerusalem, and by a Synechdoche of the part for the whole, implies That whole People which was in Covenant with GOD in those days, which did also figuratively represent, the Evangelical Church, the Heavenly Jerusalem, *Heb.* 12. 32. Now Choosing is an act of Freedom and Liberty in GOD; and a Testimony of Love and Mercy, to such, as are Chosen; by which he is inclined to help them in Misery.

Secondly, HIS Particular Favour, in delivering Joshua and them, from the Babylonish Captivity, *Is not this a Brand, &c.* Where GOD hath begun to shew special favour, he will compleat, it in opposition to Earth and Hell. As he said, so the Lord's People find it, GOD is not a Man that he should Lye, *Numb.* 23. 19. (i.e.) as to his Promise, nor that he should fail in his Providence, to carry on those works, in which he hath made such Blessed beginnings. *Is not this a brand pluckt out, &c.* (i. e.) with an holy pitty rescued, when all on a light fire, now CHRIST is brought in, using this argument in his Intercession for his People, who in imitation of him may also use it for themselves, and it seems thus to be framed (q.d.) *KNOW O Satan, GOD the FATHER, hath begun to own Joshua and the People, in their deliverance in part, and that may encourage them to expect all that remains, for the LORD will perfect what concerns them, and will not forsake the works of his own Hands, because His Mercies endure for ever. Psal.* 138. 8. The force of argument then, for clearing the Proposition lyes in these Two Assertions.

First, GOD in choosing Of and Covenanting With a Person or People, doth engage all his Glorious Attributes, for their good as the matter doth require. When he Declareth he will be their GOD, all his Sufficiency and Efficiency, is for them, (i. e.) to the utmost of what he hath Engaged by Covenant: Hence his Negative, Positive, and Relative Attributes, do recommend him as a proper Object of Faith, for present help to his People in time of Trouble, *Psal.* 46, 1. So that humble Reminding him of his Covenant, doth in its own Nature prevail with him to exert His Wisdom, Power, Goodness, Truth and Faithfulness, &c. in a proportionable degree, to Relieve the Distressed; as their occasion doth or may require: For he Remembred his Covenant, and Repented according to the Multitude of his Mercies, *Psal.* 106. 45.

Secondly, Where GOD hath given some Experience of his Mercy, it is to be used as an Argument to prevail with him, for what we may further stand in need of. Thus in the Text, Joshua is as a Brand pluckt out of the Fire, and therefore may Depend on it, to be Established in the Priesthood, and Owned accordingly. Thus then the scope of the Proposition is cleared up, viz. When God hath taken a person or people into Covenant, and shewed them special Favour, *The Gates of Hell* (as our Saviour saith, Mat. 16. 18.) *shall Never prevail against them.* Lastly,

PROPOSITION VI.

The GREAT GOD, doth mannage all his designs of Mercy to his People, under the Gospel dispensation, in and through the Mediator.

The very Tenure of the Gospel Covenant, is such; and the Terms thereof, are so Methodized, as to introduce a necessity of depending on a Mediator. The whole Transaction of the Gospel Covenant, betwixt the GREAT GOD, and Fallen Man, is by the Mediator; hence it is on better Termes, than the Covenant of Works, *Heb.* 8. 6. Under the New Covenant, all Addresses To God, are by the Mediator, *Heb.* 4. 15, 16. and all Communications of Grace From God, are by the Mediator, *John* 1. 16. Here then three things are briefly to be considered.

First, JESUS CHRIST is appointed according to the method of the Covenant of Grace, to be the only Mediator betwixt God and Man, 1 *Tim.* 2. 5. For there is ONE GOD, and ONE MEDIATOR, betwixt GOD and Man, the Man Christ-Jesus. And He is the Mediator of the New Covenant, *Heb.* 12. 24. To his Mediatorial Office, is to be referred; His Intercession with GOD the FATHER, for all Good to his Elect; which he Ever Liveth to Discharge, *Heb.* 7. 25. By Him our Prayers Ascend to GOD, *Heb.* 4. 14. By Him all Answers of Grace from GOD Descend to us. Hence he promiseth, *Whatsoever ye shall ask the Father in my Name, he will give it, John* 16. 23.

Secondly, In the Management of this Office, He is invested with Kingly Power. He is a KING for Dignity, *Psal.* 2. 6. A KING for Authority of Government: KING of KINGS, and LORD of LORDS, *Rev.* 19. 16. A King for Judgment, All Judgment is Committed unto Him, *John* 5. 22. And it shall finally be Managed by Him, *Mat.* 25. 34, & 41.

Thirdly, It is one special Administration of CHRIST's Mediatorial Kingdom, to Oppose, Suppress, and Destroy the Kingdom and Power of Satan, that Grand Enemy of the Souls, and Salvation of Men. Betwixt CHRIST's Kingdom and Satan's Kingdom, there is a direct Contrariety and Opposition: Now Contraries do mutually endeavour to Overcome each other, and bring them to Nought. Hence, when CHRIST's Kingdom goes up, Satan's must go down; on this special Errand, our Saviour is said to come into the World: *For this the Son of God was manifested, that he might destroy the Works of the Devil,* 1 John 3. 8. He was Incarnate, not only to Oppose his most Secret Insinuations and Temptations; but to Over power his most Violent motions, and hostile Invasions, when he ruffles in; the Titles of the God of this World 2 *Cor.* 4. 4. And the Prince of this World, who is by CHRIST Dismantled of his Dignity, and Cast out of all his Power and Dominion, which he had over the Children of Men, *John* 12. 31. The Reason is, by CHRIST'S Execution of his Kingly Office in Heaven, Satan's Power is Suppressed, and the Prince of this World is judged, *John* 16.8. (i. e.) Condemned to Lose all his Authority, that His Kingdom may be no more; such then Was and Is the Divine Authority and Power of CHRIST-MEDIATOR; that he could have Rebuked, and Totally Vanquished Satan by his own Power, Who is over All God Blessed for ever, *Rom.* 9. 5. But was pleased rather, to Magnify his Mediatorial Capacity, presenting it to us, as a blessed Rule to direct us in our Addresses to GOD; the Name and Merits of the LORD JESUS, being so Acceptable with the FATHER, because every way corresponding with his Designs of Grace to the Souls of men Revealed in the Gospel.

The APPLICATION, of this Doctrine to our selves remains now to be Attended.

USE I.

And First, Let it be for solemn WARNING, and Awakening, to all of us that are before the Lord at this time, and to all other of this whole People, who shall come to the Knowledge of these direful Operations of Satan, which the HOLY GOD hath permitted in the midst of us.

The LORD doth Terrible things amongst us, by lengthening the Chain of the Roaring Lyon, in an Extraordinary manner; so that the Devil is come down in Great Wrath, *Rev.* 12, 12. Endeavouring to set up his Kingdom, and by Racking Torments on the BODIES, and Affrightning Representations to the Minds of many amongst us, to Force and Fright them to become his Subjects. I may well say then, in the Words of the Prophet, *Mich.* 6. 9. *The LORD'S Voice Crieth to the City, and to the Country also, with an Unusual and Amazing Loudness,* and the Man of Wisdom (or Substance) will see his Name: *Hear ye the Rod and Who hath appointed it.* Surely it warns us, to Awaken out of all Sleep, of Security or Stupidity; to Arise, and take our bibles, turn to, and Learn that Lesson, not by Rote only, but by Heart, 1 *Pet.* 5. 8. *Be SOBER, be VIGILANT; because your Adversary the Devil, goes about as a ROARING LYON, seeeking whom amongst you he may Distress, Delude, and Devour.* And let this Warning have suitable Impressions on us all.

First, According to our Spiritual State, respecting our Regeneracy, or Unregeneracy: And therefore, 1. Let Regenerate Souls, that are in good hope of their Interest in GOD, and his Covenant, stir up themselves to Confirm and Improve, that Interest to the Utmost. Under shaking Dispensations, we should take the faster hold of

GOD by Faith, and cleave the closer to him, that Satan may not, by any of his Devices or Operations, draw us from our stedfastness of Hope, and Dependance on the GOD of our Salvation. We would hope we are Interested in the Everlasting Covenant of GOD, and Delivered from the Raging Tyranny of the Roaring Lyon. It is good to be sure, and too sure we cannot be at any time, much less at such a time as this: That it may appear before Angels and Men, that we are Chosen unto Salvation by the GOD of Jerusalem, and are accordingly Devoted to him and to his service in an Unviolable Covenant, against which the Gates of Hell shall never have any power. And the clearing up that we are in Covenant with GOD, is a Sovereign Antidote, against all Attempts of Satan, to bring us into Covenant with him or subjection To him. And in order to this, let us be Awakened.

First, To put our selves upon Faithful and Thorow Tryal and Examination, what hath been amiss. We all, even the Best of us, have by sin a hand and share, in Provoking GOD thus to let Satan Loose, in an unusual Manner, WHO can say he is Clean? This is a time then, for Solemn-Self-Examination.

In this time of Sore Affliction, there should be great Searchings of Heart, as there was for the Divisions of Reuben, *Judg.* 5. 19. GOD is a GOD of Wisdom, A Righteous and Holy GOD, and he never Afflicts the People of his Covenant without a Cause, and that Cause is always Just: We should go as far as we can in the Search, by the Light of Conscience, Conducted by the Rule of the Word, and when we can go no farther, we should Pray that Prayer of Job; Chap. 10. 2. *Do not Condemn me; shew me wherefore thou Contendest with me.* Yet was he Upright, and (even in GOD's Account;) One that Feared GOD, and Eschewed Evil Chap. 1. 8. The like Prayer David makes, *Psal.* 139. 23, 24. *Search me Oh GOD, and know my Heart, try me and know my thoughts. And see if there be any wicked way in me, &c.* These malicious operations of Satan, are the sorest afflictions can befal a person or people: And if under the Consideration of Grievous Calamities, upon the People of GOD, the Nations round about, will Inquire with amazement after the Cause: Then surely the People themselves, ought strictly to Examine, as *Deut.* 29. 24. *What meaneth the heat of this Great Anger?* And to the making this Improvement of remarkable Afflictions, we are directed by the Example of the Church, *Lam.* 3. 40. *Let us Search and Try our ways, and Turn again unto the Lord.* Which leads to the second thing.

2. Add then to the former, True and Unfeigned Reformation, of whatsoever appears to be the Provoking Evils we fall into. He or They that to Serious Examination, (which must be supposed to include Hearty Confession of what hath been done amiss) Adds Thorow Reformation, may only hope to obtain Pardoning Mercy at the Hand of God, *Prov.* 28. 13. And may it not be said, even to the Purest Churches, as he said to them, 2 *Chron.* 28. 10. *But are there not with You, even with You, Sins against the LORD your God.* And certainly, no Provokings are so Abhorred of the Lord, as those of his Sons and Daughters, *Deut.* 32. 19. This Returning and Reforming then, is the Duty Required of, and Pressed upon Israel, or the visible Covenant People of God, when by sin they had departed from him, *Hosea* 14. 1. *O ISRAEL, Return unto the Lord thy God, for thou hast fallen by thine Iniquity.* Hence the neglect of this Returning,

in those that are under many and great Afflictions, is very displeasing unto God, *Amos* 4. 11. *And ye were as a Firebrand pluckt out of the Burning, yet have ye not returned unto me, saith the Lord.* Insomuch, that obstinate persisting, in the neglect of it after Frequent Warnings, provokes the Lord to punish those that are guilty thereof, Seven and seven times more, *Lev.* 26. 23, 24. If we would then, avoid the Displeasure, and obtain the Covenant Favour of GOD, we must both in Profession, and Practice, fall in with the Example, of the formerly Degenerous, but afterwards Reformed Ephraim, *Jer.* 31. 18, 19. *Turn thou me, and I shall be turned; for thou art the Lord my God. Surely after that I was turned, I Repented, and after that I was instructed, I smote upon my Thigh, &c.* Then, and not till then, will the Bowels of the LORD, be turned within him, and his Repentings kindled together for us. Now that our Reformation may be unto Divine Acceptation, it must

First, Personal and particular. (*In Universalibus latet Dolus*) We commonly say, *that which is every Bodies work, is no Bodies work.* Every one is Guilty, in the Provocation, and therefore every one should apply themselves to Reformation. Every one of us should set our selves to do our Own Duty, and Repent of our Own Sins. There is an inclination in the best, to Charge the Sins of others, as the procuring cause of GOD's Judgments, and to reflect severely on the Pride, Lukewarmness, Covetousness, Contention, Intemperance, and Uneven Conversation of others; but we can hardly be brought, to smite upon our own Breast, and say, *What have I done?* Unless we be, in particular Charged, and Convicted, as David was by the Prophet Nathan, in 2 *Sam.* 12. 7. *Thou art the man. Thou art he* (q. d.) that art concerned in this

Provocation by thy Transgression.

Secondly, Reformation, (by which we may clear up, that we are the Covenant People of God) must be Universal. We must turn from All and Every sin which hath been Committed, and apply our selves to the discharge of Every Duty, which hath been neglected. We must have no sinful Reserves, as he, 2 *Kings* 5. 18. *In this thing pardon thy Servant, &c.* He was Convicted it was a Sin, that needed Pardon, and yet would fain be Excused in the Commission thereof. Thus Junius, and Trem. and the Dutch Annotators translate it, and Pisc. Interprets it of his desire to continue in that Office, which he could not with good Conscience discharge. Though some Learned and Judicious understand it as a craving of pardon for what he had therein done amiss in time past. In short, so far as we are guilty of Reservations in our Reformation, so far will there remain a Cloud upon the Evidences of our Covenant Interest in GOD that hath Chosen Jerusalem. This to Regenerate Souls.

Secondly then Let Unregenerate Sinners, be warned and awakned, to get out of that Miserable state of sin, and consequently of subjection to Satan, (That Tyrannical, Implacable, and Indefatigable, Enemy of Souls) in which you are. O break off your sins by Repentance, and your Iniquities by a saving closure with the LORD JESUS CHRIST, for Justification, Sanctification and Salvation, That ye may be delivered, from the Power, and Dominion of Satan, under which you are ensnared, to do his will, altho' utterly cross to the will of GOD, and may be Translated, into the Kingdom of the Lord Jesus; the Dear Son of God, and Blessed Saviour of the Souls of men, Col. 1. 13. Being by infinite mercy, Recovered out of the snare of the Devil, who are (now) taken Captive by him at his will. 2 *Tim.* 2. 26. Awake, Awake then, I beseeeh you, and remain no longer under the Dominion of that Prince of Cruelty and Malice, whose Tyrannical Fury, we see thus exerted, against the Bodies and Minds of these afflicted persons. Surely no Sinner in this Congregation, who is sensible of his Bondage to Satan, that cruel (and worse than Egyptian) Task-master, and Tyrant, can be willing, to continue quietly, in subjection to him one day or hour longer. Thus much in respect of the Spiritual State of men.

Secondly, This Warning is directed to all manner of persons, according to their condition of life, both in Civil and Sacred Order: Both High and Low, Rich and Poor, Old and Young, Bond and Free. O let the observation of these amazing Dispensations of GOD's unusual and strange Providence, quicken us to our Duty at such a time as this, in our respective Places and Stations, Relations, and Capacities. The GREAT GOD, hath done such things amongst us, as do make the Ears of those that hear them to Tingle; *Jer.* 1. 3. and serious Souls, are at a loss to what these things may grow; and what we shall find to be the end, of this dreadful visitation, in the permission whereof the Provoked GOD as a Lyon hath Roared; who can but Fear? The LORD hath spoken, who can but Prophesy? *Amos* 3. 8. The Loud Trumpet of God, in this Thundering Providence, is Blown in the City, and the Eccho of it, heard through the Country, surely then, the People must, and ought to be afraid, *Amos* 3. 6.

USE II.

Let it be for DEEP HUMILIATION, to the people of

this place, which is in special under the Influence of this Fearful Judgment of GOD. The LORD doth at this day, manage a great controversy with You, to the astonishment of your selves and others, You are therefore to be deeply humbled, and sit in the dust Considering

First, The signal hand of God, in singling out this place, this poor Village, for the first seat of Satan's Tyranny, and to make it (as 'twere) the Rendezvous of Devils, where they Muster their infernal forces appearing to the afflicted, as coming Armed, to carry on their malicious designs, against the Bodies, and if God in mercy prevent not, against the Souls of many in this place. Great Afflictions, attended with Remarkable Circumstances, do surely call for, more than ordinary degrees of Humiliation.

But Secondly be humbled also, That so many Members of this Church, of the LORD JESUS CHRIST, should be under the Influences of Satan's malice, in these his Operations; some as the Objects of his Tyrranny, on their Bodies to that degree of Distress, which none can be sensible of, but those that see and feel it, who are in the mean time also, sorely distressed in their Minds, by frightful Representations, made by the Devils unto them. Other professors, and visible Members of this Church, are under the awful Accusations, and Imputations of being the Instruments of Satan in his mischevious actings. It cannot but be matter of deep humiliation, to such as are Innocent, that the Righteous and Holy GOD, should permit them to be named, in such pernicious and unheard of practices, and not only so, but that HE who cannot but do right, should suffer the stain of suspected Guilt, to be as it were Rubbed on, and Soaked in, by many sore and amazing

Circumstances; and it is matter of soul abasement, to all that are in the Bond of GOD's Holy Covenant in this place, that Satan's seat should be amongst them, where he attempts to set up his Kingdom, in opposition to Christ's Kingdom, and to take some of the Visible Subjects of our LORD JESUS, and use at least their shapes and appearances, instrumentally, to Afflict and Torture, other Visible Subjects of the same Kingdom. Surely his design is, that CHRIST's Kingdom, may be Divided against it self, that being thereby weakened, he may the better take Opportunity to set up his own Accursed powers and Dominions. It calls aloud then, to all in this place, in the Name of the Blessed JESUS and words of his Holy Apostle; 1 *Pet.* 5. 6. *Humble your selves under the mighty hand of God, thus lift up in the midst of you, and he shall Exalt, Save, and Deliver you, in due time.*

USE III.

It is matter of TERROR, Amazement, and Astonishment, to all such wretched Souls (If there be any here in the Congregation, (and God of his infinite mercy grant that none of you may ever be found such) as have given up their Names, and Souls to the Devil: Who by Covenant Explicite or Implicite, have bound themselves to be his Slaves and Drudges, consenting to be Instruments, in whose shapes, he may Torment and Afflict their Fellow-Creatures (even *of their Own kind,) to the amazing and astonishing of the standers by.*

I would hope, I might have spared this Use, but I desire (by divine assistance) to declare the whole Counsel of God; and if it come not as Conviction where it is so, it may serve for Warning, that it may never be so: For it is a most dreadful thing to consider, that any should change the Service of GOD, for the service of the Devil, the worship of the Blessed GOD for the worship of the Cursed Enemy, of GOD and Man. But Oh! (which is yet a thousand times worse) how shall I name it? If any that are in the Visible Covenant of God, should break that Covenant, and make a League with Satan, if any that have set down and eat at CHRIST's Table should so lift up their Heel against him, as to have Fellowship at the Table of Devils; and (as it hath been represented to some of the Afflicted) Eat of the Bread, and Drink of the Wine, that Satan hath mingled. Surely if this be so, the Poet is in the right; *Audax Omnia perpeti, Gens Humana ruit, per Vetitum nefas. Audacious Mortals are grown to a fearful height of Impiety.* And we must cry out in Scripture Language, and that Emphatical Apostrophe of the Prophet Jeremy; chap. 2. 12. *Be astonished O ye Heavens at this, and be Horribly afraid; be ye very Desolate, saith the Lord.*

Now Terrors may justly seize upon those, that have so done, on these accounts. First, All Mankind is now (as well by God's Authority, as their own Interest) set against you. You have proclaimed your selves Mortal Enemies to all men, and they cannot but Mortally Hate and Abominate you. If you are in League with the DESTROYER, what is said of Ishmael is true, not only of Satan, but also of you, Gen. 16. 12. *His Hand will be against every man and every man's hand against him:* So every man's hand is, and will be against you, to Accuse, Condemn, Destroy and cut you off, from the Land of the Living. The Enmity that God in just Judgment placed; betwixt the Old Serpent and the Woman, and betwixt her Seed, and his Seed, Gen. 3. 15. is Improved to the Height against you, as you Stand, Look and Act, like your Father and King the Devil.

2. If you have been guilty of such Impiety, The Prayers of the People of God, are against you on that account. It is their Duty to pray daily, that Satan's Kingdom may be Suppressed, Weakned, brought down, and at last Totally destroyed; hence that all Abetters, Subjects, Defenders, and Promoters thereof, may be utterly Crushed and Confounded. They are constrained, to Suppress that Kindness and Compassion, that in their Sacred Addresses, they once bare unto you (as those of their own kind, and framed out of the same mould) Praying with one consent, as the Royal Prophet did against his malicious Enemies (the Instruments of Satan) *Psal.* 109. 6. *Set thou a wicked man over him, and let Satan stand at his Right-hand* (i. e.) to withstand all that is for his good, and promote all that is for his hurt, and verse 7. When he is Judged, let him be Condemned, and let his Prayer become Sin. What a miserable condition must they be in, who have all the Faithful, that have Interest in Heaven thus engaged against them? But

Thirdly, If this seems a light thing KNOW, That if you are in Covenant with the Devil, the Intercession of the BLESSED JESUS is against you, for your Contract with his Grand Implacable Enemy. His Prayer is for the Subduing of Satan's Power and Kingdom, and the utter Confounding of all his Instruments. He is exalted at the Right-hand of GOD, to make Intercession for his Elect, as also expecting, till all his Enemies (and such are All the Sworn Subjects and Vassals of Satan) be made his Footstool (i.e.) put to shame, and everlasting Contempt, *Psal.* 110. 1. *Heb.* 10. 13. Hence in the Text, He intercedes with GOD the FATHER for Joshua and the People, against Satan and all his Powers and Instruments. *And the LORD* (i.e. the INTERCESSOR) *said unto Satan, the Lord Rebuke thee, &c.*

Lastly, if it be so, Then the GREAT GOD is set against you. The Omnipotent JEHOVAH, One God in Three Persons, FATHER, SON, and HOLY GHOST, in their Several Distinct Operations, and all Their Divine Attributes, are ingaged against you: As it hath been already noted, they are against Satan: Even so because you are his Offspring, Officers, and Instrument of mischiefs, cruelty; murther, &c. Against you. You justifie the Old Subjection, made by our first Parents in the Transgression, of themselves (and for theirs) to the Dominion of Satan, and shew, that if it were to be done again you would do the same. Therefore KNOW YE, that are guilty of such Monstrous Iniquity, That since you are the People, that have no more understanding, than to forsake the Covenant of your God, to enter into Covenant with Satan; He that made you will not save you, and he that formed you will shew you no favour, *Isa.* 27. 11. And so you are utterly undone for ever, unless by the Infinite Power and Mercy of GOD, you are rescued out of the horrible Pit, and snare of THE Destroyer. Be assured, that although you should now Evade, the Condemnation of man's Judgment, and escape a violent death by the Hand of Justice: Yet unless God shall give you Repentance, (which we heartily pray for) there is a day coming, when the Secrets of all Hearts shall be revealed by JESUS CHRIST, *Rom.* 2. 16. Then, Then your sin will find you out; and you shall be punished with Everlasting Destruction, from the Presence of the LORD, and Doomed to those Endless, Easeless and Remediless Torments, Prepared for the Devil and his Angels, *Mat.* 25. 41.

The Reverend Mr. Simmes, sometime since Minister of this Country, coming into Prison to a Condemned Witch; tho' he knew her not, yet she took Knowledge of him, and said, O Mr. Simmes, I remember a Text you Preached on in England Twenty Four Years since, from those Words, Your Sin will find you out, for I find it to be true in my own Case.

USE IV
Let it be for CAUTION to all of us that are before the Lord: As ever we would prevail with GOD, to prevent the spreading of this sore Affliction, and to Rebuke Satan for us let us take heed of Sideing with, or giving place unto the Devil, Eph. 4. 27.

Neither give place to the Devil, yield no subjection to him, No not for an Hour. Thus we may be said to do in general, when we give way voluntarily, to the Comission of any sin, he that Committeth sin (i.e.) sineth *sciens, volens,* wittingly and willingly is of the Devil, 1 *John* 3. 8. (i. e.) Joyns with him in his Rebellion against GOD, hence the more there is of a Man's Will in any sin, the more he is renderd like Satan, who willeth nothing but sin from the beginning. *Ibid.* And it gratifies the Devil, because the Man appears Captivated by that sin, hence so far as the Regenerate fall into Known sin, they please the Devil, and are (in a sort) guilty of Yielding to him, and siding with him.

And we do especialy give place to him by these sins. First, By giving way unto Sinful and unruly Passions, such as Envy, Malice, or Hatred of our Neighbours and Brethren. These Devil-like, corrupted Passions, are Contrary unto, and do endanger the letting in Satan and his Temptations, yea he generally, comes into the soul at these Doors, to captivate any person to the Horrid sin of Covenanting with him. These are greedy and Insatiable Passions, that strike at the Being as well as the good of the Object, and to gratifie these, many have been Overcome by Satan's temptations, so that (as the wise man saith in another case) *He hath cast down many Wounded, yea many strong men have been slain by him, Prov. 7. 26.* And as for you of this place, you may do well seriously to Examine, whether the LORD hath not in Righteous Judgment sent this Fire of his Holy displeasure, to put out some Fires of Contention, that have been amongst you, by which the Fruits of the Spirit *Gal. 5. 22.* Have been (as I may say) much Blasted, and the Fruits of the Flesh Cherished to maturity, so as to threaten the Cheaking of All that is good, with the Priniples thereof; through the malice of your Adversary the Devil, who is now come down among you, with Open mouth as a Roaring Lyon to Devour you: By setting you one against another with earnestness, He sows discord amongst Brethren (both in Civil and Sacred Order) *Prov. 6. 19.* Stirring them up to Bite and Devour one another, that they may be Consumed one of another, *Gal. 5. 15.* Upon this ground the Apostle brings in this Caution *Eph. 4. 26.[27.] Let not the Sun go down upon your wrath. Neither give place to the Devil.* Inveterate Anger and Ill-will, makes way for the Devil, and gives place to him.

And the same we do Secondly, By using Indirect means to Prevent or Remove this Affliction; and trying Unwarrantable projects, to reveal Secrets, or Discover future events. When persons have been under long exercise, those about them are very desirous, to Relieve them out of, or Prevent those grievous fits, of Diabolical tortures, with which they are distressed. And hence do not consider the Efficacy or Tendency of those things they use. I call such Indirect means, as being duely observed, cannot be found to have any Natural or Physical virtue in them, to produce the Desired Effect of themselves: Nor yet have any warrant from the word of GOD, which if they had; ought to be believed and depended upon, to produce the Effect for which they were Instituted; tho' never so mean in their own Nature. Because the Power of the GREAT GOD is engag'd, to uphold the decisive influence of his own instituted Means, as we find in the bitter Water which caused the Curse, *Numb.* 5. 17. which was only compounded, of Holy Water, (or common Water set apart unto sacred use) and the duct of the Floor of the Sanctuary; this we may imagine had not any Physical Influence in its own Nature, proportionable, to such a solemn effect or consequence, as was in that case appointed thereunto; it must then depend, wholly and only, on the Divine Institution of it, to be for the Cursing, or Clearing of the Woman as she was in the sight of GOD, Guilty or Not Guilty; as we read, ver. 27 and 28. viz. if Guilty, her Belly should Swell, and her Thigh should Rot; if Clear, she should be Free, (i. e.) from any hurt, and should conceive Seed. But seeing we find no means instituted of GOD, to make Tryal of Witches, or to Charm away Witchcraft,(both which are a kind of Witchcraft) we are to expect Effects in the ordinary course of Providence, suitable to the natural Virtue of Causes, and means used accordingly; but what is otherwise, must be of the Nature of Inchantments; these indirect means, are such as, Burning the Afflicted Persons Hair; pairing of Nails, stopping up and boyling the Urine. Their Scratching the Accused, or otherwise Fetching Blood of them, with many more, which I forbear to mention, least unwary Persons should be inclined to try these Diabolical Feats. But as to the Effect, this is plainly found, a Giving place to the Devil; for he giving way to it, and Ceasing to Afflict, upon the use of it, brings such Projects into esteem, and Gains to his own Devices (for I can call them no better) too much Credit and Observance: For hence such as use them, finding him flee thereupon, are encouraged to the Frequent use of them, and are (as a Learned Writer saith) made Witches, by endeavouring, to Defend themselves against Witchcraft, and using the Devil's Shield, against the Devil's Sword, or (as I may allude) going down to the Philistines, to have those Weapons sharpened and pointed with which we intend to Fight against them. In a Word, is it because there is not a GOD in the midst of us, able to Rebuke and Vanquish Satan, in all his Operations? If there be, then away with whatsoever hath not Scripture Precept or President for its Warrantee.

And let us use those Weapons, which are not Carnal but Mighty through GOD, to the pulling down strong Holds, &c. 2 *Cor.* 10. 4. Thus may we put to the worse, those Principalities and Powers of Darkness which do in such a fearful manner, Wrestle and Contend with us at this time, *Eph.* 6. 12.

But I must not Conclude this Particular, without testifying against some other Practices amongst us Condemned by the Rule of GOD, and Writings of Learned and Judicious Men as yielding to, and tampering with the Devil, viz. the Sieve and Scyssers; the Bible and Key; the white of an Egge in the Glass; the Horse-shoe nailed on the Threshold; a stone hung over the Rack in a Stable, with many more; which I would not make known to any, that are ignorant of them; because they are no better than Conjurations, and if in the use of them Discoveries are made; or Effects produced, to the gratifying their sinful Curiosity in any degree it must be from the Devil, and not from GOD; who never instituted any such ways, by and in which, to discover Secret Things or Future Events to the Children of Men: Hence such as by these Experiments, adventure to play on the hole of the Asp, and approach unto the Den of the Dragons; are in great danger to become a Prey unto Satan's Malice, being (or ever they are aware) seduced by his subtlety, into an entire subjection to his Infernal Powers, [Illegible word] as at last to be destroyed by him, and cast with him, into the Lake that Burneth with Fire and Brimstone for Ever.

Thirdly, Give no place to the Devil by Rash Censuring of others, without sufficient Grounds, or False Accusing any willingly. This is indeed to be like the Devil, who hath the Title [unintelligible] in the Greek, because he is the Calummator, or False Accuser. Hence when we read of such Accusers in the Latter Days, they are in the Original called [unintelligible] Calumnatores, 2 Tim. 3. 3. It is a time of Temptation amongst you such as never was before: Let me intreat you not to be lavish or severe in reflecting, on the Malice or Envy of your neighbours, by whom any of you have been accused, lest whilst you falsely charge one another, viz. The Relations of the Afflicted, and Relations of the Accused; the Grand Accuser (who loves to Fish in Troubled Waters) should take advantage upon you. Look at Sin the procuring cause, GOD in Justice the Soveraign Efficient, and Satan THE Enemy, the principal Instrument, both in Afflicting some, and Accusing others:

And if Innocent Persons be suspected, it is to be ascribed to GOD's Pleasure, supreamly permitting, and Satan's Malice subordinately troubling, by Representation of such to the Afflicting of others, even of such as have all the while, we have reason to believe, (especially some of them) no kind of Ill-will, or Disrespect, unto those that have been complained of by them. This giving place to the Devil Avoid, for it will have uncomfortable and Pernicious Influence, upon the Affairs of this place, by letting out Peace, and bringing in Confusion, and every evil Work, which we Heartily pray GOD, in Mercy, to prevent.

Fourthly and Lastly, Then we give place to the Devil, When we are guilty, of Unbelief of GOD, and his Power Promise and Providence; for our benefit and relief under our Troubles. Unbelief betrayed our first Parents, to the first sin. The Devil in the Serpent, first moved them to Question the truth of the Threatening, and so they came to Deny it, *Gen.* 3. 1, & yielding to the God of this World, the Author and main Fomenter of Unbelief, by and in which he Reigns over the Children of Perdition, 2 *Cor.* 4. 4: Unbelief is a Mother Sin, and there are many Sins, to which Men could not be drawn, were it not for the Unbelief of the Threatenings, denounced in the Word of GOD, against that sin, which they do so boldly perpetrate, and of the Promise made unto the contrary Duty, which they do so abominably neglect.

Indeed Unbelief of the Truth of GOD's Promise, or Efficacy of His Providence, extending towards us (these being Inseperable Attributes of the Blessed GOD) brings in Question, whether he is, or hath a Being. For he can as soon cease to Be, as to be most Powerful, most Faithful, most Gracious, and Bountiful, which are all Attributes relating to his Providence, and this is to go away from GOD, For he that cometh to GOD must believe that he is, *Heb.* 11. 6. Hence the Apostle Cautions even the Brethren that they may not be Guilty of it, *Heb.* 3. 12. *Take heed Brethren, lest there be in any of you, an evil Heart of Unbelief, Departing from the Living God.* Intimating, that so far as the best fall into Unbelief, they go from GOD, and so far must needs give place to the Devil. For there are but these Two Rulers, over all Men in the World, and all that leave the one, go to the other. But to proceed.

USE V.

Let it be for EXHORTATION, and Direction, to this whole Assembly, and to all others that shall come to the Knowledge of these Amazing Dispensations; Here then give me leave to press those special Duties, which all Persons are concerned to put in Practice, at such a time as this.

First, Be we Exhorted and Directed, To Exercise True Spiritual Sympathy with, and Compassion towards, those Poor Afflicted Persons, that are by Divine Permission, under the Direful Influences of Satan's Malice. A Deep sense of all these things, and being Heartily affected with them, makes way for, and stirs up unto, those other Duties which are now incumbent on us. I fear we are not enough affected with this solemn Providence, unless it be those few that have seen these fearful things who by their Eyes, have had their Hearts affected accordingly. There is a Divine Precept enjoyning the practice of this Duty, *Heb.* 13. 2. *Remember them that suffer Adversity, as being your selves also in the Body*; (i. e.) being of the same Mould; in the same mortal and frail Estate; and therefore liable to the same Affliction, if the Holy GOD should please to permit Satan to bring it upon us: Let us then be deeply sensible, and as the Elect of GOD, put on Bowels of Mercy, towards those in Misery, *Col.* 3. 12. *Oh Pitty, Pitty them, for the Hand of the LORD hath touched them, and the Malice of Devils hath fallen upon them.*

Secondly, Let us be sure to take unto us, and PUT ON the whole Armour of GOD, and every piece of it, let none be wanting. Let us labour to be in the Exercise and Practice, of the whole company of Sanctifying Graces, and Religious Duties. This Important Duty is pressed, and the particular pieces, of that Armour recited, *Eph.* 6. 11. & 13, to the 18. Satan is Representing his Infernal Forces, and the Devils seem to come Armed, mustering amongst us. I am this day Commanded to Call and Cry an Alarm unto you, ARM; ARM; ARM; handle your Arms, see that you are fixed and in a readiness, as Faithful Soldiers under the Captain of our Salvation, that by the Shield of FAITH, Ye and We All may Resist the Fiery Darts of the Wicked. And may be Faithful unto Death, in our Spiritual Warfare, so shall we assuredly Receive the Crown of Life, *Rev.* 2. 10.

Thirdly, Let us be Watchful, to take all advantages and strenuously to improve all means (unto which the Word directs us) for the managing our Spiritual Conflict, with the Powers of Darkness. Let us admit no Parly, give no Quarter, let none of Satan's Forces or Furies, be more vigilant to hurt us, than we are to Resist and Repress them, in the NAME, and by the Spirit, Grace and Strength, of Our LORD JESUS CHRIST. Let us watch the first motions of the Enemy, for if we let him get within us, he will certainly be too hard for us. Let us take the Apostles' Counsel; *James*

4. 7. *Resist the Devil and he will flee from you.* But (q.d.) if you yield to him by Flight, he will pursue you, to the very Death: Avoid therefore all fellowship with him, under any of his insinuating pretences, and let us Wrestle, vigorously, against Principalities and Powers, &c. *Eph.* 6. 12. Let us make sure, that in nothing we give them advantage against us, seeing (through Grace) we are not Ignorant of Satan's Devices, 2 *Cor.* 2, 11.

Fourthly, Let us Ply the Throne of Grace, in the Name and Merit, of Our Blessed Mediator, With our Frequent, Faithful, and Fervent Prayers. Let us be frequent in the Duty, taking all possible Opportunities, Publick, Private and Secret, to pour out our Supplications, to the GOD of our Salvation; Prayer is the most Proper, and Potent Antidote, against the Old Serpent's Venomous Operations. When Legions of Devils, do come down amongst us, Multitudes of Prayers should go up to GOD; for suitable Grace and strength, to defend us, from being deceiv'd, and destroyed by them, in that case of the Apostle Paul, when he was under the violent Assaults of a Messenger of Satan. He doubled and trebled his Ordinary Devotions; *For this I besought the Lord thrice, that it might depart from me.* 2 *Cor.* 12. 8.

Again, Let us be Faithful in Prayer. The life of Prayer, lies in the Exercise of Faith therein. It is to the Prayer of Faith that the promise of Answer is made; by him in whom all the Promises, are Yea and Amen; *Mat.* 28. 21. *Whatsoever ye ask, Believing in my Name ye shall receive it.* Besides, it is said *the Prayer of Faith, shall save the sick; James* 5.15. (i. e.) Whatsoever kind of sickness it is, under which they labour, Faith in Prayer engageth the Glorious Intercessor on our behalf, according to his Promise, and thereby makes way for us to be accepted with the FATHER, in all our Requests, Faith in CHRIST Exercised in Prayer, is the Token of GOD's Covenant, with his Elect under the Gospel, as the Bow in the Clouds, was the Token of his Covenant with the whole World, in the days, of Noah; *Gen.* 9. 12, 13. And through Christ it is prevalent, for him the Father heareth always, *John* [unintelligible] And therefore us also through him. For he hath made us *accepted, in the Beloved*, Eph. 1. 6.

Yet once more, Let ours be Fervent Prayers; even with our whole Heart, *Psal.* 119. 10. For such Prayer (only) hath the promise, of finding GOD and his Salvation. *Then shall ye find me, when you seek me with all your Heart*, Jer. 29. 13.

Hence David pronounceth all those Blessed, that thus seek the LORD, *Psal.* 119. 2. This is when we do Rouse up our Soul, with all its Faculties unto Prayer, as the Psalmist doth unto Praise, *Psal.* 103. 1, 2. When our whole Soul, in all its Affections, are poured out before the Lord, as Hannah, 1 *Sam.* 1. 15. This Prayer is like to speed, we say amongst Men, *Qui timide rogat, docet negare; he that begs faintly, may expect a denyal.* And in this Case Justly; the Apostle James tells us, *Let not such a Man as is Faint, Weak, Doubting in Prayer, Expect any thing of the LORD, James* 1, 7. yet on the other hand, the same Apostle assures us *the Effectual Fervent Prayer of a Righteous Man AVAILETH MUCH*, Chap. 5. 16. This Faithful and Fervent Prayer, frequently put in practice, is the most Powerful Exorcisme, to drive away Devils; some of which, will not stir without it, *Mark* 9. 29. *This Kind can come forth by nothing, but by Prayer and Fasting.*

Let us then use this Weapon; It hath a kind of

Omnipotency, because it interesteth us, in the help of THE OMNIPOTENT: Satan, the worst of all our Enemies, is called in Scripture a DRAGON, to note his Malice; a SERPENT to note his Subtilty; a LYON to note his Strength. But none of all these can stand before Prayer, the most inveterate Malice, (as that of Maman) sinks under the Prayer of Esther; Chap. 4. 16. The deepest policy (the Counsel of Achitophel) Withers before the Prayer of David. 2 *Sam.* 15. 31. And the Vastest Army (an Host of a Thousand Thousand Ethiopians) *Ran away like so many Cowards, before the Prayer of Asa.* 2 *Chron.* 14. 11, 12. What therefore I say unto one, I say unto all, in this Important Case; PRAY, PRAY, PRAY.

Fifthly, and Lastly; To Our HONORED MAGISTRATES, here present this day, to Enquire into these things; Give me leave much Honoured; to offer One Word, to your Consideration, Do all that in you lies, to Check and Rebuke Satan; Endeavouring by all ways and means, that are according to the Rule of GOD, to discover his Instruments in these Horrid Operations: You are Concerned in the Civil Government of this People, being invested with Power, by their Sacred MAJESTIES; under this Glorious JESUS, (the King and Governour of his Church) for the Supporting, of CHRIST's Kingdom, against all Oppositions of Satan's Kingdom, and his Instruments. Being Ordained of GOD to such a Station, *Rom.* 13. 1. We entreat you, Bear not the Sword in vain, as v. 4. But approve your selves, a Terrour Of, and Punishment To, Evil doers; and a Praise to them that do well, 1 *Pet.* 2. 14. Ever Remembring, that ye Judge not for Men, but for the Lord; 2 *Chron.* 19. 6. And as his promise is, so our Prayer shall be for you, without Ceasing, that he would be With you in the Judgment, as He that can and will, Direct, Assist, and Reward you. Follow the Example of the Upright Job, Chap. 29. 16. Be a Father to the Poor; to these poor Afflicted Persons, (in pittiful and painful Endeavours to help them) and the Cause that seems to be so dark, as you know not how to determine it, do your utmost in the use of all Regular means to Search it out. And if after all, it still remains too hard for you, carry it unto GOD by Christ, as the Israelites were ordered, to do theirs by Moses; *Deut*. 1. 17. *For the Judgment is GOD's, and the Cause that is too hard for you, bring it unto me and I will hear it.*

USE VI.

The Sixth and Last USE, is in two Words of Comfort, to bear up the fainting Souls of those that are Personally under, or Relatively Concerned in, these direful Operations, of the GRAND Enemy of Mankind.

First, There is Comfort for you, in that ye are the Visible Covenant People of GOD. In General, this whole People of New-England, As to the main bulk of them (or in and by their Godly Leaders, who engage themselves and all under them both in Civil and Sacred Order) are in Covenant with GOD, and have many times (as such) been Signally owned by him; notwithstanding all their Defections and Degeneracies. Besides, there are many that have both Explicitely, and Implicitely; Visibly and Really Devoted themselves to GOD: And are indeed of the Number Chosen by the GOD of Jerusalem; true Citizens of that Jerusalem; that is above, which is the Mother of us all, *Gal.* 4. 26. Yea, some of those, that are under these Afflictions, may plead these Priviledges, to prevail with the LORD, to Rebuke Satan, and Deliver them and theirs, from these his malicious and woeful Oppressions. Add to this, that there are scarce any, who are under the influence, of this Affliction, but are also under the Solemn Obligation, of a Baptismal Covenant, which in its own Nature, Obligeth them, to be For God, and is a valid Argument to plead with GOD to be for them, and against Satan. Put all these together, and surely we shall not cast away our Confidence in GOD, for Deliverance from these sore Calamities. For we are all his People on one account or other: *And the LORD will not forsake his People, because it hath pleased him to make you his People,* 1 *Sam,* 12. 22.

But Secondly, 2. There is Comfort, in Considering, that the LORD JESUS the Captain of our Salvation, hath already Overcome the Devil. CHRIST that Blessed Seed of the Woman, hath given this Cursed Old Serpent called the Devil, and Satan a Mortal and Incurable, Bruise on the Head, *Gen.* 3. 15. He was too hard for him in a single Conflict, *Matth.* 4. [illegible] He Opposed his Power and Kingdom in the Possessed; he *suffered not the Devils to speak, Because they knew him Mark* 1. 34. He compleated his Victory, by his Death on the Cross, and Destroyed his Dominion, *Heb.* 2. 14. That through Death he might destroy Death, and him that had the Powers of Death, that is the DEVIL; and by and after His Resurrection, made shew openly unto the World, that he had spoiled Principalities and Powers, Triumphing over them, *Col.* 2. 15. Hence, if we are by Faith united to him, his Victory is an earnest and revelation of our Conquest at last. All Satan's strugglings now, are but those of a Conquered Enemy; to a Believer: And although

He may give a Child of GOD, great Exercise, in his way to the Kingdom, such as may often bring him to his Knees, in earnest prayers to GOD for more Grace, yet it may be truly said of him, which was Prophetically said of God, *Gen. 49. 19. A Troop shall overcome him, but he shall overcome at the last.* The Exaltation also, of Our LORD JESUS, doth assure us, that we shall be Exalted, to the Throne of Glory with him, *Rev.* 3. 21. Comfort we then, one another with these Words, That the GOD of Peace, even JESUS the Prince of Peace, will Totally and Finally, Bruise Satan under our Feet, and that shortly, *Rom.* 16. 20. It will be but a Little, Little while, before we shall enter Into, and take Possession Of, that place, into which *there shall in no wise enter, any thing that defileth, neither worketh Abomination, or maketh a Lye, Rev.* 21. 27. where we shall sin no more, sorrow no more, nor the Spiritual Wickednesses, afflict us any more for ever.

To Conclude; The Lord is known by the Judgments which he Executes in the midst of us. The Dispensations of his Providence, appear to be unsearchable, and his Doings past finding out. He seems to have allowed Satan, to afflict many of our People, and that thereupon he is come down in Great Wrath, threatning the Destruction of the Bodies, (and if the Infinite Mercy of GOD prevent not) of the Souls of many in this place. Yet may we say, in the midst of all the Terrible things which he doth in Righteousness; He alone is the GOD of our Salvation, who represents himself, as the Saviour of all that are in a low and distressed Condition, because he is good, and His Mercie endureth for ever.

Let us then Return and Repent, rent our Hearts, and not our Garments. Who can tell if the LORD will Return in Mercy unto us? And by his Spirit lift up a Standard, against the GRAND Enemy who threatens to come in like a Flood, among us, and overthrow all that is Holy, and Just, and Good. It is no small comfort to consider, that Job's Exercise of Patience, had it's Beginning from the Devil; but we have seen the end to be from the LORD. *James* 5. 11. That We also, may find by experience, the same Blessed Issue, of our present Distresses, by Satan's Malice. Let us repent of every Sin, that hath been Committed, and Labour to practice, every Duty which hath been Neglected And when we are Humbled, and Proved for for our good in the latter end: Then we shall assuredly, and speedily find, that the Kingly Power of Our LORD and SAVIOUR, shall be Magnifyed, in delivering his Poor Sheep and Lambs, out of the Jaws and Paws of the Roaring Lyon.

Then will JESUS the Blessed Antitype of Joshua, the Redeemer, and Chooser of Jerusalem, Quell, Suppress, and utterly Vanquish, this Adversary of ours, with Irresistable Power and Authority, according to our Text. *And the LORD said unto Satan, the LORD Rebuke thee O Satan, Even the LORD that hath Chosen Jerusalem, Rebuke thee: Is not this a Brand pluckt out of the FIRE?*

An extract from the Diary of Lady Anne Halkett: Wednesday, 12th October, 1698.

This shows how one particular person - Lady Anne Halkett' from Fife - reacted, at the time of its publication, to reading: A True Narrative of the Sufferings and Relief of a Young Girle. (1698) *She says she was inclined to believe it because of the various people who were cited as the witnesses to the troubles and torments of the child. A profound and morbid religiosity might have been the actual reason.*

When Lady Anne talks of Bourignianisme, she is alluding to Antoinette Bourignon (1616-1680) who was a Belgian writer and preacher. She lived a live of devotion and self-sacrifice. She developed a philosophy of Christian mysticism. William James, the brother of the novelist Henry James classified her, in his writings on religion, as a saint. She did not, however, favourably impress her ladyship.

Dr Suzanne Trill of the Department of English Literature in the School of Literature, Languages and Cultures at Edinburgh University very kindly and perceptively drew this passage to my attention. It is taken from her book: Lady Anne Halkett: Selected Self-Writings *(Ashgate, forthcoming).*

H.V.McL

Having yesterday read the Narative of the sufferings and releefe of Christian Shaw, Daughter to John Shaw Laird of Bargaren in the West. Who, from August 22 1696 to March beeing Su[n]day 28 1697, was by unheard of ways in all that time so tormented by the divell and his associates, that itt were increditable to beleeve were itt nott attested by unquestionable wittneses: And that none that truly feares God; butt knows hee can suport those that belong to him under the greatest tryalls, And deliver them when hee sees itt most for his glory & there good. And upon the Christian Sabath day which is generally called Sunday, the Lord thought fitt on that day to give her deliverance as the marke of favor from him Who is the Sun of righeousnese, and on her hee did arise & came to her with healing in his wing. How fitly doth that psalme (beeing one of th[e]m that falls to bee read this day of the Month) teach mee under any troubles, for what I have heard hath arived to others or what may arive to my selfe to say, Heare my voice O God in my prayer preserve my life from feare of the enemy: which are the wicked & workers of iniquity who whet th[e]re tongues to shoot bitter words. The[y] shoot in secrett &c: All these have beene practised by the enemys of that young Girle butt God hath made there owne toungs to fall upon themselves many of them having beene executed. That all men that heare of itt should feare & declare the worke of God & wisely consider of his doing. For The righteous shall bee glad in the Lord and shall trust in him and all the upright in heart shall glory.

Just as I had done reading this I had the occation to see & read Dr Cockburnes account Bourignianisme. I had heard before of many of the high things shee pretended to w[hi]ch was such as made me tremble when I heard of them and so much abhorre them, that I would nott either read any of her bookes my selfe; nor aproue of any reading th[e]m that I was concerned in. Nor had I read any thing of itt now butt that I expected Dr Cockburne had in this, to every dram of Poison, ministerd a sufficient dose of Counterpoison to prevent the contagion of any beeing infected with itt. Butt itt seemes hee intends to performe this in-another Narative.

All that I will aply to both these persons, the young and the older is, That all hath great need to bee sober and vigilant because our adversarys the divell as a roaring lion goeth aboutt seeking whom hee may devoure. And since Satan himselfe is transformed into an Angell of light, Therfore itt is noe great thing if his Ministers allso bee transformed as the Ministers of righteousnese whose end shall bee according to ther workes. Butt from all his assaults Good Lord deliver us.

Appendix to Christ's Fidelity the Only Shield Against Satan's Malignity

by

Deodat Lawson

This is the appendix to the 1704, London Edition of Christ's Fidelity the Only Shield Against Satan's Malignity. *It is a re-statement by Lawson, after a time for calm reflection of what he witnessed of the events in Salem village in 1692. Although he does not retract his former claims – far from it – there is a notably defensive tone in what he writes. It would appear that the Salem witchcraft trials were not generally approved of by the public that Lawson had been and was once again addressing.*

Lawson became, even by the standards of his own day, a poor man. His association with Salem did him no good. The Rev. James Brisbane, the busy-body who involved himself so much with the Renfrewshire witchcraft accusations and, I have argue, wrote the Narrative about Christian Shaw believed that one of his babies was killed by witchcraft. As this appendix shows, the Rev. Deodat Lawson believed that his wife and one of his children were killed by witchcraft. He was goaded, perhaps, in his warring against Satan by a festering, personal grievance.

Interesting comparisons between witchcraft in Renfrewshire, Scotland and witchcraft in New England can again be made by reading this Appendix and reflecting upon A True Narrative of the Sufferings and Relief of a Young Girle.

'Deodat' is, obviously, a strange Christian name, at a time when one's Christian name was, literally, that: the name one was Christened with. 'Deodat' means gift of God. This might be evidence that, from birth, his life was steeped in religion.

*Puritans in the 17ᵗʰ century did not feel obliged to name
their children after saints. It even seems as if they were keen to
advertise their disregard for what they might have thought of as
a Romanist superstition. Notice, below, further references to the
curiously named father and son: the Rev. Increase and the Rev.
Cotton Mather.*

H.V.McL

At the Request of several Worthy Ministers, and
Christian Friends, I do here Annex by way of Appendix
to the preceeding Sermon, some Brief Account of those
Amazing things, which occasioned that Discourse to be
Delivered. Let the Reader please therefore to take it in the
Brief Remarks following, and Judge as GOD shall incline
him.

It pleased God in the Year of our Lord 1692 to visit
the People at a place called Salem Village in NEW
ENGLAND, with a very Sore and Grievous Affliction,
in which they had reason to believe, that the Soveraign
and Holy GOD was pleased to permit Satan and
his Instruments, to Affright and Afflict, those poor
Mortals in such an Astonishing and Unusual manner.
Now, I having for some time before, attended the work
of the Ministry in that Village, the Report of those Great
Afflictions, came quickly to my notice; and the more readily,
because the first Person Afflicted, was in the Minister's
Family, who succeeded me, after I was removed from them;
in pitty therefore to my Christian Friends, and former
Acquaintance there, I was much concerned about them,
frequently consulted with them, and fervently (by Divine
Assistance) prayed for them; but especially my Concern

was augmented, when it was Reported, at an Examination of a Person suspected for Witchcraft, that my Wife and Daughter, who Dyed Three Years before, were sent out of the World under the Malicious Operations of the Infernal Powers; as is more fully represented in the following Remarks. I did then Desire, and was also Desired, by some concerned in the Court, to be there present, that I might hear what was alledged in that respect; observing therefore, when I was amongst them, that the Case of the Afflicted was very amazing, and deplorable; and the Charges brought against the Accused, such as were Ground of Suspicions yet very intricate,and difficult to draw up right Conclusions about them; I thought good for the satisfaction of my self, and such of my Friends as might be curious to inquire into those Mysteries of God's Providence and Satan's Malice, to draw up and keep by me, a Brief Account of the most Remarkable things, that came to my Knowledge in those Affairs; which Remarks were afterwards, (at my Request) Revised and Corrected by some who Sate Judges on the Bench, in those Matters; and were now Transcribed, from the same Paper, on which they were then Written. After this, I being by the Providence of God called over into ENGLAND, in the Year 1696; I then brought that Paper of Remarks on the Witchcraft with me; upon the sight thereof, some Worthy Ministers and Christian Friends here, desired me to Reprint the Sermon and subjoyn the Remarks thereunto, in way of Appendix, but for some particular Reasons I did then Decline it; But now, forasmuch as I my self had been an Eye and Ear Witness, of most of those Amazing things, so far as they came within the Notice of Humane Senses; and the Requests of my Friends were

Renewed since I came to Dwell in London: I have given way to the Publishing of them; that I may satisfy such as are not resolved to the Contrary; that there may be (and are) such Operations of the Powers of Darkness on the Bodies and Minds of Mankind; by Divine Permission; and that those who Sate Judges in those Cases, may by the serious Consideration, of the formidable Aspect and perplexed Circumstances, of that Afflictive Providence; be in some measure excused; or at least be less Censured, for passing Sentence on several Persons, as being the Instruments of Satan in those Diabolical Operations, when they were involved in such a Dark and Dismal Scene of Providence, in which Satan did seem to Spin a finer Thred of Spiritual Wickedness, than in the ordinary methods of Witchcraft; hence the Judges desiring to bear due Testimony, against such Diabolical Practices, were inclined to admit the validity of such a sort of Evidence, as was not so clearly and directly demonstrable to Human Senses, as in other Cases is required, or else they could not discover the Mysteries of Witchcraft; I presume not to impose upon my Christian or Learned Reader; any opinion of mine, how far Satan was an Instrument in God's Hand, in these amazing Afflictions, which were on many Persons there, about that time; but I am certainly convinced, that the Great GOD was pleased to lengthen his Chain to a very great Degree, for the hurting of Some and reproaching of Others, as far as he was permitted so to do: Now, that I may not grieve any, whose Relations were either Accused or Afflicted, in those times of Trouble and Distress; I chuse to lay down every Particular at large, without mentioning any Names or Persons concerned (they being wholly unknown here) resolving to confine my self, to such a proportion of Paper, as is assigned to these Remarks, in this impression of the Book; yet that I may be distinct, shall speak briefly to the Matter under three Heads, viz.

(1.) Relating to the Afflicted.

(2.) Relating to the Accused. And

(3.) Relating to the Confessing Witches

To Begin with the Afflicted.

1. One or two of the first that were Afflicted, Complaining of unusual Illness, their Relations used Physick for their Cure, but it was altogether in vain.

2. They were oftentimes, very stupid in their Fits, and could neither hear nor understand, in the apprehension of the Standers by, so that when Prayer hath been made, with some of them, in such a manner as might be audible in a great Congregation; yet when their Fit was off, they declared they did not hear so much as one Word thereof.

3. It was several times Observed, that when they were discoursed with, about GOD or CHRIST, or the Things of Salvation, they were presently afflicted at a dreadful Rate, and hence were oftentimes Outragious, if they were permitted to be in the Congregation, in the Time of the Publick Worship.

4. They sometimes told at a considerable Distance, yea, several Miles off, that such and such Persons were afflicted, which hath been found to be done according to the Time, and Manner they related it; and they said, the Spectres of the suspected Persons told them of it.

5. They affirm'd, That they saw the Ghosts of several departed Persons, who at their appearing, did instigate them,

to discover such as (they said) were Instruments to hasten their Deaths; threatning sorely to afflict them, if they did not make it known to the Magistrates; they did affirm at the Examination, and again at the Tryal of an accused Person, that they saw the Ghosts of his two Wives (to whom he had carryed very ill in their Lives, as was proved by several Testimonies) and also that they saw the Ghosts of My Wife and Daughter, (who dyed above three Years before) and they did affirm, that when the very Ghosts looked on the Prisoner at the Bar, they looked red, as if the Blood would fly out of their Faces, with Indignation at him: The Manner of it was thus; Several Afflicted being before the Prisoner at the Bar, on a sudden they fixed all their Eyes together, on a certain Place of the Floor before the Prisoner; neither moving their Eyes nor Bodies, for some few Minutes, nor answering to any Question which was asked them; so soon as that Trance was over, some being removed out of Sight and Hearing, they were all one after another asked what they saw, and they did all agree, that they saw those Ghosts abovementioned; I was present, and heard and saw the whole of what passed upon that Account, during the Tryal of that Person who was accused to be the Instrument of Satan's Malice therein.

6. In this (worse than Gallick) Persecution by the Dragoons of Hell, the Persons afflicted were harrassed at such a dreadful rate, to write their Names in a Devil-Book, presented by a Spectre unto them; and One in my hearing said, *I will not, I will not Write, it is none of God's Book, it is none of God's Book; it is the Devil's Book for ought I know*: And when they stedfastly refused to sign, they were told if they would but touch or take hold of the Book it should do:

And Lastly, The Diabolical Propositions were so low and easy, that if they would but let their Clothes, or any thing about them, touch the Book, they should be at ease from their Torments, it being their Consent that is aimed at by the Devil in those Representations and Operations.

7. One who had been long afflicted at a stupendious rate, by two or three Spectres, when they were (to speak after the manner of Men) tyred out with tormenting of her, to Force or Fright her to sign a Covenant with the Prince of Darkness, they said to her, as in a Diabolical and Accursed Passion, *Go your ways and the Devil go with you, for we will be no more pestred and plagued about you.* And ever after that she was well, and no more afflicted that ever I heard of.

8. Sundry Pins have been taken out of the Wrists and Arms of the Afflicted; and one in time of Examination of a suspected Person, had a Pin run through both her Upper and her Lower Lip, when she was called to speak; yet no apparent festering followed thereupon, after it was taken out.

9. Some of the Afflicted, as they were striving in their Fits, in open Court, have (by invisible means) had their Wrists bound fast together with a real Cord, so as it could hardly be taken off without cutting. Some Afflicted have been found with their Arms tyed, and hanged upon an Hook, from whence others have been forced to take them down that they might not expire in that Posture.

10. Some Afflicted have been drawn under Tables and Beds, by undiscerned Force, so as they could hardly be pulled out: And one was drawn half way over the Side of a Well, and was with much difficulty recovered back again

11. When they were most grievously afflicted, if they were

brought to the Accused, and the suspected Persons Hand but laid upon them, they were immediately relieved out of their Tortures; but if the Accused did but look on them, they were instantly struck down again: Wherefore, they use to cover the Face of the Accused, while they laid their Hands on the Afflicted, and then it obtained the desired Issue; for it hath been experienced (both in Examinations and Tryals) that so soon as the Afflicted, came in sight of the Accused, they were immediately cast into their Fits; yea, though the Accused were among the Crowd of People unknown to the Sufferers, yet on the first view were they struck down; which was observed in a Child of four or five Years of Age, when it was apprehended, that so many as she could look upon, either directly or by turning her Head, were immediately struck into their Fits.

12. An iron Spindle of a woollen Wheel, being taken very strangely out of an House at Salem Village, was used by a Spectre, as an Instrument of Torture to a Sufferer, not being discernable to the Standers by; until it was by the said Sufferer snatched out of the Spectres Hand, and then it did immediately appear to the Persons present to be really the same iron Spindle.

13. Sometimes in their Fits, they have had their Tongues drawn out of their Mouths to a fearful length, their Heads turned very much over their Shoulders; and while they have been so strained in their Fits, and had their Arms and Legs, &c. wrested, as if they were quite dislocated, the Blood hath gushed plentifully out of their Mouths, for a considerable time together; which some, that they might be satisfied that it was real Blood, took upon their Finger and rubbed on their other Hand. I saw several together

thus violently strained and bleeding in their Fits, to my very great astonishment, that my fellow-Mortals should be so grievously distressed by the invisible Powers of Darkness. For certainly, all considerate Persons, who beheld these things, must needs be convinced, that their Motions in their Fits were Præternatural and Involuntary, both as to the Manner which was so strange, as a well Person could not (at least without great Pain) screw their Bodies into; and as to the violence also, they were Præternatural Motions, being much beyond the ordinary Force of the same Persons when they were in their right Minds. So that being such grievous Sufferers, it would seem very hard and unjust to censure them of consenting To, or holding any voluntary Converse or Familiarity with the Devil.

14. Their Eyes were for the most part left closed in their Trance Fits, and when they were asked a Question, they could give no Answer; and I do verily believe, they did not hear at that time, yet did they discourse with the Spectres as with real Persons; asserting Things, and receiving Answers, affirmative or negative, as the Matter was. For Instance, One in my hearing thus argued with, and railed at a Spectre, *Goodn- be gone! be gone! be gone! Are you not ashamed, a Woman of your Profession, to afflict a poor Creature so? What hurt did I ever do you in my Life? You have but two Years to live, and then the Devil will torment your Soul for this: Your Name is blotted out of God's Book, and it shall never be put into God's Book again. Be gone for shame, are you not afraid of what is coming upon you? I know, I know, what will make you afraid, the Wrath of an angry God: I am sure that will make you afraid. Be gone, do not torment me; I know what you would have,* (we judged she meant her Soul:) *but it is out of your reach, it is clothed with the*

white Robes of Christ's Righteousness. This Sufferer I was well acquainted with, and knew her to be a very sober and pious Woman, so far as I could judge; and it appears that she had not in that Fit, voluntary Converse with the Devil; for then she might have been helped to a better Guess about that Woman above-said, as to her living but two Years, for she lived not many Months after that time; Further, this Woman in the same Fit, seemed to dispute with a Spectre about a Text of Scripture; the Apparition seemed to deny it, she said she was sure there was such a Text, and she would read it, and then said she to the Apparition, *I am sure you will be gone, for you cannot stand before that Text;* then was she sorely afflicted, her Mouth drawn on one side, and her Body strained violently for about a Minute, and then said *It is, It is, It is,* three or four times, and then was afflicted to hinder her from telling; at last, she broke forth and said, It is the third Chapter of the Revelations: I did manifest some Scruple about reading it, least Satan should draw any thereby, superstitiously to improve the Word of the Eternal GOD; yet judging I might do it once for an Experiment, I began to read, and before I had read through the first Verse, she opened her Eyes and was well: Her Husband and the Spectators told me, she had often been relieved by reading Texts pertinent to her Case; as *Isaiah* 40. 1. Ch. 49. 1. Ch. 50. 1. and several others. These things I saw and heard from her.

15. They were vehemently afflicted, to hinder any Persons Praying with them, or holding them in any Religious Discourse: The Woman mentioned in the former Section, was told by the Spectre I should not go to Prayer, but she said I should; and after I had done, reasoned with

the Apparition, *did not I say he should go to Prayer?* I went also to visit a Person afflicted in Boston, and after I was gone into the House to which she belonged, she being abroad and pretty well, when she was told I was there, she said, *I am loth to go in, for I know he will fall into some good Discourse, and then I am sure I shall go into a Fit;* accordingly when she came in, I advised her to improve all the Respite she had, to make her Peace with GOD, and sue out her Pardon through JESUS CHRIST, and beg Supplies of Faith and every Grace, to deliver her from the Powers of Darkness: And before I had uttered all this, she fell into a fearful Fit of Diabolical Torture.

16. Some of them were asked how it came to pass that they were not affrighted when they saw the Black-man, they said they were at first, but not so much afterwards.

17, Some of them affirmed, they saw the Black-man sit on the Gallows, and that he whispered in the Ears of some of the Condemned Persons when they were just ready to be turn'd off; even while they were making their last Speech.

18. They declared several things to be done by Witchcraft, which happened before some of them were born; as strange Deaths of Persons, Casting away of Ships, &c. and they said the Spectres told them of it.

19. Some of them, have sundry times seen a White-man appearing amongst the Spectres, and as soon as he appeared, the Black-Witches vanished: They said; This White-man had often foretold them, what respite they should have from their Fits; as sometimes a day or two, or more, which fell out accordingly. One of the Afflicted said she saw him in her Fit, and was with him in a Glorious Place, which had no Candle nor Sun, yet was full of Light

and Brightness; where there was a multitude in white Glitterring Robes, and they sang the Song in *Rev.* 5. 9. Psal. 110. *Psal.* 149. she was loth to leave that Place, and said *how long shall I stay here, let me be along with you?* She was grieved, she could stay no longer in that Place and Company.

20. A young Woman that was afflicted at a fearful rate, had a Spectre appeared to her, with a white Sheet wrapped about it, not visible to the Standers by, until this Sufferer (violently striving in her Fit) snatch'd at, took hold, and tore off a Corner of that Sheet; her Father being by her, endeavoured to lay hold upon it with her, that she might retain what she had gotten; but at the passing away of the Spectre, he had such a violent Twitch of his Hand, as if it would have been torn off; immediately thereupon appeared in the Sufferer's hand, the Corner of a Sheet, a real Cloth, visible to the Spectators, which (as it is said) remains still to be seen.

Remarkable Things relating to the Accused.

1. A Woman being brought upon publick Examination, desired to go to Prayer; the Magistrates told her they came not there to hear her Pray, but to examine her in what was alledged against her, relating to Suspitions of Witchcraft.

2. It was observed, both in times of Examination and Tryal, that the Accused seemed little affected with what the Sufferers underwent, or, what was Charged against them, as being the Instruments of Satan therein; so that the Spectators were grieved at their unconcernedness.

3. They were sometimes their own Image, and not always practizing upon Puppits made of Clouts, Wax or other

Materials (according to the old Methods of Witchcraft) for natural Actions in them, seemed to produce Præternatural Impressions on the Afflicted; as Biting their Lips in time of Examination and Tryal, caused the Sufferers to be Bitten so as they produced the Marks before the Magistrates and Spectators; the Accused Pinching their Hands together, seemed to cause the Sufferers to be Pinched, those again stamping with their Feet: These were tormented in their Legs and Feet, so as they stamped fearfully: After all this, if the Accused did but lean against the Bar at which they stood; some very sober Women of the Afflicted complained of their Breasts, as if their Bowels were torn out: Thus, some have since confessed, they were wont to afflict such as were the Objects of their Malice.

4. Several were accused of having Familiarity with the Black-man in time of Examination and Tryal and that He Whispered in their Ears, and therefore they could not hear the Magistrates; and that one Woman accused hid (in her Shape and Spectre) by the place of Judicature, behind the Black man in the very time when she was upon Examination.

5. When the Suspected were standing at the Bar, the Afflicted have affirmed that they saw their Shapes in other Places, suckling a yellow Bird; sometimes in one Place and Posture, and sometimes in another. They also foretold, that the Spectre of the Prisoner was going to afflict such or such a Sufferer, which presently fell out accordingly.

6. They were Accused by the Sufferers, to keep Days of Hellish Fasts and Thanksgivings, and upon one of their Fast-days they told a Sufferer, she must not Eat, it was Fast-day; she said she would, they told her they would Choak

her then; which when she did Eat was endeavoured.

7. They were also Accused, to hold and Administer Diabolical Sacraments, viz. a Mock-Baptism, and a Devil-Supper, at which Cursed Imitations of the Sacred Institutions of our Blessed Lord, they used Forms of Words to be trembled at, in the very Rehearsing, concerning Baptism shall speak elsewhere. At their Cursed Supper, they were said to have Red Bread, and Red Drink, and when they pressed an Afflicted Person to Eat and Drink thereof, she turned away her Head, and Spit at it, and said, *I will not Eat, I will not Drink, it is Blood, that is not the Bread of Life, that is not the Water of Life, and I will have none of yours.* Thus Horribly doth Satan endeavour to have his Kingdom and Administrations to resemble those of Our LORD JESUS CHRIST.

8. Some of the most Sober Afflicted Persons when they were well, did Affirm the Spectres of such and such, as they did Complain of in their Fits did appear to them, and could relate what passed betwixt them, and the Apparitions, after their Fits were over, and give account after what manner they were hurt by them.

9. Several of the Accused would neither in time of Examination, nor Tryal, Confess any thing of what was laid to their Charge; some would not admit of any Minister to Pray with them, others refused to pray for themselves: It was said by some of the Confessing-Witches that such as have received the Devil-Sacrament can never Confess, only one Woman Condemned, after the Death Warrant was signed, freely Confessed, which occasioned her Reprieval for sometime; and it was observable, This Woman had one Lock of Hair, of a very great length, viz. Four Foot and

Seven Inches long, by measure, this Lock was of a different colour from all the rest, (which was short and grey) it grew on the hinder part of her Head, and was matted together like an Elf-Lock; the Court ordered it to be cut off, to which she was very unwilling, and said, she was told if it were cut off, she should Dye, or be Sick, yet the Court ordered it so to be.

10. A Person who had been frequently Transported to and fro by the Devil for the space of near Two Years, was struck Dumb for about Nine Months of that time; yet he after that had his Speech restored to him, and did Depose upon Oath, that in the time while he was Dumb, he was many times Bodily Transported, to places where the Witches were gathered together, and that he there saw Feasting and Dancing, and being struck on the Back or Shoulder, was thereby made fast to the Place, and could only see and hear at a distance; he did take his Oath, that he did with his Bodily Eyes, see some of the Accused at those Witch-meetings several times; I was present in Court when he gave his Testimony, he also proved by sundry Persons that at those times of Transport, he was Bodily absent from his Abode, and could no where be found, but being met with by some on the Road at a distance from his home; was suddenly conveyed away from them.

11. The Afflicted Persons related that the Spectres of several Eminent Persons had been brought in amongst the rest, but as the Sufferers said, the Devil could not hurt them in their Shapes, but two Witches seemed to take them by each hand, and lead them or force them to come in.

12 Whiles a Godly Man was at Prayer with a Woman Afflicted, the Daughter of that Woman (being a Sufferer

in the like kind) Affirmed that she saw Two of the Persons Accused at Prayer to the Devil.

13. It was proved by substantial Evidences, against One Person Accused; that he had such an unusual strength, (though a very little Man) that he could hold out a Gun with one hand, behind the Lock, which was near seven Foot in the Barrel, being as much as a lusty Man could Command with both hands, after the usual manner of shooting; it was also proved, that he lifted Barrels of Meat, and Barrels of Molasses, out of a Canoe alone; and that putting his Fingers into a barrel of Molasses (full within a fingers length according to Custom) he carryed it several paces. And that he put his finger into the muzzle of a Gun which was more than five Foot in the Barrel, and lifted up the But end thereof, Lock, Stock and all, without any visible help to raise it. It was also Testified that being abroad with his Wife, and his Wife's Brother, he occasionally staid behind, letting his Wife and her Brother walk forward, but suddenly coming up with them, he was angry with his Wife, for what Discourse had passed betwixt her, and her Brother, they wondring how he should know it, he said, *I know your thoughts*, at which Expression, they (being Amazed) asked him how he could do that, he said, *My God whom I serve makes known your Thoughts to me*.

I was present when these things were Testified against him, and observed that he could not make any plea for himself (in these things) that had any weight: He had the Liberty of Challenging his Jurors, before empannelling, according to the Statute in that case, and used his Liberty in Challenging many; yet the Jury that were Sworn brought him in Guilty.

450

14. The Magistrates privately Examined a Child of Four or Five Years of Age, mentioned in the Remarks of the Afflicted, Sect. 11. and the Child told them it had a little Snake, which used to suck on the lowest Joynt of its Fore-Finger, and when they (inquiring where) pointed to other places, it told them not there but here, pointing on the lowest Joint of the Fore Finger, where they observed a deep Red Spot about the bigness of a Flea-Bite, they asked it, who gave it that Snake? Whether the Black Man gave it, the Child said, no, its Mother gave it: I heard this Child Examined by the Magistrates.

15. It was proved by sundry Testimonies against some of the Accused; that upon their Malicious Imprecations, Wishes, or Threatnings, many observable Deaths and Diseases, with many other odd Inconveniences, have happened to Cattle, and other Estate, of such as were so Threatned by them, and some to the Persons of Men and Women.

Remarkable things Confessed, by some suspected of being Guilty of Witchcraft.

1. It pleased GOD for the clearer discovery of those Mysteries of the Kingdom of Darkness, so to dispose, that several Persons Men, Women and Children, did Confess their Hellish Deeds, as followeth.

2. They Confessed against themselves, that they were Witches, Told how long they had been so; and how it came about, that the Devil appeared to them, *viz.* Sometimes upon Discontent at their mean Condition in the World; Sometimes about fine Cloaths, Sometimes for

the gratifying other Carnal and Sensual Lusts, Satan then upon his appearing to them made them Fair, (though False) Promises, that if they would yield to him, and sign his Book their Desires should be answered to Uttermost whereupon they signed it; and thus the Accursed Confederacy was confirmed betwixt them and the Prince of Darkness.

3. Some did affirm that there were some Hundreds of the Society of Witches, considerable Companies, of whom were affirmed to muster in Arms, by beat of Drum; in time of Examinations and Tryals, they declared that such a Man was wont to call them together, from all Quarters to Witch-Meetings with the sound of a Diabolical Trumpet.

4. Being brought to see the Prisoners at the Bar, upon their Tryals, they did affirm in open Court, (I was then present) that they had oftentimes seen them at Witch-meetings, where was Feasting, Dancing and Jollity, as also at Devil Sacraments, and particularly that they saw such a Man — amongst the rest of the Cursed Crew and affirmed that he did administer the Sacrament of Satan to them, encouraging them to go on in their way, and they should certainly prevail; they said also that such a Woman — was a Deacon, and served in distributing the Diabolical Element; they affirmed that there were great numbers of the Witches.

5. They affirmed that many of those Wretched Souls, had been Baptized at Newberry Falls; and at several other Rivers and Ponds; and as to the manner of Administration, the Great Officer of Hell took them up by the Body, and putting their Heads into the Water, said over them, *Thou art mine, and I have Full Power over thee*, and thereupon, they Engaged and Covenanted to Renounce GOD, CHRIST,

their Sacred Baptism, and the whole way of Gospel Salvation, and to use their utmost Endeavours, to Oppose the Kingdom of CHRIST, and to set up and Advance the Kingdom of Satan.

6. Some after they had Confessed were very Penitent, and did wring their Hands, and manifest a distressing sense of what they had done, and were by the Mercies of GOD recovered out of those Snares of the Kingdom of Darkness.

7. Several have Confessed against their own Mothers, that they were instruments to bring them into the Devil's Covenant to the undoing of them Body and Soul. And some Girls of Eight or Nine Years of Age did declare that after they were so betrayed by their Mothers, to the Power of Satan, they saw the Devil go in their Own Shapes to Afflict others.

8. Some of those that Confessed, were immediately Afflicted at a dreadful rate, after the same manner with the other Sufferers.

9. Some of them Confessed, that they did Afflict the Sufferers, according to the Time and Manner they were Accused thereof, and being asked what they did to Afflict them, some said that they pricked Pins into Puppits, made with Rags, Wax, and other Materials. One that Confessed after the signing the Death Warrant, said, the use to Afflict them by Clutching and Pinching her hands together, and Wishing in what Part and after what Manner she would have them Afflicted, and it was done.

10. They Confessed, the Design was laid by this Witchcraft, to root out the Interest of CHRIST in New England, and that they began at the Village, in order to

settling the Kingdom of Darkness, and the Powers thereof, declaring that such a Man — was to be Head Conjurer, and for his Activity in that Affair was to be Crowned King of Hell, and that such a Woman — was to be Queen of Hell.

THUS, I have given my Reader a Brief and True account of those Fearful and Amazing Operations, and Intreagues of the Prince of Darkness; and I must call them so, for let some Persons be as incredulous as they please, about the Powerful and Malicious influence of Evil Angels upon the Minds and Bodies of Mankind, Sure I am, none that observed those things abovementioned, could refer them to any other Head, than the Sovereign Permission of the HOLY GOD, and the Malicious Operations of His and Our Implacable Enemy.

I have here related nothing more, than what was acknowledged to be true, by the Judges that sat on the Bench, and other Credible Persons there, which I have without Prejudice or Partiality, represented:

I Therefore Close all, with my Uncessant Prayers, that the Great and Everlasting JEHOVAH, would for the Sake of his Blessed Son, our Most Glorious Intercessor, Rebuke Satan, and so vanquish him from time to time, that his Power may be more and more every day Suppressed, his Kingdom destroyed, and that all his Malicious and Accursed Instruments, in those Spiritual Wickednesses, may Gnash their Teeth, Melt away, and be Ashamed in their secret places, till they come to be Judged and Condemned unto the Place of Everlasting Burning, prepared for the Devil and his Angels, that they may there be Tormented with him for Ever and Ever. FINIS.

The Bargarran Witchcraft Trial - A Psychiatric Re-assessment

By

S. W. McDonald, A. Thom and A. Thom

This was first published in The Scottish Medical Journal, 1996, Vol. 41, pp. 152-158. *Whether or not it is a correct interpretation of Christian Shaw's behaviour, it shows how behaviour like that attributed to her might be explicable in terms of current medical knowledge.*

H.V.McL

Three hundred years ago, one of the last trials for witchcraft in Scotland took place at Paisley and six people were hanged and burned. The case centred around the supposed possession of Christian Shaw, the 11 year old daughter of John Shaw, laird of Bargarran. In this article, we retell the story and consider whether Christian's condition can be explained by modern psychiatry. Excellent overviews of the celebrated case of Bargarran's Daughter were given by John Millar in his *"History of the Witches of Renfrewshire"* and by Robert Chambers in *"The Domestic Annals of Scotland"*.

Bargarran was a modest estate in the parish of Erskine on the south side of the Clyde. The small mansion house, occupied by John Shaw and his wife, Christian McGilchrist, and their children, belonged to an earlier period and was, with adjacent ancillary buildings, surrounded by a semi-defensive wall. Christian was said to be lively and "well-inclined" and seems to have had a normal childhood up to

455

the time of the events to be described.

The troubles started on Monday, 17th August 1696 when Christian reported to her mother that Catherine Campbell, a servant girl, had stolen some milk. Campbell swore at Christian with oaths of terrible violence, calling the curse of God upon her and hoping her soul would be dragged through Hell. The following Saturday, these words were to have terrible repercussions.

On the Friday of the same week, in the early morning, a malicious, ignorant old woman, Agnes Naismith, who lived in the neighbourhood, appeared at Bargarran House. She frequently threatened people and it was believed that deaths had followed. When she arrived at Bargarran, she found Christian and her little sister playing in the courtyard. 'She asked how the young lady and the young child did, and how old the suckling child was; to which Christian replied, *"What do I know?"* Agnes then asked, how herself did, and how old she was; to which she answered she was well and in the eleventh year of her age.'

The next day, the Saturday, shortly after going to bed, Christian suddenly awoke shouting *"Help! Help!"* and immediately sprang up into the air with enormous force, astonishing her parents and others in the room. She was put back to bed but remained stiff and appeared unconscious for half an hour. For the next forty-eight hours, she was restless and complained of violent pains throughout her body and, if she fell asleep, she immediately awoke again crying in terror *"Help! help!"*

For eight days, Christian had violent seizures in which the pain localised in her left side and in which she was "often so bent and rigid that she stood like a bow on her feet and neck at once," and lost the power of speech. There seemed to be a short period of delirium as the fits came and went and they were interspersed by short intervals in which she seemed perfectly well. A doctor, John Johnstone, and an apothecary, John White, a relation of the Shaws, were called from Paisley but their bleedings and medications had no effect.

Presently Christian's condition changed and she appeared to fight against an invisible enemy. Her abdomen rose and fell, with a motion like that of a pair of bellows, and her whole body shook alarmingly. In these fits, she started to denounce Catherine Campbell and Agnes Naismith, claiming that they were cutting the sides of her body even though they were actually elsewhere. It was at this crisis, two months after the start of the symptoms, that Christian's parents took her to see the eminent Glasgow physician Matthew Brisbane.

For the eight days in which Christian remained in Glasgow after consulting Brisbane and for eight days after her return home, she was well. The fits then returned with increased violence. She would become stiff as a corpse and be senseless and motionless. Her tongue would stick out to a great length and her teeth would close on it. At other times her tongue was drawn far back into her mouth.

The parents decided to take her back to Dr Brisbane but, as they were going, there was a new development in Christian's condition. From time to time, she spat or took from her mouth balls of hair of various colours, which she claimed had been forced down her throat by her assailants. There were large quantities of hair, some of it was curly and some of it was plaited or knotted. Soon other material was to appear from her mouth. She also had fainting fits every quarter of an hour. During this visit to Glasgow, as well consulting Dr Brisbane, Christian was also seen by an apothecary Henry Marshall. Dr Brisbane's medical evidence was to be an important document in condemning seven people to be burned for witchcraft.

Reports of Matthew Brisbane and Henry Marshall reproduced from: A History of the Witches of Renfrewshire

"The subscribed attestations of Dr Matthew Brisbane, Physician, and Mr Henry Marshall, Apothecary in Glasgow, did influence the belief of an extraordinary cause of these events."

"The doctor, on the 31 December 1696, tells, that at first sight, when he was brought to the girl she appeared so brisk in motion, so florid in colour, so chearful, and in a word every way healthful, that he could hardly be persuaded she had need of a physician; but within ten minutes he found himself obliged to alter his thoughts, for she rose from her seat and advertised she was instantly to be seized with a fit, according whereunto he observed a considerable distension in the left hypochondre, which in a trace falling, she was forthwith taken with horrid convulsive motions and heavy groans at first; which afterwards as soon as she was able to frame words, turned into an expostulatory mourning against some women; particularly Campbell and Naesmith. Yet he thought these symptoms were reducible to the freaks of hypochondriac melancholy, and therefore put her in such a course proper (i.e. appropriate treatment) *against that kind of malady. Upon which being freed for some time: he was alarmed that the child was returned to town worse than ever for having his assistance.*

"He was then frequently with her, and observed her narrowly, so that he was confident she had no visible correspondent to subminister hair, straw, coal, cinders, hay, and such like trash unto her; all which upon several occasions he saw her put out of her mouth without being wet; nay rather as they had been dried with artifice, and actually hot above the natural warmth of the body; sometimes after severe fits, and other times without trouble when discoursing with him. When she had only light convulsive motions, but to a high degree, such rigidity of the whole body, as we call tetivo (tetanus), she did not fancy as at other times, she saw these persons already named about her; but the upcasting of the trash above-mentioned, did no sooner cease, than in all her fits, when she was able to speak any, she always cried out they were pricking or pinching her. He saw her also when free of fits suddenly seized with dumbness, etc. And this he solemnly declares himself to have seen and handled, and were it not for the hay, straw etc he should not despair to reduce the other symptoms to their proper classes, in the catalogue of human diseases.

"Mr Marshall the apothecary concurs with the doctor; and gives some particular instances of his own observation; and among the rest, that the girl having fallen headlong on the ground, as (if) she had been thrown down with violence, fell a reasoning very distinctly thus: "Katie what ails thee at me, I am sure I never did thee wrong; come let us agree, let there be no more difference betwixt us, let us shake hands together (putting forth her hand) said, well Katie, I cannot help it, ye will not agree with me ". And immediately she cried, fell into a swoon, and out of that into a rage, wherein she continued without intermission for about half an hour; and perfectly recovered. Then she told him that she saw Katie Campbell, Nancy Naismith, etc and many more; Campbell was going to thrust a sword into her side, which made her so desirous

*to be agreed with her; and when the girl told him this, she instantly
fell into another fit as formerly, in which she continued another half
hour, etc. . . .dated 1st Jan, 1697 "*

As well as the items pulled from her mouth in the presence
of Dr Brisbane, on other occasions Christian regurgitated
small sticks of candle-fir (a type of fir which burns like a
candle), stable-dung mixed with hay, hens' feathers, gravel,
a whole gallnut and egg-shells. The Laird of Kellie witnessed
Christian's fits and during one of them he gave her a sore pinch
in the arm to which Christian seemed totally insensitive.
During her fits, she sometimes tried to reason with the
invisible Catherine Campbell, pleading for a return to their
old friendship and quoting much Scripture. Witnesses were
surprised at the child's command of the Scriptures. In an
old account of the case, the narrator says, "*We doubt not that
the Lord did, by his good spirit, graciously afford her a more than
ordinary measure of assistance.*" Interestingly, the account also
tells that Christian's fits became worse if there was talk about
religion and that, if someone prayed with her, she initially did
a lot of loud talking, whistling, singing and roaring, to drown
the voice of the person praying but usually subsequently
quietened down.

John Millar in his "*History of the Witches of Renfrewshire*"
gives an account of some of Christian's dialogue with the
invisible entities; the speech is said to have been written
down as well as could be remembered around the time of
the events. The following extract gives a flavour of such a
conversation with Catherine Campbell:

"Thou sittest there with a stick in thy hand to put in my
mouth, but through God's strength thou shall not get leave:
thou art permitted to torment me, but I trust in God thou

460

shall never get my life, though it is my life thou designest" (And at that time calling for a Bible and candle), said; "Come near me Katie and I'll let thee see where a godly man was given up to Satan to be tormented, but God kept his life in his own hand; and so I trust in God thou shall never get my life, and all that thou shall be permitted to do unto me, I hope through God's mercy shall turn to my advantage. This man was robbed of all, and tormented in body, and had nothing left him but an ill wife. Come near me, Katie, and I'll read it to thee " And reading that passage of Job, when she came to the place where his wife said to him, "Curse God and die!" the damsel considering these words a little, said; "O! what a wife this has been, that bids her goodman curse God and die? she who should have been a comfort to him in his trouble, turned to cross to him. "Then, after reading of the chapter to the end, she looks toward the foot of the bed and said; "Now, Katie, what thinkest thou of that? Thou seest for all the power the Devil got over Job, he gained no ground on him; and I hope he shall gain as little on me. Thy master the Devil deceives thee; he is a bad master whom thou servest, and thou shall find it to thy smart, except thou repent before thou die. There is no repentance to be had after death. I'll let thee see, Katie, there is no repentance in hell." And turning over the book, citing Luke, Chap xvi, near the latter end thereof, and reading the same over, said; "Katie, thou seest there is no repentance in hell, for this rich man besought Abraham to testify to his five brethren, that they come not to the place of torment, where he was, but repent and turn to the Lord, for there was no winning out, if once they come there; now, Katie, thou heard this, what thinkest thou of it?"

Before leaving Glasgow for the second time, she started to mention four other people as being among her tormentors. These were Alexander and James Anderson and two others whose names she did not know.

Following her return to Bargarran about 12th December, Christian was well for around a week before her fits became worse than ever. The Devil appeared to her in various forms and threatened to devour her. Her face and body would become dreadfully contorted and she would point to where her tormentors were standing and could not understand why no-one else could see them. Agnes Naismith, whom Christian accused of being one of her tormentors came in the flesh to visit the girl and spoke kindly to her, praying that God would soon restore her health. Thereafter, Christian believed that Agnes Naismith had ceased to be among her tormentors and that she actually protected her from the rest. Catherine Campbell was less benevolent, cursing Christian and hoping that the Devil would never let her get better for all the trouble she had brought on her. Shortly afterwards, Campbell was imprisoned and from that time Christian seemed to stop regarding her as a tormentor. It was claimed that a ball of hair was found in her pocket and was burnt on a fire and from that time on the child ceased to regurgitate hair.

By now public attention was starting to focus on Bargarran and it was becoming generally held that Christian Shaw was the victim of witches colluding with the Devil. Representatives of the Presbytery were sent to Bargarran to lend all possible spiritual help. One evening, Christian was reported to have been carried, laughing wildly, and with unaccountable motion through the bedroom and hall and down the long winding stairs to the outer gate. Witnesses claimed "... *her feet did not touch the ground, so far as anyone was able to discern* ". At the gate she was rigid and, on being brought back, said she felt as if she had been carried on a swing. The next evening, in a similar episode, she appeared to be carried to the top of the house and then back down to the outer gate where she lay as if dead. She said that some men and women had been trying to throw her in the well so that everyone would think that she had drowned herself. On a third occasion, Christian went into the cellar where a minister who tried to restrain her said he felt as if someone was pulling her back from his arms. It was said that on several occasions she spoke of things of which she had no means of knowing, but which were found to be true. This phenomenon was regarded as a sign of possession. She said that someone spoke over her head and distinctly gave her the information.

Some of incidents, which seem to have been regarded as supernatural at the time, have a distinct atmosphere of deceit. An entry for 21st January in *"The History of the Witches of Renfrewshire"*, says that Christian's fits again altered and started with her making heavy sighs, groans and hideous cries and saying that cats, ravens, owls and horses were pushing her down in the bed. Her mother and another woman declared that when they took Christian out of the bed, they saw something about the size of a cat moving under the bedclothes.

John Millar's book also reports that sometimes she cried out in pain because of violent blows from her invisible tormentors and that bystanders distinctly heard them.

One night, Christian was sitting with several people

including her parents when she cried out that something was wounding her thigh. Her mother found that her folding knife was open in her pocket. Her uncle closed the knife and put it back in her pocket and presently she suddenly cried out as before that the knife was cutting her thigh. The uncle searched the pocket and found that the knife was opened again. Christian said it had been unfolded by her tormentors and it is said that those present could not account for its having been opened.

According to the contemporary narrative, on 18th February:

"She being in a light-headed fit, said the Devil now appeared to her in the shape of a man; whereupon being struck in great fear and consternation, she was desired to pray in an audible voice: "The Lord rebuke thee, Satan!" which trying to do, she presently lost the power of her speech, her teeth being set, and her tongue drawn back into her throat; and attempting it again, she was immediately seized by another severe fit, in which, her eyes being twisted almost round, she fell down as one dead, struggling with her feet and hands, and, getting up again suddenly, was hurried violently to and fro through the room, deaf and blind, yet was speaking to some invisible creature about her, saying: "With the Lord's strength, thou shall neither put straw nor sticks into my mouth." After this she cried in a pitiful manner: "The bee hath stung me." Then, presently sitting down, and untying her stockings, she put her hand to that part which had been nipped or pinched; upon which the spectators discerned the lively marks of nails, deeply imprinted on that same part of her leg. When she came to herself, she declared that something spoke to her as if it were over her head, and told her it was Mr M. in a neighbouring parish (naming the place) that had appeared to her, and pinched her leg in the likeness of a bee."

Another time, while addressing an invisible assailant, she suddenly asked the entity where she had got her red sleeves.

There was a ripping sound and Christian was suddenly holding two pieces of red cloth. It seemed as if they had been torn from a witch's arms and astonished those present in the room, who were certain that there had been no such cloth there beforehand. The case was referred by the Presbytery to the Privy Council who set up a special commission, chaired by Lord Blantyre, the principal man in the parish. The commissioners came to Bargarran on 5th February 1697. Catherine Campbell, Agnes Naismith, a man called Anderson and his daughter Elizabeth, Margaret Fulton, James Lindsay and a Highland beggar, were all accused of being among Christian's tormentors. Each was confronted with the girl and when they touched her, she fell into fits; this did not happen when she was touched by others. When blindfolded, she could still recognise that the Highland beggar had touched her. Three other people were also implicated.

A boy in the neighbourhood, Thomas Lindsay, who used to say charms for a halfpenny, was called in and quickly confessed to being in league with the Devil and bearing his marks. Elizabeth Anderson also confessed to attending meetings with the Devil and said that her father and the Highland beggar were involved in tormenting Christian Shaw. The plan to torment Christian had been devised at a meeting with the Devil in the orchard at Bargarran House.

Two other women were also accused, Margaret Lang and her daughter Martha Semple. Margaret Lang had a better background than the others and was a midwife. Hearing that she had been accused she came to Bargarran to plead her innocence. At first Christian did not accuse Maggie further. However, a ball of hair was found under the chair where she had been sitting. Christian declared that this was a charm which prevented her from saying that Mrs Lang was indeed one of her tormentors. The two women were later to be pricked to detect the Devil's marks, insensitive areas of skin; it seems that no such areas were found on Martha Semple.

During these proceedings, the Presbytery held a fast in Erskine parish with special services in the church. Christian was present throughout the day but nothing happened to her. On 28th March, Christian recovered her former health and had no further fits or hallucinations.

Presently the case was compiled and seven people were summoned to appear at an assize in Paisley. The Lord Advocate was prosecutor and, as was customary in Scotland, an advocate was appointed to represent the accused. A new commission had been appointed to judge the case; it was composed of several persons of honour with special knowledge and experience. The charges were for several murders including children and a minister and for tormenting several people, particularly Christian Shaw. Reading the account of the charges and the confessions, one gets a distinct impression that the confessions may have been forced as they show general agreement about a conspiracy with the Devil to torment Christian Shaw and others and describe the Devil as a dark man whom they met several times, once in the orchard at Bargarran House. The reports that the defendants bore the marks of the Devil suggests that they had been pricked.

The minister who was said to have been murdered was John Hardie, minister of Dumbarton who died in November, 1696. He had been ordained in March 1693 and died unmarried. The Bargarran witches were said to have met one night in his manse garden. The basis of the belief that the Rev Mr Hardie and some children had been murdered is not clear; it seems more likely that they suffered sad and untimely deaths from natural causes.

For twenty hours, witnesses were carefully questioned and the jury took six hours to reach the verdict that the defendants were guilty. In his address to the jury, the Lord Advocate, Sir James Steuart, claimed that all the instances of clairvoyance and of flying locomotion were completely proven. He had no doubt about the murders and torments carried out by the accused. He stressed that the Devil's marks had been found on the witches and pointed out the many coincidences between what Christian Shaw alleged and what the accused confessed. On 10th June 1697, a gibbet and fire were prepared on the Gallow Green of Paisley. This was the scene of the execution of six of the condemned, including Maggie Lang. Each was strangled on a gibbet for a few minutes and was then thrown on the flames. A seventh victim, John Reid, was found hanged in his cell by his handkerchief attached to a nail in the wall; he was believed to have been strangled by the Devil. A horseshoe in the cross-roads at the intersection of Maxwellton Street and George Street in Paisley is said to mark the place where the witches' ashes were buried.

Further information about those who died has been obtained from Poll Tax Records of 1695:

Margaret Lang, wife of William Semple, cottar in Cartympen in Orbistoune's lands, Parish of Erskine.

John Lindsay, cottar in Barloch of Bargarran, Parish of Erskine.

James Lindsay, cottar in Billboe in Orbistoune's lands, Parish of Erskine.

John Reid, smith in the Laird of Hapland's lands, Parish of Inchinnan.

Catherine Campbell, Margaret Fulton and **Agnes Naismith** do not appear in these rolls. It is thought that Catherine Campbell may have become a servant to the Laird of Bargarran at Whitsun 1696, that Margaret Fulton may have been a resident of Dumbarton and that Agnes Naismith may have lived in Kilpatrick across the Clyde from Bargarran.

Christian Shaw seems to have suffered no recurrences of her condition after her symptoms ceased on 28th March, while the enquiries of the commission were still in progress. She later became Mrs Miller, wife of the minister of Kilmaurs in Ayrshire, whom she married in 1718. The Rev John Miller died in 1721 on a visit to his wife's family and was buried at Erskine. Christian learned the techniques of spinning thread and, in the early 1720s, she and the Shaw family set up a mill producing Bargarran thread. The product became famous in its day and brought good prices. It had a special mark which bore the arms of the Shaw family, "azure, three covered cups *or*".

Psychiatric assessment

Comments on history

This is an 11 year old pre-pubertal girl of well-to-do parents. Christian is assumed to be normal developmentally and to have no significant medical or psychiatric history, including sexual abuse. There is no evidence of premorbid personality dysfunction and she is described as lively and well-inclined. She seems to have suffered no long term sequelae after this seven month episode. No drug history is available including the substances administered by the physicians.

17th August 1697

Christian suffers acute stress after Catherine Campbell's anger was displaced onto Christian. This may have caused her to feel guilty and at fault. Apart from the visit of Agnes Naismith, there is no history of events in the five days between the verbal attack and the onset of illness (e.g. personality change, head injury, infection, further confrontation). There is also no information about the parents' mental state or whether there is any marital stress, important considerations when dealing with ill health in a child. Misidentifications, visual hallucinations and peculiar time distortions often occur to children who have experienced single intense, unexpected shocks.

The prodromal period of Christian's illness appears to be when she awakes with night terrors and remains restless for the next eight days complaining of non-specific symptoms. Accounts indicate there were episodes of opisthotonus and aphonia. Bleeding and treatment by a doctor and an

469

apothecary from Paisley fail. Christian then develops acute delirium, convulsions and visual hallucinations. Anaemia or, more likely, the psychological stress induced by the treatment, may have precipitated further seizures. Tongue-biting, incontinence and self-injury can occur in conversion non-epileptic seizures as well as in epilepsy. It is claimed that the tolerance of pain conferred by dissociation can account for substantial self-injury including bony fractures. Non-epileptic seizures (NES) are less likely to lead to discrete gaps in memory that are characteristic of complex partial seizures. NES are usually of longer seizure duration and vocalisations are associated with emotional content. There is also more frequent crying, yelling and use of profanity in NES.

October 1696
Around the time of the consultation with Matthew Brisbane, Christian develops generalised seizures associated with pica. Patients with pica may have a false or craving appetite and deliberately ingest a bizarre selection of foods and non-food items. It is more common in women and may be associated with iron-deficiency anaemia. During seizures, Christian quotes scriptures and names those she implicates in witchcraft. There is no mention of her cognitive state although she seems to be aware of her surroundings, with her vocalisations influenced by the attention and subsequent reactive behaviour of her carers. On presentation to Dr Brisbane, Christian is noted to be well. Five minutes into the consultation she develops convulsions, heavy groanings and murmurings against two women. She had announced the oncoming event previously, a feature more common in pseudo-seizures than in epilepsy.

470

12th December 1696

For one week, Christian remains symptom-free, then develops fits, visual hallucinations and bizarre behaviour resembling trance disorder. She appears to sleepwalk for a considerable distance (with dim light and tired carers, this is the most likely explanation for her moving across the ground). Her behaviour confirmed existing beliefs of witchcraft within the parish.

February 1697

Christian falls into fits whenever any of the alleged perpetrators touch her. When blind-folded she is only able to positively identify the Highland beggar by his touch. There is no mystery in this, as his smell, clothes and manner would differentiate him from local people. Thomas Lindsay confesses to being in league with the Devil, however, it would seem that he was a young, impressionable boy. Elizabeth Anderson also testifies but there is no note of her level of intelligence nor of the methods used to obtain her confession, although its nature suggests it was extracted under duress.

More interestingly, when Maggie Lang, a lady of superior character, challenges Christian, she is initially unwilling to identify her as a perpetrator. A ball of hair is taken as evidence that Maggie made Christian initially silent. It would seem that Christian, who was now of special significance to the townspeople, was believed implicitly with alternative explanations discounted.

18th February 1697

Christian is delirious and visually hallucinating, witnessing the Devil appearing in human form. She experiences tactile hallucinations and seizure activity is noted. Her self-injurious behaviour has religious significance attached to it. A degree of suggestibility of her carers and manipulative behaviour by Christian is demonstrated on several occasions, particularly when supernatural significance is given to a simple conjuring trick with two pieces of red cloth.

28th March 1697

Christian becomes symptom free. A new commission is appointed. Its members are honourable, experienced and less likely to be controversial in a case of notoriety. Crimes are attributed to the defendants which seem unrelated to the case and with no evidence proffered other than supposed confessions. The Lord Advocate instructed the jury in forceful terms as to the decision expected. In particular, his evidence was based on Christian's bizarre behaviour and the coincidences between what Christian stated and the confessions obtained from the accused.

10th June 1697

Six people executed and one suicide.

Diagnoses

While the story is bizarre, modern psychiatry could certainly explain Christian Shaw's condition. Because of the incomplete history and the inability to examine the patient, diagnosis can only be tentative but the following would be likely. The definitions are those given in the appropriate classification.

F44 (ICD 10) Dissociative disorder/ 300.11 (DSM IV) Conversion Disorder with mixed presentation (which encompasses NES). Following the DSM IV classification, diagnosis of "300.11 Conversion disorder" is dependent on the following:

A One or more symptoms or deficits affecting voluntary motor or sensory function that suggest a neurological or other medical condition.

B Psychological factors are judged to be associated with the symptom or deficit because the initiation or exacerbation of the symptom or deficit is preceded by conflicts or other stresses.

C The symptom or deficit is not intentionally produced or feigned (as in factious disorder or malingering).

D The symptom or deficit cannot, after appropriate investigation, be fully explained by a general medical condition, or by the direct effects of a substance, or as a culturally sanctioned behaviour or experience.

E The symptom or deficit causes clinically significant distress or impairment in social, occupational, or other important areas of functioning or warrants medical evaluation.

F The symptom or deficit is not limited to pain or sexual dysfunction, does not occur exclusively during the course of a somatisation disorder, and is not better accounted for by another mental disorder.

F44.3 (ICD 10) Trance and possession disorder.

Disorder is which there is a temporary loss of the sense of personal identity and full awareness of surroundings.

Pica of infancy and childhood.

Persistent eating of non-nutritive substances (such as soil, paint chippings etc.). It may occur as one of many symptoms that are part of a more widespread psychiatric disorder or as a relatively isolated psychopathological behaviour (F98.3, ICD 10).

G40.0 (ICD 10) Localisation-related (focal) (partial) idiopathic epilepsy and epileptic syndromes with seizures of localised onset.

Benign childhood epilepsy with centrotemporal EEG spikes. Childhood epilepsy with occipital EEG paroxysms.

F23 (ICD 10) Acute and transient psychotic disorder.

A heterogeneous group of disorders characterised by the acute onset of psychotic symptoms such as delusions, hallucinations and perceptual disturbances, and by the severe disruption of ordinary behaviour. Acute onset is defined as a crescendo development of a clearly abnormal clinical picture in about two weeks or less. For these disorders there is no evidence of organic causation. Perplexity and puzzlement are often present but disorientation for time, place and person is not persistent or severe enough to justify a diagnosis of organically caused delirium. Complete recovery usually occurs within a few months, often within a few weeks or even days. If the disorder persists, a change in classification will be necessary. The disorder may or may not be associated with acute stress, defined as unusually stressful events preceding the onset by one to two weeks.

Christian's age would mitigate against diagnosing personality disorder as this does not fully develop until the age of eighteen.

Investigations and treatment

If Christian were to be seen today, in order to diagnose an organic disorder, there would be a full range of haematological investigations including serum prolactin, and a 24 hour EEG. A CT scan would be helpful. Full thyroid investigations would be carried out if merited by the clinical picture. Hypocalcaemia secondary to anxiety-based hyperventilation would not be of sufficient severity to account for the opisthotonus. Assuming normal renal function, it would be unlikely that significant hypercalcaemia would result from pica involving eggshells.

In modern psychiatry, initial investigation would be a mental state examination, with a history from both parents and any other significant carer. Educational assessment would be important along with information about her friendships, religious teaching and her interaction with siblings. Information would be corroborated with the patient's general practitioner and with her school. A psychometric assessment would also be warranted at the beginning and end of the episode to elucidate any cognitive decline. Due to the severity of these symptoms, she would most likely be admitted to a child in-patient unit for observation and would be detainable under Section 25 (1) Mental Health (Scotland) Act 1984.

Treatment may consist of individual work for Christian and family work, possibly marital counselling, and minimal use of sedative drugs until the diagnosis was clarified. A social work colleague may be involved as a co-worker for the family and to offer practical advice. Liaison with the school would be important to ensure that Christian would not fall behind with schoolwork and also to guide the teachers how to deal with Christian on her return. When her symptoms resolved she would be followed-up at psychiatric out-patients and thereafter by her general practitioner.

Biographical note: Dr Matthew Brisbane

Matthew Brisbane was a very successful and well respected Scottish medic of the later half of the 1600s and was the city of Glasgow's physician in the last two decades of the century. He was the son of the manse of Erskine in Renfrewshire, where his father Matthew had succeeded his own father, William, as minister. William Brisbane was minister of Erskine from 1592 to c 1640-2 and his son held the charge from 1642 to 1648. The Brisbanes were well connected and were a scion of the family of the Brisbanes of nearby Bishopton, believed to be descendants of one William Brisbane who was chancellor of Scotland in 1332. In addition, the Rev Matthew Brisbane's wife, the mother of the physician, was the youngest daughter of John Napier of Merchiston, the famous inventor of logarithms. The main Brisbane line also had property in Ayrshire, the estate of Brisbane at Largs, and later the family resided there as Brisbane of that ilk. Last century, one of their descendants, Sir Thomas Brisbane, was to become famous as the Governor of New South Wales in Australia and the city of Brisbane is named after him. Little is known of Matthew Brisbane's early career but he received a classical education at the College of Glasgow and was awarded the degree of M.D from the University of Utrecht in the Netherlands in 1661; his thesis was entitled *"De Calalepsi"*. At this time there was little opportunity for studying medicine in the Scottish universities and presumably his choice of the Netherlands was related to its being a country whose religion was reformed and, therefore, sympathetic to a Scottish presbyterian.

Clearly Matthew Brisbane was well-respected. There is

a record in the Glasgow City Accounts for 1682 that he was the town physician and was paid the same salary as the surgeon, John Robisoune, and the stone-cutter, Evir McNeill. Each received £66 13s 4d. Scots. About 1684, he was entered in the roll of the Glasgow Faculty of Physicians and Surgeons. His name appears on a list of *"The names of such worthie persons as have gifted books to the Chierurgions Librarie in Glasgow"*. He also held office in the University, being Dean of Faculty in 1675-76 and Rector in 1677-81. Matthew Brisbane died in 1699.

A pamphlet entitled *"A relation of the diabolical practices of the witches of the Sheriffdom of Renfrew in the Kingdom of I Scotland contained in their tryalls, examinations, and confessions; and for which several of them have been execulec this present year 1697."* contains a horrific section in its preface in which the trial of the witches by pricking is described fearsome detail. It makes clear that Dr Brisbane had at first disbelieved that witches bore the mark of the Devil but it seems that he was called to witness the pricking of two of the women and shown the evidence. A three-inch long needle was inserted at the top of the vertebrae in one victim and into the lower abdomen a hands-breadth below the ribs in Margaret Lang; neither woman, the writer claims, felt pain or bled.

BIBLIOGRAPHY

Bargarran witchcraft trial and Dr Matthew Brisbane.

Anderson, W. *The Scottish Nation*. A. Fullarton and Co., London 1863.

Chambers, R. *Domestic Annals of Scotland*. W.& R. Chambers, Edinburgh 1861

Clark, S. *Paisley: A History*. Mainstream Edinburgh 1988

Duncan, A. *Memorials of the Faculty of Physicians and Surgeons of Glasgow 1599-1850* James Maclehose and Sons, Glasgow 1896.

Gardner, A. *A History of the Witches of Renfrewshire* (New Edition).Alexander Gardner, Paisley 1877.

Innes Smith, R. W. *English-Speaking Students of Medicine at the University of Leyden*. Oliver and Boyd, Edinburgh 1932.

Lang, A. *History of Scotland*, William Blackwood and Sons. Edinburgh 1907.

Larner, C., Lee, C. H. and McLachlan, H. V. *A Source-Book of Scottish Witchcraft*, University of Glasgow 1977. [reprinted 2005]

Metcalfe, W. M. *A History of Paisley 600 - 1908*. Alexander Gardner, Paisley, 1909.

Millar, John. *A History of the Witches of Renfrewshire*. John Millar Paisley, 1809.

Scott, H. *Fasti Ecclesiae Scoticanae*. Oliver and Boyd, Edinburgh 1920.

T. P. *A Relation of the Diabolical Practices of the Witches of the Sheriffdom of Renfrew in the Kingdom of Scotland*. Hugh Newman at the Grashopper in the Poultry, London 1697.

Psychiatric assessment.

Alper, K. 'Nonepileptic seizures'. *Neurologic Clinics* 12 153-173, 1994. j

Diagnostic and Statistical Manual of Mental Disorders, 4th Ed., American Psychiatric Association, Washington D. C. 1994.

Hare, E. 'The history of "nervous disorders" from 1600 to 1840, and a comparison with modern views'. *British Journal of Psychiatry*, 159 37-45, 1991.

Hornstein, N L. and Putnam, F. W. 'Clinical phenomenology

of child and adolescent dissociative disorders'. *American Academy of Child and Adolescent Psychiatry*; 31: 1077-1085, 1992.

International Classification of Diseases and Related Health Problems, 10th Ed., World Health Organisation, Geneva 1992

Mace, C. J. 'Hysterical conversion I: a history'. *British Journal of Psychiatry*; 161:369-377,1992.

Mace, C. J. 'Hysterical conversion II: a critique'. *British Journal of Psychiatry*; 161:378-389,1992.

Parry-Jones, B. and Parry-Jones, W. L. 'Pica: symptom or eating disorder? A historical assessment'. *British Journal of Psychiatry*; 160: 341 -354,1992.

Small, G. W., Propper, M. W., Randolphs, E. T. and Eth, S. 'Mass hysteria among student performers: social relationship as a symptom predictor'. *American Journal of Psychiatry*; 148: 1200-1205, 1991.

Terr, L. C. 'Childhood traumas: an outline and overview'. *American Journal of Psychiatry*; 148: 10-20. 1991.

Exonerate the Erskine one!

By

Hugh V. McLachlan and J. Kim Swales

This paper is, with minor alterations, one that was presented at: Twisted Sisters: Women Crime and Deviance Since 1400 *Scottish Women's History Network Conference at Glasgow Caledonian University, 14th October, 2000. See http://www.swhn.org.uk/shaw.html*

A fuller version of it appeared as 'The Bewitchment of Christian Shaw: A Re-assessment of the Famous Paisley Witchcraft Case of 1697' *in* Twisted Sisters: Women, Crime and Deviance in Scotland Since 1400, *edited by Yvonne Brown and Rona Ferguson, Tuckwell, 2002, pp. 54-83*

H.V.McL.

Introduction

Christian Shaw - 'The Bargarran Impostor'- has been treated harshly by commentators on the famous Paisley witchcraft trial of 1697. The daughter of the Laird of Bargarran, she lived in Erskine. She is commonly thought to have been responsible, through her cunning and malicious allegations concerning them, for the deaths of several people who were executed as witches.

Her reputation as a spectacularly evil child, is based upon an interpretation which later generations, following Arnot, have put upon a book entitled: A *True Narrative of the Sufferings and Relief of a Young Girle; Strangely molested by*

Evil spirits and their instruments in the West: With a preface and postscript containing Reflections on what is most Material or Curious either in the history or trial of the Seven Witches who were Condemn'd to be Execute in the country. It was published in Edinburgh in 1698. Both the *Narrative*, and Arnot's comments are reprinted in this book.

The Evidence

On the 21st of August, 1696, when the strange afflictions and behaviour of Christian Shaw were reported to have commenced, the child was only ten or eleven years old. She accused particular people of tormenting her. They, it was said, bit her, and their bite marks and the effects of their nipping of her could be seen on the girl's body, tore her flesh and forced various things – for instance, straw, pins, egg shells, orange pills, hair, bones and another substance which we shall return to – into her mouth. Later, the child removed the stuff from her mouth in the presence of witnesses. Christian's tormentors, it should be noted were said in the *Narrative* to be visible to Christian while they were tormenting her but to be invisible to Christian's parents and to the other people who were said to be there at the time.

It is narrated that she fell into 'sore fits', in some of which she seemed to be dead. In others, she seemed, deaf or blind and could not speak. She had 'swooning fits' and would laugh and giggle when the Scriptures were read out to her. Sometimes, she would go as stiff as a board and her head would bend backwards towards her heels. In some of her fits, her belly swelled '... as like a woman with child.

Her eyes were pulled into her head so far that spectators thought she should never have used them more'.

The Devil would appear to the child and people would observe the girl holding lengthy theological discussions with him. Christian is said to have reported that the Devil, who was unseen by the other people who were present, had hairy arms and hairs like the bristles of a pig on his face.

She tried to throw herself into a fire during one of her fits and, the *Narrative* says, it took four strong men to restrain her. It says too that she was seen to fly around the room without her feet touching the ground. It is said that she dropped her glove on the ground and one of her invisible tormentors picked it up and gave it back to her.

A highlander, who was said by Christian to be one of her tormentors was brought before Christian and a blanket was placed over her head. Various people then, in turn, touched the child and nothing happened. However, whenever the highlander touched her, she went into a fit.

Christian is said to have predicted events which turned out as she predicted they would and revealed the occurrence of events of which she could not have had knowledge in any obvious natural way. For instance, she said that, at a particular time, her tormentors were then holding a meeting in Bargarran Orchard at which the Devil was present. What she said was latter discovered to have been true. Sometimes too, when her tormentors were arrested, they immediately ceased to torment her even although, it is noted, she could have had no natural way of knowing that they had been arrested.

Between her fits, she is said to have been normal and well. Local ministers prayed with her and held services in her house. Her parents and other concerned people did all they could, it is said, to explain these events but they were unable to do so. They took her to a famous medical authority, Dr. Brisbane, in Glasgow. Here, the child spat out a coal cinder which was as big as a chestnut and, warmer than body temperature, was almost too hot to handle. After conducting a thorough examination of the child and the case, so the *Narrative* infers, Dr. Brisbane announced that her affliction was preternatural.

On the 28th of March, 1997, Christian Shaw was said to be, 'by God's great mercy toward her', perfectly recovered.

The Bargarran Impostor?

The traditional interpretation of the reported events is that Christian Shaw was a trickster. According to Arnot: 'She seems to have displayed an artifice above her years... and to have been aided by accomplices, which dullness of apprehension or violence of prejudice forbade the bystanders to discover'. (Arnot, 1785, p.202). There might also, he considers, have been an element of hysteria behind the girl's behaviour.

Notice that even if Arnot's interpretation were true, it would be most unfair to focus on Christian Shaw as the central villain of the piece. After all, the pre-teenaged child was not the judge in the case nor a member of the jury. She did not arrest the particular people concerned nor was she the one who exercised the authority to have them tried for witchcraft. Furthermore, a child would not have adult accomplices in the sort of situation which Arnot envisages; she would, rather, be the stooge of adult manipulators.

However, Arnot's interpretation is not very plausible. At the very least, one can say that it does not compel one's belief. If the child was an impostor, why did she do what she did? It is all very well to say that she did it, say, out of spite and to attract attention to herself but some of the things which were reported to have happened must have been if they did happen as reported, extremely unpleasant. Less unpleasant actions could have attracted as much attention and vented as much spite. For instance, among the things which Christian is said to have removed from her mouth were lumps of excrement.

One might, of course, want to explain such incidents in terms of hysteria rather than of fraud. However, if one does this, it is difficult to avoid making the unlikely claim that the child was simultaneously a rational, methodical, amazingly skilful conjurer and a passionate hysteric. One explanation tends to cancel out rather than reinforce the other.

If she was an impostor, then how was she, a young girl of ten or eleven years old, able to perform such tricks? How did she learn them? Who taught her? It is possible that someone of the experience, training and unusual talent of, say, Paul Daniels could perform the sorts of tricks which might deceive an inquiring and sceptical audience and a learned authority such as Dr. Brisbane into thinking that supernatural actions were taking place before their very eyes. It is implausible to say that Christian Shaw could have performed them. For instance – and other examples could be cited – could you drop a glove onto the ground and than make it jump back into your hand as if an invisible tormentor had replaced it there? We could not (with or

484

without the help of accomplices). Could you fly through the air without touching the ground or give the impression that you were doing so?

Four strong men, it is said, were required to stop Christian Shaw from ending up in the fire. How could the child, through trickery, give the impression that such amazing physical force was required to subdue her ten or eleven year old frame?

Mental Illness?

Recently, the interpretation that Christian Shaw was suffering from some sort of mental illness has been focused upon. For instance, Adam writes: 'If Christian's bewitchment happened now, it would be diagnosed at once as a case for psychotherapy. She was suffering from hysteria...'. (Adam, 1978, p. 222) See too 'The Bargarran Witchcraft Trial: A Psychiatric Reassessment', by McDonald, Thom and Thom. It has been reprinted in this book.

Some aspects of the case, for instance, the levitation cannot be explained, according to Adam, in terms of mental illness and rather than putting them down to Christian's trickery, she says that they were paranormal. She writes: 'Much of the reporting in the Narrative, once considered exaggerated and credulous can now be seen as factual and accurate'.

Now, it is possible that some of the events described in the Narrative could be accounted for in terms of Christian Shaw's mental health. However – as in the case of the theory of the child as an impostor – not all of the events could be. Various events, furthermore, can be explained by neither the theory that she was mentally ill nor that she was an impostor.

For instance, reconsider some of the incidents which we have noted. Suggested mental illness on the part of Christian Shaw would not explain, say, how she was able to fool adult spectators into believing that a glove dropped from her hand was replaced there by an invisible tormentor nor how she was able to seem to fly around the room without touching the ground. Mental illness too would not have given her the ability to predict occurrences nor could mental illness have enabled her to know, when she was covered with a blanket, whether the highlander or some other person was touching her.

In a reported theological conversation with one of her tormentors, Katherine Campbell, who was said to have been visible in this incident only to Christian Shaw and who was later burnt as a witch, the child said:

'"Thou sittest there with a stick in thy hand to put in my mouth, but through God's strength thou shalt not get leave; thou are permitted to torment me, but I trust in God thou shalt never get my life though it is my life thou designest... Come near me Katie, and I'll let thee see where a godly man was given up to Satan to be tormented but God kept his life in His own hand...'".

The child then, it is narrated, read from the relevant passages in Job and then said to her:

'"Now, Katie, what thinkest thou of that? thou seest for all the power the Devil got over Job, he gained no ground on him: and I hope he shall gain as little on me. Thy master the Devil deceives thee; he is a bad master whom thou servest, and thou shalt find it to thy smart, except thou

486

repent before thou die. There is no repentance to be had after death. I'll let thee see, Katie, there is no repentance in hell". And turning over the book, citing *Luke*, Chap. xvi, near the latter end thereof, and reading the same over, said...".

The *Narrative* claims:

'Thus she continued for more than two hours space, reasoning at this rate, and exhorting her to repent, quoting many places of Scripture through the Revelation and the Evangelists'

The passage in *Luke*, chapter sixteen, which the girl is said to have referred to is particularly relevant to the point which the girl is said to have been making. It contains the story of the rich man and Lazarus and of the torment the rich man suffered in hell

In another similar reported conversation with her tormentors, Christian is said to have argued as follows:

'It is God that gives us every good gift. We have nothing of our own. I submit to His will, though I never be better, for God can make all my trouble turn to my advantage, according to His Word, *Romans* viii 28'.

Again, when we consult the *Bible*, we find that this text is particularly appropriate. It is: 'And we know that all things work together to them that love God, to them who are called according to His purpose'.

It does not seem plausible that an eleven year old child – whether or not an impostor and whether or not suffering from a mental illness – could possess sufficient knowledge of the Scriptures to realise the pertinence of these passages to the highly sophisticated theological points which she was said to be making. It is plausible that other adults – for instance, local ministers – could have had the required level of scriptural knowledge, linguistic sophistication and theological acumen to devise monologues like these.

The Bewitchment of Christian Shaw: a Re-assessment

Arnot talks of gullible people being deceived by Christian Shaw. We suggest that, perhaps, the gullible people are those like Arnot and Adam who believe too readily that what is written in the *Narrative* is an authentic account of what people who were observing Christian Shaw believed they saw.

Some of the events described in the *Narrative* are, we would suggest, fantasies: they did not occur or, at least, did not happen quite as they are described. They do not require an explanation. What requires to be explained, perhaps, is why it was said that the events occurred. In so far as there were hoaxes and impostures going on, they were carried out by those who said that Christian Shaw did the things which she was said to have done and not by Christian Shaw.

Who wrote the *Narrative*? It is an anonymous document. Commentators tend not to mention this anonymity nor to speculate on its authorship. Our research leads us to suggest that it was written, or compiled, collated and/or edited by the Rev. Andrew Turner, minister at Erskine and the Rev. James Brisbane, minister at Kilmacolm. The latter was a young relative of Dr. Brisbane.

In the Record of the Presbytery of Paisley for the 13th of December, 1696 (reprinted in this book), it is noted that Christian Shaw, of the parish of Erskine has 'been under a very sore and unnatural distemper' and the Presbytery '... appoints Mr. Turner and Mr. Brisbane to repair to Bargarran, Friday next, there to take up a particular narrative of her whole trouble, of its rise and progress...'.

There are other mentions of 'the revising of the narrative of Christine Shaw's trouble' and of producing copies of it. The Rev. John Wilson, it is noted in the Record for the 10th of May, 1997, wrote a preface to the *Narrative*, which was handed over to Mr. Turner.

There are important features of the Bargarran witchcraft case which tend to overlooked and which we would like to highlight. It is most unlike the Scottish witchcraft cases which preceded it (and which, by and large, had died out decades before). In the Scottish context, it is, to our knowledge, unique. For instance, it was not usual for children to be involved as both victims and accusers. Usually in Scottish witchcraft cases, when a child is said to have been bewitched, the allegation came from the parents of the child, one of whom – usually the mother – is usually said to have had a pre-existing grievance with the accused witch. Furthermore, the sorts of fits and other bizarre occurrences which are described are not mentioned in the preceding Scottish witchcraft cases.

However, the Bargarran case bears some striking resemblances to the famous Salem witchcraft case in New England in 1692. The earliest known account of the Salem case was written by the Rev. Deodat Lawson and published in Boston in 1692. It is entitled: *A Brief and True Narrative of some Remarkable Passages Relating to Sundry Persons Afflicted by Witchcraft, at Salem Village which happened from the Nineteenth of March, to the Fifth of April, 1692.* (It is reprinted, along with Lawson's other relevant writings, in this book.)

Mr. Lawson had previously been a minister at Salem. He believed that his wife and daughter, who died there three years previously, had been killed by witchcraft. We have discovered from a manuscript relating to other unpublished witchcraft cases – which were deserted before they came to trial – that the Mr. Brisbane concerned himself with witchcraft cases, gave evidence in them and believed that his own child had been killed by witchcraft. [See *NAS manuscript JC/26/81/D9*, reprinted in this book.])

In his appendix to his treatise on witchcraft, *Christ's Fidelity the Only Shield Against Satan's Malignity*, Lawson says that he published his account of the Salem case in order to: '... satisfy such as are not resolved to the Contrary, that there may be (and are) such Operations of the Powers of Darkness on the bodies and Minds of Mankind, by Divine Permission'. (Note that Christian Shaw expresses a similar theological outlook.) There is, as the minutes of the Presbytery of Paisley would lead one to expect, a preface to the Bargarran *Narrative* which is similar in tone to Mr. Lawson's sermon. In the preface, the existence of God, the Devil and witchcraft is affirmed and the then current atheism and disbelief in witchcraft – and these two things are united in the mind of the preface's author – are deplored. It is indicated that the subsequent *Narrative* will furnish proof of the existence of witchcraft and, by implication, of the existence of God.

The *Narrative*, the preface says, will serve to glorify God's name. It asserts that: '... the abundant and efficacious grace of God is conspicuous in enabling a young girl to resist to the utmost the best laid assaults of the evil one, as it is

490

certain that he shews the greatest malice in countries where he is hated and hateth most, and the nearer his reign be to an end'.

Notice that it is often said that, in the past, at the time of the witchcraft trials, everybody believed in witchcraft – as if there were more uniformity of thought in the past than now. This is far from the case. The *Narrative* was written, not because everyone believed in witchcraft but precisely because not every did. As we have indicated already, various other witchcraft cases were instigated but not proceeded with around this time and this also lends weight to the view that beliefs concerning witchcraft and witchcraft accusations were not universally uncritically held.

Both in style and content, as well as in rationale, the Salem *Narrative* and the later Bargarran one are remarkably similar. For instance, it says in Mr. Lawson's *Narrative*:

'Abigail Williams, (about 12 years of age) had a grievous fit; she was at first hurried with Violence to and fro in the room (though Mrs. Ingerson endeavoured to hold her) sometimes making as if she would fly...she said there was Goodw. N. and said, "Do you not see her? Why, there she stands!".... After that, she ran to the Fire, and began to throw Fire Brands, about the house; and run against the Back, as if she would run up the chimney, and, as they said, she had attempted to go into the Fire in other Fits'.

In relation to another accused witch, Goodwife C., the alleged victims: '... did vehemently accuse her ... of afflicting them, by Biting, Pinching, Strangling, etc. And that they did in their Fit see her likeness coming to them'.

It is a myth, incidentally, that the supposed victims of witchcraft in Salem were, invariably, children. Of the ten afflicted females that Mr. Lawson indicates, only three of them were young pre-teenaged girls; four were said to be married and , of the remainder, two of them were seventeen. This pattern is similar to that in Renfrewshire in the 1690s when one views the Bargarran case along with the other contemporary cases which were deserted before they reached trial.

Conclusion

We suggest that what propelled this famous witchcraft case was not the actions and intentions of Christian Shaw but those of the person or people who was or were aware of Mr. Lawson's Salem *Narrative* and wanted to produce a Scottish equivalent. He or they chose Christian Shaw as the central figure in his or their story, a story which he or they quite possibly considered to be true, at least in essence and which probably did contain some elements of truth which he or they consciously or unconsciously polished, revised and exaggerated upon.

The *Narrative*, we suggest, is not completely true. Whether or not it was completely truthful – whether the errors of fact were deliberate or not – remains an open question. If there were liars, it remains an open question who they were. Notice that Mr. Turner and Mr. Brisbane (or one or other of them) might well have had a clerical rather than a creative role in the production of the book. We are not trying to free Christian Shaw from unfair blame at the expense of unfairly blaming some one else.

That some strange things happened to or concerning Christian Shaw – whether they were paranormal, the result of mental illness, merely mysteriously co-incidental or whatever - seems to us to be likely. The account given in the *Narrative* is not a complete fabrication.

We are not sceptical in general about the possibility of attaining knowledge of long since passed events but in the particular case of the alleged bewitching of Christian Shaw, a degree of scepticism is appropriate. We do not know, no one, we would say, knows precisely what happened. However, we think it can be said with justified confidence that the claim that Christian Shaw was an impostor cannot be sustained. It is not credible. It is a nasty, unfair and unsubstantiated allegation.

Christian Shaw was a wonderful woman who, as the brains behind the Bargarran Thread company, can be regarded as a founder of the sewing thread industry on which the prosperity of Paisley was based. Feminists - but not only they - should celebrate her. However, she is regarded more as an embarrassment than a heroine in Paisley because of her imagined pivotal role in the witchcraft trials.

It would be fitting if an appropriate plaque were to be placed in or near Paisley to mark the repudiation of the accusation that she was 'The Bargarran Impostor'. Parade the placards, chant the mantra: 'Exonerate the Erskine One!'

Other Related Publications by McLachlan and Swales:

McLachlan, Hugh V. and Swales, J. Kim. (forthcoming) *Women, Crime and Witchcraft: Scotland After the Reformation and Before the Enlightenment*, Humming Earth.

McLachlan, Hugh V. and Swales, J. Kim. (1978), 'Lord Hale, Witches and Rape: A Comment', *British Journal of Law and Society*, Vol. 5, No. 2, pp. 251-261.

McLachlan, Hugh V. and Swales, J. Kim. (1979a),'Stereotypes and Scottish Witchcraft', *Contemporary Review*, Vol. 234, No. 1357, February, pp. 88-94.

McLachlan, Hugh V. and Swales, J. Kim. (1979b), 'Witchcraft and the Status of Women: A Comment', *British Journal of Sociology*, Vol. 30, No. 3, pp. 349-358.

McLachlan, Hugh V. and Swales, J. Kim. (1980), 'Witchcraft and Anti-Feminism', *Scottish Journal of Sociology*, vol. 4, no. 2, pp 141-166.

McLachlan, Hugh V. and Swales, J. Kim. (1982), 'Tibbetts's Theory of Rationality and Scottish Witchcraft', *Philosophy of the Social Sciences*, Vol. 12, No. 1, pp 75-79.

McLachlan, Hugh V. and Swales, J. Kim. (1983), 'Rationality and the Belief in Witches: A Rejoinder to Tibbetts', *Philosophy of the Social Sciences*, Vol. 13, No. 4, pp 475-477.

McLachlan, Hugh V. and Swales, J. Kim. (1984), 'Review of Witch-Hunting, Magic and the New Philosophy by Brian Easlea', *Philosophy of the Social Sciences*, Vol. 14, No. 4, 577-580.

McLachlan, Hugh V. and Swales, J. Kim. (1992), 'Scottish Witchcraft: Myth or Reality?', *Contemporary Review*, vol. 260, no. 1513, February, pp. 79-84.

McLachlan, Hugh V. and Swales, J. Kim. (1994), 'Sexual Bias the the Law: The Case of Pre-Industrial Scotland', *International Journal of Sociology and Social Policy*, Vol. 14, No. 9, pp. 20-39.

Bibliography

Adam, Isabel (1978), *Witch Hunt: The Great Scottish Witchcraft Trials of 1697*, London, Macmillan.

Alper, K. (1994) 'Nonepileptic seizures', *Neurologic Clinics* 12: pp 153-173.

Anderson, W. (1863), *The Scottish Nation*, London, A. Fullarton and Co.

Anon. (ed.) (1877) *A History of the Witches of Renfrewshire* (New Edition), Paisley, Alexander Gardner.

Apps, L. and Gow, A. (2003), *Male Witches in Early Modern Europe*, Manchester, Manchester University Press.

Arnot, Hugo (1785), *A Collection of Celebrated Criminal Trials in Scotland, 1536-1784*, Edinburgh.

Chambers, R. (1861), *Domestic Annals of Scotland*, Edinburgh, W. and R. Chambers.

Clark, S. (1988), *Paisley: A History*, Edinburgh, Mainstream.

Duncan, A. (1896), *Memorials of the Faculty of Physicians and Surgeons of Glasgow 1599-1850*, Glasgow, James Maclehose and Sons.

Ewan, E., Innes, S., Reynolds. S and Pipes, R. (2006), *The Biographical Dictionary of Scottish Women*, Edinburgh, Edinburgh University Press.

Francis, Richard (2005), *Judge Sewall's Apology: The Salem Witch Trials and the Forming of a Conscience*, Fourth Estate.

Godbeer, Richard (2005), *Escaping Salem: The Other Witch Hunt of 1692*, Oxford and New York, Oxford University Press.

Goodare, Julian (2002), 'Witch-hunting and the Scottish State' in J. Goodare (ed.) *The Scottish Witch-Hunt in Context*, Manchester University Press.

Goodare, Julian (2005) 'The Scottish witchcraft act', *Church History*, 74, pp. 39-67.

Goodare, J., Martin, L., Miller J. and Yeoman, L. 'The Survey of Scottish Witchcraft', *http://www.arts.ed.ac.uk/witches*

Hare, E. (1991), 'The history of "nervous disorders" from 1600 to 1840, and a comparison with modern views', *British Journal of Psychiatry*, No. 159 pp 37-45.

Hornstein, N L. and Putnam, F. W. (1992), 'Clinical phenomenology of child and adolescent dissociative disorders', *American Academy of Child and Adolescent Psychiatry*, No. 31, pp 1077-1085.

Houston, R.A. (2000), *Madness and Society in Eighteenth-Century Scotland*, Oxford, Clarendon Press.

James VI and I,(1597), *Deamonologie*.

Innes Smith, R. W. (1932) *English-Speaking Students of Medicine at the University of Leyden*, Edinburgh, Oliver and Boyd.

Lang, A. (1907) *History of Scotland*, Edinburgh, William Blackwood and Sons.

Larner, C., Lee, C. H. and McLachlan, H. V. (2005), *A Source-book of Scottish Witchcraft*, Glasgow, The Grimsay Press. First published 1977, Glasgow University.

Macdonald, Stuart (2002), *The Witches of Fife: Witch-Hunting in a Scottish Shire*, 1560-1710, East Linton, Tuckwell Press.

McDonald, S.W., Thom, A. and Thom, A. (1996), 'The Bargarran Witchcraft Trial: A Psychiatric Reassessment', *The Scottish Medical Journal*, Vol. 41, pp. 152-158.

Mclachlan, Hugh V., (2006) 'Language, Truth and Meaning: A Defence of Modernism', *International*

Journal of Sociology and Social Policy, vol 25, no. 12, pp 114-135

McLachlan, Hugh V. and Swales, J. Kim (2006), *Women, Crime and Witchcraft: Scotland After the Reformation and Before the Enlightenment*, Humming Earth.

McLachlan, Hugh V. and Swales, J. Kim (1978), 'Lord Hale, Witches and Rape: A Comment', *British Journal of Law and Society*, Vol. 5, No. 2, pp. 251-261.

McLachlan, Hugh V. and Swales, J. Kim (1979), 'Stereotypes and Scottish Witchcraft', *Contemporary Review*, Vol. 234, No. 1357, February, pp. 88-94.

McLachlan, Hugh V. and Swales, J. Kim (1980), 'Witchcraft and Anti-Feminism', *Scottish Journal of Sociology*, vol. 4, no. 2, pp 141-166.

McLachlan, Hugh V. and Swales, J. Kim (1982), 'Tibbetts's Theory of Rationality and Scottish Witchcraft', *Philosophy of the Social Sciences*, Vol. 12, No. 1, pp 75-79.

McLachlan, Hugh V. and Swales, J. Kim (1983), 'Rationality and the Belief in Witches: A Rejoinder to Tibbetts', *Philosophy of the Social Sciences*, Vol. 13, No. 4, pp 475-477.

McLachlan, Hugh V. and Swales, J. Kim (1984), 'Review of Witch-Hunting, Magic and the New Philosophy by Brian Easlea', *Philosophy of the Social Sciences*, Vol. 14, No. 4, pp 577-580.

McLachlan, Hugh V. and Swales, J. Kim (1992), 'Scottish Witchcraft: Myth or Reality?', *Contemporary Review*, vol. 260, no. 1513, February, pp. 79-84.

McLachlan, Hugh V. and Swales, J. Kim (1994), 'Sexual Bias the the Law: The Case of Pre-Industrial Scotland', *International Journal of Sociology and Social Policy*, Vol. 14, No. 9, pp. 20-39.

McLachlan, Hugh V. and Swales, J. Kim (2002), 'The Bewitchment of Christian Shaw: A Re-assessment of the Famous Paisley Witchcraft Case of 1697' in Y.G. Brown and R. Ferguson (eds.) *Twisted Sisters: Women Crime and Deviance in Scotland since 1400*, East Linton, Tuckwell Press.

Mace, C. J. (1992) 'Hysterical conversion I: a history'. *British Journal of Psychiatry*, No. 161, pp 369-377.

Mace, C. J. (1992) 'Hysterical conversion II: a critique', *British Journal of Psychiatry*, No. 161, pp 378-389.

Maxwell-Stuart, P.G.(2001), *Satan's Conspiracy: Magic and Witchcraft in Sixteenth-Century Scotland*, East Linton, Tuckwell Press.

Metcalfe, W. M. (1909), *A History of Paisley 1600 – 1908*, Paisley, Alexander Gardner.

Metcalfe, W. M. (1909, reprinted 2003), *A History of Paisley 1600 – 1908*, Paisley, Alexander Gardner, Glasgow: The Grimsay Press.

Millar, John (ed.) (1809), *A History of the Witches of Renfrewshire* Paisley.

Morgan, Edumnd S. (1979) 'The Witch trials', *New York Review of Books*, Vol. 26, No. 4, March 22.

Parry-Jones, B. and Parry-Jones, W. L. (1992) 'Pica: symptom or eating disorder? A historical assessment'. *British Journal of Psychiatry*, No. 160, pp 341 -354.

Russell, S. (2001), 'Witchcraft, Genealogy and Foucault', *The British Journal of Sociology* 52(1), pp 121-37.

Scott, H.(1920), *Fasti Ecclesiae Scoticanae*, Edinburgh, Oliver and Boyd.

Small, G. W., Propper, M. W., Randolphs, E. T. and Eth, S. (1991), 'Mass hysteria among student performers: social relationship as a symptom predictor', *American Journal of Psychiatry*, No. 148, pp 1200-1205.

Swales, J. Kim and McLachlan, Hugh V. (1979), 'Witchcraft and the Status of Women: A Comment', *British Journal of Sociology* 30(3), pp 349-58.

T. P.(1697), *A Relation of the Diabolical Practices of the Witches of the Sheriffdom of Renfrew in the Kingdom of Scotland*, London, Hugh Newman at the Grashopper in the Poultry.

Terr, L. C. (1991), 'Childhood traumas: an outline and overview', *American Journal of Psychiatry*, No. 148, pp 10-20.

Trill, Suzanne (forthcoming), *Lady Anne Halkett: Selected Self-Writings*, Ashgate.

Wasser, Michael (2002), 'The western witch-hunt of 1697-1700: the last major witch-hunt in Scotland' in J Goodare (ed.) *The Scottish Witch-Hunt in Context*, Manchester University Press, pp 146-165.

Index to new material

The facsimiles are not indexed.

mental illness 20, 60, 63, 64, 65, 66, 469-475, 485, 486, 487, 493

Miller, Joyce 36, 50, 496

Minister 13,17,18,19, 20, 22, 23, 24, 25, 37, 44, 56, 57 64, 323, 326, 329, 330. 339, 342, 344, 347, 373, 417, 436, 448

N

Naismith, Agnes 56, 57, 456, 457, 459, 462, 465, 468, 469

Narrative, of Christian Shaw 10 13, 16, 17, 55, 56, 60, 323, 432, 435, 464, 480, 481, 482, 483, 485, 487, 488, 489, 490, 491, 492, 493, 500

necromancy 36, 38, 57

P

Paisley 15, 16, 17, 35, 50, 58, 59, 61, 62, 65, 97, 337, 351, 455, 457, 466, 467, 470, 478, 480, 488, 490, 493, 495, 498

Parris, Elizabeth 19, 325

Parris, Samuel 19, 20, 332, 334

Presbytery/Presbyterian, Presbyterianism, 16, 36, 55, 56, 462, 465, 466, 476, 488,489, 490

Privy Council 43, 44, 48, 49, 56, 58, 465

R

Reid, Annabell 64, 336, 337, 343,344

Reid, John 56, 57. 467, 468

Reid, 63

Renfrewshire 3, 5, 13, 15, 16, 17, 21, 25, 30, 55, 58, 61, 62, 69, 97, 336, 435, 455, 458, 460, 463, 476, 478, 492, 495, 498

Roman Catholic 37, 55

Russell, S 42, 43, 45, 46, 47, 48, 49, 50, 498

Printed in the United Kingdom
by Lightning Source UK Ltd.
113470UKS00001B/42

9 781845 300357